INTERVENTIONS
FOR
**Reading
Success**

INTERVENTIONS
FOR
Reading
Success

by

Diane Haager, Ph.D.

Joseph A. Dimino, Ph.D.

and

Michelle Pearlman Windmueller, Ph.D.

Baltimore • London • Sydney

Paul H. Brookes Publishing Co.
Post Office Box 10624
Baltimore, Maryland 21285-0624

www.brookespublishing.com

Typeset by Integrated Publishing Solutions, Grand Rapids, Michigan.
Manufactured in the United States of America by
Sheridan Books, Inc., Chelsea, Michigan.

The case studies in this book are fictionalized composites that are based on the authors'
experience and do not represent the lives of specific individuals, and no implications
should be inferred.

Library of Congress Cataloging-in-Publication Data
Haager, Diane.
Interventions for reading success / by Diane Haager, Joseph A. Dimino, and Michelle
Pearlman Windmueller.
    p.   cm.
    Includes bibliographical references and index.
    ISBN-13: 978-1-55766-678-9 (spiral)
    ISBN-10: 1-55766-678-4 (spiral)
    1. Reading-Remedial teaching.   2. Reading disability.   I. Dimino, Joseph A.
II. Windmueller, Michelle Pearlman.   III. Title.

    LB1050.5.H255 2007
    372.43-dc22   2006035052

British Library Cataloguing in Publication data are available from the British Library.

Contents

About the Authors

Diane Haager, Ph.D., Professor, Charter College of Education, California State University, Los Angeles, 5151 State University Drive, Los Angeles, California 90032

Diane Haager is a researcher and teacher educator in reading and learning disabilities. She is a professor at California State University, Los Angeles, where she instructs teachers in methods for teaching students with high-incidence disabilities. Dr. Haager has worked in the public schools and clinics as a reading specialist and special educator. She has had extensive experience working with English language learners who have reading difficulties. She is editor of *Evidence-Based Reading Practices for Response to Intervention* (co-edited with Janette Klingner and Sharon Vaughn, Paul H. Brookes Publishing Co., 2007) and author of the textbook *Differentiating Instruction in Inclusive Classrooms: The Special Educator's Guide* (co-authored with Janette Klingner, Allyn & Bacon, 2004). She has written numerous book chapters and research articles. Her research interests include issues related to effective reading instruction for English language learners, students with learning disabilities, and students at risk for reading failure.

Dr. Haager directs the PLUS Project (Promoting Literacy in Urban Schools), a federally funded project to develop and validate a response-to-intervention approach for identifying struggling readers in the primary grades and providing intervention to prevent reading failure. Other current projects include an investigation of the impact of teacher study groups on the quality of reading instruction in urban schools, an investigation of the quality of reading instruction in special education classrooms, and the impact of using a web-based system for assessing reading fluency. Dr. Haager has served on the Reading First National Panel of Experts and is on the editorial review board of three journals in the field of learning disabilities.

Joseph A. Dimino, Ph.D., Research Associate, Instructional Research Group, and Research Associate, RG Research Group, 2525 Cherry Avenue, Suite 300, Signal Hill, California 90755

Since the early 1970s, Joseph A. Dimino has had experience as a general education teacher, special education teacher, administrator, behavior consultant, and researcher. He has extensive experience working with teachers, parents, administrators, and instructional assistants in the areas of instruction and early literacy, reading comprehension strategies, and classroom and behavior management in urban, suburban, and rural communities.

Dr. Dimino is a part-time research associate at the Instructional Research Group in Signal Hill, California, where he is the coordinator of a national research project investigating the impact of teacher study groups as a means to enhance the quality of reading instruction for first graders in schools in high-poverty areas. He is also a part-time research associate at the RG Research Group, where he is involved in a national evaluation investigating the effects of reading comprehension programs. In addition, Dr. Dimino is Principal Investigator for a large-scale study exploring the effects of explicit reading comprehension instruction on English language learners' reading comprehension and vocabulary development. He serves as one of the seven professional development staff members for the National Center on Student Progress Monitoring, a technical assistance and dissemination center funded by the Office of Special Education Programs within the U.S. Department of Education.

He is co-author of a book on reading comprehension and has published in *Elementary School Journal, Reading Research Quarterly, The Journal of Learning Disabilities, Educational Leadership, Remedial and Special Education, Learning Disabilities Research and Practice, Learning Disability Quarterly, Exceptional Children, The Journal of Special Education,* and *Reading and Writing Quarterly.* Dr. Dimino has delivered papers at numerous state, national, and international conferences including the American Educational Research Association annual meeting, the National Reading Conference, the Council for Exceptional Children convention, and the Association for Supervision and Curriculum Development conference. He consults nationally in the areas of early literacy and reading comprehension instruction.

Michelle Pearlman Windmueller, Ph.D., Elementary School Administrator, Los Angeles Unified School District, Los Angeles, California

Michelle Pearlman Windmueller is an adjunct professor in the areas of reading, learning disabilities, assessment, instruction, and technology at California State University, Los Angeles and Mount St. Mary's College in Los Angeles. Dr. Windmueller completed her Ph.D. in education at the University of Southern California in 2004, where her dissertation titled *Early Reading Predictors of Literacy Achievement for English Learners: A Longitudinal Study from First Through Third Grade* won the Dissertation Award of Merit. Her research interests include issues related to effective reading instruction for English language learners, students at risk for reading failure, and second language learning. Dr. Windmueller serves as a consultant in reading for state and local education agencies.

In 2002, Dr. Windmueller received the Distinguished Alumna Award from the Charter College of Education at California State University, Los Angeles. She has published in *Learning Disability Quarterly, The Urban Education Journal,* and *The Mentor.* Dr. Windmueller has delivered papers at state and national conferences, including the AERA annual meeting, the Council for Exceptional Children convention, the Conference on Learning Disabilities, and the DIBELS Summit.

Dr. Windmueller taught reading and special education for 23 years in the urban public schools of East Los Angeles. She is currently an administrator in a public elementary school in South Central Los Angeles, where she coordinates the special education and reading intervention programs. She is working on publishing a reading intervention program focused on a balanced approach to instruction.

Acknowledgments

We offer heartfelt thanks to the students, teachers, and administrators of the PLUS Project schools in Southern California, with particular appreciation for the teachers who provided feedback and ideas about reading intervention. We give special thanks to Tisa Jimenez, Jennifer Mahdavi, and Marta Reinoso, whose assistance in the implementation of this project was invaluable. We gratefully acknowledge the funding provided by the U.S. Department of Education, Office of Special Education Programs, Grants H325P990019 and H324R030083, which supported the development of the PLUS reading intervention model. The views expressed in this book are those of the authors and do not represent those of the funding agency.

Overview

1

Introduction to Reading Intervention

Helping students overcome reading difficulty is one of the most important and rewarding aspects of being a teacher. If you are a general or special education teacher, you may have students who have not shown adequate progress in reading. You are probably aware that these students are likely to have academic and social difficulty later in life if they do not develop a solid foundation of basic reading skills. Studies have shown that more than 40% of students nationwide fail to meet grade-level standards in reading (National Assessment of Educational Progress, 2005). For these students, a basic reading program may not be enough. They will need additional support with the fundamentals of reading. *Interventions for Reading Success* will help you provide supplemental reading intervention for your struggling readers.

This book includes information, strategies, and ideas that are derived from the most current research in beginning reading. With the No Child Left Behind Act of 2001 (PL 107-110) requiring that all schools hold teachers and students to higher standards, research-based reading instruction has become a top priority in today's classrooms. The content of this book reflects our current understanding of why some students experience reading difficulty, how to prevent reading failure, and what constitutes effective reading instruction. Intervention activities are provided in the areas of reading considered as building blocks for more advanced reading skills. The "Big Ideas" of reading include phonological awareness, alphabetic principle, fluency with connected text, vocabulary development, and comprehension. We offer guidance on making the home–school connection in reading intervention. In addition, we provide a simple strategy called STAR in Chapter 2 for working with English language learners.

This handbook on reading intervention is for classroom teachers who want to provide supplemental instruction in reading for students who are lagging behind. The activities are most appropriate for kindergarten through third-grade students, but teachers of other grades who have students reading significantly below grade level may find this guide useful. Special education teachers, reading specialists, speech and language specialists, and anyone who wants to help struggling readers will be able to use the activities with small groups or individual students who need additional support in reading.

THE PLUS PROJECT: BRINGING
RESEARCH-BASED STRATEGIES INTO REAL CLASSROOMS

When using this book, you can be confident that the ideas and activities are research based and readily applicable to your real-life classroom. Reading initiatives such as Reading First, the federal reading initiative included in the No Child Left Behind Act of 2001, call for scientifically based reading research to guide reading instruction. Implementing strategies validated by research is critically important in reading intervention with struggling readers. The activities included in this book were field tested and evaluated as part of a federally funded research project called The PLUS Project (Promoting Literacy in Urban Schools; Haager, 2006; Oh, Haager, & Windmueller, 2006). This project provided an opportunity for groups of classroom teachers to participate in professional development and then try various strategies in their classrooms. Through a process of observation, in-class coaching and support, and evaluative feedback, these strategies were modified and refined by teams of teachers and researchers. The activities and strategies in this book not only represent principles of effective reading instruction as outlined in the National Reading Panel Report (National Institute of Child Health and Human Development [NICHD], 2000) and other research reports but also have the added benefit of being classroom based and easy to implement.

WHAT IS READING INTERVENTION?

Reading intervention is *supplemental instruction* for students struggling with basic early reading skills. It is not meant to replace regular reading instruction provided by the teacher. We recommend an additional 20–30 minutes of daily intervention instruction beyond the regular reading program. Intervention should be provided in small-group or one-to-one sessions before or after the normal classroom reading instruction. This book could also be used in an after-school intervention program. Some activities could be done with the entire class to provide extra practice for all students, but the activities are primarily meant for small-group instruction. Intervention instruction should be focused on the Big Ideas of reading—phonological awareness, alphabetic principle, fluency with connected text, vocabulary development, and comprehension—according to students' academic learning needs.

HOW TO USE THIS BOOK

Section I of this book is designed to build your knowledge about reading intervention. The next two chapters present basic information about early reading intervention. Chapter 2 provides the research base for beginning reading and reading intervention. Chapter 3 shows how to plan and organize assessment and intervention. Chapter 4 describes the nuts and bolts of implementing a reading intervention program in your school and explains in detail how to prepare for and use the activities in this book. Sections II and III include the classroom and home activities, respectively, that you will use to implement reading intervention.

All of the intervention activities within Sections II and III are arranged from easier to more advanced. Word lists for the activities are included. Any materials that you may need are listed in the activities. Templates for some of the materials are provided in the appendix and are discussed in Chapter 4. The rest of the materials are likely to be the kind of things you would have on hand in your classroom or that parents would have readily available at home.

Chapter 5 includes activities for phonological awareness. In this chapter, you will find many activities to teach the phonological concepts of rhyming, onset-rime, segmenting, and blending. Chapter 6 has activities related to the alphabetic principle, or decoding. Chapter 7, on reading fluency, includes activities to develop students' word-level fluency and text-level processing. Having automatic recognition of words facilitates fluency with text; thus, Chapter 7 includes many activities to teach sight words as well as guidance to help students to become fluent in reading connected text, using sentences or short reading passages.

Interventions for Reading Success is not meant to be a lock-step reading program implemented in sequential order. The classroom activities in Chapters 5–7 represent a menu of activities to choose from to tailor reading intervention for students' specific areas of need. For any intervention session, you may want to pull activities from more than one place in the book. In fact, most at-risk students have needs in more than one area of reading, and you may want to construct a session that covers two or more of the Big Ideas.

Students struggling with early reading typically need critical support in the basic skills of phonological awareness, decoding, or fluency. In a 20- to 30-minute intervention session, it is not feasible to cover all five Big Ideas of reading. Yet, some students may need extra support in vocabulary and comprehension. Therefore, Chapter 8 provides ideas for incorporating vocabulary and comprehension into intervention activities. Many of these ideas can also be used to enhance the vocabulary and comprehension instruction for your whole class. Students learning English as a second language also often need extra vocabulary support. The STAR strategy discussed in Chapter 2 describes how to integrate vocabulary development into activities at the word level specifically for English language learners.

Teachers often say that struggling students learn best when they have opportunities to practice new skills at home. For this purpose, the essential reading skills of phonological awareness, alphabetic principle and fluent word recognition are addressed in Home–School Connection activities that teachers can send home with students for extra practice. Corresponding Home–School Connection activities are provided for many of the intervention activities included in this book. The Home–School Connection activities can be photocopied and sent home on an as-needed basis. When a student is struggling with a particular skill, the teacher can teach it during intervention time and then send home a corresponding simple activity for practice at home. (See Chapter 4 for more instructions on how to prepare materials for and introduce parents to the home activities.)

The appendix contains photocopiable templates that can be used with some of the activities. The templates are discussed in detail in Chapter 4.

Each activity in this book provides a step-by-step instructional sequence for conducting the intervention. This design was developed as a guideline, not an instructional script. Before teaching an intervention, read the activity to understand its structure, purpose, and content. How you present the intervention is your decision. You can use our language or your own words.

We know that experienced teachers often modify strategies and activities to fit their own teaching styles. We hope you will make these activities your own by adding your own special touches and flair. Making these activities fun for your students with a game-like atmosphere will certainly help. We hope you will see your students become enthusiastic readers right before your eyes.

2

Providing Classroom-Based Reading Intervention

Like many elementary teachers, Ms. Russell has a few students in her class who are falling behind in reading even though a solid schoolwide reading program is in place. She knows that if these students do not get a boost now, in the early years, they may struggle throughout their academic careers. Ms. Russell wants to organize a reading intervention program to provide extra help to her struggling readers. She is planning to structure time for small groups so that she can provide extra assistance to students who might need help along the way. She wants the groups to be flexible so that she can move students in and out of groups as needed. She does not have a lot of experience with individualizing instruction. She wonders what evidence exists to guide her intervention.

WHAT THE RESEARCH SAYS ABOUT STRUGGLING READERS

Children who do not acquire basic proficiency in the early grades are likely to struggle with reading and other academic skills throughout their school years (Juel, 1988; Snow, Burns, & Griffin, 1998). Stanovich (1986) described this phenomenon as the "Matthew effect," or "the rich get richer while the poor get poorer," meaning that students who fail to develop proficiency in reading will fall further and further behind in both academic and cognitive development. After the primary grades, the academic and cognitive demands of schooling increase rapidly. As students move through school, their cognitive development becomes more and more dependent on academic skills as students are expected to use their reading and writing skills to acquire new knowledge. By the middle school years, teachers assign independent reading of long, dense chapters and students must write informational reports. In high school, students are responsible for reading and committing to memory large amounts of text. Students who fail to get a good start in reading may struggle through their entire school career and fall behind, not just in academics but also in their knowledge of the world. Preventing early reading failure is a high priority in today's classrooms.

A significant number of students do not learn to read even with a sound core reading program and competent teachers (Snow et al., 1998). Despite a decade of change in reading practices across the nation, 25%–40% of students across the grades scored below a basic level in the 2002 National Assessment of Educational Progress study (U.S. Department of Education, 2002). The alarming news is that students who fall behind in the early years of reading rarely catch up with their peers (Foorman, Francis, Fletcher, Schatschneider, & Mehta, 1998; Francis, Shaywitz, Stuebing, Shaywitz, & Fletcher, 1996; Torgesen & Burgess, 1998). Not surprisingly, the number of students provided with special education services has risen steadily since 1976 (Hunt & Marshall, 2006). This is especially true for students of minority backgrounds, who often come from disadvantaged educational backgrounds in urban schools (National Research Council, 2002).

Recent studies have focused on preventing reading difficulties by providing intervention before problems become insurmountable. When early reading problems go undetected, students often fall so far behind that they never catch up. These students may appear to have a learning disability and often are referred to and receive special education services for intensive help. Yet, special education may be preventable for a significant number of students if they are provided with early intensive intervention in reading. Without systematic screening and assessment, we miss many students who would benefit from early assistance (O'Connor & Jenkins, 2002). An alternative to the "wait and fail" model is to catch reading problems early and provide sufficient intervention supplemental to the regular reading program. Studies have shown that providing early intervention in critical early reading skills can prevent or lessen reading problems later (Haager & Windmueller, 2001; O'Connor, 2000). The key to preventing the devastating effects of reading failure is intervening early. Torgesen (1998) asserted that we must "catch them before they fall" to make a significant difference in the outcomes for such students.

A THREE-TIERED MODEL OF READING INTERVENTION

Reading intervention should be readily available to students who need it. With the use of early reading assessment tools (see Chapter 3), we are able to identify students who need assistance and pinpoint their reading difficulties. A three-tiered reading intervention model allows schools to provide early assistance to students and increase the intensity of intervention as needed for persistent reading problems (Haager, Klingner, & Vaughn, 2007; Texas Education Agency, 2003). Figure 1 shows the three-tiered reading intervention model.

Tier One

The first tier of intervention is for all students. It consists of having a solid, research-based core reading program in place in the early elementary grades taught by qualified teachers who have the knowledge and skills to provide effective instruction. National reports highlight the importance of applying the collective knowledge gained from 30 years of research on effective reading instruction (NICHD, 2000; Snow et al., 1998; Stanovich & Stanovich, 2003). With the No Child Left Behind Act of 2004 (PL 107-110) and Reading First legislation, many schools are implementing reading programs based on scientifically based reading research. Reading First guidelines specify that schools must select reading programs that have a proven track record in promoting reading success, dedicate a significant uninterrupted

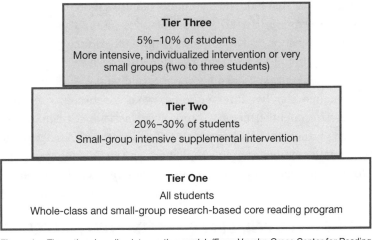

Figure 1. Three-tiered reading intervention model. (From Vaughn Gross Center for Reading and Language Arts at the University of Texas at Austin. [2005]. *Implementing the 3-tier reading model, presenter guide;* adapted by permission.)

block of time to reading instruction, and implement reading via highly qualified teachers. Thus, in Tier One, all children have an opportunity to develop basic reading skills.

Tier Two

Despite the best reading programs and early reading instruction, 20%–30% of students may experience difficulty in the early stages of reading (O'Connor, 2000; Vaughn, Linan-Thompson, & Hickman, 2003). The second tier of intervention is designed to provide supplemental reading intervention for these students to accelerate their reading development. With appropriate intervention, many of these students will catch up with their peers. This intervention occurs prior to consideration of special education services and is often called *prereferral intervention.* Tier Two intervention consists of systematic, intensive instruction focused on the key components of early reading. Small-group instruction with three to six students would be ideal for this level of intervention. Many teachers fit this in when they break their students into small groups or have students rotate to different centers. Tier Two intervention occurs during 20–30 minutes of daily supplemental instruction *in addition to* the core reading program. Ongoing assessment allows teachers to monitor students' progress closely and adjust instruction along the way (see Chapter 3).

Interventions for Reading Success provides many ideas for implementing Tier Two reading intervention. This book provides many small-group activities that can be used to reinforce the key components of reading development.

Tier Three

Despite secondary intervention, a small number of students, 5%–10%, will continue to experience difficulty in reading (Vaughn et al., 2003). After a period of Tier Two intervention, ongoing progress monitoring and adjusting instruction to meet students' individual needs, it may become clear that individual students require a more intensive approach. At this point, students may be referred to the third tier of intervention. This level is what is usually thought of as special education, but some schools have other remedial services available. School or district policy should dictate the procedures for identifying and referring students to the third tier of intervention. Decisions about an individual student, such as how long he or she would remain in Tier Two intervention or what constitutes a severe reading problem warranting referral, might be made by a prereferral assistance team (sometimes called a student study team or a student assistance team). Consider the advantage of having implemented the secondary intervention program: Implementing Tier Two intervention and ongoing progress monitoring assessment provides extensive data for team decisions.

GUIDING PRINCIPLES FOR EFFECTIVE READING INTERVENTION

This book helps teachers provide supplemental instruction to meet the needs of individual students. There are five key principles for implementing an effective reading intervention program. These five principles are discussed in detail in this chapter:

1. Focus on the essential components of early reading, or the "Big Ideas."

2. Use assessment data to identify students who need intervention, strategically group students, and monitor progress.

3. Provide systematic and explicit reading instruction during intervention.

4. Organize the classroom routine and environment.

5. Use school and classroom resource staff, such as instructional assistants or volunteers, to assist with intervention.

Principle 1: Focus on the Big Ideas of Reading

There are five essential components of early reading instruction: phonological awareness, alphabetic principle, fluency with connected text, vocabulary development, and comprehension. We can think of these components as the Big Ideas of beginning reading instruction (Simmons & Kame'enui, 1998). Reading instruction in all three tiers should focus on the Big Ideas. During reading intervention for struggling readers, however, it is critically important to provide systematic and explicit instruction in these key areas.

Phonological Awareness

Phonological awareness is an important prerequisite to learning to read. Phonological awareness is knowledge of the structure of language. People often confuse *phonological awareness* and *phonemic awareness* and use the terms synonymously. Technically, they are not the same. Phonemic awareness is one type of phonological awareness. It involves understanding that words contain individual speech sounds, or phonemes, and being able to manipulate these sounds. Other phonological skills that fall into the category of phonological

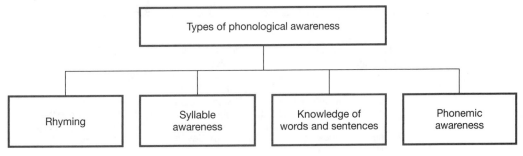

Figure 2. Types of phonological awareness.

awareness are rhyming, syllable awareness, and knowledge of words and sentences (see Figure 2).

Rhyming develops naturally in many children through word play and songs. Recognizing rhymes is an easier skill than producing rhymes. Rhyme recognition activities involve having students identify whether or not words rhyme. This could be done with matching games, word sorts, or various interactive activities. Here is an example of rhyme recognition taught in an intervention group.

Teacher (to a small group):   I am going to say two words. If you think these two words rhyme, put your thumbs up. Ready? *mow-go*

    (Students put thumbs up in the air.)

Teacher: Good job, everyone. Now listen to these words: *mop-pan*.

    (Students do not put thumbs up.)

Rhyme production involves asking students to make rhymes. A teacher might give students a word and ask for one or more words that rhyme with the target word. Another rhyme production activity would be to use fill-in-the-blank sentences requiring students to think of a rhyming word.

Syllable awareness occurs when students segment or blend words orally into syllables. Syllable segmenting involves hearing the syllables in words. Clapping names and words is an example of this kind of activity. For example, Marisa's name would be clapped with three syllables: *Ma ris a.* Syllable blending is the opposite skill. When the teacher says a word in segmented form, the students can say the whole word.

Breaking sentences into individual words represents word awareness. We can teach students to separate a sentence into word components. For example, students may stomp their feet along with the words in this sentence: *The book is red.*

Phonemic awareness is a very important part of phonological awareness. Research has shown that this skill is an important precursor to decoding. Understanding that the words of English are made up of individual sounds, or phonemes, is probably the most important skill for reading acquisition for several reasons. We know that it is a powerful predictor of later reading (NICHD, 2000). Children who develop phonemic awareness in preschool and kindergarten are likely to be skilled readers in the later grades. Phonemic awareness assessment tools help identify students who might benefit from intervention. Students with deficits in phonemic awareness benefit from systematic explicit intervention in these skills.

Table 1. Developmental sequence for phonological awareness development

Skill	Example
Onset recognition: recognition of initial sounds	"*Cap* begins with the sound /k/. Find all of the pictures in this set that begin with the same sound as *cap*." (Show students a group of picture cards.)
Onset–rime segmentation: saying the beginning sound (the onset) separate from the rest of the word (the rime, i.e., the vowel and any subsequent consonant sounds)	Teach students to separate words based on their onset or rime. "Listen to me say this word in parts: *kite,* /k/ /īt/. Now it's your turn. Say this word in parts: *rake.*" /r/ /āk/
Onset–rime blending: identifying the complete word after hearing a segmented onset and rime	"Tell me what whole word I am saying." /c/ /āk/, *cake;* /l/ /īf/, *life*
Phoneme segmentation: saying the individual phonemes or sounds of a word	"Say the sounds in the word *cap*." /c/ /ă/ /p/
Phoneme blending: saying the complete word after hearing the segmented word	"Tell me what whole word I am saying: /m/ /ă/ /p/." *map*
Phoneme addition	"Add the /m/ sound to /ăt/." *mat*
Phoneme deletion	"Say the word *bike* without /b/." /īk/
Phoneme substitution	"Change the /m/ in *man* to a /t/ sound." *tan*

Table 1 explains the different skills that make up phonemic awareness and a suggested developmental sequence.

Alphabetic Principle

The second Big Idea, the alphabetic principle, is often referred to as *decoding, word recognition,* or *phonics.* The alphabetic principle is really a type of knowledge that underlies phonics or word recognition skills. It is an awareness that words are made up of sounds and are represented by letters. In a nutshell, this means that beginning readers need to understand the code of our language—the alphabet—and its function in reading.

Teaching the alphabetic principle has many facets. We may begin by teaching *letter-sound correspondence.* This is the ability to look at single letters or common letter combinations (e.g., *th*) and say the sound represented by the letter(s). Learning letter-sound correspondence usually occurs in kindergarten. Children who struggle with reading in first or second grade may not have a well-developed understanding of this principle.

Phonics is the ability to associate sounds with letters and letter patterns and then blend them into whole words. Once children have a clear understanding of the alphabetic principle, they can begin to work on phonics and learn to sound out words. It is not necessary to learn all 26 letters of the alphabet before beginning to learn phonics. Teachers should introduce a few sounds and then begin blending right away so that children learn the habit of sound blending. *Decoding* is the ability to look at the letters in a word, pronounce the sounds associated with the letters or letter patterns, and blend them into a recognizable word. Decoding involves using the sounds of letters to arrive at word meaning. Again, children should be taught that the ultimate goal of sounding out is to figure out the word and how it makes sense in the written context.

Word recognition is the ability to look at a word and automatically generate its pronunciation. This may happen by recognizing a whole word by sight (i.e., visually recognizing words in their whole form) or by automatic decoding. *Automaticity* occurs when the decoding process is so automatic or well refined that the reader appears to recognize the word instantly. This is different from sight recognition in that the reader actually processes the individual letters and sounds but does so in a rapid, automatic manner. This skill is very important to becoming a proficient reader because with automaticity the reader is able to focus attention on comprehension rather than on decoding. Much of a beginning reader's cognitive resources, or brain power, is devoted to the decoding process and little is left for comprehension. Automaticity develops gradually during the first few years of reading instruction.

Onset-rime manipulation is linguistic terminology that refers to breaking a syllable or a short word into any beginning sounds (the onset) before the vowel and the rest of the syllable (the rime). This skill is developed through phonological awareness, but we include it here because it is common to teach students decoding by using rime patterns. The onset is the beginning sound(s) in a syllable before the vowel, such as /m/ in *man*. The rime is the vowel plus the ending sound(s), such as /ān/ in *man* or /ĭlk/ in *milk*. All words have rimes, but not all words have onsets. Words that begin with vowels, such as *it* or *and* do not have onsets. The syllables in a multisyllabic word also each may have onsets and rimes. For example, in the word *basket*, the first syllable, *ba*, has an onset of /b/ and a rime of /ă/. The second syllable, *sket*, has an onset of /sk/ and a rime of /ĕt/. Learning to decode words by onset-rime patterns reflects the process of natural language development. It is easier to learn words in sets of rime patterns, or word families, such as *chip, dip, hip, lip, nip, rip, sip, ship, tip,* and *whip.*

Fluency with Connected Text

Reading fluency is defined as reading with speed, accuracy, and expression. A fluent reader can read words and phrases fluidly and with ease. This is a critical aspect of reading instruction because fluent readers have a better chance of comprehending what they read. Even though 40%–45% of fourth-grade students fail to develop fluency in grade-level materials, fluency is often a neglected area of reading instruction (Pinnell, Lyons, DeFord, Bryk, & Seltzer, 1995). Most teachers do not allocate instructional time to activities aimed at building fluency because they assume that students will acquire fluency naturally as they begin to read independently. Opportunity to practice by reading independently is important in fluency development but is not sufficient. This is particularly true for struggling readers. An important component of reading intervention for students beyond the beginning first-grade level is fluency-building exercises.

Accurate decoding is an important aspect of fluency. Accurate reading leads to ready access to the meaning of a passage. This in turn helps further with decoding by establishing a meaningful context. There are two prongs to accurate word recognition. One is having a well-developed bank of sight words, or words recognized from memory as whole units, and the other is ease of decoding unfamiliar words. Another important component of fluency is the ability to process meaningful units of text, or phrases. Through guided practice and modeling, students learn to hold a string of words in memory while processing the meaning of the connected words. Reading rate is another component of fluency. When readers process words quickly, the text flows smoothly. Although some students need a little encouragement to get their speed up to this point, it would be unwise to encourage them to speed-read. Accessing meaning is always the goal.

Automaticity is the ability to decode text with such ease that the decoding appears to happen automatically. Automatic, effortless word recognition frees cognitive resources for comprehension (LaBerge & Samuels, 1974). Imagine a young reader going through a story word by word, finger-pointing at each word, and struggling to pronounce many of the words. In this scenario, most of the student's mental energy is going to decoding the letter-sound relationships, blending the sounds together, and remembering sight words. By the time this student gets to the end of a sentence, much of the meaning is lost. Compare this scenario with one in which a skilled reader can breeze through a paragraph and focus mainly on the meaning of the text. When students are reading quickly and accurately while getting the meaning from text, they are then able to add expression, or prosody, to their skills.

Vocabulary Development

The Big Idea of vocabulary development is one that is taught and reinforced throughout every school day. Vocabulary development is highly related to reading comprehension (NICHD, 2000). Though students learn many words from context and exposure, we know that a certain amount of explicit teaching of unknown words is important for reading growth. Children in kindergarten learn 2,500–5,000 new words in their first year of school. On average, primary grade children learn about seven new words per day (Beck, McKeown, & Kucan, 2002). There is a great disparity, however, between children of different backgrounds. First-grade children of lower socioeconomic status know about half as many words as children of higher socioeconomic status (Beck et al., 2002). Differences such as this persist throughout the grades, and the gap widens between high- and low-performing students.

Vocabulary development is an especially important aspect of intervention for students who are learning English as a second language, or English language learners (ELLs). Many such students begin to learn English when they enter school, at the same time they are expected to learn to read. It is important to build students' English language skills in order to ensure their success in reading. There are various models for English language development instruction. We find that many ELLs who are identified as needing intervention also need English language development instruction.

How does vocabulary fit into reading intervention? For both native English speakers and ELLs, we recommend that teachers integrate oral language activities into intervention rather than plan specific intervention activities for isolated words. The STAR strategy (discussed next) can help teachers to do this. Vocabulary intervention is more effective when students are engaged in active responding. It is also important to create an environment in which students feel safe to try out new words. While conducting an intervention activity, teachers should select words that might need further explanation and discuss them during the activity.

STAR: A Strategy for English Language Learners

ELLs often fall behind native English speaking peers in acquiring basic reading skills. A bilingual reading program may not be feasible because of practical considerations or policy. To accelerate their reading development, ELLs must acquire English rapidly. This means teaching vocabulary concepts along the way, as a supplement to a structured English development program. STAR is a simple strategy for integrating English language development into reading intervention activities. It involves four simple steps.

Set the Stage

Prepare your ELLs for the intervention activity by *preteaching* vocabulary words used in the activity. You will not need to preteach all the words; some are not used frequently in English and may come later in development. Focus on words that you think are critical for early language development. Select additional words as you wish, based on your students' specific needs.

Begin by selecting words from the activity ahead of time. Be selective. It is best to teach only a few words. Then, introduce these words orally to your ELLs *before* the intervention activity. It is not important to teach the students to read the words. Instead, focus on oral language and concept development. It might be helpful to use picture cards, real objects, or simple line drawings to illustrate word meanings. Practice using the words in oral sentences or phrases with the students. Most important, make learning new words fun and exciting for your ELLs.

Teach as You Go

Once you have pretaught the words, it is a simple matter to reinforce word meanings throughout the activity. As you engage students in the intervention activity, review and reinforce the target words with your ELLs by using simple sentences, pictures, phrases, or other simple items. If you have used pictures to introduce the words earlier, be sure to have the pictures handy during the activity. This reinforcement of word meanings should be very brief and to the point, almost an aside. It is important not to interrupt the flow of the activity or detract from the reading task at hand.

Apply the Concept

At the end of the activity, take a few moments to have your students form simple sentences, phrases, or pantomimes to illustrate that they understand the word meaning. The goal is to have the students say and use the words for themselves.

Review and Repeat

Vocabulary is learned best when students have repeated opportunities to hear and say new words. Revisit words several times during the following days and weeks. Be sure to notice and praise students when they use newly acquired vocabulary in their daily learning tasks.

Comprehension

Comprehension, the fifth Big Idea, is the goal of reading instruction. The whole purpose of reading is to get meaning from print. During the early grades, students need to learn strategies for monitoring their understanding. Reading comprehension instruction occurs as a regular part of the core reading program. During intervention, teachers should reinforce and support students' comprehension in an ongoing way. Interactive discussion and corrective feedback are important aspects of comprehension intervention. In addition, some students may need to start with comprehension at the phrase and sentence levels before going on to reading longer passages.

Principle 2: Use Assessment to Guide Intervention

Ongoing assessment is essential for making important intervention decisions. The three basic purposes of reading assessment will guide reading intervention: screening, diagnosis, and ongoing progress monitoring. We discuss these purposes in Chapter 3. There are several assessment tools available that can serve these purposes. For the Reading First national initiative, a panel of experts conducted a review of existing reading assessments to determine their reliability and validity for each of these purposes in relation to each of the Big Ideas. The assessment tools that a teacher or school selects should reflect the curriculum or standards for grade-level instruction. An assessment tool should do more than give a number or a score—it needs to indicate what skills students have and what skills need more work. We discuss assessment in more detail in Chapter 3.

Principle 3: Provide Systematic and Explicit Reading Intervention

There are two qualities of a good intervention program for at-risk readers: Such a program is systematic and explicit. Systematic intervention means that intervention happens frequently, routinely, and follows a well-defined sequence. The most effective reading intervention programs occur daily or several times per week and are of sufficient duration to allow for concept development and practice with skills.

Explicit instruction occurs when the teacher provides direct and focused instruction. The teacher makes it clear what is being taught, models and explains the task, provides opportunities for students to practice the skill, and provides specific feedback. Learning is most effective when students are fully engaged in the task. Intervention activities should be focused rather than merely touching on a concept or providing exposure to an idea. Intensive instruction also involves the students in *active responding* rather than passive learning. Instead of telling students how to do something, explicit instruction requires that students perform a skill or engage in dialogue about or explanation of that skill.

Principle 4: Organize the Classroom Routine and Environment

Teachers consistently report that their greatest challenge is finding time to reach all students. There is no magic formula for creating more time in the school day; it is important for teachers to make the best use of the time they have. Twenty to thirty minutes per day devoted to intervention is well worth the investment. Most teachers include small-group time during their language arts time. This time is ideal for group intervention activities.

A successful reading intervention program must be planned into the classroom routine with systematic implementation. Consistency is important. Some schools run their intervention programs before or after school. In addition to having planned group time, there may be occasional small blocks of time that can be captured for intervention. Perhaps during the 5–10 minutes before recess or lunch, the teacher could work with three or four struggling readers while other students finish seatwork. This would provide one more learning opportunity for intervention students. Most of the games and activities in this guide take around 10 minutes.

Efficiency is a key ingredient in finding more time for reading intervention. Typically, a great deal of time is wasted during transition from one activity to the next. Teachers often spend several minutes on behavior management between activities. The longer transitions take, the more management is required. Making swift and seamless transitions can buy more time for important intervention activities.

Principle 5: Use School and Classroom Resource Staff for Intervention

Providing reading intervention for students having difficulty with specific skills should not always be relegated to support personnel, such as paraprofessionals, and instead should be conducted consistently by the classroom teacher. Support personnel such as paraprofessionals, classroom volunteers, or itinerant specialists can certainly be helpful in providing intervention, but we recommend that the classroom teacher work consistently with intervention groups. *Consistent contact with intervention students allows the teacher to remain abreast of student growth or specific difficulties through ongoing observation of student performance.* Ongoing monitoring of student progress through assessment and observation is a key to intervention success.

Paraprofessionals can be very helpful in implementing intervention, and their services should be used strategically. Paraprofessionals should never *replace* the classroom teacher, instead *supplementing* the classroom teacher's intervention. It is helpful to provide specific training and explanation to paraprofessionals to ensure that the activities are done appropriately and well. When working with a paraprofessional, it is also very helpful for the classroom teacher to work with the intervention students in proximity to the paraprofessional to model the techniques for the paraprofessional, then rotate groups so the paraprofessional will work with the group later or the next day. By rotating groups, the teacher maintains consistent contact with intervention students but can still use the valuable help of support personnel while providing repeated exposure to intervention students.

A resource specialist or reading specialist can also bring valuable help to the classroom during intervention time. Resource specialists using a collaborative approach in which they visit general education classrooms might work with intervention students while providing special education services to students on their caseload. Similarly, some schools have reading specialists on staff to work with students who need additional help. Taking these services into the classroom in a collaborative teaching model provides additional opportunities for students to receive intervention. Again, classroom teachers should not overrely on specialists to implement intervention in the classroom, nor should the specialists *replace* the classroom teacher. Rather, the teacher should use specialists' services to *supplement* their intervention.

MAKING IT FUN

Students like to play games. Rather than using the intervention activities as "drill and kill" activities, consider incorporating games to practice the interventions. In this way, the intervention activities can be both memorable and fun.

The games described next are easy to play and require a minimum of preparation and materials. In fact, most of the things teachers will need are already in the classroom. The games are meant to be examples of how easy it is to make the interventions fun for students. We hope that these ideas will stimulate teachers to create their own games and incorporate them regularly into their intervention programs.

GAMES

1. Make or buy a game board. After giving a correct response to an intervention activity (e.g., providing a rhyme), a child throws the dice and moves his or her game piece the designated number of spaces. If the response is not correct, the teacher models the correct response before the next child takes a turn. The first person to get around the game board is the winner.

   What you will need: Game board
   Dice
   Game pieces

2. Collect objects such as plastic chips or blocks. After giving a correct response, a child earns a chip for the group. If a child does not respond correctly, the teacher models the correct response and earns the chip. At the end of the game, whoever has the most chips is the winner.

   What you will need: Plastic chips, small blocks, and so forth

3. Provide one score sheet for the students and one for the teacher. After giving a correct response, a child earns one point for the group. The teacher or a student colors in one space on the students' score sheet. If a child does not respond correctly, the teacher models the correct response and colors in one space on the teacher's score sheet. At the end of the game, whoever has the most spaces colored in is the winner.

   What you will need: Two score sheets
   Crayon or colored pencil

4. Gather dice and one score sheet for the students and one for the teacher. After giving a correct response, a child throws the dice. The teacher or student colors in the corresponding number of spaces on the students' score sheet. If a student does not respond correctly, the teacher models the correct response and colors in the corresponding number of spaces on the teacher's score sheet. At the end of the game, whoever has the most spaces colored in is the winner.

   What you will need: Two score sheets
   Crayon or colored pencil

5. Draw a T-chart on the board or on sheet of paper. Have the students choose a name for their team. It can be a professional sports team, cartoon character, or personality. Write the team's name on the left side of the chart. Write the teacher's name on the right side of the chart. When a child responds correctly, mark one tally in the students' column. If a child does not respond correctly, the teacher models the correct answer and marks one tally in the teacher's column. At the end of the game, count the number of tallies in each column. The team with the most tallies is the winner.

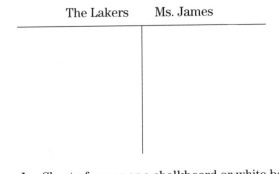

The Lakers   Ms. James

What you will need: Sheet of paper or a chalkboard or white board
Pen or chalk

6. Play a Hangman-type game. You will need two sheets of 8½″ × 11″ paper, one for the teacher and one for the students (or you can use the board). When a student gives a correct response, the student draws one part of a stick figure on the students' paper. If a child does not respond correctly, the teacher models the correct answer and draws one part of a stick figure on the teacher's paper. The team who completes drawing the stick figure first is the winner.
What you will need: Two sheets of 8½″ × 11″ paper or a chalkboard or white board

Variation: Rather than drawing, the students and the teacher can each be given the pieces of a simple jigsaw puzzle. After giving a correct response, a student adds a piece to the students' puzzle. If a child does not respond correctly, the teacher models the correct answer and adds a piece to her/his puzzle. The team completing the puzzle first is the winner.
What you will need: Two simple jigsaw puzzles

Using Assessment to Guide Intervention

We use assessment data in many aspects of our daily lives. How do we know what to wear when we go out for the day? We look at the weather forecast to see the temperature. How do we know when our cars need gas? We read the fuel gauge. How much carpeting do we buy when we redecorate a room? We measure the dimensions and calculate the square yards. These are all examples of making decisions based on data. The same notion applies to planning intervention for struggling readers. Teachers need to know *what skills* students need more work on and *how much* intervention will meet their needs.

Teachers make an average of 4,000 decisions per day (Dimino, 2004). It is not surprising that teachers feel exhausted at the end of the day! Sometimes teachers wonder if they are making the *right* decisions about individual students or wish that they had more depth of information about a student's skills. In this chapter, you will see how using accurate and targeted reading assessments will help you to plan and implement more effective reading intervention, particularly for the second tier of reading intervention (supplemental instruction).

THREE KINDS OF ASSESSMENT FOR EARLY READING INTERVENTION

In a three-tiered intervention model, teachers use three kinds of assessment to make critical decisions about reading intervention. *Screening assessment* is used to catch struggling readers early. At the beginning and midpoint of the school year, a teacher screens all of his or her students and examines the data to see which students are failing to meet specified benchmarks. These data, along with judgment based on personal experience with students during reading activities, help the teacher identify which students may have significant reading difficulties. In the early grades, this may be 20%–30% of the students (Vaughn et al., 2003). *Diagnostic assessment* is then conducted for these students. In this process, the teacher would conduct individualized assessment covering specific developmental reading skills to determine areas of need for individual students. This helps the teacher to better understand why a student is struggling. Then, intervention can be targeted to meet those specific skill needs. *Ongoing progress monitoring assessment* consists of short tasks that represent the identified area of need in the continuum of reading skills. Students are assessed on these grade-level skills frequently, and progress is charted or monitored to ensure adequate progress toward goals. In this chapter, we illustrate these types of assessment in more detail and give examples to demonstrate the process of making intervention decisions based on assessment data.

IDENTIFYING STUDENTS' LEARNING NEEDS

Although there are several commercial reading assessment tools that are appropriate for use in the beginning reading stages, we use the Dynamic Indicators of Basic Early Literacy Skills (DIBELS; Good & Kaminski, 2002) in our examples in this book for several reasons. DIBELS is a widely used and highly respected assessment system for kindergarten through sixth grade. Reliability and validity have been established over years of research (Good, Simmons, & Kame'enui, 2001; Kaminski & Good, 1996). The subtests of the DIBELS assessment system represent a sound, research-validated sequence of reading skills that align with most states' curriculum standards. The DIBELS assessment system uses established benchmarks, or performance standards, to indicate at what point a student should master the skills. Last, we use the DIBELS assessments in our examples here because this assessment system is available free of charge at http://dibels.uoregon.edu. Although it is very helpful to go through a DIBELS training session, teachers can download this assessment and learn how to use it from the web-based information.

The DIBELS assessments cover what are widely referred to as the five Big Ideas, or key skill areas of early reading: phonological awareness, alphabetic principle, fluency with connected text, vocabulary development, and comprehension (see Chapter 2). Across Grades K–2, these five Big Ideas are assessed as they would occur in the developmental sequence of skills in the curriculum. For Grades 3–6, oral reading fluency assessment is conducted. Table 2 shows the skill areas assessed at each grade level. For each assessment, benchmarks allow an individual score to be compared with an expected level of performance. Students scoring below benchmarks are candidates for Tier Two or Tier Three reading intervention. The DIBELS system also indicates the degree of severity of the reading problem. Students' scores are classified according to whether the students have low risk, some risk, or are very likely to be at risk for reading problems. In addition, students' scores are classified according to instructional recommendations. A *Benchmark* score means the student has reached the established performance level for that grade and time point. A *Strategic* score indicates the student is a little behind for that time point and may need some extra attention to accelerate learning. An *Intensive* score indicates that the student is in serious danger of experiencing reading failure and needs intensive, focused intervention to catch up.

Teachers have a wide array of choices of assessment tools. There are other tools that would serve the same purpose as DIBELS. Some are commercially available. Others are included in basal reading programs. It is important to select an assessment tool that addresses critical grade-level skills. The advantage of DIBELS and some commercially available tools is that they have benchmarks and standard administration procedures for making systematic intervention decisions. For many textbook assessments (assessments that accompany reading curricula or basal readers), district-developed assessments and other informal tools,

Table 2. Areas of reading instruction addressed in the Dynamic Indicators of Basic Early Literacy Skills (DIBELS) assessment system

Big Idea of reading instruction	DIBELS subtests	Grade levels assessed
Phonological awareness	Initial Sounds Fluency *Measures beginning sound recognition*	Kindergarten
	Phoneme Segmentation Fluency *Measures ability to separate the sounds in spoken words*	Kindergarten through first grade
Alphabetic principle	Letter Naming Fluency *Measures rapid, automatic letter naming*	Kindergarten through first grade
	Nonsense Word Fluency *Measures the use of the alphabetic code*	Kindergarten through first grade
Fluency with connected text	DIBELS Oral Reading Fluency *Measures words read correctly in a timed reading of a passage*	First through sixth grades
Vocabulary development	Word Use Fluency *Measures the ability to use common vocabulary words in sentences or phrases*	Kindergarten through second grade
Comprehension	Retell Fluency *Measures the ability to recall information in a reading passage*	First through sixth grades

performance benchmarks either do not exist or have been chosen arbitrarily rather than through a research validation process.

In the following two vignettes, we demonstrate how teachers make intervention decisions regarding individual students. Read about each student and examine the assessment data.

Nicole

Nicole's first-grade teacher, Ms. Franco, has been worried about her since the beginning of the school year. Ms. Franco first discovered that Nicole was having significant difficulty with phonemic awareness, an important foundational skill for reading, when she gave the DIBELS as a screening assessment in the fall. In the first month of school, Nicole scored as At Risk on the Phoneme Segmentation Fluency subtest in the DIBELS first-grade battery, with an instructional recommendation of Intensive. Nicole's scores in Letter Naming Fluency and Nonsense Word Fluency were also very low. Ms. Franco gave Nicole extra attention by having Nicole sit near her during phonological activities and did some individual follow-up with Nicole. Recently, Ms. Franco gave the mid-year assessment, and Nicole is still highly at risk in phonological and alphabetic areas. Ms. Franco has formed a small group of students with similar needs. She will meet with these students daily to do 20–30 minutes per day of intensive instruction in phonemic awareness and decoding.

Following are Nicole's scores on the DIBELS subtests (see Table 3) and a detailed look at her performance on Phoneme Segmentation Fluency (see Figure 3). Nicole's performance in Table 3 shows that she has serious phonological difficulties. In 1 minute, she got nine phonemes correct on the mid-year assessment, which indicates a need for intensive intervention. This is consistent with Nicole's classroom performance and is significantly below the benchmark of 35 for the middle of first grade. In terms of screening assessment scores, Nicole's score jumps out as a red flag that she needs help.

Digging a little deeper, we can look at Nicole's score diagnostically (see Figure 3). In a diagnostic perspective, a teacher looks for a student's strengths as well as areas of weakness. What patterns are apparent in Nicole's scores? Nicole was able to produce the beginning sounds in words fairly consistently. In three of the words, *man, kite,* and *kill,* she was able to segment the word into its onset (any sounds before the vowel) and rime (vowel and any remaining consonant sounds). Although her score indicates that she needs intensive assistance, we conclude that Nicole has some phonological ability that will provide a starting place for instruction. Segmenting words into onsets and rimes is the first step in developing phonemic awareness. Chapter 5 of this book contains a number of phonological activities that focus on onset–rime patterns. Starting with these activities would strengthen Nicole's existing skills and would provide a stronger foundation for moving on to other segmentation and blending activities.

Nicole's performance on the other subtests of DIBELS indicates that she is significantly below grade-level expectations across the range of skills assessed in first grade. However, by winter, Nicole has some automatic recognition of letters, a sign that she is developing the automatic processing skills necessary for reading. Ms. Franco would be

Table 3. Nicole's DIBELS scores

DIBELS subtest	DIBELS intervention recommendations by score	Nicole's scores	
		Fall	Winter
Letter Naming Fluency	Beginning of first grade:	18	26
	< 25 Intensive		
	25–36 Strategic		
	37+ Benchmark Met		
	Middle of first grade: N/A		
Phoneme Segmentation Fluency	Beginning and middle of first grade:	2	9
	< 10 Intensive		
	10–34 Strategic		
	35+ Benchmark Met		
Nonsense Word Fluency	Beginning of first grade:	0	6
	< 13 Intensive		
	13–23 Strategic		
	24+ Benchmark met		
	Middle of first grade:		
	< 30 Intensive		
	30–49 Strategic		
	50+ Benchmark Met		
DIBELS Oral Reading Fluency	Beginning of first grade: N/A	Not tested	0
	Middle of first grade:		
	< 8 Intensive		
	8–19 Strategic		
	20+ Benchmark met		
	Note: 40 or more correct words per minute by the end of first grade is the goal.		

Source: University of Oregon Center on Teaching and Learning. (n.d.).

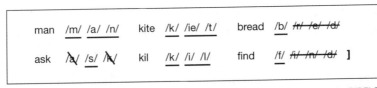

Figure 3. A diagnostic look at Nicole's Phoneme Segmentation Fluency subtest in the DIBELS first-grade battery. Ms. Franco scored this subtest by drawing lines under the sounds exactly as Nicole said them. A horizontal line drawn through a sound means that Nicole did not provide a response for that sound. A slanted line through a sound means that she gave an incorrect sound. The bracket at the end indicates the stopping place at the end of 1 minute.

wise to engage Nicole in a range of intervention activities that include both phonological and decoding skills. Given that more than half the school year has passed, it is urgent for Nicole to receive intensive assistance. At this point, using progress-monitoring assessment would allow Ms. Franco to have frequent data points to evaluate the effectiveness of intervention. The DIBELS system has a progress monitoring booklet that can be used for this purpose. This consists of multiple forms of each assessment so that Ms. Franco could assess Nicole frequently, as often as once per week, and chart her progress.

Figure 4 is a chart of Nicole's Phoneme Segmentation Fluency progress during a 6-week period in which Ms. Franco provided 30 minutes per day of supplemental instruction. In this chart, the dashed trend line indicates the desired slope of her performance over time. The solid line across the chart at 35 indicates the goal, or benchmark, for

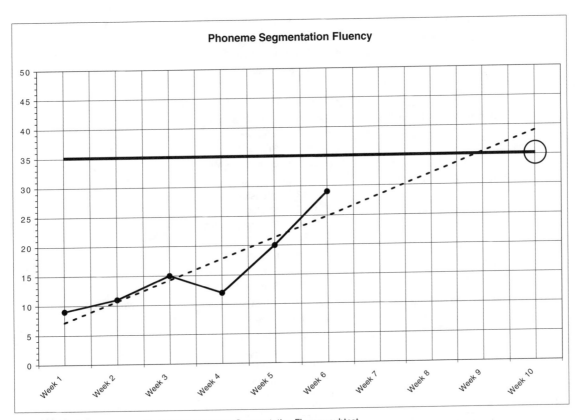

Figure 4. Nicole's progress on the DIBELS Phoneme Segmentation Fluency subtest.

this assessment. The circle at 35 at Week 10 shows what Nicole's goal would be for a 10-week intervention. If Nicole were to maintain her rapid rate of progress in intervention, she would easily meet the goal by the end of a 10-week period.

Jermaine

Jermaine is another student in Ms. Franco's first-grade class. In Letter Naming Fluency and Phoneme Segmentation Fluency (see Table 4), Jermaine did not appear to be highly at risk in the fall, although his Nonsense Word Fluency was in the Intensive range. By the winter assessment, he was not acquiring the decoding skills needed to be successful. Ms. Franco has decided mid-year to put Jermaine in an intervention group focusing on decoding and word recognition. She will do some additional phonological awareness practice with the intervention group to reinforce these skills.

Table 4 shows Jermaine's scores on the DIBELS subtests, and Figure 5 gives a detailed look at his performance on Nonsense Word Fluency. In the Nonsense Word Fluency assessment, the teacher puts a line under each sound read correctly. If the student gives an incorrect sound, the letter for that sound gets a slash mark through it. If the stu-

Table 4. Jermaine's DIBELS scores

DIBELS subtest	DIBELS intervention recommendations by score	Jermaine's scores	
		Fall	Winter

Letter Naming Fluency	Beginning of first grade:
	  < 25 Intensive
	  25–36 Strategic
	  37+ Benchmark Met
	Middle of first grade: N/A
		32	37

Phoneme Segmentation Fluency	Beginning and middle of first grade:
	  < 10 Intensive
	  10–34 Strategic
	  35+ Benchmark Met
		33	38

Nonsense Word Fluency	Beginning of first grade:
	  < 13 Intensive
	  13–23 Strategic
	  24+ Benchmark met
	Middle of first grade:
	  < 30 Intensive
	  30–49 Strategic
	  50+ Benchmark Met
		5	12

Oral Reading Fluency	Beginning of first grade: N/A
	Middle of first grade:
	  < 8 Intensive
	  8–19 Strategic
	  20+ Benchmark met
	Note: 40 or more correct words per minute by the end of first grade is the goal.
		Not tested	0

Source: University of Oregon Center on Teaching and Learning. (n.d.).

Figure 5. Jermaine's performance on the Nonsense Word Fluency subtest of the DIBELS first-grade battery. Ms. Franco scored this subtest in the winter testing period by drawing lines under the sounds exactly as Jermaine read them. When he read a word sound by sound, she marked each letter. When he read a word by blending the sounds together as a whole word, she marked it with a continuous line. Slanted lines indicate errors. In one place, Ms. Franco wrote a tiny *b* above the *d* to show that he read the word with a /b/ sound. The bracket at the end indicates the stopping place at the end of 1 minute.

dent reads sound by sound rather than blending the sounds in the word into a whole word, the teacher marks the letters individually. If the student reads the whole word, the teacher puts a solid line under the word. A bracket is used to indicate the place the student has reached in the passage when the timer goes off.

Jermaine's score of 12 correct sounds in 1 minute puts him in the Intensive range for first grade and in need of intervention in the area of decoding. Unlike Nicole, however, Jermaine does not have significant difficulties with phonological awareness or letter naming. Ms. Franco has placed him with two other students with similar decoding difficulties.

It is helpful to analyze Jermaine's performance diagnostically. First, Jermaine does not have fluency, or automaticity, with the alphabetic code. Getting only 12 sounds in 1 minute on the Nonsense Word Fluency subtest means that he reads very slowly. This will seriously affect his reading fluency, or rate. There are some other consistencies in the types of Jermaine's correct and incorrect responses. Jermaine consistently got the initial consonant sound correct. He knows several consonant sounds, but he confused /d/ with /b/ and missed several final consonant sounds (see Figure 5). Jermaine knows a few vowels, although his performance is inconsistent in this area. Ms. Franco will want to do some informal assessment to see if Jermaine does, in fact, know all of the sounds of the letters. Figure 5 also shows that Jermaine attempted to blend the nonword *nim*, which indicates that he is somewhat aware of the blending process.

What aspects of decoding are difficult for Jermaine? What does he need to work on in intervention? Jermaine consistently missed final consonant sounds and had difficulty with several vowel sounds. He has not mastered the blending process, and this is slowing him down. Ms. Franco has concluded that Jermaine needs intervention activities that move beyond initial sounds and that emphasize the blending process. Ms. Franco will use activities from Chapter 6 of this book to boost Jermaine's decoding skills.

How to Use the Activities in This Book

The Nuts and Bolts of Implementing Intervention

To be an effective reading intervention teacher, you will need to know how to organize and manage intervention. In this chapter, we provide what we call the "nuts and bolts" of intervention. It is important to think through the implementation process. The following topics, which are discussed in this chapter, are important if you are going to establish, maintain, and manage an effective intervention program in your classroom and provide parents with the guidance and materials they need to do the home activities with their children.

- How to prepare and organize materials

- How to use the classroom activities in Chapters 5–7

- Activity design and process for the classroom activities

- How to use the Home–School Connections in Section III (activities for students and their parents that correspond to the classroom activities)

- Activity design and process for the activities conducted by parents at home

- Time management for intervention

- A weekly intervention activity-planning tool

In addition, at the end of this chapter, we provide answers to some of the most common questions we have received from teachers:

1. What do I do with the other students while I'm working with my intervention group?

2. How do I make transitions between intervention activities?

3. How do I teach all students to work independently during intervention time?

4. How do I teach students to use each center?

5. How do I organize my time to fit intervention into my reading period?

6. How do I teach intervention when my students are working at many different levels?

We have worked with hundreds of teachers who have implemented reading intervention in their classrooms. We have taken practical advice from these teachers, and their answers to these questions appear at the end of this chapter.

HELPFUL HINTS REGARDING THE ACTIVITIES IN THIS BOOK

Throughout the classroom and home activities in this book, the following apply:

- Letters placed between slash marks represent letter sounds. For example, /ă/ represents the vowel sound of the letter *a* in the word *hat*, and /th/ represents the first sound in the word *thin*.

- Upper- and lowercase letters that are not between slash marks represent letter names rather than sounds, such as the letter *B* or the letter *g*.

- Short vowel sounds are indicated using a breve (˘) over the vowel, and long vowel sounds are indicated using a macron (‾) over the vowel. The unstressed schwa vowel sound is indicated using this symbol: ə.

These conventions are also explained to parents in a photocopiable letter that explains the use of the Home–School Connection activities. (This letter is discussed further later in this chapter, and a photocopiable version appears in the appendix.)

MATERIALS

The activities in this book call for the use of materials that are easily prepared, such as color tiles and letter tiles. Many of the other materials used in the activities in this book are readily available in classrooms and homes.

How to Prepare Intervention Materials

This book contains photocopiable templates (see the appendix) that will be useful in implementing some of the classroom intervention activities. These materials include the following:

1. *A blank bingo board:* This bingo board can be used for a variety of activities. Because it is blank, you can fill the squares with whatever is needed for the focus of the activity, or you can have the students write in the spaces. You can use it to work on letters, decoding words, or sight words. The blank spaces help organize giving directions when dictating words (e.g., "Boys and girls, write the word *was* in the first column, row 1").

2. *Color tiles:* Some of the phonological awareness activities in Chapter 5 call for the use of color tiles, such as to show segmenting and blending of sounds or word parts. The color tile template can be copied onto red, green, and blue construction paper or tag board and then cut apart.

3. *Lower- and uppercase letter tiles:* These letter tiles can be cut apart and placed in snack-size zip-top bags for easy storage and management. The letter tiles can be used with the bingo board for spelling words, with the sound templates (mentioned next) for segmenting and blending words, and simply on the table to play matching games or to spell words that are dictated by the teacher.

4. *Two-, three-, and four-sound templates:* The sound templates contain boxes, sometimes called Elkonin boxes, that are used for segmenting and blending two, three, and four-sound words. These boxes provide a visual prompt for outlining how the materials should look when the students perform the task. In this case, the boxes represent empty cells that should be filled by color or letter tiles. Color or letter tiles are placed above the line at the top of a sound template, and letters are pulled down into the boxes as a student says each letter sound aloud. The words may then be blended and segmented depending on the skill level of the student.

5. A *fluency graph:* This blank graph can be used with a variety of activities, especially those in Chapter 7 and the matching home activities at the end of Section III. Students can complete the graph by coloring in a bar when a timed fluency exercise has been completed. If students are working at the letter knowledge level, then they complete the graph with how many letters they can identify in a minute. If students are working at the word level, then they fill in the graph with the number of words read in a minute. At the sentence level, students graph how many words correct per minute they read.

6. A *high-frequency word bank:* The high-frequency word bank is a tool that can be used by all students who need to memorize and master these words with automaticity. It is very important that all students be able to read the high-frequency word list. These words constitute about 50% of what is written in decodable texts. Reading with mastery is essential to good reading fluency. Place this list or a high-frequency word bank from your core reading program in each fluency kit (described on p. 32) so that students can have quick access to it at any time during intervention.

7. Several sheets of *high-frequency word cards:* These word cards can be cut apart and used to review high-frequency words during intervention or as a take-home assignment. The cards can be used as flash cards to help a student develop rapid word reading skills, or two sets of these cards can be used in a concentration game with a partner, in which the words are matched and then read aloud and used in complete sentences.

8. A *word bank of high-frequency nouns:* This word bank of high-frequency nouns is a list of words that students will need to read with automaticity. The words in this list should be used in 1-minute timed tests until mastery of the list is achieved.

9. Various *graphic organizers:* Chapter 8 describes and provides examples of a number of different graphic organizers and other tools that you can use when working on vocabulary development and comprehension with your students.

These materials will need to be made for each student in your intervention groups or for every student in your classroom. It is recommended that the materials be duplicated on tag board. They will last longer as the students use them throughout the school year.

If you are working with a group of teachers and want to make intervention materials for many students, assign tasks to each teacher so that no one teacher is responsible for duplicating the materials for an entire grade level. Set up a meeting at which materials will be cut, hole-punched, assembled into intervention kits, and made ready for classroom use.

In addition to preparing classroom materials, it is useful to assemble kits for students to take home to use when doing the Home–School Connection activities with their parents. The Home–School Connection activity pages are photocopiable so that students can take the activity pages home with them. See the section later in this chapter called Implementing the Home–School Connection Program for a discussion of how to prepare these materials and activity pages.

How to Organize Intervention Materials

After intervention materials are made and sorted, they can be placed in individual gallon-size zip-top bags and stored either in a central box in the classroom or at students' desks. These intervention kits are an easy and inexpensive way to gather and store the materials needed for students to work independently or in small groups during the independent work time provided daily in the reading program. The bags are also a convenient means of organizing and storing materials for daily use during intervention, allowing for fluid transitions between activities. Students simply pick up their bags and move them from center to center, ultimately bringing the bags to the teacher's table to use for fluency checks and assessment.

Some teachers have purchased inexpensive tackle boxes at a hardware or do-it-yourself store. A tackle box is an excellent means of organizing letter and color tiles for easy access for intervention. In addition, many teachers have developed intervention folders. These folders typically have pockets in which to store center work and usually have a record sheet where students can check off completed work. This tracking system helps teachers in monitoring and organizing student work. In the intervention folders, teachers have also placed a fluency graph, a reading passage, a list of high-frequency words, and any other materials that students will need to work during the intervention period.

The fluency activities in Chapter 7 in particular call for numerous materials to be used during the activities. It is helpful to have all of these materials assembled into fluency kits that contain the following:

1. Resealable Ziploc baggie (gallon size or larger)

2. One high-frequency word bank

3. Two sets of high-frequency word cards, preferably in two different colors

The Home–School Connection activities that focus on fluency also involve numerous prepared materials. Similar fluency kits can be provided for students to take home; these kits should also include additional lists of high-frequency words, with 10 words on a page, to be posted weekly on the refrigerator.

Alternative Materials that You May Have in Your Classroom

Teachers are very resourceful people. You may have purchased manipulatives, puzzles, word games, student white boards, and so forth that you can use to accompany any number of the interventions in this book. We recommend that you use any materials that meet the needs of your students. We once visited a classroom where a teacher used small puzzles to teach words beginning with consonant blends and short vowels. Each puzzle displayed a picture, and the letters spelling the name of the pictured object were color coded so that students could tell the difference between the consonant blends and the vowel sounds. The teacher had purchased these puzzle materials at a local teacher supply store.

HOW TO USE THE CLASSROOM ACTIVITIES

Classroom Activity Design and Process: A Walk Through an Activity

Each classroom activity in this book is constructed in the same way and in the same sequence. Following are outlines of the components of a classroom activity and the activity design. The only design features that may differ from activity to activity are that some activities have variations, whereas others do not, and certain activities do not require the use of a word bank.

Activity Components

1. Big Idea

2. Focus On

3. Title

4. Goal(s)

5. Materials

6. Teacher Steps: Describe It

7. Student Steps: Do It

8. Variation(s) (for selected activities)

9. Word Bank (for most activities)

The activities in this book are grouped into the five Big Ideas of reading intervention—phonological awareness, alphabetic principle, fluency with connected text, vocabulary development, and comprehension. Chapters 5–7 contain classroom activities that relate to the first three Big Ideas, and the last two Big Ideas are covered in Chapter 8. Because there are so many phonological awareness and alphabetic principle activities, the Big Ideas are further subdivided into "Focus On" headings in Chapters 5 and 6 to indicate which subskill of the Big Idea is the target for intervention. Shaded bars on the margins of the classroom activity pages are designed to help you navigate through the various Focus On subsections, and the home activity pages carry matching shaded bars.

On the classroom activity pages, a small image of a sun bearing the letters *HS* indicates that the activity has a corresponding Home–School Connection activity. The Home–School Connection activities have numbers and titles that are identical to their corresponding classroom activities. (Because not every classroom activity has a home activity, the numbering of the home activities is not consecutive in some places.)

Activity Design

1. Model the intervention.

    a. Teacher Steps: Describe It

2. Guide students through the intervention.

    a. Student Steps: Do It

3. Provide independent practice.

4. Incorporate correction procedures.

5. Integrate and fade scaffolds.

6. Try the variations.

Sample Classroom Activity: Segmenting and Blending Three-Sound Words

Following is an example of how a typical activity is written, accompanied by a discussion of each phase in the activity. (The sample activity, Segmenting and Blending Three-Sound Words, is Activity 18 in Chapter 5.) Keep in mind that you can integrate and fade the scaffolds that are at your fingertips.

Modeling

In the first phase of each activity, you must get students' attention and demonstrate the task by serving as a model. In the activities in this book, this phase is listed as Teacher Steps: Describe It. Let's look at this step in the sample activity.

Teacher Steps: Describe It

Here, the teacher demonstrates the task by saying the word and manipulating the tiles for one word. The instructions that you will see in the book look like this:

- Place three blank tiles above the bold line on the three-sound template.
- Say a word from the word bank (e.g., *sip*).
- Move one tile into each square for every sound you say (/s/ /ĭ/ /p/).
- Move the tiles together as you blend the sounds (*sip*).

Here is an example of what a teacher might say to students at this stage of the activity:

Teacher: Today we are going to listen for the sounds in words. All of our words will have three sounds. I have three tiles in front of me. The word is *sip . . . sip.* Watch me put down tiles for each sound in the word: /s/ [first tile goes down] . . . /ĭ/ [second tile goes down] . . . /p/ [third tile goes down]. [The teacher puts a tile down on the table each time he or she says a sound.] Now I will blend the sounds and say the whole word: *sip.* [While the teacher says the whole word, he or she pushes the tiles together to demonstrate visually that the sounds "smoosh" together to make a whole word.]

Guided Practice

In the guided practice phase, the students perform the task simultaneously with the teacher. It is important to have the materials needed for the activity ready ahead of time so that the activity does not lose momentum while you search for the right materials. Guide the students through the task by providing clear directions while performing the task. These instructions are listed in each activity in the section called Student Steps: Do It. Of course, you would also give corrective feedback if students do not seem to grasp the concept.

Student Steps: Do It

The instructions that you will see in the book look like this:

- Distribute three tiles and a three-sound template to each student.
- Say the following:
  - "What are the sounds in the word _____?" (e.g., *sip*)
  - "Put one tile in each square for every sound you say." (/s/ /ĭ/ /p/)
  - "Blend the sounds as you move the tiles together." (*sip*)

- As the students become proficient, say the following instead:
  - "What are the sounds in the word _____?" (e.g., *sip*)

The teacher might say something like this:

Teacher: Now it's your turn to say the sounds in the word. Listen to the word: *sip.* What are the sounds in *sip?* Let's put down a tile for every sound we hear. Let's do it together. Ready? /s/ [first tile goes down] . . . /ĭ/ [second tile goes down] . . . /p/ [third tile goes down]. Now, let's blend the sounds and say the whole word. Ready? [The teacher pushes his or her tiles together. Students follow suit while saying the word.] *Sip.*

Independent Practice

In the independent practice phase, students practice the task while you provide the target words and give feedback to individuals as necessary. First, the students perform the task together as a group. Then, after a few words, ask individuals to perform the task alone to ensure that each student has grasped the concept. A word bank is provided for each activity so you will not have to think of words on the spot.

Teacher: Here's your next word. Let's do it together. Ready? The word is *cup. Cup.* What are the sounds in the word *cup?* Now, put down a tile for every sound. [Students put down tiles as they say the sounds: /k/ /ŭ/ /p/.] Good job, everyone. Now, let's blend the sounds together and say the whole word. Ready? *Cup.*

Correction Procedure

When individual students have difficulty with a task, it is necessary to break it down further. Here is an example of how to break down the task for a student. In this step, the teacher talks an individual student, Jonathan, through each sound:

Teacher: Jonathan, the word is *bat.* Listen: *bat.* The sounds in the word bat are /b/ /ă/ /t/. What is the first sound?

Jonathan: /b/

Teacher: Now, put down one tile for the /b/ sound just like I did. Say /b/ while you put down the tile. Good job.

Teacher: What is the second sound in bat? [Jonathan does not say the sound.] Jonathan, listen: /b/ . . . /ă/ . . . /t/. Put down a tile for the /ă/ sound. Say it with me . . . /ă/. Good job. Now, what is the last sound in *bat?*

Jonathan: /t/

Teacher: Put down a tile for the /t/ sound. Say sounds in *bat* as you point to each tile. Blend the sounds. Ready? *Bat.*

Integration and Fading of Scaffolds

In this section we describe materials or ideas for scaffolding intervention instruction. Each of these scaffolds could be used as a variation of an activity. On the activity pages, you will sometimes see suggestions for variations.

A scaffold is something that provides temporary support while students are learning a task. Scaffolding is used during or as a follow up to a lesson when a student or group of students is having difficulty grasping a concept. These items and activities will help to make the abstract reading concepts or ideas more concrete to students. Once students become independent with a skill, you will want to fade, or gradually phase out, the concrete scaffold and have students perform the tasks without a visual prompt.

Sound Templates

Sound templates are useful when a student is just beginning the blending and segmenting tasks. For example, in the activity described in this chapter, teaching three-sound words, the teacher would tell the student to take out three blue tiles. The student would place each tile above the line at the top of the three-sound template. When the teacher asks the student to sound out the word *bat*, the student would pull down one tile into each box at the bottom of the sound template while making the sounds of the word and then would blend the word. Once the student becomes independent with blending and segmenting, the teacher can gradually phase out the use of the template and just use the tiles on the table without the prompt provided by the template.

Color Tiles

To use color tiles in an activity to teach three-sound words, the teacher would ask the student to take out three color tiles and place them on the table. Without the use of other scaffolds, the students would move each color tile downward slightly while saying the sounds of the word, for example, /b/ /ă/ /t/. Then the student would "smoosh" the tiles together while saying the word *bat*.

Slinky

A Slinky is a useful kinesthetic scaffold for assisting students to segment and blend words. In some activities the students are to hold a Slinky in front of themselves horizontally as if they were playing an accordion and pull apart and push together the slinky while saying the sounds of a word such as /b/ /ă/ /t/. We recommend the small Slinkies rather than the large ones. The larger Slinkies droop down in the middle when doing the segmenting activity, whereas the smaller ones maintain their shape.

Kinesthetic Activities

Students often use their arm as another scaffold. For example, in an activity about three-sound words, students can point to their shoulder while saying the sound /b/, point to the middle of their arm while voicing the sound /ă/, and point to their hand when voicing the sound /t/. Sweeping the hand from shoulder to hand while blending the entire word *bat* concludes the use of the scaffold.

Self-Phones

These tools are called *self-phones* because students are typically talking to themselves while using them. A self-phone is made from 4″ PVC pipe with one elbow fitting on either end. These supplies can be purchased from any home improvement store or from school supply catalogs. Students use self-phones simply to amplify sounds so that pronunciation and sound discrimination can be mastered. As students speak into their self-phones, they can hear the sounds that they are making more clearly than they would without the devices. Speech therapists often use these tools in therapy.

How to Use the Word Banks

There are word banks at the end of most of the intervention activities that you can use when needed. Word banks are critical to the success of your implementation of the intervention, as you will not need to look for words or make them up on the spot for any activity. Each bank of words is appropriate for the activity it is attached to, and you can use some or all of the words depending on your goal for that activity. If your goal is skill mastery, then you might want to use all of the words to test students' skills in performing the task with a number of words. If you are just reviewing or practicing a certain skill, then using a partial list may be more appropriate.

HOW TO USE THE HOME-SCHOOL CONNECTIONS

The connection between home and school is a critical part of any intervention activity. Research shows that children are more likely to succeed in school when their families are actively supporting them at home (U.S. Department of Education, 2002). The U.S. Department of Education offers homework tips to teachers and parents at the following web site: http://www.ed.gov/parents/academic/help/homework/index.html.

In Section III, Home–School Connection activities are provided for parents to work with their children at home to reinforce and review activities that have already been covered in your class. Each Home–School Connection activity follows a uniform sequence in both the components of the activity and the design of the activity. Parents are asked to model the task, guide their child through the steps of the task, and then incorporate a correction procedure if necessary.

The purpose of the Home–School Connections is to have adults reinforce the interventions with a child at home. Selected interventions have been written in a format that makes it easy for adults to practice the interventions with a child.

Activity Design and Process: A Walk Through a Home-School Connection Activity

The design of the home activities is similar to that of the interventions delivered by the teacher, but the Home–School Connection activities are more directive in that they are in a more scripted format. Following is a listing of the typical components and design of a Home–School Connection activity.

Activity Components

1. Big Idea

2. Focus On

3. Title

4. Goal

5. Materials

6. Model

7. Now It's Your Turn (guided practice)

8. Extra Support (correction procedure)

9. Variations (for some activities)

10. Word Bank (for most activities)

Activity Design

1. The parent models the intervention at the beginning of the activity: "I'm going to say a three-sound word: /s/ /ă/ /t/. Now I'm going to say the word together: *sat.*" The parent actually says the word aloud, segmenting the word as /s/ /ă/ /t/ and then blending the word together as *sat.*

2. The parent guides the child through the intervention: "Now it's your turn to say the sounds of the word and then say the whole word."

3. The parent incorporates correction procedures if needed: "Listen to me say the sounds of the word *sat.* The sounds in the word *sat* are /s/ /ă/ /t/."

Sample Home–School Connection Activity: Segmenting and Blending Three-Sound Words

Following is an example of a typical Home–School Connection Activity. The sample activity, Segmenting and Blending Three-Sound Words, is Activity 18 on page 283 in the phonological awareness activities in Section III.

Modeling

The Model section provides specific language the adult uses to demonstrate the intervention. For the phonological awareness and alphabetic principle interventions, it is recommended that the adult provide three demonstrations before asking the child to complete the task.

Say the following:
- "I'm going to break apart the word *sat.*"
- "Listen and watch while I put down one square for each sound I say: /s /ă/ /t/."
- "The word is *sat.*" (Say the word while pushing the squares together.)

Guided Practice

The section titled Now It's Your Turn gives the child an opportunity to practice the intervention with the adult. Again, the activity provides the specific language that the adult should use to guide the child through the process. The Now It's Your Turn portion of the activity also contains directions to the adult on the use of the word bank as the child practices the targeted skill:

- Say the following:
  - "Put down one square for each sound in the word _____." (Say a word from Column 1. See the answer in Column 2.)
- Say the word and push the squares together.

Correction Procedure

The Extra Support portion of the activity contains a straightforward, consistent correction procedure that the adult can use when the child makes an error. The adult simply models the correct response and asks the child to repeat each step.

- If the child has difficulty moving one square for each sound, model the correct response and ask the child to repeat after you.

Word Bank

Word banks are provided for most of the phonological awareness and alphabetic principle home activities. The structure of each word bank depends on the complexity of the skill being taught. A number of the phonological awareness word banks contain a column of words and a column showing how the word is segmented into onset and rime or individual phonemes. If the intervention requires the child to add, delete, or substitute a phoneme, there is a column listing those phonemes. The adult is directed to the appropriate column in the word bank throughout the activity. The following example word bank would be used in an activity in which the child practices adding an initial consonant sound:

1. Word pairs	2. Sounds	3. Added sound
at-mat	/m/ /ă/ /t/	/m/
an-pan	/p/ /ă/ /n/	/p/

There are two types of word banks for the alphabetic principle activities. The first is similar to the word banks just described for the phonological awareness activities. They are composed of two columns, one containing the target words and a second listing the sounds that were added, deleted, or substituted. The second type simply lists words used for interventions in which the child is asked to spell and/or read words.

Implementing the Home–School Connection Program

Orientation

Because most of the adults who will be working with your students at home will not be reading teachers, it is important to conduct a short training session on teaching these activities. Parents will need to know how to conduct the interventions, how to say the sounds correctly, and understand rudimentary concepts in beginning reading. It is important to prepare the materials that adults will need to conduct the interventions (described later in this section) and give these materials out at the orientation session. The appendix contains photocopiable masters of some of these materials.

In addition, it is a good idea to provide parents with a brief letter that they can take home with the materials. This letter can serve as a reminder for parents on how to use the materials and also is useful if more than one adult will be doing activities with the child at home and only one adult is able to come to the orientation session. Parents who are unable to attend the orientation may also find the letter helpful. A photocopiable letter can be found in the appendix.

Training for parents should include not only an explanation of the skills students will be learning but also hands-on practice and time to ask questions. Be sure to have materials ready to demonstrate sample Home–School Connection activities. Following is a possible format for a 30-minute orientation session for parents:

10 minutes	Explain the five Big Ideas of reading and give examples of each skill.
5 minutes	Describe the steps of the Home–School Connection activities. Model two or three activities for parents, using an overhead projector to show how letter or color tiles are used.
10 minutes	Give parents materials and a photocopied Home–School Connection activity. Have them work in pairs, taking turns in the roles of parent and child.
5 minutes	Lead a group discussion and answer questions.

Providing Materials and Activity Pages to Parents

Like the classroom activities, the Home–School Connection activities involve the use of some materials that are available around the house and some prepared materials. So that students and parents will have all of the latter materials needed for the activities, prepare these materials ahead of time and give them to parents at the orientation session.

The Home–School Connection activity pages are photocopiable so that you can make as many copies as you need for your students. It is best to send these activity pages home with students in batches rather than all at once. This way parents will know which activities you want them to focus on and will not try to do too many activities with their child at one time.

Phonological Awareness Intervention Materials

For the phonological awareness interventions, adults will need a two-sound, a three-sound, and a four-sound template. They will also need eight red paper squares and four blue paper squares instead of the blank plastic tiles or cubes that you use in the classroom. You can make these squares by duplicating the color tile master template on red and blue construction paper or tag board. For each participant, cut out these 12 squares and place them in a small plastic baggie. This small baggie is then placed in a gallon-size zip-top bag along with the sound templates. The photocopied phonological awareness Home–School Connection activities can be stored in this bag as they are sent home in batches.

Alphabetic Principle Intervention Materials

Each adult will need two sets of lowercase letters. You can make these paper letters by duplicating the lowercase letter template on white construction paper or tag board. Cut out the sets of letters and place each set in a small plastic baggie, one set for the child and one for the adult. The two small baggies are placed in a gallon-size zip-top bag. The photocopied alphabetic principle Home–School Connection activities can be stored in this as they are sent home in batches.

Fluency Intervention Materials

The fluency interventions focus on reading high-frequency words and connected text. Not all reading programs introduce high-frequency words in the same order, but the appendix has a high-frequency word bank and master high-frequency word cards that can be duplicated on construction paper or tag board and made into flash cards and/or reading lists. Similarly, some of the fluency Home–School Connection activities call for reading passages at the students' independent and instructional level. You will have to duplicate the appropriate passages for these interventions. (Chapter 7 describes how to determine students' independent and instructional reading levels.) A master of a reading fluency graph is provided in the appendix so that students can monitor their progress in reading high-frequency words and connected text. A timer is also needed for some of these interventions. Most homes have one that is readily available.

Ongoing Communication

Each time that you assign a Home–School Communication activity, you will need to communicate clearly about which activity you would like parents to do with students and which materials will be required. It is important that you communicate which interventions you would like reinforced at home, such as through a brief note indicating the name of the intervention(s) with which a child needs help. For example, if a child is experiencing difficulty segmenting three-sound words, write a note asking the adult to work on the Home–School Connection activity called Segmenting and Blending Three-Sound Words.

TIME MANAGEMENT FOR INTERVENTION

Every teacher knows that time management can make or break any activity. It is important to be able to structure an activity for just the right amount of time so that students are engaged in an optimal learning environment. To get in 20–30 minutes of daily intervention, you may need to plan two short intervention activities to be conducted at separate times of the day. Some teachers find it easier to do this than to carve out a half hour to work with one group. Changing the activities frequently can also aid in keeping the students' attention, thereby avoiding any unpleasant behavior. Effective time management also sends a clear message that the teacher is in charge. (For additional tips on time management, see Common Question 5, "How do I organize my time to fit intervention into my reading period?" at the end of this chapter.)

INTERVENTION PLANNING TOOLS

Planning is critical to the success of any intervention program. Weekly activity plans help you as the teacher to adjust your instruction to the changing needs of your students. As students progress and master the intervention skills, you will need to plan for new learning. Figure 6 is a lesson planning worksheet. The goal is to complete the worksheet weekly and keep a record of the sequence of student intervention activities. Figure 7 lists each skill included in *Interventions for Reading Success*. This tool is suggested as a weekly or bimonthly assistant to managing your interventions. (For more on gauging student progress, see Common Question 6, "How do I know if my students have mastered all of the skills for intervention?" at the end of this chapter.)

COMMON QUESTIONS FROM TEACHERS

Following are some of the most common questions we have received from teachers.

1. What do I do with the other students while I am working with my intervention group?

We often hear teachers say, "If the other 17 students weren't in the room, I could really work with my students who are most at risk." This is simply not possible, but there are less drastic methods for managing the rest of the class while teaching an at-risk intervention group.

This task can be one of the most challenging for teachers. Providing meaningful activities and work for students and keeping them busy so that you can work with the most at-risk students is an art. Setting up centers and activities throughout the classroom is a very effective way of managing the independent work time of all students. Some centers are permanent, such as a listening center, writing center, computer center, and library center. Other centers are dynamic and will change from week to week. These might include a word-making center, a game center, and individual intervention kits for each student. The dynamic centers can be adjusted weekly so that the letters, words, and/or books that children read are changed with their weekly progress and skill mastery. When activities are geared at students' instructional levels, frustration is limited to isolated instances.

Managing student traffic at each center is easily remedied by having a student check-off card at the centers. Students are then reminded that if they have checked off their name on the card, they must choose a different center to visit. This cuts down on having more than two students working at any one center at one time. Here is an example of a card for a center that Mary and Bryan have already visited:

Name	Check-off
Ashley	
Bryan	✓
David	
Mary	✓

Intervention Lesson Plan

Teacher: _____ Dates: From _____ to _____

Big Idea	Time (minutes)	Intervention	Materials	Students
PA AP Vocab. ELD				
PA AP Vocab. ELD				
PA AP Vocab. ELD				
PA AP Vocab. ELD				
PA AP Vocab. ELD				

PA = phonological awareness; AP = alphabetic principle; Vocab. = vocabulary development; ELD = English language development.

Interventions for Reading Success by Diane Haager, Joseph A. Dimino, and Michelle Windmueller

Figure 6.   Intervention lesson plan.

Goals	Page numbers	
	Classroom activities	Home–School Connection activities
Rhyming		
Students will develop an understanding of the concepts of rhyme and rhyming and how rhyme is typically used.	58–61	269
Students will practice rhyming word pairs.		270
Students will make rhymes using objects around the room.		271
Onset and Rime		
Students will segment and blend onsets and rimes.	66–73, 82–84	272–273
Segmenting and Blending		
Students will segment and blend words with two sounds.	85–86, 93–119	282, 285–296
Students will segment and blend words with three sounds.	87–89, 93–119	283, 285–296
Students will segment and blend words with four sounds.	90–119	284–296
Students will identify the initial sound that has been added to a word to make a new word.	74–75, 105–108	274–275, 285–288
Students will identify the sound that has been added to a word to make a new word.	109–112	289–290
Students will identify the final sound that has been added to a word to make a new word.	76–77	276–277
Students will identify the initial sound that has been deleted from a word to make a new word.	78–79, 113–117	278–279, 291–294
Students will identify the sound that has been deleted from a word to make a new word.	118–119	295–296
Students will identify the final sound that has been deleted from a word to make a new word.	80–81	280–281
Students will identify the initial consonant sound that has been substituted to make a new word.	120–121	297–298
Students will identify the final consonant sound that has been substituted to make a new word.	122–123	299–300
Students will identify the medial sound that has been substituted to make a new word.	124–125	301–302
Letter–Sound Correspondence		
Students will spell two-sound words in which each sound is represented by one letter.	129	303
Students will spell three-sound words in which each sound is represented by one letter.	130–131, 134	304–305
Students will spell four-sound words in which each sound is represented by one letter.	132–134	306–307
Adding Sounds		
Students will spell new words by adding an initial consonant sound.	135–136	308–309
Students will spell new words by adding a final consonant sound.	137–138	310–311
Students will spell new words by adding a sound to form an initial consonant blend.	139–140, 143–144	312–313, 316–317
Students will spell new words by adding an initial consonant blend.	141–142	314–315
Deleting Sounds		
Students will spell new words by deleting an initial consonant sound.	145–146	318–319
Students will spell new words by deleting a final consonant sound.	151–152	324–325

Figure 7. Goals included in *Interventions for Reading Success.*

continued

Figure 7. *(continued)*

Goals	Page numbers	
	Classroom activities	Home–School Connection activities
Deleting Sounds *(continued)*		
Students will spell new words by deleting the first sound from an initial consonant blend.	147–148	320–321
Students will spell new words by deleting the second sound from an initial consonant blend.	149–150	322–323
Substituting Sounds		
Students will spell new words by substituting an initial consonant sound.	153–154, 160–161	326–327
Students will spell new words by substituting a final consonant sound.	155–157, 160–161	328–329
Students will spell new words by substituting a medial sound.	158–160	330–331
Long Vowel Spelling Patterns		
Students will spell words with the long *a* sound.	162–163, 172–175	332–333, 342–345
Students will spell words with the long *e* sound.	164–165, 172–173 178–181	334–335, 342–343 348–351
Students will spell words with the long *i* sound.	166–167, 172–173 182–183	336–337, 342–343 352–353
Students will spell words with the long *o* sound.	168–169, 172–173 184–187	338–339, 342–343 354–357
Students will spell words with the long *u* sound.	170–173	340–343
Students will spell words containing the *ay* digraph.	176–177	346–347
Variant Vowel Spelling Patterns		
Students will spell long *o* words containing the *ow* digraph.	188–189	358–359
Students will spell words containing the murmur diphthong *ar.*	190–191	360–361
Students will spell words containing the murmur diphthong *or.*	192–193	362–363
Students will spell words containing the murmur diphthong *er.*	194–195	364–365
Students will spell words containing the murmur diphthong *ir.*	196–197	366–367
Students will spell words containing the murmur diphthong *ur.*	198–199	368–369
Students will spell words containing the short *oo* sound.	200–201, 204–205	370–371, 374–375
Students will spell words containing the long *oo* sound.	202–205	372–375
Students will spell words containing the *oy* diphthong.	206–207	376–377
Students will spell words containing the *oi* diphthong.	208–209	378–379
Students will spell words containing the *ou* diphthong.	210–211	380–381
Students will spell words containing the *ow* diphthong.	212–213	382–383
Students will spell words containing the *ew* digraph.	214–215	384–385
Students will spell words containing the *au* digraph.	216–217	386–387
Fluency with Connected Text		
Students will read high-frequency words accurately and fluently.	230	390
Students will read and recognize high-frequency words with mastery and fluency.	231–239	391–396
Students will write, read, and recognize high-frequency words with mastery and fluency.	228	388
Students will increase fluency and accuracy.	229, 240–246	389, 397–400

The check-off card is also a helpful tool to teach all students to work independently and make good choices throughout the intervention period. This simple tool also ensures that students reach each center during an entire week of intervention. At the end of a week, students who have completed all centers may receive a sticker or a stamp from the teacher in their intervention folder.

The centers also help you, the teacher, differentiate instruction for all learners in your classroom. Students are working at many different levels in your classroom. Having different levels of materials at each center will help to better meet the differing needs of each student. For example, at the listening center, some students can listen to taped anthologies, and others can listen to a decodable text. The differentiated text helps to individualize the activity so that an at-risk reader is not reading text at the frustration level and is still benefiting from the intervention activity.

2. How do I make transitions between intervention activities?

This is a question asked by most teachers. We have observed in numerous classrooms that teachers use a variety of techniques for transitions from one activity to another. One first-grade teacher had the students recite the words to a nursery rhyme while they walked to their next station. By the time the students finished reciting the nursery rhyme, they needed to be in their seats. This accomplished two tasks for the teacher: First, the students made the transition without talking and walking aimlessly, and second, students learned many nursery rhymes throughout the year, which provides good phonological practice.

A second technique for making transitions from one intervention activity to another is in the use of music. We have witnessed a group of second graders moving from one station to the next to taped music. By the time the music stopped, the students needed to be in their new seat. This was calming and effective in getting students to transition to the next activity.

3. How do I teach all students to work independently during intervention time?

Sometimes you can teach students the skill of working independently by teaching the behaviors you want your students to have and by reinforcing on-task behavior when you see it. Then you can begin to introduce all of the activities that the students will be working on during the intervention period. Make sure that you tell your students the rules for how to get help if they get stuck. You will want to make it clear that students cannot interrupt you while you work with an intervention group. Simulation often is a precursor to beginning intervention. Have students rotate through the activity centers and pretend to work at completing a task so that they know what the expectations are for working by themselves or with a partner. When students exhibit appropriate behavior in the simulation, it is then time to introduce real centers and intervention activities. For the first few days, stop regularly to reinforce students who are displaying on-task behavior so that the students who are still struggling with independent work habits will see what is expected.

4. How do I teach students to use each center?

We teach center use by introducing one center at a time during a demonstration before beginning an intervention work period. Begin the week by introducing the students to one center. In this introduction, you will teach the rules of the center and the actual academic skills needed for this center. You will also model the actual use of the materials followed by having individual students demonstrate how to do the activities and ask any unanswered questions. If there are multiple activities within a center, we recommend that you introduce only a few activities at a time to ensure that students have mastered them and then slowly introduce more activities over time. If the center has only one main focus, such as a listening center, introduce that center and go on to a new center the next day. When students have a sufficient number of activities to choose from (four to five), then vary the activities as needed each week or every other week.

Here is an example of how Ms. Shaw, a second-grade teacher, introduced the centers in her classroom during 1 week. By Friday of that week, the students knew how to operate all centers and she launched her complete intervention program with groups rotating to centers. The time she invested in teaching students how to use the centers was well spent.

Monday   *Listening center*

The purpose of the listening center is for students to listen to tape-recorded books to hear models of fluent reading. There are several things that students must learn in order to function in this center:

- How to use the equipment

- How to find and put away the books and tapes

- Behavior rules

- How to record what students have done each day on a simple checklist

Tuesday   *Writing center*

The writing center has all of the materials necessary for students to work independently with the writing process. Directions are posted, with an example of the step-by-step procedures for the writing process. There are certain things that students must learn in order to function in this center:

- How to use the materials that are clearly labeled in the center

- Behavior rules

- How to use a writing folder

- How to record what students have done each day on a simple checklist

Wednesday   *Fluency center*

The purpose of the fluency center is to practice fluency activities using words and materials posted throughout the room and in a specific place in the classroom. There are certain things that students must learn in order to function in this center:

- How to work with a partner in timing fluency exercises

- How to record fluency scores on a fluency graph

- How to use the word wall and/or sight word cards for fluency practice

- How to record activities on a simple checklist

Thursday   *Word games center*

The word games center is stocked with word puzzles and games that allow the students to practice decoding concepts taught in class. Teachers might also include lists of decodable words to use in pairs with a timer. Students can work in pairs or individually. We do not recommend using larger groups because doing so could get disruptive. Teachers will need to demonstrate the following:

- How to play the games or do the puzzles

- Rules for playing games and maintaining order in the center

- How to clean up materials

- How to record activities on a simple checklist

5. How do I organize my time to fit intervention into my reading period?

Intervention is a critical and necessary element to any reading program. You must consider this essential to your reading program, not peripheral. Let's look at a day in the life of Ms. Shaw and see how she fits intervention into her daily teaching schedule.

Morning   When students enter the classroom, Ms. Shaw begins the day with one of the ten-penny fluency activities (see Chapter 7). This focuses the entire class on beginning the day with a quick intervention activity (e.g. One Minute, Please; Echo Reading).

Before recess   The time between the start of school and recess is typically spent in a reading block. Structured intervention is usually part of this time unless it is scheduled for after recess or after lunchtime.

After recess   Ms. Shaw usually conducts her math lessons after recess. When students are working independently on their follow-up assignment, she pulls a student or two aside for 5–10 minutes and gives them extra help in reading intervention.

After lunch	Students come in from lunch and have sustained silent reading for about 10 minutes. Ms. Shaw pulls a few more students to conduct 10 minutes of reading intervention at this time. She typically works with the students who have difficulty reading alone, focusing on needed early reading intervention activities.
End of day and after school	While the homework monitors in Ms. Shaw's class are busy distributing the day's homework assignment and students are readying themselves to go home, Ms. Shaw pulls a few students aside to read words from the word wall. Ms. Shaw has said that whenever there is a spare minute in the day, it is filled with reading intervention activities. There are a few students who always have permission to stay after school. When Ms. Shaw is free at the end of the day, she grabs those students to work on 10 more minutes of reading intervention.

6. How do I teach intervention when my students are working at many different levels?

The answer to this question is differentiating instruction. It would be ideal to have everyone working on the same level, but this is unrealistic. Although Ms. Shaw assigns a spelling task to her group of five intervention students, there are two in the group who need the assignment modified even further. For example, instead of writing eight words, these two students write only five. When Ms. Shaw assigns partner work in reading fluency, one student may be reading a passage slightly below grade level, whereas another student may be practicing high-frequency words. Having students work at their own level helps to minimize behavior problems and prescribes the appropriate intervention work for each student. Reading intervention is *not* a one-size-fits-all model.

Classroom Activities

Phonological Awareness

FOCUS ON: Rhyming

FOCUS ON: Onset-Rime and Phonemic Awareness

FOCUS ON: Segmenting and Blending

INTRODUCTION

Phonological awareness is the understanding of different ways that oral language can be manipulated and divided into smaller components. Spoken language can be broken down in many different ways, including sentences into words and words into syllables (e.g., in the word table, /tā/ and /bəl/), onset and rime (e.g., in the word *brănch*, /br/ and /ănch/), and individual phonemes (e.g., in the word pump, /p/, /ŭ/, /m/, /p/). Manipulating sounds includes deleting, adding, or substituting syllables or sounds (e.g., "say *tăn;* say it without the /t/; say *tăn* with /m/ instead of /t/"). When students have good phonological awareness, they have an understanding at all levels on the continuum (see Figure 8).

At the less complex end of the continuum are activities that demonstrate an awareness that speech can be broken down into individual words. These activities include rhyming and song and segmenting sentences. At the middle of the continuum are activities related to segmenting words into syllables and blending syllables into words. Next are activities such as segmenting words into onsets and rimes and blending onsets and rimes into words.

At the top of the continuum is the highest level of phonological awareness, which is phonemic awareness. Phonemic awareness is the understanding that words are made up of individual sounds or phonemes that can be manipulated and that by segmenting, blending, or changing individual phonemes within words, new words are created. Chapter 5 is designed to move from less complex activities to more complex activities and follows this sequence: rhyming, onset and rime, and finally blending and segmenting activities.

Continuum of Complexity

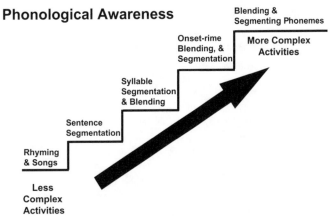

Figure 8. A continuum of complexity of phonological awareness activities (From Chard, D.J., & Dickson, S.V. [1999]. *Phonological awareness: Instructional and assessment guidelines.* Retrieved August 3, 2006, from http://www.ldonline .org/article/6254; adapted by permission.)

Rhyming Assessment

Children do not have to know the term *rhyme* in order to understand rhyming activities. Begin with whole-group activities in which rhyming or "words that sound the same at the end" are introduced. At the end of this assessment, you'll have a good idea which students understand rhyme and which have not reached mastery.

Play with nursery rhymes and other verses, helping the children fill in the blanks.

Jack and Jill went up the _____ (hill).

The itsy, bitsy, spider went up the waterspout.

Down came the rain and washed the spider _____ (out).

See ya later,

Alli-_____ (gator)

After a while

Croco-_____ (dile)

After the children have had some exposure to whole group rhyming activities, meet with each student individually to play some rhyming games.

IDENTIFICATION ACTIVITIES

"Do *dog* and *hog* end the same?"

"Do *kite* and *cook* end the same?"

"Do *pot* and *cot* end the same?"

"Do *mom* and *gone* end the same?"

RECOGNITION ACTIVITIES

"I am going to say three words; tell me the ones that end the same."

- cat   hat   dog
- ship   boot   sip
- frog   rode   toad

RHYMES WITH SEMANTIC CLUES

"I'm thinking of a word that rhymes with *kite* and *height*, and it means 'when you go to bed.'"

RHYMES WITHOUT SEMANTIC CLUES

"What words do you know that rhyme with or end the same as *sad*?"

1 Rhyming with Books

GOAL

- **Students will develop an understanding of the concepts of rhyme and rhyming and how rhyme is typically used.**

MATERIALS

○ A children's picture book with many rhymes, such as *The Great Pancake Escape*, written by Paul Many and illustrated by Scott Goto (see the list of rhyming books at end of the Focus On: Rhyming section), with word prompts for rhyming, such as those listed in Describe It, and a blank line after each

TEACHER STEPS: Describe It

- Seat students on the floor as a group. Start by asking if they know of any words that sound like the word *hat*.
- List the words that students come up with on a chalkboard or overhead (e.g., *mat, cat, sat, fat, brat, that*).
- Explain to the students that words that sound alike or repeat the same sound at the end are said to rhyme.
- Spell the target word (*hat*), and write it on the chalkboard or overhead.
- Explain that rhymes are often used in poems and songs because they sound good and they help people remember the next line. Show them the book *The Great Pancake Escape*, and read the first verse aloud.
- Ask students which of the words sound alike and explain that these words rhyme.
- Repeat the first verse, stopping before the last word and asking the students to supply it.
- Explain that they were able to remember the last word more easily because it rhymed.
- Repeat this procedure with the second verse.
- Read the rest of the book, stopping at every other page or so to elicit from students which words rhyme.
- You may also wish to occasionally repeat a verse and have students supply the last word.

STUDENT STEPS: Do It

Say the following:
- "Now I'm going to reread the book *The Great Pancake Escape*, and when I stop, I want you to fill in the missing word that rhymes."

VARIATION

- Introduce other rhyming picture books in the classroom following procedures just described.

2 Rhyming Word Families

GOAL

- **Students will develop an understanding of the concepts of rhyme and rhyming and how rhyme is typically used.**

MATERIALS

○ Word bank for this activity

TEACHER STEPS: Describe It

- Introduce the first word from the word bank (e.g., *bowl*). Have students rhyme this word, beginning a word that starts with the next letter in the alphabet that would rhyme (e.g., *coal, dole, foal, goal, hole, knoll, mole, poll/pole, role/roll, sole/soul*).
- Continue until the class has rhymed as many words as they can, using initial letters from the entire alphabet.

STUDENT STEPS: Do It

Say the following:
- "Now I'm going give you another word (e.g., *cat*). I want you to rhyme as many words as you can, using the alphabet as your guide." (Say a word from the word bank.)
- "cat" (*at, bat, fat, hat, mat, pat, rat, sat, vat*)

Word Bank: Words with Possible Rhyming Answers

1. bowl (coal, hole, mole, pole/poll, role/roll, sole/soul)
2. cat (at, bat, fat, hat, mat, pat, rat, sat, vat)
3. spoon (baboon, cartoon, dune, goon, June, moon, noon, raccoon)
4. flour (cower, glower, hour, our, power, scour, sour, tower)
5. egg (beg, leg, peg)
6. milk (bilk, ilk, silk; not many others)
7. butter (apple butter, bread and butter, cutter, clutter, flutter, gutter, mutter, peanut butter, shutter)
8. pan (an, Ann, bran, can, Dan, fan, flan, Japan, man, pecan, pelican, plan, ran, tan, van)
9. spatula (Ashtabula, Dracula, hula)
10. stove (cove, dove, drove, grove, wove)
11. syrup (cheer up, I give up)
12. batter (chatter, clatter, fatter, matter, patter)
13. flipper (clipper, dipper, hipper, kipper, nipper, ripper, slipper, zipper)

3 The Ants Go Marching

GOAL

- **Students will develop an understanding of the concepts of rhyme and rhyming and how rhyme is typically used.**

MATERIALS

- ○ Poem: "The Ants Go Marching"

TEACHER STEPS: Describe It

- Explain to students that they are going to learn a new poem that has rhyme and repeating patterns.
- Teach the first verse to the students so that they become familiar with the repeating parts.
- Tell the students that the verses also involve counting, beginning with 1 and finishing with 10.

STUDENT STEPS: Do It

Say the following:
- "Now we're going to say the poem together, and when we get to the parts that repeat, we're going to raise our voices without shouting."

VARIATION

- Use any repeating poem to emphasize these rhyming skills.

THE ANTS GO MARCHING

The ants go marching one by one.
Hurrah! Hurrah!
The ants go marching one by one.
Hurrah! Hurrah!
The ants go marching one by one;
The little one stops to suck his thumb,
And they all go marching
down
into the ground
to get out
of the rain.
Boom, boom, boom!

The ants go marching two by two.
Hurrah! Hurrah!
The ants go marching two by two.
Hurrah! Hurrah!
The ants go marching two by two;

The little one stops to tie his shoe,
And they all go marching
down
into the ground
to get out
of the rain.
Boom, boom, boom!

The ants go marching three by three.
Hurrah! Hurrah!
The ants go marching three by three.
Hurrah! Hurrah!
The ants go marching three by three;
The little one stops to ride a bee,
And they all go marching
down
into the ground
to get out

Activity continued on following page

of the rain.
Boom, boom, boom!

The ants go marching four by four.
Hurrah! Hurrah!
The ants go marching four by four.
Hurrah! Hurrah!
The ants go marching four by four;
The little one stops to ask for more,
And they all go marching
down
into the ground
to get out
of the rain.
Boom, boom, boom!

The ants go marching five by five.
Hurrah! Hurrah!
The ants go marching five by five.
Hurrah! Hurrah!
The ants go marching five by five;
The little one stops to jump and dive,
And they all go marching
down
into the ground
to get out
of the rain.
Boom, boom, boom!

The ants go marching six by six.
Hurrah! Hurrah!
The ants go marching six by six.
Hurrah! Hurrah!
The ants go marching six by six;
The little one stops to pick up sticks,
And they all go marching
down
into the ground
to get out
of the rain.
Boom, boom, boom!

The ants go marching seven by seven.
Hurrah! Hurrah!

The ants go marching seven by seven.
Hurrah! Hurrah!
The ants go marching seven by seven;
The little one stops to write with a pen,
And they all go marching
down
into the ground
to get out
of the rain.
Boom, boom, boom!

The ants go marching eight by eight.
Hurrah! Hurrah!
The ants go marching eight by eight.
Hurrah! Hurrah!
The ants go marching eight by eight;
The little one stops to roller-skate,
And they all go marching
down
into the ground
to get out
of the rain.
Boom, boom, boom!

The ants go marching nine by nine.
Hurrah! Hurrah!
The ants go marching nine by nine.
Hurrah! Hurrah!
The ants go marching nine by nine;
The little one stops to drink and dine,
And they all go marching
down
into the ground
to get out
of the rain.
Boom, boom, boom!

The ants go marching ten by ten.
Hurrah! Hurrah!
The ants go marching ten by ten.
Hurrah! Hurrah!
The ants go marching ten by ten;
The little one stops to shout
"THE END!!"

More About Rhyming

These are rhymes, poems, or songs that will be useful when teaching the individual letters of the alphabet. These rhymes and others can be found on the web sites and in the books listed on page 65.

A
All Around the Mulberry Bush
The Ants Go Marching
As I Was Going to St. Ives
As I Went Over Lincoln Bridge
As I Went to Bonner
As White as Milk

B
Baa, Baa, Black Sheep
Barber, Barber, Shave a Pig
Bat, Bat, Come Under My Hat
Bell Horses
Birds of a Feather
Bobby Shaftoe
Bow, Wow, Says the Dog
Boys and Girls, Come Out to Play
Bum, Bum, Bailey, O!
Butterfly, Butterfly
Pat-a-Cake, Pat-a-Cake
Sing a Song of Sixpence

C
A Cat Came Fiddling Out of a Barn
The Cats Went Out to Serenade
Cobbler, Cobbler, Mend My Shoe
The Cock Doth Crow
The Cock's on the Housetop
Come to the Window
Cross Patch, Draw the Latch
Curly Locks, Curly Locks
Cut Thistles in May

D
Daffy Down Dilly
Dame Trot and Her Cat
Dance to Your Daddy
Davy Davy Dumpling
Dickery Dickery Dare
Did You Ever See a Lassie?
Diddle, Diddle, Dumpling
A Diller, a Dollar
Ding, Dong, Bell
Do You Know the Muffin Man?
Do Your Ears Hang Low?

Doctor Foster
Down at the Station
The Farmer in the Dell
Hey, Diddle, Diddle
Hickory Dickory Dock!

E
Eensy Weensy Spider
Elizabeth, Elspeth, Betsey, and Bess
Elsie Marley's Grown So Fine
Every Lady in This Land

F
The Farmer in the Dell
Father and Mother and Uncle John
Fee! Fi! Fo! Fum!
Fiddle Dee Dee
For Want of a Nail
Four Stiff-Standers
Little Bunny Foo Foo

G
Georgie Porgie
Go to Bed, Tom
Good Night, Sleep Tight
Goosey, Goosey Gander
Gray Goose and Gander
Green Cheese
Three Grey Geese

H
Handy Spandy Jack-A-Dandy
Hark! Hark! The Dogs Do Bark
The Hart, He Loves the High Wood
Hector Protector was Dressed All in
    Green
Here I Am, Little Jumping Joan
Here We Go 'Round the Mulberry Bush
Hey, Diddle, Diddle
Hi! Hi! Says Anthony
Hickory Dickory Dock!
Higglety, Pigglety
High in the Pine Tree
The Hokey Pokey
Horsie, Horsie, Don't You Stop

Hot Cross Buns
The House that Jack Built
How Many Miles to Babylon?
Humpty Dumpty
Hush-A-Bye, Baby
Hush, Baby, My Dolly
Hush, Little Baby

I

I Am a Pretty Little Dutch Girl
I Do Not Like Thee, Doctor Fell
I Don't Want to Go to Mexico
I Had a Little Hen
I Had a Little Nut Tree
I Love Little Pussy
I Saw a Ship A-sailing
I Saw Esau
I See the Moon
I Sing, I Sing
Ice Cream
Ice Cream, a Penny a Lump
If All the World Were Paper
If I Had a Donkey
If I'd as Much Money as I Could Spend
If Wishes Were Horses
In Marble Walls
In Spring I Look Gay
It's Raining, It's Pouring
I've Been Workin' on the Railroad

J

Here I Am, Little Jumping Joan
Jack and Jill Went up the Hill
Jack Be Nimble
Jack Sprat
Jerry Hall
John Jacob Jingleheimer Schmidt

K

King Boggen, He Built a Fine New Hall
Kookaburra
This Old Man

L

Ladybug! Ladybug!
Lavender's Blue
Lend Me Thy Mare to Ride a Mile
The Lion and the Unicorn
Little Bo Peep
Little Boy Blue
Little Bunny Foo Foo
Little Jack Horner
Little Miss Muffet
Little Nancy Etticoat
Little Poll Parrot

Little Polly Flinders
Little Robin Redbreast Sat Upon a Rail
Little Robin Redbreast Sat Upon a Tree
Little Tommy Tittlemouse
London Bridge Is Falling Down

M

Little Miss Muffet
Mademoiselle Went Down to the Well
The Man in the Moon
A Man in the Wilderness
Mares Eat Oats
Mary Had a Little Lamb
Mary, Mary, Quite Contrary
Matthew, Mark, Luke, and John
Michael, Row the Boat Ashore
Monday's Child
Mother Goose Had a House
Mother, May I Go Out to Swim?
My Bonnie Lies Over the Ocean
My Grandfather's Clock

N

The North Wind Doth Blow
Now I Lay Me Down to Sleep

O

Oats, Peas, Beans, and Barley Grow
Oh, Dear, What Can the Matter Be?
   (Apple tree version)
Oh, Dear, What Can the Matter Be?
   (Johnny version)
Oh, the Grand Old Duke of York
Oh Where, Oh Where Has My Little Dog
   Gone?
Old King Cole
Old MacDonald Had a Farm
Old Mother Goose
Old Mother Hubbard
On Top of Old Smokey
On Top of Spaghetti
Once I Saw a Little Bird
One for Sorrow
One for the Mouse
One I Love
One Little, Two Little, Three Little Indians
One Misty Moisty Morning
One to Make Ready
One, Two, Buckle My Shoe
One, Two, Three, Four, Five
Over the River and Through the Woods

P

Pat-a-Cake, Pat-a-Cake
Pease Porridge Hot

Continued on following page

Peter, Peter, Pumpkin Eater
Peter Piper Picked a Peck of Pickled Peppers
Piping Hot, Smoking Hot
Polly, Put the Kettle on
Pop! Goes the Weasel
Punch and Judy Fought for a Pie
Pussycat, Pussycat, Where Have You Been?

Q
The Queen of Hearts

R
Rain on the Green Grass
Rain, Rain Go Away
Riddle Me, Riddle Me, Ree
Ride a Cock Horse
Ring Around the Rosie
Robin and Richard
Row, Row, Row Your Boat
Rub-a-Dub-Dub

S
Sailing, Sailing
The Seasons
See, Saw, Marjorie Daw
See, Saw, Sacradown
See, See!
She'll Be Comin' Round the Mountain
A Shoe Maker Makes Shoes
Simple Simon
Sing a Song of Sixpence
Sing, Sing, What Shall I Sing
Sippity Sup, Sippity Sup
Six Little Mice Sat Down to Spin
Skip, Skip, Skip to My Lou
Sleep, Baby, Sleep
Smiling Girls, Rosy Boys
Solomon Grundy
Spring Is Showery
Star Light, Star Bright
Swan Swam Over the Sea
A Swarm of Bees in May

T
Taffy Was a Welshman
Teddy Bear, Teddy Bear
Ten Little Indians
The Owl and the Pussycat
There Was a Crooked Man
There Was a Jolly Miller Once
There Was a Little Man
There Was a Maid on Scrabble Hill
There Was an Old Crow
There Was an Old Woman Tossed in a
    Blanket

There Was an Old Woman Who Lived in a
    Shoe
There's a Neat Little Clock
Thirty Days Hath September
The House that Jack Built
This Little Froggy
This Little Piggy
This Old Man
Three Blind Mice
Three Grey Geese
Three Little Kitten
Three Wise Men of Gotham
Three Young Rats With Black Felt Hats
Tinker, Tailor
A Tisket, a Tasket
To Bed, to Bed
To Market, to Market
Tom, Tom, the Piper's Son
Trip Upon Trenches
Trot, Trot, to Boston
Tweedledum and Tweedledee
Twinkle, Twinkle, Little Star

U
Up the Wooden Hill to Blanket Fair
Upstairs, Downstairs

V
Vintery, Mintery, Cutery, Corn

W
Warm Hands, Warm
Wash the Dishes
Wee Willie Winkie
What Are Little Boys Made of?
What Are Little Girls Made of?
What Did I Dream?
When That I Was but a Little Tiny Boy
When Little Fred Went to Bed
When the Wind Lies in the East
Where is Thumbkin
Whether the Weather
Wibbleton to Wobbleton
Winken, Blinken, and Nod
A Wise Old Owl

X
X, Y, and Tumbledown Z

Y
Yankee Doodle

Z
Zum Gali Gali Gali

Rhyming Books and Web Sites

RHYMING BOOKS

Anglund, J.W. *In a pumpkin shell: A Mother Goose ABC.* New York: Harcourt & Brace.

Craft, K. (Illus.). *Mother Goose ABC.* New York: Platt & Munk.

Craig, H. (1992). *I see the moon, and the moon sees me . . .* New York: Willa Perlman Books/HarperCollins.

Daiken, L. (1976). *Children's games throughout the year.* New York: Arno Press. (Original work published 1949 by Batsford, London)

de Paola, T. (1985). *Tomie de Paola's Mother Goose.* New York: G.P. Putnam & Sons.

Fowke, E. (1969). *Sally go round the sun: Three hundred children's songs, rhymes and games.* New York: Doubleday.

Fremont, V. (Ed.). (1992). *Nursery rhymes coloring book* (N. Barbaresi, Illus.). New York: Dover Publications.

Larche, D.W. (1985). *Father Gander nursery rhymes* (C.M. Blattel, Illus.). Santa Barbara, CA: Advocacy Press. (Available from the publisher, Post Office Box 236, Department A, Santa Barbara, CA 93102)

Many, P. (2002). *The great pancake escape* (S. Goto, Illus.). New York: Walker & Co.

Mother Goose's melodies: Facsimile edition of the Munroe and Francis "Copyright 1833" version (1970). (Introduction and bibliographic note by E.F. Bleiler). New York: Dover Publications.

Opie, I. (1996). *My very first Mother Goose* (Rosemary Wells, Illus.). Cambridge, MA: Candlewick Press.

Opie, I., & Opie, P. (1977). *The Oxford nursery rhyme book.* New York: Oxford University Press. (Original work published 1951)

Opie, I., & Opie, P. (1992). *I saw Esau: The schoolchild's pocket book* (Maurice Sendak, Illus.). Cambridge, MA: Candlewick Press. (Original work published 1947)

Rey, H.A. (1995). *Humpty Dumpty, and other Mother Goose songs.* New York: HarperFestival. (Original work published 1943)

Rosetti, C. (1968). *Sing-song: A nursery rhyme book.* New York: Dover Publishing. (Original work published 1872)

Singing games and play party games (R. Chase, Compiler; Joshua Tolford, Illus.). (1967). New York: Dover Publications. (Original work published 1949)

Smith, J.W. (1991) *The Jessie Willcox Smith Mother Goose.* Gretna, LA: Pelican. (Original work published 1914)

Ward, H. (1995). *Helen Ward's nursery treasury.* Dorking, Surrey, England: The Templar Company.

Wright, B.F. *The real Mother Goose.*

Yeatman, L. *A treasury of Mother Goose rhymes.*

RHYMING WEB SITES

The following web sites contain suggestions for incorporating rhyming activities into instruction and/or contain the text of many common rhymes, poems, and songs that can be used in rhyming activities.

http://www.amherst.edu/~rjyanco94/literature/mothergoose/rhymes/menu.html

http://www.enchantedlearning.com/Nurseryrhymes.html

http://www.hubbardscupboard.org/dr_seuss.html

http://www.hubbardscupboard.org/letter_and_rhyme_a_day.html

http://www.mothergoose.com/

http://rbeaudoin333.homestead.com/files/Cando/rhyme_1.html

http://www-personal.umich.edu/~pfa/dreamhouse/nursery/rhymes.html

http://webtech.kennesaw.edu/jcheek3/mother_goose.htm

http://www.zelo.com/family/nursery/index.asp

4 Who Is It?

GOAL

- **Students will segment and blend onsets and rimes.**

MATERIALS

○   No materials are needed for this activity.

TEACHER STEPS: Describe It

- Tell students you are going to say the name of someone in the classroom in a fun and different way. Then, they have to figure out whose name you are saying.
- Tell students that if you say /j/ /ān/, you are saying "Jane." If you say /k/ /āt/, you are saying "Kate."

STUDENT STEPS: Do It

- Choose a student.
- Say the following to the student:
  - "Break apart someone's name." (e.g., /l/ /ĭndə/)
  - "Raise your hand if you know who it is."
- Call on someone whose hand is raised.
  - "What's the student's name?" (*Linda*)
- If the name is said correctly, the student who has responded gets a turn to break down a student's name and choose someone whose hand is raised.
- Continue this process until all students have had at least one turn.

VARIATIONS

- Have students hold a contracted Slinky with one hand on either end. Tell students to pull the ends of the Slinky apart as they break apart the name and push the ends together as they put the name together.
- Have students put their hands together in front of them. Tell them to move their hands apart as they break apart the name and clap once as they put the name together.
- Have students segment and blend the word parts into a self-phone. (See Chapter 4 for a description of a self-phone.)

5 | I Spy

GOAL

- **Students will segment and blend onsets and rimes.**

MATERIALS

○ No materials are needed for this activity.

TEACHER STEPS: Describe It

- Tell students you are going to give them a clue about something in the room by saying, "I spy something that begins with the sound _____." (e.g., /l/)
- Say the word and segment the onset and rime (*light, /l/ / īt/*).
- Blend the parts (*light*).

STUDENT STEPS: Do It

- Choose a student to give a clue.
- Say the following:
  - "Give us a clue by saying, 'I spy something that begins with the sound _____.'"
- The student gives a clue.
  - "Raise your hand if you know what the object is."
- Call on a student to respond.
  - "Say the word."
  - "Break apart the word."
  - "Blend the parts."

VARIATIONS

- Have students hold a contracted Slinky with one hand on either end. Tell students to pull the ends of the Slinky apart as they break apart the word and push the ends together as they put the word together.
- Have students put their hands together in front of them. Tell them to move their hands apart as they break apart the word and clap once as they put the word together.

6   Creatures from Outer Space

GOAL

- **Students will segment and blend onsets and rimes.**

MATERIALS

○ Word bank for this activity   ○ Puppet (optional)

TEACHER STEPS: Describe It

- Tell students that friendly creatures from outer space came to earth. They have a different way of talking. For example, for *cake* they say /k/ /āk/. For *dog* they say /d/ /ŏg/.
- Tell students that you will say a word the way the creatures do and that the students have to say it the way we do.
- "The creatures say, '_____.'" (e.g., /d/ /ŏg/)
- "We say, '_____.' (e.g., *dog*)
- "The creatures say, '_____.'" (e.g., /k/ /āk/)
- "We say, '_____.'" (e.g., *cake*)

STUDENT STEPS: Do It

Say the following:
- "The creatures say, '_____.'" (e.g., /j/ /ŭmp/)
- "We say, '_____.'" (*jump*)
- "How do the creatures say the word?" (/j/ /ŭmp/)

VARIATIONS

- Introduce a puppet as the creature from outer space. Have the puppet segment the words into onset and rime. Then, have the students blend the parts.
- Say a word from the word bank. Ask the students to say it the way the creature would say it.
- Have students hold a contracted Slinky with one hand on either end. Tell the students to pull the ends of the Slinky apart as they break apart the word and push the ends together as they put the word together.
- Have students put their hands together in front of them. Tell them to move their hands apart as they break apart the word and clap once as they put the word together.

Word Bank on following page

Word Bank

ad	**an**	**ant**	**ed**	**est**	**ig**	**ink**	**ob**	**ot**	**um**
bad	ban	can't	bed	best	big	link	Bob	cot	bum
dad	can	pant	fed	jest	dig	mink	cob	dot	gum
fad	Dan	rant	led	nest	fig	pink	job	got	hum
had	fan		red	rest	jig	rink	lob	hot	sum
lad	man	**ap**	wed	vest	pig	sink	mob	lot	
mad	pan	cap		west	rig	wink	nob	not	**un**
pad	ran	gap	**en**		wig		rob	pot	bun
sad	tan	lap	den	**et**		**ip**	sob	rot	fun
	van	map	hen	bet	**im**	dip			pun
ag		nap	men	get	dim	hip	**old**	**ub**	run
bag	**and**	sap	pen	jet	him	nip	bold	cub	sun
gag	band	tap	ten	let	Tim	sip	cold	hub	
lag	hand			met		tip	fold	rub	**ut**
nag	land	**ask**	**end**	net	**in**		gold	sub	but
rag	sand	mask	bend	pet	bin	**it**	hold	tub	cut
sag		task	lend	set	fin	bit	mold		gut
tag	**ank**		mend	vet	pin	fit	sold	**ug**	hut
wag	bank	**at**	send	wet	sin	hit	told	bug	jut
	rank	bat	tend	yet	tin	kit		dug	nut
am	sank	cat	vend		win	lit	**op**	hug	rut
ham	tank	fat		**id**		pit	hop	jug	
jam		hat		did	**ing**	sit	mop	mug	
Pam		mat		hid	king	wit	pop	rug	
ram		pat		kid	ring		top	tug	
Sam		rat		lid	sing				
		sat		rid	wing				

7 Choose a Picture/Object

GOAL

- **Students will segment and blend onsets and rimes.**

MATERIALS

○ Picture cards or objects

TEACHER STEPS: Describe It

- Choose a picture card or an object, and identify it (e.g., *hand*).
- Tell the students you are going to break apart the word.
- Segment the word into onset and rime (/h/ /ănd/).
- Tell students you are going to blend the sounds.
- Blend the onset and the rime (*hand*).

STUDENT STEPS: Do It

Say the following:
- "What is that picture/object?" (e.g., *monkey*)
- "Break apart the word." (/m/ /ŭnkē /)
- "Blend the parts." (*monkey*)

VARIATIONS

- Have students hold a contracted Slinky with one hand on either end. Tell students to pull the ends of the Slinky apart as they break apart the word and push the ends together as they put the word together.
- Have students put their hands together in front of them. Tell them to move their hands apart as they break apart the word and clap once as they put the word together.
- Students place the card/object in front of them if they segment and blend the word correctly. At the end of the activity, ask students to count their cards/objects.
- Students place the card/object in the class pile if they segment and blend the word correctly. The card/object is placed in the teacher's pile if the word is not segmented and blended correctly. At the end of the activity, count the cards to see who has won!

8 Find the Picture: Listening for Initial Consonant Sounds

GOALS

- Students will segment and blend onsets and rimes.
- Students will choose a picture that begins with a specific consonant sound.

MATERIALS

○ Picture cards

TEACHER STEPS: Describe It

- Choose several picture cards that each begin with a different beginning consonant sound.
- Place the cards face up on the table.
- Tell students you will find a picture that begins with the sound _____ (e.g., /k/).
- Choose the picture that begins with the targeted sound (e.g., *cat*).
- Tell students you are going to break apart the word.
- Segment the word into onset and the rime (/k/ /ăt/).
- Tell students you are going to blend the sounds.
- Blend the onset and the rime (*cat*).

STUDENT STEPS: Do It

Say the following:
- "Find a picture that begins with the sound _____" (e.g., /m/)
- "What is the picture?" (*moon*)
- "Break apart the word." (/m/ /ōon/)
- "Blend the parts." (*moon*)

VARIATIONS

- Have students hold a contracted Slinky with one hand on either end. Tell students to pull the ends of the Slinky apart as they break apart the word and push the ends together as they put the word together.
- Have students put their hands together in front of them. Tell them to move their hands apart as they break apart the word and clap once as they put the word together.
- Students place the card in front of them if they segment and blend the word correctly. At the end of the activity, ask students to count their cards.
- Students place the card in the class pile if they segment and blend the word correctly. The card is placed in the teacher's pile if the word is not segmented and blended correctly. At the end of the activity, count the cards to see who has won!
- Have students segment and blend the word parts into a self-phone.

9 Segmenting and Blending Words with Onsets and Rimes

GOAL

- **Students will segment and blend onsets and rimes.**

MATERIALS

- Word bank for this activity
- Blank colored tiles

TEACHER STEPS: Describe It

- Tell the students you are going to say a word, break it apart, and blend it back together.
- Say a word from the word bank (e.g., *mat*).
- Put down one tile as you say the onset (/m/) and a tile of a different color as you say the rime (/ăt/).

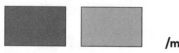

/m/ /ăt/

Blend the parts together. (*mat*)

STUDENT STEPS: Do It

Say the following:
- "The word is _____." (e.g., *dig*)
- "Break apart the word." (/d/ /ĭg/)
- "Blend the parts." (*dig*)

VARIATIONS

- Have students hold a contracted Slinky with one hand on either end. Tell students to pull the ends of the Slinky apart as they break apart the word and push the ends together as they put the word together.
- Have students put their hands together in front of them. Tell them to move their hands apart as they break apart the word and clap once as they put the word together.
- Have students segment and blend the word parts into a self-phone.

Word Bank on following page

Word Bank

ad	**an**	**ant**	**ed**	**est**	**ig**	**ink**	**ob**	**ot**	**um**
bad	ban	can't	bed	best	big	link	Bob	cot	bum
dad	can	pant	fed	jest	dig	mink	cob	dot	gum
fad	Dan	rant	led	nest	fig	pink	job	got	hum
had	fan		red	rest	jig	rink	lob	hot	sum
lad	man	**ap**	wed	vest	pig	sink	mob	lot	
mad	pan	cap		west	rig	wink	nob	not	**un**
pad	ran	gap	**en**		wig		rob	pot	bun
sad	tan	lap	den	**et**		**ip**	sob	rot	fun
	van	map	hen	bet	**im**	dip			pun
ag		nap	men	get	dim	hip	**old**	**ub**	run
bag	**and**	sap	pen	jet	him	nip	bold	cub	sun
gag	band	tap	ten	let	Tim	sip	cold	hub	
lag	hand			met		tip	fold	rub	**ut**
nag	land	**ask**	**end**	net	**in**		gold	sub	but
rag	sand	mask	bend	pet	bin	**it**	hold	tub	cut
sag		task	lend	set	fin	bit	mold		gut
tag	**ank**		mend	vet	pin	fit	sold	**ug**	hut
wag	bank	**at**	send	wet	sin	hit	told	bug	jut
	rank	bat	tend	yet	tin	kit		dug	nut
am	sank	cat	vend		win	lit	**op**	hug	rut
ham	tank	fat		**id**		pit	hop	jug	
jam		hat		did	**ing**	sit	mop	mug	
Pam		mat		hid	king	wit	pop	rug	
ram		pat		kid	ring		top	tug	
Sam		rat		lid	sing				
		sat		rid	wing				

10 Adding an Initial Consonant Sound

GOAL

- Students will identify the initial sound that has been added to a word to make a new word.

MATERIALS

○ Word bank for this activity   ○ Blank colored tiles, small blocks, or paper squares

TEACHER STEPS: Describe It

- Tell students you can do a magic trick with sounds because you can make a new word by adding one sound to the beginning of a word.
- Put down one tile as you say the first word in a pair of words (e.g., *old* in *old-mold*).
- As you segment the second word, place the tile representing the onset (/m/) to the left of the tile representing the first word in the pair.
- Point to the second tile as you say the rime (/ōld/). As a prompt, the tile representing the rime should be a different color.

 /m/ /ōld/

- Remove and add the first tile as you say both words (*old-mold*).
- Tell students what sound you added (/m/).

STUDENT STEPS: Do It

- Say the following:
  - "The words are _____-_____" (e.g., *old-mold*)
  - "Put down a tile for the word _____." (Say the first word in the pair, e.g., *old*.)
  - "The new word is _____." (Say the second word in the pair, e.g., *mold*.)
  - "Put down a tile to show where you added a sound to change _____ to _____." (*old* to *mold*)
  - "What sound did you add to change _____ to _____?" (*old* to *mold*; ANSWER: /m/)
- As students become proficient, conduct this activity without the tiles.
- Say the following:
  - "_____-_____" (e.g., *old-mold*)
  - "What sound do you add to change _____ to _____?" (*old* to *mold*; ANSWER: /m/)

VARIATIONS

- Have students hold a contracted Slinky with one hand on either end. Tell students to pull the ends of the Slinky apart as they break apart the word and push the ends together as they put the word together.
- Have students put their hands together in front of them. Tell them to move their hands apart as they break apart the word and clap once as they put the word together.
- Have students segment and blend the word parts into a self-phone.

Word Bank on following page

Word Bank

ace	am	ash	ear	end	in	oh
ace-base	am-ham	ash-bash	ear-dear	end-bend	in-bin	oh-bow
ace-case	am-jam	ash-cash	ear-fear	end-lend	in-fin	oh-go
ace-face	am-lamb	ash-dash	ear-gear	end-mend	in-pin	oh-hoe
ace-lace	am-Pam	ash-gash	ear-hear	end-send	in-sin	oh-low
ace-race	am-ram	ash-hash	ear-leer	end-tend	in-tin	oh-no
	am-Sam	ash-lash	ear-near	end-vend	in-win	oh-row
ache	am-yam	ash-mash	ear-pier			oh-sew
ache-bake		ash-rash	ear-rear	**eye**	**ink**	oh-toe
ache-cake	**an**	ash-sash	ear-tear	eye-by	ink-link	
ache-fake	an-ban		ear-year	eye-die	ink-mink	**oil**
ache-lake	an-can	**ask**		eye-guy	ink-pink	oil-boil
ache-make	an-Dan	ask-mask	**eat**	eye-high	ink-rink	oil-coil
ache-rake	an-fan	ask-task	eat-beat	eye-lie	ink-sink	oil-foil
ache-sake	an-man		eat-feet	eye-my	ink-wink	oil-loyal
ache-take	an-pan	**at**	eat-heat	eye-pie		oil-royal
ache-wake	an-ran	at-bat	eat-meat	eye-rye	**it**	oil-soil
	an-tan	at-cat	eat-neat	eye-sigh	it-bit	oil-toil
ad		at-fat	eat-Pete	eye-tie	it-fit	
ad-bad	**and**	at-hat	eat-seat		it-hit	**old**
ad-dad	and-band	at-mat		**ice**	it-kit	old-bold
ad-fad	and-hand	at-pat	**Ed**	ice-dice	it-lit	old-cold
ad-had	and-land	at-rat	Ed-bed	ice-lice	it-pit	old-fold
ad-lad	and-sand	at-sat	Ed-fed	ice-mice	it-sit	old-gold
ad-mad			Ed-led	ice-nice	it-wit	old-hold
ad-pad	**ant**	**ate**	Ed-Ned	ice-rice		old-mold
ad-sad	ant-can't	ate-bait	Ed-red		**oak**	old-told
	ant-pant	ate-date	Ed-Ted	**ill**	oak-Coke	
aim	ant-rant	ate-gate	Ed-wed	ill-bill	oak-joke	**own**
aim-fame		ate-hate		ill-dill	oak-soak	own-bone
aim-game	**art**	ate-late	**eel**	ill-fill	oak-woke	own-cone
aim-lame	art-cart	ate-mate	eel-deal	ill-gill		own-loan
aim-name	art-dart	ate-rate	eel-feel	ill-hill		own-moan
aim-same	art-heart	ate-wait	eel-heal	ill-Jill		own-phone
aim-tame	art-mart		eel-kneel	ill-kill		own-tone
	art-part		eel-meal	ill-mill		
	art-tart		eel-peel	ill-pill		
			eel-reel			
			eel-seal			

11 Adding a Final Consonant Sound

GOAL

- **Students will identify the final sound that has been added to a word to make a new word.**

MATERIALS

○ Word bank for this activity

○ Blank colored tiles, small blocks, or paper squares

TEACHER STEPS: Describe It

- Tell students you can do a magic trick with sounds because you can make a new word by adding one sound to the end of a word.
- Say a pair of words in which the second word is identical to the first word except that a final consonant sound has been added. Accentuate the final sound as you say the second word (e.g., *bell-bel**t***).
- As you segment the second word, put down one tile to represent the first part (/běl/). As a prompt, the tile representing the final sound should be a different color (/t/).

 **/běl/ /t/**

- Remove the second tile as you say the first word, and add it back as you say the second word (*bell-belt*).
- Tell students the added sound (/t/).

STUDENT STEPS: Do It

- Say the following:
  - "Accentuate the final sound in the second word." (*bel**t***)
  - "The words are _____-_____." (e.g., *bell-bel**t***).
  - "Put down a tile for each part in the word _____" (*belt*). Say the second word in the pair (/běl/ /t/).
  - "What sound did you add to change _____ to _____?" (*bell* to *belt*; ANSWER: /t/)

- As students become proficient, conduct this activity without the tiles.
- Say the following:
  - "_____-_____" (e.g., *bell-bel**t***)
  - "What sound did you add to change _____ to _____?" (*bell* to *bel**t***; ANSWER: /t/)

Activity and Word Bank continued on following page

Adding a Final Consonant Sound continued

VARIATIONS

- Have students hold a contracted Slinky with one hand on either side. Tell students to pull the ends of the Slinky apart as they break apart the word and push the ends together as they put the word together.
- Have students put their hands together in front of them. Tell them to move their hands apart as they break apart the word and clap once as they put the word together.
- Have students segment and blend the word parts into a self-phone.

Word Bank

/d/
an-and
ban-band
Ben-bend
car-card
for-ford
high-hide
may-made
men-mend
moo-mood
rye-ride
see-seed
sigh-side
wee-weed
why-wide

/f/
bee-beef
cell-self
say-safe

/k/
bar-bark
bay-bake
bee-beak
by-bike
for-fork
free-freak
high-hike
lay-lake
mill-milk
my-mike
par-park
pie-pike
sill-silk
spar-spark

/l/
hay-hail
he-heal
may-mail
me-meal
pay-pail
ray-rail
say-sail
see-seal

/m/
die-dime
far-farm
for-form
lie-lime
say-same
tie-time

/n/
bar-barn
bee-bean
core-corn
fir-fern
gray-grain
me-mean
moo-moon
my-mine
pie-pine

/p/
gray-grape
hoe-hope
lamb-lamp
roe-rope
she-sheep
so-soap

/ər/
farm-farmer
ham-hammer
high-hire
paint-painter
pitch-pitcher
play-player
ranch-rancher
sneak-sneaker
teach-teacher
tie-tire
why-wire

/s/
for-force
how-house
lay-lace
moo-moose
my-mice
tray-trace

/t/
bee-beet
bell-belt
Ben-bent
boo-boot
bow-boat
by-bite

car-cart
den-dent
fell-felt
go-goat
gray-great
her-hurt
lay-late
me-meat
my-might
no-note
she-sheet
shore-short
ten-tent
tie-tight
tree-treat
two-toot
when-went

/v/
die-dive
high-hive
say-save

/z/
free-freeze
pry-prize

77

12 Deleting an Initial Consonant Sound

GOAL

- **Students will identify the initial sound that has been deleted from a word to make a new word.**

MATERIALS

- ○ Word bank for this activity
- ○ Blank colored tiles, small blocks, or paper squares

TEACHER STEPS: Describe It

- Tell students you can do a magic trick with sounds because you can make a new word by taking away one sound from the beginning of a word.
- Say a pair of words (e.g., *sit-it*).
- As you segment the first word, put down one tile as you say the onset of the first word (/s/). As a prompt, the tile representing the rime (/ĭt/) should be a different color.

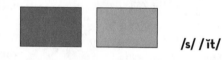

/s/ /ĭt/

- Say the first word, then remove the first tile as you say the second word (*sit-it*).
- Tell students the deleted sound (/s/).

STUDENT STEPS: Do It

- Say the following:
  - "The words are _____-_____." (e.g., *sit-it*)
  - "Put down a tile for each part in the word." Say the first word, then say the second word in the pair (*sit-it*).
  - "What sound do you take away to change _____ to _____?" (*sit* to *it*; ANSWER: /s/)

- As students become proficient, conduct this activity without the tiles.
- Say the following:
  - " _____-_____ " (e.g., *sit-it*)
  - "What sound do you take away to change _____ to _____?" (*sit* to *it*; ANSWER: /s/)

VARIATIONS

- Have students hold a contracted Slinky with one hand on either end. Tell students to pull the ends of the Slinky apart as they break apart the word and push the ends together as they put the word together.
- Have students put their hands together in front of them. Tell them to move their hands apart as they break apart the word and clap once as they put the word together.
- Have students segment and blend the word parts into a self-phone.

Work Bank on following page

Word Bank

ace
base-ace
case-ace
face-ace
lace-ace
race-ace

ache
bake-ache
cake-ache
fake-ache
lake-ache
make-ache
rake-ache
sake-ache
take-ache
wake-ache

ad
bad-ad
dad-ad
fad-ad
had-ad
lad-ad
mad-ad
pad-ad
sad-ad

aim
fame-aim
game-aim
lame-aim
name-aim
same-aim
tame-aim

am
ham-am
jam-am
lamb-am
Pam-am
ram-am
Sam-am
yam-am

an
ban-an
can-an
Dan-an
fan-an
man-an
pan-an
ran-an
tan-an

and
band-and
hand-and
land-and
sand-and

ant
can't-ant
pant-ant
rant-ant

art
cart-art
dart-art
heart-art
mart-art
part-art
tart-art

ash
bash-ash
cash-ash
dash-ash
gash-ash
hash-ash
lash-ash
mash-ash
rash-ash
sash-ash

ask
mask-ask
task-ask

at
bat-at
cat-at
fat-at
hat-at
mat-at
pat-at
rat-at
sat-at

ate
bait-ate
date-ate
gate-ate
hate-ate
late-ate
mate-ate
rate-ate
wait-ate

eat
beat-eat
feet-eat
heat-eat
meat-eat
neat-eat
Pete-eat
seat-eat

Ed
bed-Ed
fed-Ed
led-Ed
Ned-Ed
red-Ed
Ted-Ed
wed-Ed

eel
deal-eel
feel-eel
heal-eel
kneel-eel
meal-eel
peel-eel
reel-eel
seal-eel

end
bend-end
lend-end
mend-end
send-end
tend-end
vend-end

eye
by-eye
die-eye
guy-eye
high-eye
lie-eye
my-eye
pie-eye
rye-eye
sigh-eye
tie-eye

ice
dice-ice
lice-ice
mice-ice
nice-ice
rice-ice

ill
bill-ill
dill-ill
fill-ill
gill-ill
hill-ill
Jill-ill
kill-ill
mill-ill
pill-ill

in
bin-in
fin-in
pin-in
sin-in
tin-in
win-in

ink
link-ink
mink-ink
pink-ink
rink-ink
sink-ink
wink-ink

it
bit-it
fit-it
hit-it
kit-it
lit-it
pit-it
sit-it
wit-it

oak
Coke-oak
joke-oak
soak-oak
woke-oak

oh
bow-oh
go-oh
hoe-oh
low-oh
no-oh
row-oh
sew-oh
toe-oh

oil
boil-oil
coil-oil
foil-oil
loyal-oil
royal-oil
soil-oil
toil-oil

old
bold-old
cold-old
fold-old
gold-old
hold-old
mold-old
told-old

own
bone-own
cone-own
loan-own
moan-own
phone-own
tone-own

13 Deleting a Final Consonant Sound

GOAL

- **Students will identify the final sound that has been deleted from a word to make a new word.**

MATERIALS

○ Word bank for this activity

○ Blank colored tiles, small blocks, or paper squares

TEACHER STEPS: Describe It

- Tell students you can do a magic trick with sounds because you can make a new word by taking away a sound at the end of a word.
- Say a pair of words, accentuating the final sound as you say the first word (e.g., bee**t**-bee).
- As you segment the first word, put down one tile to represent the first part (/bē/). As a prompt, the tile representing the final sound should be a different color (/t/).

/bē/ /t/

- Remove the second tile as you say the second word (beet-bee).
- Tell students the deleted sound (/t/).

STUDENT STEPS: Do It

- Say the following, accentuating the final sound in the first word:
  - "The words are _____-_____." (e.g., beet-bee)
  - "Put down a tile for each part in the word." Say the phonemes, then say the whole word. (/bē/ /t/, beet)
  - "What sound do you take away to change _____ to _____?" (beet to bee; ANSWER: /t/)

- As students become proficient, conduct this activity without the tiles.
- Say the following:
  - "_____-_____" (e.g., beet-bee)
  - "What sound do you take away to change _____ to _____?" (beet to bee; ANSWER: /t/)

VARIATIONS

- Have students hold a contracted Slinky with one hand on either end. Tell students to pull the ends of the Slinky apart as they break apart the word and push the ends together as they put the word together.
- Have students put their hands together in front of them. Tell them to move their hands apart as they break apart the word and clap once as they put the word together.
- Have students segment and blend the word parts into a self-phone.

Word Bank on following page

Word Bank

/d/
and-an
band-ban
bend-Ben
card-car
ford-for
hide-high
made-may
mend-men
mood-moo
ride-rye
seed-see
side-sigh
weed-wee
wide-why

/f/
beef-bee
safe-say
self-cell

/k/
bake-bay
bark-bar
beak-bee
bike-by
fork-for
freak-free
hike-high
lake-lay
mike-my
milk-mill
park-par
pike-pie
silk-sill
spark-spar

/l/
hail-hay
heal-he
mail-may
meal-me
pail-pay
rail-ray
sail-say
seal-see

/m/
dime-die
farm-far
form-for
lime-lie
same-say
time-tie

/n/
barn-bar
bean-bee
corn-core
fern-fir
grain-gray
mean-me
mine-my
moon-moo
pine-pie

/p/
grape-gray
hope-hoe
lamp-lamb
rope-row
sheep-she
soap-so

/ər/
farmer-farm
hammer-ham
hire-high
letter-let
painter-paint
pitcher-pitch
player-play
rancher-ranch
sneaker-sneak
teacher-teach
tire-tie
wire-why

/s/
force-for
house-how
lace-lay
mice-my
moose-moo
trace-tray

/t/
beet-bee
belt-bell
bent-Ben
bite-by
boat-bow
boot-boo
cart-car
dent-den
felt-fell
goat-go
great-gray
hurt-her
late-lay
meat-me
might-my
note-no
sheet-she
short-shore
tent-ten
tight-tie
toot-two
treat-tree
went-when

/v/
dive-die
hive-high
save-say

/z/
freeze-free
prize-pry

14 Sound Stew

GOAL

- **Students will segment and blend onsets and rimes.**

MATERIALS

○ Objects or picture cards   ○ Sauce pan

TEACHER STEPS: Describe It

- Place objects or picture cards in a sauce pan.
- Tell the students you have made sound stew and that you need help emptying the stew from the sauce pan.
- Choose a picture or object from the sauce pan and identify it (e.g., *cat*).
- Tell students you are going to break apart the word.
- Segment the word into onset and rime (/k/ /ăt/).
- Tell students you are going to blend the parts.
- Blend the onset and the rime (*cat*).

STUDENT STEPS: Do It

Say the following:
- "Close your eyes and choose an object/picture from the pan."
- "What is it?" (e.g., *cat*)
- "Break apart the word." (/k/ /ăt/)
- "Blend the parts." (*cat*)

VARIATIONS

- Have students hold a contracted Slinky with one hand on either side. Tell students to pull the ends of the Slinky apart as they break apart the word and push the ends together as they put the word together.
- Have students put their hands together in front of them. Tell them to move their hands apart as they break apart the word and clap once as they put the word together.
- Students place the card/object in front of them if they segment and blend the word correctly. At the end of the activity, ask students to count their cards.
- Students place the card/object in the class pile if they segment and blend the word correctly. The card is placed in the teacher's pile if the word is not segmented and blended correctly. At the end of the activity, count the cards to see who has won!
- Have students segment and blend the word parts into a self-phone.

15 Stretchy Sounds

GOAL

- **Students will segment and blend onsets and rimes.**

MATERIALS

○ Word bank for this activity, picture cards, or objects

○ Slinky spring toy for each student and the teacher

TEACHER STEPS: Describe It

- Tell students you are going to use the Slinky to help you break down and blend words together.
- Choose a word from the word bank, a picture card, or an object (e.g., *fan*).
- Hold a contracted Slinky with one hand on either side.
- Expand the Slinky as you segment the word into the onset and rime (/f/ /ăn/).
- Contract the Slinky as you blend the onset and rime (*fan*).

STUDENT STEPS: Do It

- Demonstrate how to hold the contracted Slinky.
- Say a word from the word bank or identify an object or picture.
- Say the following:
  - "Pull the ends of the Slinky as you say the sounds in the word." (/b/ /ā/)
  - "Push the Slinky together as you blend the sounds/say the word." (*bee*)

VARIATIONS

- Students place the card/object in front of them if they segment and blend the word correctly. At the end of the activity, ask students to count their cards.
- Students place the card in the class pile if they segment and blend the word correctly. The card/object is placed in the teacher's pile if the word is not segmented and blended correctly. At the end of the activity, count the cards to see who has won!
- Have students segment and blend the word parts into a self-phone.

Word Bank on following page

CLASSROOM ACTIVITY
PHONOLOGICAL AWARENESS · Onset-Rime and Phonemic Awareness

Word Bank

ad	**an**	**ant**	**ed**	**est**	**ig**	**ink**	**ob**	**ot**	**um**
bad	ban	can't	bed	best	big	link	Bob	cot	bum
dad	can	pant	fed	jest	dig	mink	cob	dot	gum
fad	Dan	rant	led	nest	fig	pink	job	got	hum
had	fan		red	rest	jig	rink	lob	hot	sum
lad	man	**ap**	wed	vest	pig	sink	mob	lot	
mad	pan	cap		west	rig	wink	nob	not	**un**
pad	ran	gap	**en**		wig		rob	pot	bun
sad	tan	lap	den	**et**		**ip**	sob	rot	fun
	van	map	hen	bet	**im**	dip			pun
ag		nap	men	get	dim	hip	**old**	**ub**	run
bag	**and**	sap	pen	jet	him	nip	bold	cub	sun
gag	band	tap	ten	let	Tim	sip	cold	hub	
lag	hand			met		tip	fold	rub	**ut**
nag	land	**ask**	**end**	net	**in**		gold	sub	but
rag	sand	mask	bend	pet	bin	**it**	hold	tub	cut
sag		task	lend	set	fin	bit	mold		gut
tag	**ank**		mend	vet	pin	fit	sold	**ug**	hut
wag	bank	**at**	send	wet	sin	hit	told	bug	jut
	rank	bat	tend	yet	tin	kit		dug	nut
am	sank	cat	vend		win	lit	**op**	hug	rut
ham	tank	fat		**id**		pit	hop	jug	
jam		hat		did	**ing**	sit	mop	mug	
Pam		mat		hid	king	wit	pop	rug	
ram		pat		kid	ring		top	tug	
Sam		rat		lid	sing				
		sat		rid	wing				

16 Segmenting and Blending Two-Sound Words

GOAL

- **Students will segment and blend words with two sounds.**

MATERIALS

- ○ Word bank for this activity
- ○ Blank tiles, small blocks, or paper squares
- ○ Two-sound templates

TEACHER STEPS: Describe It

- Place two blank tiles above the bold line on the two-sound template.
- Say a word from the word bank (e.g., go).
- Move one tile into each square for every sound you say (/g/ /ō/).
- Move the tiles together as you blend the sounds (go).

STUDENT STEPS: Do It

- Distribute two tiles and a two-sound template to each student.
- Say the following:
  - "What are the sounds in the word _____?" (e.g., go)
  - "Put one tile in each square for every sound you say." (/g/ /ō/)
  - "Blend the sounds as you move the tiles together." (go)

- As the students become proficient, say the following instead:
  - "What are the sounds in the word _____?" (go)

VARIATIONS

- Have students hold a contracted Slinky with one hand on either side. Tell students to pull the ends of the Slinky as they say the sounds in the word and push the ends together as they put the sounds together.
- Have students put their hands together in front of them. Tell them to move their hands apart as they say the sounds in the word and clap once as they put the sounds together.
- Tell students to hold one arm out with their palm up. With the opposite hand, have them touch their shoulder as they say the first sound and the middle of their arm as they say the second sound. Tell them to slide their hand down their arm as they blend the sounds.
- Have students segment and blend the sounds into a self-phone.

Word Bank										
bee	day	eat	hay	jay	may	oak	ray	see	tie	way
bow	die	fee	he	knee	me	pay	row	sew	toe	we
bye	do	go	hi	lie	my	pea	rye	show	two	
chew	doe	guy	hoe	low	no	pie	say	tea		

17 Stretchy Sounds: Segmenting and Blending Two-Sound Words

GOAL

- **Students will segment and blend words with two sounds.**

MATERIALS

○ Word bank for this activity   ○ Slinky spring toy

TEACHER STEPS: Describe It

- Hold a contracted Slinky with one hand on either side.
- Say a word from the word bank (e.g., *no*).
- Expand the Slinky as you segment the word (/n/ /ō/).
- Contract the Slinky as you blend the sounds (*no*).

STUDENT STEPS: Do It

- Demonstrate how to hold the contracted Slinky.
- Say the following:
  - "Pull the ends of the Slinky as you say the sounds in the word." (/n/ /ō/)
  - "Push the Slinky together as you blend the sounds." (*no*)

Word Bank

bee	day	eat	hay	jay	may	oak	ray	see	tie	way
bow	die	fee	he	knee	me	pay	row	sew	toe	we
bye	do	go	hi	lie	my	pea	rye	show	two	
chew	doe	guy	hoe	low	no	pie	say	tea		

18 Segmenting and Blending Three-Sound Words

GOAL

- **Students will segment and blend words with three sounds.**

MATERIALS

- ○ Word bank for this activity
- ○ Blank tiles, small blocks, or paper squares
- ○ Three-sound templates

TEACHER STEPS: Describe It

- Place three blank tiles above the bold line on the three-sound template.
- Say a word from the word bank (e.g., *sip*).
- Move one tile into each square for every sound you say (/s/ /ĭ/ /p/).
- Move the tiles together as you blend the sounds (*sip*).

STUDENT STEPS: Do It

- Distribute three tiles and a three-sound template to each student.
- Say the following:
  - "What are the sounds in the word _____?" (e.g., *sip*)
  - "Put one tile in each square for every sound you say." (/s/ /ĭ/ /p/)
  - "Blend the sounds as you move the tiles together." (*sip*)

- As the students become proficient, say the following instead:
  - "What are the sounds in the word _____?" (e.g., *sip*)

VARIATIONS

- Have students hold a contracted Slinky with one hand on either side. Tell students to pull the ends of the Slinky as they say the sounds in the word and push the ends together as they put the sounds together.
- Have students put their hands together in front of them. Tell them to move their hands apart as they say the sounds in the word and clap once as they put the sounds together.
- Tell students to hold one arm out with their palm up. With the opposite hand, have them touch their shoulder as they say the first sound, the middle of their arm as they say the second sound, and their wrist as they say the third sound. Tell them to slide their hand down their arm as they blend the sounds.
- Tell students to touch their head as they say the first sound, their waist as they say the second sound, and their knees as they say the third sound. Tell them to blend the sounds as they stand up straight and tall!
- Have students segment and blend the sounds into a self-phone.

Word Bank on following page

Word Bank

ad	am	ate	eel	ine	itch	ot	ug
fad	ham	bait	deal	dine	ditch	cot	bug
lad	jam	gate	feel	fine	pitch	dot	dug
mad	Sam	hate	heel	line	rich	hot	hug
pad		late	meal	mine	witch	lot	jug
sad	**an**	wait	real	nine		not	mug
tad	ban		seal		**ock**	tot	rug
	Dan	**ed**	wheel	**ip**	dock		tug
ail	fan	bed		dip	lock	**ub**	
fail	man	fed	**ill**	hip	rock	cub	**um**
mail	pan	led	bill	sip	sock	hub	bum
nail	ran	red	chill	tip		rub	gum
pail	tan	wed	fill		**op**	sub	hum
	van		pill	**it**	hop	tub	sum
ake		**eed**	will	bit	mop		
bake	**ap**	deed		fit	pop	**uck**	
cake	cap	feed	**in**	hit	top	buck	
fake	lap	need	chin	kit		duck	
lake	map	seed	shin	pit		luck	
	nap		win	sit		puck	
	sap			wit		suck	
	tap					tuck	

19 Stretchy Sounds: Segmenting and Blending Three-Sound Words

GOAL

- **Students will segment and blend words with three sounds.**

MATERIALS

- ○ Word bank for this activity, objects, or picture cards
- ○ Slinky spring toy

TEACHER STEPS: Describe It

- Hold a contracted Slinky with one hand on either side.
- Say a word from the word bank or identify an object or a picture (e.g., *sun*).

STUDENT STEPS: Do It

- Demonstrate how to hold the contracted Slinky.
- Say the following:
  - "Pull the end of the Slinky as you say the sounds in the word _____." (/s/ /ŭ/ /n/)
  - "Push the Slinky together as you blend the sounds." (*sun*)

Word Bank

ad	**am**	**ate**	**eel**	**ine**	**itch**	**ot**	**ug**
fad	ham	bait	deal	dine	ditch	cot	bug
lad	jam	gate	feel	fine	pitch	dot	dug
mad	Sam	hate	heel	line	rich	hot	hug
pad		late	meal	mine	witch	lot	jug
sad	**an**	wait	real	nine		not	mug
tad	ban		seal		**ock**	tot	rug
	Dan	**ed**	wheel	**ip**	dock		tug
ail	fan	bed		dip	lock	**ub**	
fail	man	fed	**ill**	hip	rock	cub	**um**
mail	pan	led	bill	sip	sock	hub	bum
nail	ran	red	chill	tip		rub	gum
pail	tan	wed	fill		**op**	sub	hum
	van		pill	**it**	hop	tub	sum
ake		**eed**	will	bit	mop		
bake	**ap**	deed		fit	pop	**uck**	
cake	cap	feed	**in**	hit	top	buck	
fake	lap	need	chin	kit		duck	
lake	map	seed	shin	pit		luck	
	nap		win	sit		puck	
	sap			wit		suck	
	tap					tuck	

20 Segmenting and Blending Four-Sound Words

GOAL

- **Students will segment and blend words with four sounds.**

MATERIALS

- ○ Word bank for this activity
- ○ Blank tiles, small blocks, or paper squares
- ○ Four-sound templates

TEACHER STEPS: Describe It

- Place four blank tiles above the bold line on the four-sound template.
- Say a word from the word bank (e.g., *last*).
- Move one tile into each square for every sound you say (/l/ /ă/ /s/ /t/).
- Move the tiles together as you blend the sounds (*last*).

STUDENT STEPS: Do It

- Distribute four tiles and a four-sound template to each student.
- Say the following:
  - "What are the sounds in the word _____?" (e.g., *last*)
  - "Move one tile into each square for every sound you say." (/l/ /ă/ /s/ /t/)
  - "Blend the sounds as you move the tiles together." (*last*)

- As the students become proficient, say the following instead:
  - "What are the sounds in the word _____?" (e.g., *last*)

VARIATIONS

- Have students hold a contracted Slinky with one hand on either side. Tell students to pull the ends of the Slinky as they say the sounds in the word and push the ends together as they put the sounds together.
- Have students put their hands together in front of them. Tell them to move their hands apart as they say the sounds in the word and clap once as they put the sounds together.
- Tell students to hold one arm out with their palm up. With the opposite hand, have them touch their shoulder as they say the first sound, the middle of their arm as they say the second sound, their wrist as they say the third sound, and their palm as they say the final sound. Tell them to slide their hand down their arm as they blend the sounds.
- Tell students to touch their head as they say the first sound, their waist as they say the second sound, their knees as they say the third sound, and their feet as they say the final sound. Tell them to blend the sounds as they stand up straight and tall!
- Have students segment and blend the sounds into a self-phone.

Word Bank on following page

Word Bank

beds	crib	flat	hens	mink	plug	skid	slit	spot	trim
best	cups	fled	hump	mops	plum	skin	slug	steak	trip
black	damp	flip	jest	nest	price	skip	smash	steal	trot
brag	drag	fret	lamp	pans	pump	skit	smile	steer	twin
bump	drop	glad	land	pigs	raft	slab	snag	stone	vest
camp	drug	great	last	pinch	ramp	slam	snail	stool	webs
cats	drum	grin	lend	pink	rest	slap	snob	stop	west
clap	fans	grip	limp	place	rink	sled	snug	swag	wigs
club	flab	groan	link	plane	rugs	slick	speak	tops	wink
crab	flag	grub	list	plate	sand	slid	spill	trace	
cram	flake	hand	lump	please	scan	slime	spin	train	
crash	flame	hats	maps	plot	sink	slip	spit	trap	

21 Stretchy Sounds: Segmenting and Blending Four-Sound Words

GOAL

- **Students will segment and blend words with four sounds.**

MATERIALS

- ○ Word bank for this activity, objects, or picture cards
- ○ Slinky spring toy

TEACHER STEPS: Describe It

- Hold a contracted Slinky with one hand on either side.
- Say a word from the word bank or identify an object or a picture (e.g., *sand*).
- Expand the Slinky as you segment the word (/s/ /ă/ /n/ /d/).
- Contract the Slinky as you blend the sounds (*sand*).

STUDENT STEPS: Do It

- Demonstrate how to hold the contracted Slinky.
- Say the following:
  - "Pull the ends of the Slinky as you say the sounds in the word _____." (/s/ /ă/ /n/ /d/)
  - "Push the Slinky together as you blend the sounds." (*sand*)

Word Bank

beds	crib	flat	hens	mink	plug	skid	slit	spot	trim
best	cups	fled	hump	mops	plum	skin	slug	steak	trip
black	damp	flip	jest	nest	price	skip	smash	steal	trot
brag	drag	fret	lamp	pans	pump	skit	smile	steer	twin
bump	drop	glad	land	pigs	raft	slab	snag	stone	vest
camp	drug	great	last	pinch	ramp	slam	snail	stool	webs
cats	drum	grin	lend	pink	rest	slap	snob	stop	west
clap	fans	grip	limp	place	rink	sled	snug	swag	wigs
club	flab	groan	link	plane	rugs	slick	speak	tops	wink
crab	flag	grub	list	plate	sand	slid	spill	trace	
cram	flake	hand	lump	please	scan	slime	spin	train	
crash	flame	hats	maps	plot	sink	slip	spit	trap	

22　Stretchy Sounds: Segmenting and Blending Two-, Three-, and Four-Sound Words

GOAL

- **Students will segment and blend words with two, three, and four sounds.**

MATERIALS

○ Word bank for this activity, objects, or picture cards

○ Slinky spring toy

TEACHER STEPS: Describe It

- Hold a contracted Slinky with one hand on either side.
- Say a word from the word bank or identify an object or a picture (e.g., *sand*).
- Expand the Slinky as you segment the word (/s/ /ă/ /n/ /d/).
- Contract the Slinky as you blend the sounds (*sand*).

STUDENT STEPS: Do It

- Demonstrate how to hold the contracted Slinky.
- Say the following:
  - "Pull the ends of the Slinky as you say the sounds in the word _____."
    (/s/ /ă/ /n/ /d/)
  - "Push the Slinky together as you blend the sounds." (*sand*)

Word Banks on following page

Two-Sound Words

Word Bank

bee	day	eat	hay	jay	may	oak	ray	see	tie	way
bow	die	fee	he	knee	me	pay	row	sew	toe	we
bye	do	go	hi	lie	my	pea	rye	show	two	
chew	doe	guy	hoe	low	no	pie	say	tea		

Three-Sound Words

Word Bank

ad	am	ate	eel	ine	itch	ot	ug
fad	ham	bait	deal	dine	ditch	cot	bug
lad	jam	gate	feel	fine	pitch	dot	dug
mad	Sam	hate	heel	line	rich	hot	hug
pad		late	meal	mine	witch	lot	jug
sad	an	wait	real	nine		not	mug
tad	ban		seal		ock	tot	rug
	Dan	ed	wheel	ip	dock		tug
ail	fan	bed		dip	lock	ub	
fail	man	fed	ill	hip	rock	cub	um
mail	pan	led	bill	sip	sock	hub	bum
nail	ran	red	chill	tip		rub	gum
pail	tan	wed	fill		op	sub	hum
	van		pill	it	hop	tub	sum
ake		eed	will	bit	mop		
bake	ap	deed		fit	pop	uck	
cake	cap	feed	in	hit	top	buck	
fake	lap	need	chin	kit		duck	
lake	map	seed	shin	pit		luck	
	nap		win	sit		puck	
	sap			wit		suck	
	tap					tuck	

Four-Sound Words

Word Bank

beds	crib	flat	hens	mink	plug	skid	slit	spot	trim
best	cups	fled	hump	mops	plum	skin	slug	steak	trip
black	damp	flip	jest	nest	price	skip	smash	steal	trot
brag	drag	fret	lamp	pans	pump	skit	smile	steer	twin
bump	drop	glad	land	pigs	raft	slab	snag	stone	vest
camp	drug	great	last	pinch	ramp	slam	snail	stool	webs
cats	drum	grin	lend	pink	rest	slap	snob	stop	west
clap	fans	grip	limp	place	rink	sled	snug	swag	wigs
club	flab	groan	link	plane	rugs	slick	speak	tops	wink
crab	flag	grub	list	plate	sand	slid	spill	trace	
cram	flake	hand	lump	please	scan	slime	spin	train	
crash	flame	hats	maps	plot	sink	slip	spit	trap	

23 Show Me! Counting Phonemes in Two-, Three-, and Four-Sound Words

GOALS

- **Students will segment words with two, three, and four sounds.**
- **Students will count the number of phonemes in words with two, three, and four sounds.**

MATERIALS

- ○ Word bank for this activity, objects, or picture cards

TEACHER STEPS: Describe It

- Say a word from the word bank or identify an object or picture (e.g., *cap*).
- Tell the students you are going to count the sounds in your head.
- Put up the number of fingers that shows how many sounds there are in the word.
- To demonstrate how you determined the number of sounds in the word, put up one finger for every sound you say (/k/ /ă/ /p/).

STUDENT STEPS: Do It

Say the following:
- "The word is _____." (e.g., *cap*)
- "Count the sounds in your head."
- "When I say, 'Show me,' put up the number of fingers that shows how many sounds there are in the word." (Give students time to think.)
- "Show me!"
- "Show how you figured out the number of sounds by putting up one finger for every sound you say." (/k/ /ă/ /p/)

VARIATIONS

- Using individual white boards, have students write a tally mark for each sound, draw a square for each sound, or make a dot for each sound.
- Have students drop one blank tile in a cup for each sound.

Word Banks on following page

Two-Sound Words

Word Bank

bee	day	eat	hay	jay	may	oak	ray	see	tie	way
bow	die	fee	he	knee	me	pay	row	sew	toe	we
bye	do	go	hi	lie	my	pea	rye	show	two	
chew	doe	guy	hoe	low	no	pie	say	tea		

Three-Sound Words

Word Bank

ad	**am**	**ate**	**eel**	**ine**	**itch**	**ot**	**ug**
fad	ham	bait	deal	dine	ditch	cot	bug
lad	jam	gate	feel	fine	pitch	dot	dug
mad	Sam	hate	heel	line	rich	hot	hug
pad		late	meal	mine	witch	lot	jug
sad	**an**	wait	real	nine		not	mug
tad	ban		seal		**ock**	tot	rug
	Dan	**ed**	wheel	**ip**	dock		tug
ail	fan	bed		dip	lock	**ub**	
fail	man	fed	**ill**	hip	rock	cub	**um**
mail	pan	led	bill	sip	sock	hub	bum
nail	ran	red	chill	tip		rub	gum
pail	tan	wed	fill		**op**	sub	hum
	van		pill	**it**	hop	tub	sum
ake		**eed**	will	bit	mop		
bake	**ap**	deed		fit	pop	**uck**	
cake	cap	feed	**in**	hit	top	buck	
fake	lap	need	chin	kit		duck	
lake	map	seed	shin	pit		luck	
	nap		win	sit		puck	
	sap			wit		suck	
	tap					tuck	

Four-Sound Words

Word Bank

beds	crib	flat	hens	mink	plug	skid	slit	spot	trim
best	cups	fled	hump	mops	plum	skin	slug	steak	trip
black	damp	flip	jest	nest	price	skip	smash	steal	trot
brag	drag	fret	lamp	pans	pump	skit	smile	steer	twin
bump	drop	glad	land	pigs	raft	slab	snag	stone	vest
camp	drug	great	last	pinch	ramp	slam	snail	stool	webs
cats	drum	grin	lend	pink	rest	slap	snob	stop	west
clap	fans	grip	limp	place	rink	sled	snug	swag	wigs
club	flab	groan	link	plane	rugs	slick	speak	tops	wink
crab	flag	grub	list	plate	sand	slid	spill	trace	
cram	flake	hand	lump	please	scan	slime	spin	train	
crash	flame	hats	maps	plot	sink	slip	spit	trap	

24 Jump to It! Counting Phonemes in Two-, Three-, and Four-Sound Words

GOAL

- **Students will segment and blend words with two, three, and four sounds.**

MATERIALS

○ Word bank for this activity, objects, or picture cards

TEACHER STEPS: Describe It

- Say a word from the word bank or identify an object or a picture (e.g., *bike*).
- Tell students you are going to jump one time for every sound you say (/b/ /ī/ /k/).
- Blend the sounds (*bike*).

STUDENT STEPS: Do It

Say the following:
- "The word (object or picture) is _____." (e.g., *bike*)
- "Jump once for every sound you say." (/b/ /ī/ /k/)
- "Blend the sounds." (*bike*)

VARIATION

- Have students jump rope, with one jump for every sound.

Word Banks on following page

Two-Sound Words

Word Bank

bee	day	eat	hay	jay	may	oak	ray	see	tie	way
bow	die	fee	he	knee	me	pay	row	sew	toe	we
bye	do	go	hi	lie	my	pea	rye	show	two	
chew	doe	guy	hoe	low	no	pie	say	tea		

Three-Sound Words

Word Bank

ad	am	ate	eel	ine	itch	ot	ug
fad	ham	bait	deal	dine	ditch	cot	bug
lad	jam	gate	feel	fine	pitch	dot	dug
mad	Sam	hate	heel	line	rich	hot	hug
pad		late	meal	mine	witch	lot	jug
sad	an	wait	real	nine		not	mug
tad	ban		seal		ock	tot	rug
	Dan	ed	wheel	ip	dock		tug
ail	fan	bed		dip	lock	ub	
fail	man	fed	ill	hip	rock	cub	um
mail	pan	led	bill	sip	sock	hub	bum
nail	ran	red	chill	tip		rub	gum
pail	tan	wed	fill		op	sub	hum
	van		pill	it	hop	tub	sum
ake		eed	will	bit	mop		
bake	ap	deed		fit	pop	uck	
cake	cap	feed	in	hit	top	buck	
fake	lap	need	chin	kit		duck	
lake	map	seed	shin	pit		luck	
	nap		win	sit		puck	
	sap			wit		suck	
	tap					tuck	

Four-Sound Words

Word Bank

beds	crib	flat	hens	mink	plug	skid	slit	spot	trim
best	cups	fled	hump	mops	plum	skin	slug	steak	trip
black	damp	flip	jest	nest	price	skip	smash	steal	trot
brag	drag	fret	lamp	pans	pump	skit	smile	steer	twin
bump	drop	glad	land	pigs	raft	slab	snag	stone	vest
camp	drug	great	last	pinch	ramp	slam	snail	stool	webs
cats	drum	grin	lend	pink	rest	slap	snob	stop	west
clap	fans	grip	limp	place	rink	sled	snug	swag	wigs
club	flab	groan	link	plane	rugs	slick	speak	tops	wink
crab	flag	grub	list	plate	sand	slid	spill	trace	
cram	flake	hand	lump	please	scan	slime	spin	train	
crash	flame	hats	maps	plot	sink	slip	spit	trap	

25　Sound Noise: Counting Phonemes in Two-, Three-, and Four-Sound Words

GOAL

- **Students will segment and blend words with two, three, and four sounds.**

MATERIALS

○ Word bank for this activity, objects, or picture cards

○ Plastic spoons, sticks, or cymbals

TEACHER STEPS: Describe It

- Say a word from the word bank or identify an object or a picture (e.g., *past*).
- Tap the spoons, sticks, or cymbals together for each sound you say (/p/ /ă/ /s/ /t/).
- Blend the sounds (*past*).

STUDENT STEPS: Do It

Say the following:
- "The word is _____." (e.g., *past*)
- "Tap the spoons, sticks, or cymbals together for each sound you say." (/p/ /ă/ /s/ /t/)
- "Blend the sounds." (*past*)

VARIATIONS

- Students place the card/object in front of them if they segment and blend the word correctly. At the end of the activity, ask students to count their cards/objects.
- Students place the card/object in the class pile if they segment and blend the word correctly. The card/object is placed in the teacher's pile if the word is not segmented and blended correctly. At the end of the activity, count the cards/objects to see who won!
- Have students segment and blend the sounds into a self-phone before tapping out the sounds.

Word Banks on following page

Two-Sound Words

Word Bank

bee	day	eat	hay	jay	may	oak	ray	see	tie	way
bow	die	fee	he	knee	me	pay	row	sew	toe	we
bye	do	go	hi	lie	my	pea	rye	show	two	
chew	doe	guy	hoe	low	no	pie	say	tea		

Three-Sound Words

Word Bank

ad	**am**	**ate**	**eel**	**ine**	**itch**	**ot**	**ug**
fad	ham	bait	deal	dine	ditch	cot	bug
lad	jam	gate	feel	fine	pitch	dot	dug
mad	Sam	hate	heel	line	rich	hot	hug
pad		late	meal	mine	witch	lot	jug
sad	**an**	wait	real	nine		not	mug
tad	ban		seal		**ock**	tot	rug
	Dan	**ed**	wheel	**ip**	dock		tug
ail	fan	bed		dip	lock	**ub**	
fail	man	fed	**ill**	hip	rock	cub	**um**
mail	pan	led	bill	sip	sock	hub	bum
nail	ran	red	chill	tip		rub	gum
pail	tan	wed	fill		**op**	sub	hum
	van		pill	**it**	hop	tub	sum
ake		**eed**	will	bit	mop		
bake	**ap**	deed		fit	pop	**uck**	
cake	cap	feed	**in**	hit	top	buck	
fake	lap	need	chin	kit		duck	
lake	map	seed	shin	pit		luck	
	nap		win	sit		puck	
	sap			wit		suck	
	tap					tuck	

Four-Sound Words

Word Bank

beds	crib	flat	hens	mink	plug	skid	slit	spot	trim
best	cups	fled	hump	mops	plum	skin	slug	steak	trip
black	damp	flip	jest	nest	price	skip	smash	steal	trot
brag	drag	fret	lamp	pans	pump	skit	smile	steer	twin
bump	drop	glad	land	pigs	raft	slab	snag	stone	vest
camp	drug	great	last	pinch	ramp	slam	snail	stool	webs
cats	drum	grin	lend	pink	rest	slap	snob	stop	west
clap	fans	grip	limp	place	rink	sled	snug	swag	wigs
club	flab	groan	link	plane	rugs	slick	speak	tops	wink
crab	flag	grub	list	plate	sand	slid	spill	trace	
cram	flake	hand	lump	please	scan	slime	spin	train	
crash	flame	hats	maps	plot	sink	slip	spit	trap	

26 Clapping Sounds: Counting Phonemes in Two-, Three-, and Four-Sound Words

GOAL

- **Students will segment and blend words with two, three, and four sounds.**

MATERIALS

○ Word bank for this activity, objects, or picture cards

TEACHER STEPS: Describe It

- Say a word from the word bank or choose an object or a picture (e.g., *bed*).
- Clap once for each sound you say (/b/ /ĕ/ /d/).
- Blend the sounds (*bed*).

STUDENT STEPS: Do It

Say the following

- "The word (object or picture) is _____." (e.g., *bed*)
- "Clap once for every sound you say." (/b/ /ĕ/ /d/)
- "Blend the sounds." (*bed*)

VARIATIONS

- Students place the card/object in front of them if they segment and blend the word correctly. At the end of the activity, ask students to count their cards/objects.
- Students place the card/object in the class pile if they segment and blend the word correctly. The card/object is placed in the teacher's pile if the word is not segmented and blended correctly. At the end of the activity, count the cards/objects to see who won!
- Have students segment and blend the sounds into a self-phone before clapping out the sounds.

Word Banks on following page

Two-Sound Words

Word Bank

bee	day	eat	hay	jay	may	oak	ray	see	tie	way
bow	die	fee	he	knee	me	pay	row	sew	toe	we
bye	do	go	hi	lie	my	pea	rye	show	two	
chew	doe	guy	hoe	low	no	pie	say	tea		

Three-Sound Words

Word Bank

ad	**am**	**ate**	**eel**	**ine**	**itch**	**ot**	**ug**
fad	ham	bait	deal	dine	ditch	cot	bug
lad	jam	gate	feel	fine	pitch	dot	dug
mad	Sam	hate	heel	line	rich	hot	hug
pad		late	meal	mine	witch	lot	jug
sad	**an**	wait	real	nine		not	mug
tad	ban		seal		**ock**	tot	rug
	Dan		wheel	**ip**	dock		tug
ail	fan	**ed**		dip	lock	**ub**	
fail	man	bed	**ill**	hip	rock	cub	**um**
mail	pan	fed	bill	sip	sock	hub	bum
nail	ran	led	chill	tip		rub	gum
pail	tan	red	fill		**op**	sub	hum
	van	wed	pill	**it**	hop	tub	sum
ake			will	bit	mop		
bake	**ap**	**eed**		fit	pop	**uck**	
cake	cap	deed	**in**	hit	top	buck	
fake	lap	feed	chin	kit		duck	
lake	map	need	shin	pit		luck	
	nap	seed	win	sit		puck	
	sap			wit		suck	
	tap					tuck	

Four-Sound Words

Word Bank

beds	crib	flat	hens	mink	plug	skid	slit	spot	trim
best	cups	fled	hump	mops	plum	skin	slug	steak	trip
black	damp	flip	jest	nest	price	skip	smash	steal	trot
brag	drag	fret	lamp	pans	pump	skit	smile	steer	twin
bump	drop	glad	land	pigs	raft	slab	snag	stone	vest
camp	drug	great	last	pinch	ramp	slam	snail	stool	webs
cats	drum	grin	lend	pink	rest	slap	snob	stop	west
clap	fans	grip	limp	place	rink	sled	snug	swag	wigs
club	flab	groan	link	plane	rugs	slick	speak	tops	wink
crab	flag	grub	list	plate	sand	slid	spill	trace	
cram	flake	hand	lump	please	scan	slime	spin	train	
crash	flame	hats	maps	plot	sink	slip	spit	trap	

27 Concentration: Segmenting and Blending Two-, Three-, and Four-Sound Words

GOAL

- **Students will segment and blend words with two, three, and four sounds.**

MATERIALS

○ Picture cards (two cards of each picture)

TEACHER STEPS: Describe It

- Place picture cards face down in the form of a square or rectangle. (Make sure there are two cards of each picture.)
- Turn over the first card and segment the word.
- Turn over a second card and segment the word
- Tell students that if the pictures are the same, they keep the cards. If not, turn them over.

STUDENT STEPS: Do It

Say the following:
- "Turn over a card."
- "What is it?" (e.g., *pig*)
- "Say the sounds." (/p/ /ĭ/ /g/)
- "Blend the sounds." (*pig*)
- "Turn over another card."
- "What is it?"
- "Say the sounds."
- "Blend the sounds."
- "Are the two words the same?"
- (Yes) "Keep the cards."
- (No) "Flip the cards over."

VARIATION

- Have students segment and blend the sounds into a self-phone.

28 Go Fish: Segmenting and Blending Two-, Three-, and Four-Sound Words

GOAL

- **Students will segment and blend words with two, three, and four sounds.**

MATERIALS

- ◯ Picture cards (two cards of each picture)

TEACHER STEPS: Describe It

- Deal five cards to each student. (Make sure there are two cards of each picture.)
- The remaining cards are placed in the middle of the playing area.
- Tell the students when it is their turn, they will ask the student to their right for a card that matches a card they have in their hand.
- Tell students they must ask for the card by saying the sounds in the word. For example, "Do you have a /d/ /ŏ/ /g/?"
- If the student who was asked has the card, he or she gives it to the player.
- The player places the pair in front of him or her.
- If the student who was asked does not have the card, he or she says, "Go Fish."
- Then, the player picks a card from the deck.
- If the player picks a card that matches one in his or her hand, the pair is placed in front of him or her.

VARIATION

- Have students segment and blend the sounds into a self-phone.

29 Adding an Initial Consonant Sound

GOALS

- **Students will segment and blend words with two, three, and four sounds.**
- **Students will identify the initial sound that has been added to a word to make a new word.**

MATERIALS

❍ Word bank for this activity

❍ Blank colored tiles, small blocks, or paper squares

TEACHER STEPS: Describe It

- Tell students you can do a magic trick with sounds because you can make a new word by adding a sound to the beginning of a word.
- Say the first word in a word pair (e.g., *at* in *at-mat*).
- As you segment the word, put down one tile for every sound you say.
- Blend the sounds as you move the tiles together (*at*).
- Say the second word in the pair (*mat*).
- As you segment the word, put down one tile for every sound you say. Place these tiles under the first set of tiles. (See the illustration below.) As a prompt, the tile representing the beginning sound of the second word should be a different color.
- Tell students the sound you added to make the new word (/m/).
- Point to the sets of tiles as you say each word (*at-mat*).

 /ă/ /t/ **Use tiles of the same color to segment the first word.**

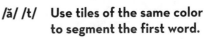 /măt/ **Use a tile of a different color to indicate the added sound.**

STUDENT STEPS: Do It

- Say the following:
  - "What are the sounds in the word _____?" (e.g., *at*)
  - "Put down a tile for each sound you say." (/ă/ /t/).
  - "Blend the sounds as you move the tiles together." (*at*)
  - "The new word is _____." (e.g., *mat*)
  - "Put down a tile for every sound you say." (/m/ /ă/ /t/)
  - "What sound did you add to change _____ to _____? (*at* to *mat*; ANSWER: /m/)
- As students become proficient, conduct this activity without the tiles.
- Say the following:
  - "What are the sounds in the word _____?" (e.g., *at*; ANSWER: /ă/ /t/)
  - "What are the sounds in the word _____?" (e.g., *mat*; ANSWER: /m/ /ă/ /t/)
  - "What sound did you add to change _____ to _____?" (*at* to *mat*; ANSWER: /m/)

Activity and Word Bank continued on following page

Adding an Initial Consonant Sound continued

VARIATIONS

- Have students hold a contracted Slinky with one hand on either side. Tell students to pull the ends of the Slinky as they say the sounds in the word and push the ends together as they put the sounds together.
- Have students put their hands together in front of them. Tell them to move their hands apart as they say the sounds in the word and clap once as they put the sounds together.
- Tell students to hold one arm out with their palm up. With the opposite hand, have them touch their shoulder as they say the first sound, the middle of their arm as they say the second sound, their wrist as they say the third sound, and their palm if there is a fourth sound. Tell them to slide their hand down their arm as they blend the sounds.
- Tell students to touch their head as they say the first sound, their waist as they say the second sound, their knees as they say the third sound, and their feet if there is a fourth sound. Tell them to blend the sounds as they stand up straight and tall!

Word Bank

ace	am	ash	ear	end	in	oh
ace-base	am-ham	ash-bash	ear-dear	end-bend	in-bin	oh-bow
ace-case	am-jam	ash-cash	ear-fear	end-lend	in-fin	oh-go
ace-face	am-lamb	ash-dash	ear-gear	end-mend	in-pin	oh-hoe
ace-lace	am-Pam	ash-gash	ear-hear	end-send	in-sin	oh-low
ace-race	am-ram	ash-hash	ear-leer	end-tend	in-tin	oh-no
	am-Sam	ash-lash	ear-near	end-vend	in-win	oh-row
ache	am-yam	ash-mash	ear-pier			oh-sew
ache-bake		ash-rash	ear-rear	**eye**	**ink**	oh-toe
ache-cake	**an**	ash-sash	ear-tear	eye-by	ink-link	
ache-fake	an-ban		ear-year	eye-die	ink-mink	**oil**
ache-lake	an-can	**ask**		eye-guy	ink-pink	oil-boil
ache-make	an-Dan	ask-mask	**eat**	eye-high	ink-rink	oil-coil
ache-rake	an-fan	ask-task	eat-beat	eye-lie	ink-sink	oil-foil
ache-sake	an-man		eat-feet	eye-my	ink-wink	oil-loyal
ache-take	an-pan	**at**	eat-heat	eye-pie		oil-royal
ache-wake	an-ran	at-bat	eat-meat	eye-rye	**it**	oil-soil
	an-tan	at-cat	eat-neat	eye-sigh	it-bit	oil-toil
ad		at-fat	eat-Pete	eye-tie	it-fit	
ad-bad	**and**	at-hat	eat-seat		it-hit	**old**
ad-dad	and-band	at-mat		**ice**	it-kit	old-bold
ad-fad	and-hand	at-rat	**Ed**	ice-dice	it-lit	old-cold
ad-had	and-land	at-pat	Ed-bed	ice-lice	it-pit	old-fold
ad-lad	and-sand	at-sat	Ed-fed	ice-mice	it-sit	old-gold
ad-mad			Ed-led	ice-nice	it-wit	old-hold
ad-pad	**ant**	**ate**	Ed-Ned	ice-rice		old-mold
ad-sad	ant-can't	ate-bait	Ed-red		**oak**	old-told
	ant-pant	ate-date	Ed-Ted	**ill**	oak-Coke	
aim	ant-rant	ate-gate	Ed-wed	ill-bill	oak-joke	**own**
aim-fame		ate-hate	**eel**	ill-dill	oak-soak	own-bone
aim-game	**art**	ate-late	eel-deal	ill-fill	oak-woke	own-cone
aim-lame	art-cart	ate-mate	eel-feel	ill-gill		own-loan
aim-name	art-dart	ate-rate	eel-heal	ill-hill		own-moan
aim-same	art-heart	ate-wait	eel-kneel	ill-Jill		own-phone
aim-tame	art-mart		eel-meal	ill-kill		own-tone
	art-part		eel-peel	ill-mill		
	art-tart		eel-reel	ill-pill		
			eel-seal			

CLASSROOM ACTIVITY

106

30 Adding a Sound to Form an Initial Consonant Blend

GOALS

- **Students will segment and blend words with two, three, and four sounds.**
- **Students will identify the initial sound that has been added to a word to make a new word.**

MATERIALS

○ Word bank for this activity

○ Blank colored tiles, small blocks, or paper squares

TEACHER STEPS: Describe It

- Tell students you can do a magic trick with sounds because you can make a new word by adding a sound to the beginning of a word.
- Say the first word in a word pair (e.g., *low* in *low-glow*).
- As you segment the word, put down one tile for every sound you say. Place these under the first set of tiles. (See the illustration below.)
- Blend the sounds as you move the tiles together (*low*).
- Say the second word in the pair (*glow*).
- As you segment the word, put down one tile for every sound you say. Place these tiles under the first set of tiles. (See the illustration below.) As a prompt, the tile representing the beginning sound of the second word should be a different color.
- Tell students the sound you added to make the new word. (/g/)
- Point to the sets of tiles as you say each word (*low-glow*).

 /l/ /ō/   Use tiles of the same color to segment the first word.

 /g/ /l/ /ō/   Use a tile of a different color to indicate the added sound.

STUDENT STEPS: Do It

- Say the following:
  - "What are the sounds in the word _____?" (e.g., *low*)
  - "Put down a tile for each sound you say." (/l/ /ō/)
  - "Blend the sounds as you move the tiles together." (*low*)
  - "The new word is _____." (e.g., *glow*)
  - "Put down a tile for every sound you say." (/g/ /l/ /ō/)
  - "What sound did you add to change _____ to _____?" (*low* to *glow*; ANSWER: /g/)

Activity and Word Bank continued on following page

- As students become proficient, conduct this activity without the tiles.
- Say the following:
  - "What are the sounds in the word _____?" (*low;* ANSWER: /l/ /ō/)
  - "What are the sounds in the word?" (*glow;* ANSWER: /g/ /l/ /ō/)
  - "What sound did you add to change _____ to _____?" (*low to glow;* ANSWER: /g/)

VARIATIONS

- Have students hold a contracted Slinky with one hand on either side. Tell students to pull the ends of the Slinky as they say the sounds in the word and push the ends together as they put the sounds together.
- Have students put their hands together in front of them. Tell them to move their hands apart as they say the sounds in the word and clap once as they put the sounds together.
- Tell students to hold one arm out with their palm up. With the opposite hand, have them touch their shoulder as they say the first sound, the middle of their arm as they say the second sound, their wrist as they say the third sound, and their palm if there is a fourth sound. Tell them to slide their hand down their arm as they blend the sounds.
- Tell students to touch their head as they say the first sound, their waist as they say the second sound, their knees as they say the third sound, and their feet if there is a fourth sound. Tell them to blend the sounds as they stand up straight and tall!

Word Bank

bl	dr	pl	sl	sp	sw
lack-black	raft-draft	lane-plane	lamb-slam	peak-speak	wag-swag
Lou-blue	ream-dream	lay-play	lap-slap	peer-spear	way-sway
low-blow	ride-dried	lie-ply	leap-sleep	pie-spy	weep-sweep
	rug-drug	lot-plot	led-sled	pill-spill	well-swell
br	rum-drum		lick-slick	pin-spin	wet-sweat
rag-brag	rye-dry	**pr**	lid-slid	pit-spit	wheat-sweet
raid-braid		ray-pray	lie-sly	poke-spoke	will-swill
rake-brake	**fl**	rise-prize	lied-slide		
read-bread	lame-flame	rye-pry	lip-slip	**st**	**tr**
ride-bride	Lee-flea		lit-slit	tack-stack	rack-track
right-bright	lore-floor	**sk**	low-slow	tale-stale	rail-trail
		key-ski		team-steam	rap-trap
cl	**gl**	kid-skid		tick-stick	read-tread
lap-clap	lass-glass	kill-skill	**sm**	tie-sty	Rick-trick
lay-clay	Lou-glue	kin-skin	Mack-smack	till-still	rim-trim
Lou-clue	low-glow	kit-skit		top-stop	rip-trip
			sn	tore-store	roll-troll
			knees-sneeze	tow-stow	rot-trot
cr	**gr**		nag-snag	tuck-stuck	rye-try
rain-crane	rain-grain		nail-snail		
rash-crash	rate-great		nap-snap		**tw**
rate-crate	rave-grave		nick-snick		weak-tweak
rave-crave	row-grow		nip-snip		win-twin
reap-creep			no-snow		
			nob-snob		

31 Adding a Second Sound to Form an Initial Consonant Blend

GOALS

- **Students will segment and blend words with two, three, and four sounds.**
- **Students will identify the sound that has been added to a word to make a new word.**

MATERIALS

○ Word bank for this activity

○ Blank colored tiles, small blocks, or paper squares

TEACHER STEPS: Describe It

- Tell students you can do a magic trick with sounds because you can make a new word by adding a sound to the beginning of a word.
- Say the first word in a word pair (e.g., *cap* in *cap-clap*).
- As you segment the word, put down one tile for every sound you say. (See the illustration below.)
- Blend the sounds as you move the tiles together (*cap*).
- Say the second word (*clap*).
- Point to the tiles as you say the sounds. Insert a tile of a different color to indicate the added sound. (See the illustration below.)
- Tell students the sound you added to make the new word (/l/).
- Remove and add the second tile as you say each word (*cap-clap*).

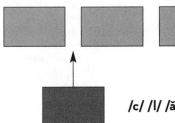

/c/ /ă/ /p/ Use tiles of the same color to segment the first word.

/c/ /l/ /ă/ /p/ Insert a tile of a different color to indicate the added sound.

STUDENT STEPS: Do It

- Say the following:
  - "What are the sounds in the word _____?" (e.g., *cap*)
  - "Put down a tile for each sound you say." (/c/ /ă/ /p/)
  - "Blend the sounds as you move the tiles together." (*cap*)
  - "The new word is _____." (e.g., *clap*)
  - "Point to the tiles as you say the sounds." (/c/ /l/ /ă/ /p/)
  - "Add a tile to show where the new sound is."
  - "What sound did you add to change _____ to _____?" (*cap* to *clap*; ANSWER: /l/)

Activity and Word Bank continued on following page

- As students become proficient, conduct this activity without the tiles.
- Say the following:
  - "What are the sounds in the word _____?" (e.g., *cap*; ANSWER: /c/ /ă/ /p/)
  - "What are the sounds in the word _____?" (e.g., *clap*; ANSWER: /c/ /l/ /ă/ /p/)
  - "What sound did you add to change _____ to _____?" (*cap* to *clap*; ANSWER: /l/)

VARIATIONS

- Have students hold a contracted Slinky with one hand on either side. Tell students to pull the ends of the Slinky as they say the sounds in the word and push the ends together as they put the sounds together.
- Have students put their hands together in front of them. Tell them to move their hands apart as they say the sounds in the word and clap once as they put the sounds together.
- Tell students to hold one arm out with their palm up. With the opposite hand, have them touch their shoulder as they say the first sound, the middle of their arm as they say the second sound, their wrist as they say the third sound, and their palm if there is a fourth sound. Tell them to slide their hand down their arm as they blend the sounds.
- Tell students to touch their head as they say the first sound, their waist as they say the second sound, their knees as they say the third sound, and their feet if there is a fourth sound. Tell them to blend the sounds as they stand up straight and tall!

Word Bank

bl-	dr-	pr-	sn-	sw-
back-black	daft-draft	pay-pray	sag-snag	sag-swag
bend-blend	deem-dream	pie-pry	sail-snail	say-sway
boo-blue	die-dry	pies-prize	sap-snap	seat-sweet
bow-blow	died-dried		seize-sneeze	seep-sweep
box-blocks	dug-drug	**sk-**	sick-snick	sell-swell
	dumb-drum	see-ski	sip-snip	set-sweat
br-		Sid-skid	sob-snob	sill-swill
bade-braid	**fl-**	sill-skill	sow-snow	
bag-brag	fame-flame	sin-skin		**tr-**
bake-brake	fee-flea	sit-skit	**sp-**	tack-track
bed-bread	four-floor		sear-spear	tail-trail
bide-bride		**sl-**	seek-speak	tap-trap
bite-bright	**gl-**	said-sled	sigh-spy	Ted-tread
	gas-glass	Sam-slam	sill-spill	tick-trick
cl-	go-glow	sap-slap	sin-spin	tie-try
camp-clamp	goo-glue	seep-sleep	sit-spit	Tim-trim
cap-clap		sew-slow	soak-spoke	tip-trip
coo-clue	**gr-**	sick-slick		toll-troll
Kay-clay	gain-grain	Sid-slid	**st-**	tot-trot
	gate-great	side-slide	sack-stack	
cr-	gave-grave	sigh-sly	sale-stale	**tw-**
camp-cramp	go-grow	sip-slip	seam-steam	teak-tweak
cane-crane		sit-slit	sick-stick	tin-twin
cash-crash	**pl-**		sigh-sty	
cave-crave	pain-plane	**sm-**	sill-still	
Kate-crate	pay-play	sack-smack	sop-stop	
keep-creep	pie-ply	sash-smash	sore-store	
	pot-plot		sow-stow	
	pump-plump		suck-stuck	

32 Making Words Grow

GOALS

- **Students will segment and blend words with two, three, and four sounds.**
- **Students will identify the sound that has been added to a word to make a new word.**

MATERIALS

○ Word bank for this activity

○ Blank colored tiles, small blocks, or paper squares

TEACHER STEPS: Describe It

- Tell students you can do a magic trick with sounds because you can make words grow.
- Say the first word in the triad (e.g., *my* in *my-mile-smile*).
- As you segment the word, put down one tile for every sound you say. (See the illustration below.)
- Blend the sounds as you move the tiles together (my).
- Say the second word (*mile*).
- Point to the tiles as you say the sounds.
- Insert a tile of a different color to indicate the added sound. (See the illustration below.)
- Blend the sounds as you move the tiles together (*mile*).
- Tell students the sound you added to make the new word (/l/).
- Say the third word (*smile*).
- Point to the tiles as you say the sounds. Use a tile of a different color to indicate the added sound. (See the illustration below.)
- Blend the sounds as you move the tiles together (*smile*).
- Tell students the sound you added to make the new word (/s/).
- Add tiles as you review each word (*my-mile-smile*).

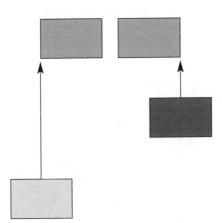

/m/ /ī/ **Use tiles of the same color to segment the first word.**

/m/ /ī/ /l/ **Insert a tile of a different color to indicate the added sound.**

/s/ /m/ /ī/ /l/ **Insert a tile of a different color to indicate the added sound.**

Activity and Word Bank continued on following page

PHONOLOGICAL AWARENESS · **Segmenting and Blending**   CLASSROOM ACTIVITY

STUDENT STEPS: Do It

- Say the following:
  - "What are the sounds in the word _____?" (e.g., *my*; ANSWER: /m/ /ī/)
  - "Put down a tile for each sound you say." (/m/ /ī/)
  - "Blend the sounds as you move the tiles together." (*my*)
  - "The new word is _____." (e.g., *mile*)
  - "Point to the tiles as you say the sounds." (/m/ /ī/ /l/)
  - "Add a tile to show where the new sound is."
  - "What sound did you add to change _____ to _____?" (*my* to *mile*; ANSWER: /l/)
  - "The new word is _____." (e.g., *smile*)
  - "Say the sounds." (/s/ /m/ /ī/ /l/)
  - "Add a tile to show where the new sound is."
  - "What sound did you add to change _____ to _____?" (*mile* to *smile*; ANSWER: /s/)

- As students become proficient, conduct this activity without the tiles.
- Say the following:
  - "What are the sounds in the word _____?" (e.g., *my*; ANSWER: /m/ /ī/)
  - "What are the sounds in the word _____?" (e.g., *mile*; ANSWER: /m/ /ī/ /l/)
  - "What sound did you add to change _____ to _____?" (*my* to *mile*; ANSWER: /l/)
  - "What are the sounds in the word _____?" (e.g., *smile*)
  - "What sound did you add to change _____ to _____?" (*mile* to *smile*; ANSWER: /s/)

VARIATIONS

- Have students hold a contracted Slinky with one hand on either side. Tell students to pull the ends of the Slinky as they say the sounds in the word and push the ends together as they put the sounds together.
- Have students put their hands together in front of them. Tell them to move their hands apart as they say the sounds in the word and clap once as they put the sounds together.
- Tell students to hold one arm out with their palm up. With the opposite hand, have them touch their shoulder as they say the first sound, the middle of their arm as they say the second sound and their wrist as they say the third sound, and their palm if there is a fourth sound. Tell them to slide their hand down their arm as they blend the sounds.
- Tell students to touch their head as they say the first sound, their waist as they say the second sound, their knees as they say the third sound, and their feet if there is a fourth sound. Tell them to blend the sounds as they stand up straight and tall!

Word Bank							
am	ear	ill	locks	pinch	seat	smile	teal
an	eat	in	mash	pit	sill	spice	tear
and	Ed	inch	mile	price	sin	spill	till
ash	eel	it	my	rain	sit	spit	toe
at	end	kill	ox	rash	skill	spy	tone
ate	fat	kin	pain	rate	skin	steal	train
blend	flat	lamb	paint	ray	slam	steer	tread
blocks	gray	led	pay	read	sled	still	twin
crash	great	lend	pie	rice	slit	stone	wheat
crate	ice	lit	pill	sand	smash	sweet	win

33 Deleting an Initial Consonant Sound

GOALS

- **Students will segment and blend words with two, three, and four sounds.**
- **Students will identify the initial sound that has been deleted from a word to make a new word.**

MATERIALS

○ Word bank for this activity

○ Blank colored tiles, small blocks, or paper squares

TEACHER STEPS: Describe It

- Tell students you can do a magic trick with sounds because you can make a new word by taking away a sound from the beginning of a word.
- Say the first word in a word pair (e.g., *sat* in *sat-at*).
- As you segment the word, put down one tile for every sound you say (/s/ /ă/ /t/). (As a prompt, the tile representing the beginning sound of the first word should be a different color. See the illustration below.)
- Blend the sounds as you move the tiles together (*sat*).
- Say the second word (*at*).
- As you segment the word, put down one tile for every sound you say. Place these tiles under the first set of tiles. (See the illustration below.)
- Tell students the sound you deleted (/s/).
- Point to the sets of tiles as you say each word (*sat-at*).

/s/ /ă/ /t/   Use a tile of a different color to indicate the beginning sound.

/ă/ /t/   Use tiles of the same color for the remaining sounds.

STUDENT STEPS: Do It

Say the following:
- "What are the sounds in the word _____?" (e.g., *sat*)
- "Put down a tile for every sound you say." (/s/ /ă/ /t/)
- "Blend the sounds as you move the tiles together." (*sat*)
- "The new word is _____." (e.g., *at*)
- "Put down a tile for every sound you say." (/ă/ /t/)
- "What sound did you take away to change _____ to _____?" (*sat* to *at*; ANSWER: /s/)

Activity and Word Bank continued on following pages

- As students become proficient, conduct this activity without the tiles.
- Say the following:
    - "What are the sounds in the word _____?" (e.g., *sat*)
    - "What are the sounds in the word _____?" (e.g., *at*)
    - "What sound did you take away to change _____ to _____?" (*sat* to *at*; ANSWER: /s/)

VARIATIONS

- Have students hold a contracted Slinky with one hand on either side. Tell students to pull the ends of the Slinky as they say the sounds in the word and push the ends together as they put the sounds together.
- Have students put their hands together in front of them. Tell them to move their hands apart as they say the sounds in the word and clap once as they put the sounds together.
- Tell students to hold one arm out with their palm up. With the opposite hand, have them touch their shoulder as they say the first sound, the middle of their arm as they say the second sound, their wrist as they say the third sound, and their palm if there is a fourth sound. Tell them to slide their hand down their arm as they blend the sounds.
- Tell students to touch their head as they say the first sound, their waist as they say the second sound, their knees as they say the third sound, and their feet if there is a fourth sound. Tell them to blend the sounds as they stand up straight and tall!

Word Bank on following page

Word Bank

ace	**an**	**ask**	**eel**	**ill**	**oh**
base-ace	ban-an	mask-ask	deal-eel	bill-ill	bow-oh
case-ace	can-an	task-ask	feel-eel	dill-ill	go-oh
face-ace	Dan-an		heal-eel	fill-ill	hoe-oh
lace-ace	fan-an	**at**	kneel-eel	gill-ill	low-oh
race-ace	man-an	bat-at	meal-eel	hill-ill	no-oh
	pan-an	cat-at	peel-eel	Jill-ill	row-oh
ache	ran-an	fat-at	reel-eel	kill-ill	sew-oh
bake-ache	tan-an	hat-at	seal-eel	mill-ill	toe-oh
cake-ache		mat-at		pill-ill	
fake-ache	**and**	pat-at	**end**		**oil**
lake-ache	band-and	rat-at	bend-end	**in**	boil-oil
make-ache	hand-and	sat-at	lend-end	bin-in	coil-oil
rake-ache	land-and		mend-end	fin-in	foil-oil
sake-ache	sand-and	**ate**	send-end	pin-in	loyal-oil
take-ache		bait-ate	tend-end	sin-in	royal-oil
wake-ache	**ant**	date-ate	vend-end	tin-in	soil-oil
	can't-ant	gate-ate		win-in	toil-oil
ad	pant-ant	hate-ate	**eye**		
bad-ad	rant-ant	late-ate	by-eye	**ink**	**old**
dad-ad		mate-ate	die-eye	link-ink	bold-old
fad-ad	**art**	rate-ate	guy-eye	mink-ink	cold-old
had-ad	cart-art	wait-ate	high-eye	pink-ink	fold-old
lad-ad	dart-art		lie-eye	rink-ink	gold-old
mad-ad	heart-art	**eat**	my-eye	sink-ink	hold-old
pad-ad	mart-art	beat-eat	pie-eye	wink-ink	mold-old
sad-ad	part-art	feet-eat	rye-eye		told-old
	tart-art	heat-eat	sigh-eye	**it**	
aim		meat-eat	tie-eye	bit-it	**own**
fame-aim	**ash**	neat-eat		fit-it	bone-own
game-aim	bash-ash	Pete-eat	**ice**	hit-it	cone-own
lame-aim	cash-ash	seat-eat	dice-ice	kit-it	loan-own
name-aim	dash-ash		lice-ice	lit-it	moan-own
same-aim	gash-ash	**Ed**	mice-ice	pit-it	phone-own
tame-aim	hash-ash	bed-Ed	nice-ice	sit-it	tone-own
	lash-ash	fed-Ed	rice-ice	wit-it	
am	mash-ash	led-Ed			
ham-am	rash-ash	Ned-Ed		**oak**	
jam-am	sash-ash	red-Ed		Coke-oak	
lamb-am		Ted-Ed		joke-oak	
Pam-am		wed-Ed		soak-oak	
ram-am				woke-oak	
Sam-am					
yam-am					

34 Deleting the First Sound from an Initial Consonant Blend

GOALS

- Students will segment and blend words with two, three, and four sounds.
- Students will identify the initial sound that has been deleted from a word to make a new word.

MATERIALS

○ Word bank for this activity

○ Blank colored tiles, small blocks, or paper squares

TEACHER STEPS: Describe It

- Tell students you can do a magic trick with sounds because you can make a new word by taking away a sound from the beginning of a word.
- Say the first word in a word pair (e.g., *snow* in *snow-no*).
- As you segment the word, put down one tile for every sound you say (/s/ /n/ /ō/).
- As a prompt, the tile representing the beginning sound of the first word should be a different color. (See the illustration below.)
- Move the tiles together as you blend the sounds (*snow*).
- Say the second word (*no*).
- As you segment the word, put down one tile for every sound you say. Place these tiles under the first set of tiles. (See the illustration below.)
- Tell students the sound you deleted to make the new word (/s/).
- Point to the sets of tiles as you say each word (*snow-no*).

/s/ n/ /ō/ Use a tile of a different color to indicate the beginning sound.

/n/ /ō/ Use tiles of the same color for the remaining sounds.

STUDENT STEPS: Do It

Say the following:
- "What are the sounds in the word _____?" (e.g., *snow*)
- "Put down a tile for every sound you say." (/s/ /n/ /ō/)
- "Blend the sounds as you move the tiles together." (*snow*)
- "The new word is _____." (e.g., *no*)
- "Put down a tile for every sound you say." (e.g., /n/ /ō/)
- "What sound did you take away to change _____ to _____?" (*snow* to *no*; ANSWER: /s/)

Activity and Word Bank continued on following page

- As students become proficient, conduct this activity without tiles.
- Say the following:
  - "What are the sounds in the word _____?" (e.g., *snow*).
  - "What are the sounds in the word _____?" (e.g., *no*).
  - "What sound did you take away to change _____ to _____?" (*snow* to *no*; ANSWER: /s/)

VARIATIONS

- Have students hold a contracted Slinky with one hand on either side. Tell students to pull the ends of the Slinky as they say the sounds in the word and push the ends together as they put the sounds together.
- Have students put their hands together in front of them. Tell them to move their hands apart as they say the sounds in the word and clap once as they put the sounds together.
- Tell students to hold one arm out with their palm up. With the opposite hand, have them touch their shoulder as they say the first sound, the middle of their arm as they say the second sound, their wrist as they say the third sound, and their palm if there is a fourth sound. Tell them to slide their hand down their arm as they blend the sounds.
- Tell students to touch their head as they say the first sound, their waist as they say the second sound, their knees as they say the third sound, and their feet if there is a fourth sound. Tell them to blend the sounds as they stand up straight and tall!

Word Bank

bl	**dr**	**pl**	**sl**	**sp**	**sw**
black-lack	draft-raft	plane-lane	slam-lamb	speak-peak	swag-wag
blow-low	dream-ream	play-lay	slap-lap	spear-peer	sway-way
blue-Lou	dried-ride	plot-lot	sled-led	spill-pill	sweat-wet
	drug-rug	ply-lie	sleep-leap	spin-pin	sweep-weep
br	drum-rum		slick-lick	spit-pit	sweet-wheat
brag-rag	dry-rye	**pr**	slid-lid	spoke-poke	swell-well
braid-raid		pray-ray	slide-lied	spy-pie	swill-will
brake-rake	**fl**	prize-rise	slip-lip		
bread-read	flame-lame	pry-rye	slit-lit	**st**	**tr**
bride-ride	flea-Lee		slow-low	stack-tack	track-rack
bright-right	floor-lore	**sk**	sly-lie	stale-tale	trail-rail
		ski-key		steam-team	trap-rap
cl	**gl**	skid-kid	**sm**	stick-tick	tread-read
clap-lap	glass-lass	skill-kill	smack-Mack	still-till	trick-Rick
clay-lay	glow-low	skin-kin		stop-top	trim-rim
clue-Lou	glue-Lou	skit-kit	**sn**	store-tore	trip-rip
			snag-nag	stow-tow	troll-roll
cr	**gr**		snail-nail	stuck-tuck	trot-rot
crane-rain	grain-rain		snap-nap	sty-tie	try-rye
crate-rate	grave-rave		sneeze-knees		
crave-rave	great-rate		snick-nick		**tw**
creep-reap	grow-row		snip-nip		tweak-weak
			snob-knob		twin-win
			snow-no		

117

35 Deleting the Second Sound from an Initial Consonant Blend

GOALS

- Students will segment and blend words with two, three, and four sounds.
- Students will identify the sound that has been deleted from a word to make a new word.

MATERIALS

○ Word bank for this activity   ○ Blank tiles, small blocks, or paper squares

TEACHER STEPS: Describe It

- Tell students you can do a magic trick with sounds because you can make a new word by taking away a sound.
- Say the first word in a word pair (e.g., *slide* in *slide-side*).
- As you segment the word, put down one tile for every sound you say. (See the illustration below.)
- Move the tiles together as you blend the sounds (*slide*).
- Say the second word (*side*).
- Point to the tiles as you say the sounds. Remove the tile representing the deleted sound. (See the illustration below.)
- Tell students the sound you deleted to make the new word (/l/).
- Add and remove the second tile as you say each word (*slide-side*).

Arrangement of tiles for segmenting the sounds in *slide*:

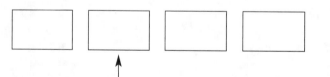

Remove the second tile when segmenting the second word in the pair.

STUDENT STEPS: Do It

- Say the following:
  - "What are the sounds in the word _____?" (e.g., *slide*)
  - "Put down a tile for each sound you say." (/s/ /l/ /ī/ /d/)
  - "Blend the sounds as you move the tiles together." (*slide*)
  - "The new word is _____." (e.g., *side*)
  - "Point to the tiles as you say the sounds." (/s/ /ī/ /d/)
  - "Take away a tile to show where the sound was taken away."
- "What sound did you take away to change _____ to _____?" (*slide* to *side*; ANSWER: /l/)

Activity and Word Bank continued on following page

- As students become proficient, conduct this activity without the tiles.
- Say the following:
  - "What are the sounds in the word _____?" (e.g., *slide* ANSWER: /s/ /l/ /ī/ /d/)
  - "What are the sounds in the word _____?" (e.g., *side* ANSWER: /s/ /ī/ /d/)
  - "What sound did you take away to change _____ to _____?" (*slide* to *side*; ANSWER: /l/)

VARIATIONS

- Have students hold a contracted Slinky with one hand on either side. Tell students to pull the ends of the Slinky as they say the sounds in the word and push the ends together as they put the sounds together.
- Have students put their hands together in front of them. Tell them to move their hands apart as they say the sounds in the word and clap once as they put the sounds together.
- Tell students to hold one arm out with their palm up. With the opposite hand, have them touch their shoulder as they say the first sound, the middle of their arm as they say the second sound, their wrist as they say the third sound, and their palm if there is a fourth sound. Tell them to slide their hand down their arm as they blend the sounds.
- Tell students to touch their head as they say the first sound, their waist as they say the second sound, their knees as they say the third sound, and their feet if there is a fourth sound. Tell them to blend the sounds as they stand up straight and tall!

Word Bank

bl	dr	pl	sl	sp	sw
black-back	draft-daft	plane-pain	slam-Sam	speak-seek	swag-sag
blow-bow	dream-deem	play-pay	slap-sap	spear-sear	sway-say
blue-boo	dried-died	plot-pot	sled-said	spill-sill	sweat-set
	drug-dug	ply-pie	sleep-seep	spin-sin	sweep-seep
br	drum-dumb		slick-sick	spit-sit	sweet-seat
brag-bag	dry-die	**pr**	slid-Sid	spoke-soak	swell-sell
braid-bade		pray-pay	slide-side	spy-sigh	swill-sill
brake-bake	**fl**	prize-pies	slip-sip		
bread-bed	flame-fame	pry-pie	slit-sit	**st**	**tr**
bride-bide	flea-fee		slow-sew	stack-sack	track-tack
bright-bite	floor-four	**sk**	sly-sigh	stale-sale	trail-tail
		ski-see		steam-seam	trap-tap
cl	**gl**	skid-Sid	**sm**	stick-sick	tread-Ted
clap-cap	glass-gas	skill-sill	smack-sack	still-sill	trick-tick
clay-Kay	glow-go	skin-sin		stop-sop	trim-Tim
clue-coo	glue-goo	skit-sit	**sn**	store-sore	trip-tip
			snag-sag	stow-sow	troll-toll
cr	**gr**		snail-sail	stuck-suck	trot-tot
crane-cane	grain-gain		snap-sap	sty-sigh	try-tie
crate-Kate	grave-gave		sneeze-seize		
crave-cave	great-gate		snick-sick		**tw**
creep-keep	grow-go		snip-sip		tweak-teak
			snob-sob		twin-tin
			snow-sow		

119

36 Substituting an Initial Consonant Sound

GOAL

- **Students will identify the initial consonant sound that has been substituted to make a new word.**

MATERIALS

○ Word bank for this activity

○ Blank colored tiles, small blocks, or paper squares

TEACHER STEPS: Describe It

- Tell students you can do a magic trick with letters because you can make new words by changing the beginning sound in a word.
- Say a word from the word bank (e.g., *sit*).
- As you segment the word, put down one tile for every sound you say. (/s/ /ĭ/ /t/)
- Blend the sounds as you move the tiles together (*sit*).
- Say another word (e.g., *pit*).
- Point to the tiles as you say the sounds. Substitute a tile of a different color to represent the new sound. (See the illustration below.)
- Blend the sounds (*pit*).
- Tell students the sound that made the new word (/p/).
- Accentuate the first sound of the first word as you say both words (**s**it-**p**it).

Substitute a tile of a different color for the new sound.

STUDENT STEPS: Do It

- Say the following:
  - "What are the sounds in the word _____?" (e.g., *sit*; ANSWER: /s/ /ĭ/ /t/)
  - "Put down a tile for each sound you say." (/s/ /ĭ/ /t/)
  - "Blend the sounds as you move the tiles together." (*sit*)
  - "The new word is _____." (e.g., *pit*)
  - "What sound changed _____ to _____?" (*sit* to *pit*; ANSWER: /p/)
  - "Use a tile of a different color to show the sound that changed _____ to _____." (*sit* to *pit*; ANSWER: /p/)

- As students become proficient, conduct this activity without the tiles.
- Say the following:
  - "_____-_____" (e.g., *sit-pit*)
  - "What sound changed _____ to _____?" (*sit* to *pit*; ANSWER: /p/)

Activity and Word Bank continued on following page

VARIATIONS

- Have students hold a contracted Slinky with one hand on either side. Tell students to pull the ends of the Slinky as they say the sounds in the word and push the ends together as they put the sounds together.
- Have students put their hands together in front of them. Tell them to move their hands apart as they say the sounds in the word and clap once as they put the sounds together.
- Tell students to hold one arm out with their palm up. With the opposite hand, have them touch their shoulder as they say the first sound, the middle of their arm as they say the second sound, their wrist as they say the third sound, and their palm if there is a fourth sound. Tell them to slide their hand down their arm as they blend the sounds.
- Tell students to touch their head as they say the first sound, their waist as they say the second sound, their knees as they say the third sound, and their feet if there is a fourth sound. Tell them to blend the sounds as they stand up straight and tall!

Word Bank

ad	an	ant	ed	est	ig	ink	ob	ot	um
bad	ban	can't	bed	best	big	link	Bob	cot	bum
dad	can	pant	fed	jest	dig	mink	cob	dot	gum
fad	Dan	rant	led	nest	fig	pink	job	got	hum
had	fan		red	rest	jig	rink	lob	hot	sum
lad	man	**ap**	wed	vest	pig	sink	mob	lot	
mad	pan	cap		west	rig	wink	nob	not	**un**
pad	ran	gap	**en**		wig		rob	pot	bun
sad	tan	lap	den	**et**		**ip**	sob	rot	fun
	van	map	hen	bet	**im**	dip			pun
ag		nap	men	get	dim	hip	**old**	**ub**	run
bag	**and**	sap	pen	jet	him	nip	bold	cub	sun
gag	band	tap	ten	let	Tim	sip	cold	hub	
lag	hand			met		tip	fold	rub	**ut**
nag	land	**ask**	**end**	net	**in**		gold	sub	but
rag	sand	mask	bend	pet	bin	**it**	hold	tub	cut
sag		task	lend	set	fin	bit	mold		gut
tag	**ank**		mend	vet	fit	fit	sold	**ug**	hut
wag	bank	**at**	send	wet	hit	hit	told	bug	jut
	rank	bat	tend	yet	kit	kit		dug	nut
am	sank	cat	vend		lit	lit	**op**	hug	rut
ham	tank	fat		**id**		pit	hop	jug	
jam		hat		did	**ing**	sit	mop	mug	
Pam		mat		hid	king	wit	pop	rug	
ram		pat		kid	ring		top	tug	
Sam		rat		lid	sing				
		sat		rid	wing				

37 Substituting a Final Consonant Sound

GOAL

- **Students will identify the final consonant sound that has been substituted to make a new word.**

MATERIALS

○ Word bank for this activity

○ Blank colored tiles, small blocks, or paper squares

TEACHER STEPS: Describe It

- Tell students you can do a magic trick with letters because you can make new words by changing the last sound in a word.
- Say a word from the word bank (e.g., *sit*).
- As you segment the word, put down one tile for every sound you say (/s/ /ĭ/ /t/).
- Blend the sounds as you move the tiles together (*sit*).
- Say another word (e.g., *sip*).
- Point to the tiles as you say the sounds. Substitute a tile of a different color to represent the new sound. (See the illustration below.)
- Blend the sounds (*sip*).
- Tell students the sound that made the new word (/p/).
- Accentuate the last sound as you say both words (si**t**-si**p**).

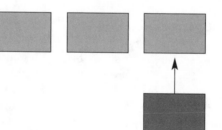

Substitute a tile of a different color for the new sound.

STUDENT STEPS: Do It

- Say the following:
  - "What are the sounds in the word _____?" (e.g., *sit*)
  - "Put down a tile for each sound you say." (/s/ /ĭ/ /t/)
  - "Blend the sounds as you move the tiles together." (*sit*)
  - "The new word is _____." (e.g., *sip*)
  - "What sound changed _____ to _____?" (*sit* to *sip*; ANSWER: /p/)
  - "Use a tile of a different color to show the sound that changed _____ to _____." (*sit* to *sip*)

- As students become proficient, conduct this activity without the tiles.
- Say the following:
  - "_____-_____" (*sit-sip;*)
  - "What sound changed _____ to _____?" (*sit* to *sip*; ANSWER: /p/)

Activity and Word Bank continued on following page

VARIATIONS

- Have students hold a contracted Slinky with one hand on either side. Tell students to pull the ends of the Slinky as they say the sounds in the word and push the ends together as they put the sounds together.
- Have students put their hands together in front of them. Tell them to move their hands apart as they say the sounds in the word and clap once as they put the sounds together.
- Tell students to hold one arm out with their palm up. With the opposite hand, have them touch their shoulder as they say the first sound, the middle of their arm as they say the second sound, their wrist as they say the third sound, and their palm if there is a fourth sound. Tell them to slide their hand down their arm as they blend the sounds.
- Tell students to touch their head as they say the first sound, their waist as they say the second sound, their knees as they say the third sound, and their feet if there is a fourth sound. Tell them to blend the sounds as they stand up straight and tall!

Word Bank

ă	ă	ă	ĕ	ĕ	ĭ	ĭ	ŏ	ŏ	ŭ	ŭ
bad	jab	rag	bed	peg	bib	lid	cob	nod	bud	mud
bag	jam	ram	beg	pen	bid	lip	cod	not	bug	mug
ban	Jan	ran	Ben	pep	big	lit	cog		bum	mum
bat		rap	bet	pet	bin		cop	pod	bun	
	lab	rat			bit	rib	cot	pop	bus	rub
dad	lad		hem	Ted		rid		pot	but	rug
Dan	lag	sad	hen	ten	did	rig	Dom			run
	lap	sag			dig	rim	don	rob	gum	rut
fad		Sam	led	web	dim	rip	dot	Rod	gun	
fan	man	sap	leg	wed	din			Ron	Gus	sub
fat	map	sat	let	wet	dip	Sid	hop	rot	gut	sum
	mat					sin	hot			sun
had		tab	men	yes	fib	sip		sob	hub	
hag	nab	tad	met	yet	fig	sit	job	sod	hug	tub
ham	nag	tag			fin		jog	sop	hum	tug
has	Nan	tan	Ned		fit	Tim	jot		hut	
hat	nap	tap	net			tin		Tom		
					hid	tip	mob	ton		
					him		mom	top		
	pad				hip	wig	mop	tot		
	pal				hit	win				
	Pam					wit				
	pan									
	pat									

38 Substituting a Medial Vowel Sound

GOAL

- **Students will identify the medial sound that has been substituted to make a new word.**

MATERIALS

- ○ Word bank for this activity
- ○ Blank colored tiles, small blocks, or paper squares

TEACHER STEPS: Describe It

- Tell students you can do a magic trick with letters because you can make new words by changing the middle sound in a word.
- Say a word from the word bank (e.g., *sit*).
- As you segment the word, put down one tile for every sound you say. (/s/ /ĭ/ /t/)
- Blend the sounds as you move the tiles together (*sit*).
- Say another word (e.g., *sat*).
- Point to the tiles as you say the sounds. Substitute a tile of a different color to represent the new sound. (See the illustration below.)
- Blend the sounds (*sat*).
- Tell students the sound that made the new word (/ă/).
- Accentuate the middle sound as you say both words (*sit-sat*).

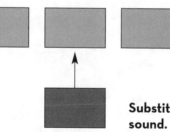

Substitute a tile of a different color for the new sound.

STUDENT STEPS: Do It

- Say the following:
  - "What are the sounds in the word _____?" (e.g., *sit*)
  - "Put down a tile for each sound you say." (/s/ /ĭ/ /t/)
  - "Blend the sounds as you move the tiles together." (*sit*)
  - "The new word is _____." (e.g., *sat*)
  - "What sound changed _____ to _____?" (*sit* to *sat*; ANSWER: /ă/)
  - "Use a tile of a different color to show the sound that changed _____ to _____." (*sit* to *sat*)

- As students become proficient, conduct this activity without the tiles.
- Say the following:
  - "_____-_____" (*sit-sat*)
  - "What sound changed _____ to _____?" (*sit* to *sat*; ANSWER: /ă/)

Activity and Word Bank continued on following page

VARIATIONS

- Have students hold a contracted Slinky with one hand on either side. Tell students to pull the ends of the Slinky as they say the sounds in the word and push the ends together as they put the sounds together.
- Have students put their hands together in front of them. Tell them to move their hands apart as they say the sounds in the word and clap once as they put the sounds together.
- Tell students to hold one arm out with their palm up. With the opposite hand, have them touch their shoulder as they say the first sound, the middle of their arm as they say the second sound, their wrist as they say the third sound, and their palm if there is a fourth sound. Tell them to slide their hand down their arm as they blend the sounds.
- Tell students to touch their head as they say the first sound, their waist as they say the second sound, their knees as they say the third sound, and their feet if there is a fourth sound. Tell them to blend the sounds as they stand up straight and tall!

Word Bank

bib	bat	Dan	hip	lag	man	pan	red	Sam	tan
Bob	bet	den	hop	leg	men	pen	rid	sum	ten
	bit	din		log		pin	rod		tin
bad	but	Don	hat	lug	map	pun		sin	
bed			hit		mop		rag	sun	tap
bid	dad	had	hot	lap		pep	rig		tip
bud	did	hid	hut	lip	Ned	pop	rug	sat	top
	dud			lop	nod	pup		set	
bag		hag	jam				ran	sit	wag
beg	fan	hog	Jim	let	nap	pat	Ron		wig
big	fin	hug		lit	nip	pet	run	tab	
bog	fun		jet	lot		pit		tub	wet
bug			jot		net	pot			wit
	gas	ham	jut	mad	not	put	rap	Tim	
ban	Gus	hem		mud	nut		rip	Tom	zap
Ben		him							zip
bin	get	hum	lad			rib	sad		
bun	got		led		Peg	rob	Sid		
	gut		lid		pig	rub	sod		
					pug				

6

Alphabetic Principle

FOCUS ON: Letter-Sound Correspondence

FOCUS ON: Adding Sounds

FOCUS ON: Deleting Sounds

FOCUS ON: Substituting Sounds

FOCUS ON: Long Vowel Spelling Patterns

FOCUS ON: Variant Vowel Spelling Patterns

INTRODUCTION

Mastering the alphabetic principle is one of the most critical tasks that young learners will face. Simply defined, the alphabetic principle is the representation of a phoneme by a graphic symbol, such as a letter or letters. Students must understand the alphabetic code in order to read and spell and thus comprehend text.

Because most of the sounds in words are predictable, it is important for students to learn the alphabetic principle. However, there are some exceptions. Some of the letters in English words do not correspond to the phonemes. Some letters make more than one sound (e.g., *e* can be /ĕ/ or /ē/, ough sounds differently in *tough* and *dough*), and certain combination of letters make single sounds (e.g., *ch, ng*). The sound of a letter can be modified by the letter or letters around it. There is no doubt that learning the alphabetic principle takes time and practice, but it is effort well spent. Students who have a strong sense of phonemes and a solid visual knowledge of the letters of the alphabet are well on their way to becoming proficient readers.

Chapter 6 moves from less complex to more complex activities. Students begin by practicing letter–sound correspondence with two-, three-, and four-sound words in which each sound is represented by one letter. They then move to adding, deleting, and substituting sounds. The students learn consonants and consonants blends and then practice with vowel sounds and patterns. The final activities target long vowel spelling patterns and variant vowel spelling patterns such as *ow, oy,* and *au.*

BIG IDEA: Alphabetic Principle	FOCUS ON: Letter-Sound Correspondence

1 Spelling Two-Sound Words

GOAL

- **Students will spell two-sound words in which each sound is represented by one letter.**

MATERIALS

○ Word bank for this activity   ○ Letter tiles or letter cards

TEACHER STEPS: Describe It

- Say a word from the word bank (e.g., *up*).
- As you segment the word, put down the corresponding letter for each sound you say (/ŭ/ /p/).

- Blend the sounds (*up*).

STUDENT STEPS: Do It

Say the following:
- "Put down a letter for each sound you say in the word _____." (e.g., *up*)
- "Blend the sounds." (*up*)

VARIATIONS

- Before putting down a letter for each sound, have students hold a contracted Slinky with one hand on either side. Tell students to pull the ends of the Slinky as they say the sounds in the word and push the ends together as they put the sounds together.
- Before putting down a letter for each sound, ask students to put their hands together in front of them. Tell them to move their hands apart as they break apart the word and clap once as they put the word together.
- Before putting down a letter for each sound, ask students to segment and blend the sounds into a self-phone. (See Chapter 4 for a description of a self-phone.)
- Before putting down a letter for each sound, ask students to hold one arm out with their palm up. With the opposite hand, have them touch their shoulder as they say the first sound and the middle of their arm as they say the second sound. Tell them to slide their hand down their arm as they blend the sounds.
- Instead of using letter tiles, ask students to spell the word on individual white boards.

Word Bank

ă	ĕ	ĭ	ŏ	ŭ
ad	Ed	if	on	up
am		in		us
an		it		
at				

BIG IDEA: Alphabetic Principle   FOCUS ON: Letter–Sound Correspondence

2 Spelling Three-Sound Words

GOAL

- Students will spell three-sound words in which each sound is represented by one letter.

MATERIALS

○ Word bank for this activity   ○ Letter tiles or letter cards

TEACHER STEPS: Describe It

- Say a word from the word bank (e.g., *bug*).
- As you segment the word, put down the corresponding letter for each sound you say (/b/ /ŭ/ /g/).

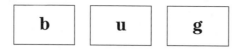

| b | u | g |

- Blend the sounds (*bug*).

STUDENT STEPS: Do It

Say the following:
- "Put down a letter for each sound you say in the word _____." (e.g., *bug*)
- "Blend the sounds." (*bug*)

VARIATIONS

- Before putting down a letter for each sound, have students hold a contracted Slinky with one hand on either side. Tell students to pull the ends of the Slinky as they say the sounds in the word and push the ends together as they put the sounds together.
- Before putting down a letter for each sound, ask students to put their hands together in front of them. Tell them to move their hands apart as they break apart the word and clap once as they put the word together.
- Before putting down a letter for each sound, ask students to segment and blend the sounds into a self-phone.
- Before putting down a letter for each sound, ask students to hold one arm out with their palm up. With the opposite hand, have them touch their shoulder as they say the first sound, the middle of their arm as they say the second sound, and their wrist as they say the third sound. Tell them to slide their hand down their arm as they blend the sounds.
- Instead of using letter tiles, ask students to spell the word on individual white boards.

Word Bank on following page

Word Bank

ă	ĕ	ĭ	ŏ	ŭ
bag	beg	bib	Bob	bud
bat	Ben	big	cod	bug
Dan	bet	bin	Don	bun
fan	den	bit	dot	bus
had	get	did	got	but
ham	hen	dip	hop	fun
jam	jet	fib	hot	gum
lap	leg	fig	job	gun
mad	let	hit	lot	Gus
map	men	lid	mop	hug
mat	net	lip	nod	hum
nap	peg	lit	not	hut
pan	pen	nip	pop	mud
pat	pet	rib	pot	nut
rag	red	rip	rob	rub
ran	set	sin	sob	rug
rap	Ted	sit	Tom	run
sad	ten	Tim	top	sum
tag	web	tip		sun
tan	wet	wig		tub
tap	yes	win		
wag	yet	zip		

3 Spelling Four-Sound Words

GOAL

- **Students will spell four-sound words in which each sound is represented by one letter.**

MATERIALS

○ Word bank for this activity   ○ Letter tiles or letter cards

TEACHER STEPS: Describe It

- Say a word from the word bank (e.g., *list*).
- As you segment the word, put down the corresponding letter for each sound you say (/l/ /ĭ/ /s/ /t/).

| l | i | s | t |

- Blend the sounds (*list*).

STUDENT STEPS: Do It

Say the following:
- "Put down a letter for each sound you say in the word _____." (e.g., *list*)
- "Blend the sounds." (*list*)

VARIATIONS

- Before putting down a letter for each sound, have students hold a contracted Slinky with one hand on either side. Tell students to pull the ends of the Slinky as they say the sounds in the word and push the ends together as they put the sounds together.
- Before putting down a letter for each sound, ask students to put their hands together in front of them. Tell them to move their hands apart as they break apart the word and clap once as they put the word together.
- Before putting down a letter for each sound, ask students to segment and blend the sounds into a self-phone.
- Before putting down a letter for each sound, ask students to hold one arm out with their palm up. With the opposite hand, have them touch their shoulder as they say the first sound, the middle of their arm as they say the second sound, their wrist as they say the third sound, and their palm as they say the final sound. Tell them to slide their hand down their arm as they blend the sounds.
- Instead of using letter tiles, ask students to spell the word on individual white boards.

Word Bank on following page

Word Bank

ă	ĕ	ĭ	ŏ	ŭ
bank	beds	drip	drop	bump
brag	best	flip	mops	club
camp	fled	grin	plot	cups
cats	fret	grip	snob	drug
clap	hens	limp	spot	drum
crab	jest	link	stop	grub
cram	lend	list	tops	hump
damp	nest	mink	trot	lump
drag	rest	pigs		plug
fans	sled	pink		plum
flab	vest	rink		pump
flag	webs	sink		rugs
flap		skid		slug
flat		skin		snug
glad		skip		spun
hand		skit		stub
hats		slid		
lamp		slip		
land		slit		
last		spin		
maps		spit		
pans		trim		
plan		trip		
raft		twig		
ramp		twin		
rank		wigs		
sand		wink		
sank				
scab				
scan				
slab				
slam				
slap				
snag				
snap				
swag				
tank				
trap				

4 Spelling Pictures

GOAL

- **Students will spell three- and four-sound words in which each sound is represented by one letter.**

MATERIALS

○ Picture cards   ○ Letter tiles or letter cards

TEACHER STEPS: Describe It

- Choose picture and identify it (e.g., *cat*).
- As you segment the word, put down the corresponding letter for each sound you say.

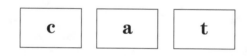

| c | a | t |

- Blend the sounds (*cat*).

STUDENT STEPS: Do It

Say the following:
- "Choose a picture and tell what it is." (e.g., *cat*)
- "Put down one letter for each sound you say in the word."

| c | a | t |

- "Blend the sounds." (*cat*)

VARIATIONS

- Before putting down a letter for each sound, have students hold a contracted Slinky with one hand on either side. Tell students to pull the ends of the Slinky as they say the sounds in the word and push the ends together as they put the sounds together.
- Before putting down a letter for each sound, ask students to put their hands together in front of them. Tell them to move their hands apart as they break apart the word and clap once as they put the word together.
- Before putting down a letter for each sound, ask students to segment and blend the sounds into a self-phone.
- Before putting down a letter for each sound, ask students to hold one arm out with their palm up. With the opposite hand, have them touch their shoulder as they say the first sound, the middle of their arm as they say the second sound, their wrist as they say the third sound, and their palm if there is a fourth sound. Tell them to slide their hand down their arm as they blend the sounds.
- Instead of using letter tiles, ask students to spell the word on individual white boards.

5 Adding an Initial Consonant Sound

GOAL

- **Students will spell new words by adding an initial consonant sound.**

MATERIALS

○ Word bank for this activity   ○ Letter tiles or letter cards

TEACHER STEPS: Describe It

- Tell students you can do a magic trick with letters because you can make a new word by adding a letter to the beginning of a word.
- Say the first word in a pair of words (e.g., *it* in *it-sit*).
- As you segment the word, put down the corresponding letter for each sound you say (/ĭ/ /t/).
- Blend the sounds (*it*).
- Say the second word in the pair (*sit*).
- Add the letter representing the initial sound (see the illustration below). Point to the other letters as you say the remaining sounds.
- Tell students the sound you added to make the new word (/s/).
- Remove and add the letter representing the initial sound of the new word as you say each word (*it-sit*).

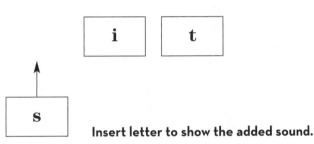

Insert letter to show the added sound.

STUDENT STEPS: Do It

Say the following:
- "Put down one letter for each sound you say in the word _____." (e.g., *it*; ANSWER: /ĭ/ /t/)
- "The new word is _____." (e.g., *sit*)
- "Add the letter that changes _____ to _____." (*it* to *sit*; ANSWER: s)

As students become proficient, say the following instead:
- "Use the letter tiles to spell _____." (e.g., *it*)
- "Change _____ to _____." (*it* to *sit*)

VARIATIONS

- Before putting down a letter for each sound, have students hold a contracted Slinky with one hand on either side. Tell students to pull the ends of the Slinky as they say the sounds in the word and push the ends together as they put the sounds together.

Activity and Word Bank continued on following page

CLASSROOM ACTIVITY
ALPHABETIC PRINCIPLE · Adding Sounds

- Before putting down a letter for each sound, ask students to put their hands together in front of them. Tell them to move their hands apart as they break apart the word and clap once as they put the word together.
- Before putting down a letter for each sound, ask students to segment and blend the sounds into a self-phone.
- Before putting down a letter for each sound, ask students to hold one arm out with their palm up. With the opposite hand, have them touch their shoulder as they say the first sound, the middle of their arm as they say the second sound, their wrist as they say the third sound, and their palm if there is a fourth sound. Tell them to slide their hand down their arm as they blend the sounds.
- Instead of using letter tiles, ask students to spell the word on individual white boards.

Word Bank

ad	an	ask	end	ink
ad-bad	an-ban	ask-mask	end-bend	ink-link
ad-dad	an-can	ask-task	end-lend	ink-mink
ad-fad	an-Dan		end-mend	ink-pink
ad-had	an-fan	**at**	end-send	ink-rink
ad-lad	an-man	at-bat	end-tend	ink-sink
ad-mad	an-pan	at-cat	end-vend	ink-wink
ad-pad	an-ran	at-fat		
ad-sad	an-tan	at-hat	**in**	**it**
		at-mat	in-bin	it-bit
am	**and**	at-pat	in-fin	it-fit
am-ham	and-band	at-rat	in-pin	it-hit
am-jam	and-hand	at-sat	in-sin	it-kit
am-Pam	and-land		in-tin	it-lit
am-ram	and-sand	**Ed**	in-win	it-pit
am-Sam		Ed-bed		it-sit
	ant	Ed-fed		it-wit
	ant-can't	Ed-led		
	ant-pant	Ed-Ned		
	ant-rant	Ed-red		
		Ed-Ted		
		Ed-wed		

6 Adding a Final Consonant Sound

GOAL

- **Students will spell new words by adding a final consonant sound.**

MATERIALS

○ Word bank for this activity

○ Letter tiles or letter cards

TEACHER STEPS: Describe It

- Tell students you can do a magic trick with sounds because you can make a new word by adding one sound to the end of a word.
- Say the first word in a pair of words (e.g., *an* in *an-and*).
- As you segment the first word, put down the corresponding letter for each sound you say (/ă/ /n/).
- Blend the sounds (*an*).
- Say the second word in the pair (*and*).
- Point to the letters as you say the sounds. Insert the letter that represents the added sound. (See the illustration below.)
- Tell students the sound you added to make the new word (/d/).
- Remove and add the letter that represents the added sound as you say each word (*an-and*).

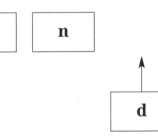

Insert letter to show the added sound.

STUDENT STEPS: Do It

Say the following:

- "Put down one letter for each sound you say in the word _____." (e.g., *an*; ANSWER: /ă/ /n/)
- "The new word is _____." (e.g., *and*)
- "Add the letter that changes _____ to _____." (*an* to *and*; ANSWER: *d*)

As students become proficient, say the following instead:

- "Use the letters to spell _____." (e.g., *an*)
- "Change _____ to _____." (*an* to *and*)

VARIATIONS

- Before putting down a letter for each sound, have students hold a contracted Slinky with one hand on either side. Tell students to pull the ends of the Slinky as they say the sounds in the word and push the ends together as they put the sounds together.

Activity and Word Bank continued on following page

Adding a Final Consonant Sound continued

- Before putting down a letter for each sound, ask students to put their hands together in front of them. Tell them to move their hands apart as they break apart the word and clap once as they put the word together.
- Before putting down a letter for each sound, ask students to segment and blend the sounds into a self-phone.
- Before putting down a letter for each sound, ask students to hold one arm out with their palm up. With the opposite hand, have them touch their shoulder as they say the first sound, the middle of their arm as they say the second sound, their wrist as they say the third sound, and their palm if there is a fourth sound. Tell them to slide their hand down their arm as they blend the sounds.
- Instead of using letter tiles, ask students to spell the word on individual white boards.

Word Bank

an-and	ban-band	Ben-bent	den-dent	pan-pant	Stan-stand	ten-tent
an-ant	Ben-bend	bus-bust	men-mend	ran-rant	ten-tend	tin-tint

7 Adding a Sound to Form an Initial Consonant Blend

GOAL

- **Students will spell new words by adding a sound to form an initial consonant blend.**

MATERIALS

○ Word bank for this activity

○ Letter tiles or letter cards

TEACHER STEPS: Describe It

- Tell students you can do a magic trick with letters because you can make a new word by adding a letter to the beginning of a word.
- Say the first word in a pair of words (e.g., *lap* in *lap-clap*).
- As you segment the word, put down the corresponding letter for each sound you say (/l/ /ă/ /p/).
- Blend the sounds (*lap*).
- Say the second word in the pair (*clap*).
- Add the letter representing the initial sound (see the illustration below). Point to the letters as you say the remaining sounds.
- Tell students the sound you added to make the new word (/k/).
- Remove and add the letter representing the initial sound as you say each word (*lap-clap*).

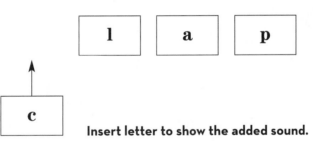

Insert letter to show the added sound.

STUDENT STEPS: Do It

Say the following:

- "Put down one letter for each sound you say in the word _____." (e.g., *lap*; ANSWER: /l/ /ă/ /p/)
- "The new word is _____." (e.g., *clap*)
- "Add the letter that changes _____ to _____." (*lap* to *clap*; ANSWER: c)

As students become proficient, say the following instead:

- "Use the letters to spell _____." (e.g., *lap*)
- "Change _____ to _____." (*lap* to *clap*)

Activity and Word Bank continued on following page

VARIATIONS

- Before putting down a letter for each sound, have students hold a contracted Slinky with one hand on either side. Tell students to pull the ends of the Slinky as they say the sounds in the word and push the ends together as they put the sounds together.
- Before putting down a letter for each sound, ask students to put their hands together in front of them. Tell them to move their hands apart as they break apart the word and clap once as they put the word together.
- Before putting down a letter for each sound, ask students to segment and blend the sounds into a self-phone.
- Before putting down a letter for each sound, ask students to hold one arm out with their palm up. With the opposite hand, have them touch their shoulder as they say the first sound, the middle of their arm as they say the second sound, their wrist as they say the third sound, and their palm if there is a fourth sound. Tell them to slide their hand down their arm as they blend the sounds.
- Instead of using letter tiles, ask students to spell the word on individual white boards.

Word Bank

bl	**cr**	**gr**	**sk**	**sn**	**sw**
lend-blend	ram-cram	rant-grant	kid-skid	nag-snag	wag-swag
limp-blimp	ramp-cramp	rip-grip	kin-skin	nap-snap	wig-swig
link-blink	rank-crank	runt-grunt	kit-skit	nip-snip	
lot-blot	rib-crib				**tr**
		pl	**sl**	**sp**	rap-trap
br	**dr**	lot-plot	lap-slap	Pam-Spam	rim-trim
rag-brag	raft-draft	lump-plump	led-sled	pan-span	rip-trip
ran-bran	rank-drank		lid-slid	pin-spin	rot-trot
rim-brim	rink-drink	**pr**	link-slink	pit-spit	
rink-brink	rip-drip	rank-prank	lip-slip	pot-spot	**tw**
	rug-drug		lit-slit	pun-spun	wig-twig
cl	rum-drum	**sc**	lot-slot		win-twin
lamp-clamp		can-scan	lug-slug	**st**	
lap-clap	**fl**		lump-slump	top-stop	
link-clink	lap-flap				
lip-clip	rip-flip		**sm**		
lot-clot			mug-smug		

8 Adding an Initial Consonant Blend

GOAL

- **Students will spell new words by adding an initial consonant blend.**

MATERIALS

❍ Word bank for this activity

❍ Letter tiles or letter cards

TEACHER STEPS: Describe It

- Tell students you can do a magic trick with letters because you can make a new word by adding two letters to the beginning of a word.
- Say the first word in a pair of words (e.g., *in* in the word pair *in-spin*).
- As you segment the word, put down the corresponding letter for each sound you say (/ĭ/ /n/).
- Blend the sounds (*in*).
- Say the second word in the pair (*spin*).
- Add the letters representing the initial sounds (see the illustration below). Point to the letters as you say the remaining sounds.
- Tell students the sounds you added to make the new word (/s/ /p/).
- Remove and add the letters as you say each word (*in-spin*).

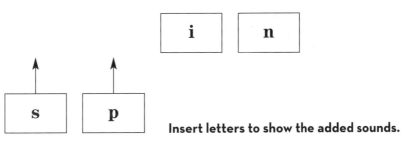

Insert letters to show the added sounds.

STUDENT STEPS: Do It

Say the following:

- "Put down one letter for each sound you say in the word _____." (e.g., *in*; ANSWER: /ĭ/ /n/)
- "The new word is _____." (e.g., *spin*)
- "Add the letters that change _____ to _____." (*in* to *spin*; ANSWER: *sp*)

As students become proficient, say the following instead:

- "Use the letters to spell _____." (e.g., *in*)
- "Change _____ to _____." (*in* to *spin*)

VARIATIONS

- Before putting down a letter for each sound, have students hold a contracted Slinky with one hand on either side. Tell students to pull the ends of the Slinky as they say the sounds in the word and push the ends together as they put the sounds together.

Activity and Word Bank continued on following page

- Before putting down a letter for each sound, ask students to put their hands together in front of them. Tell them to move their hands apart as they break apart the word and clap once as they put the word together.
- Before putting down a letter for each sound, ask students to segment and blend the sounds into a self-phone.
- Before putting down a letter for each sound, ask students to hold one arm out with their palm up. With the opposite hand, have them touch their shoulder as they say the first sound, the middle of their arm as they say the second sound, their wrist as they say the third sound, and their palm if there is a fourth sound. Tell them to slide their hand down their arm as they blend the sounds.
- Instead of using letter tiles, ask students to spell the word on individual white boards.

Word Bank

bl	cr	pl	sl	st
end-blend	am-cram	an-plan	am-slam	an-Stan
Ed-bled		ant-plant	ant-slant	ink-stink
ink-blink	**dr**	us-plus	at-slat	
	ink-drink		Ed-sled	**sw**
br		**sk**	ink-slink	am-swam
an-bran	**fl**	in-skin	it-slit	
at-brat	at-flat	it-skit		**tr**
ink-brink	Ed-fled		**sp**	am-tram
			am-spam	end-trend
cl			at-spat	
am-clam	**gr**		end-spend	**tw**
an-clan	ant-grant		in-spin	in-twin
ink-clink	in-grin		it-spit	

9 Adding a Second Sound to Form an Initial Consonant Blend

GOAL

- **Students will spell new words by adding a sound to form an initial consonant blend.**

MATERIALS

○ Word bank for this activity

○ Letter tiles or letter cards

TEACHER STEPS: Describe It

- Tell students you can do a magic trick with letters because you can make a new word by adding a letter to the beginning of a word.
- Say the first word in a pair of words (e.g., *tin* in *tin-twin*).
- As you segment the word, put down the corresponding letter for each sound you say (/t/ /ĭ/ /n/).
- Blend the sounds (*tin*).
- Say the second word in the pair (*twin*).
- Point to the letters as you say the sounds. Insert the letter that represents the new sound. (See the illustration below.)
- Tell students the sound you added to make the new word (/w/).
- Remove and add the letter representing the added sound as you say each word (*tin-twin*).

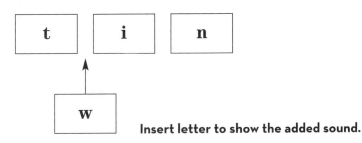

Insert letter to show the added sound.

STUDENT STEPS: Do It

Say the following:

- "Put down one letter for each sound you say in the word _____." (e.g., *tin*; ANSWER: /t/ /ĭ/ /n/)
- "The new word is _____." (e.g., *twin*)
- "Add the letter that changes _____ to _____." (*tin* to *twin*; ANSWER: *w*)

As students become proficient, say the following instead:

- "Use the letters to spell _____." (e.g., *tin*)
- "Change _____ to _____." (*tin* to *twin*)

Activity and Word Bank continued on following page

VARIATIONS

- Before putting down a letter for each sound, have students hold a contracted Slinky with one hand on either side. Tell students to pull the ends of the Slinky as they say the sounds in the word and push the ends together as they put the sounds together.
- Before putting down a letter for each sound, ask students to put their hands together in front of them. Tell them to move their hands apart as they break apart the word and clap once as they put the word together.
- Before putting down a letter for each sound, ask students to segment and blend the sounds into a self-phone.
- Before putting down a letter for each sound, ask students to hold one arm out with their palm up. With the opposite hand, have them touch their shoulder as they say the first sound, the middle of their arm as they say the second sound, their wrist as they say the third sound, and their palm if there is a fourth sound. Tell them to slide their hand down their arm as they blend the sounds.
- Instead of using letter tiles, ask students to spell the word on individual white boards.

Word Bank

bl	cr	sk	sn	sw
bend-blend	camp-cramp	Sid-skid	sag-snag	sag-swag
		sin-skin	sap-snap	
br	**dr**	sit-skit	sip-snip	**tr**
bag-brag	daft-draft			tap-trap
	dug-drug	**sl**	**sp**	Tim-trim
		sap-slap	sin-spin	tip-trip
cl	**pl**	Sid-slid	sit-spit	tot-trot
camp-clamp	pant-plant	sink-slink	sun-spun	
cap-clap	pot-plot	sip-slip	**st**	**tw**
cot-clot	pump-plump	sit-slit	sop-stop	tin-twin

10 Deleting an Initial Consonant Sound

GOAL

- **Students will spell new words by deleting an initial consonant sound.**

MATERIALS

○ Word bank for this activity   ○ Letter tiles or letter cards

TEACHER STEPS: Describe It

- Tell students you can do a magic trick with letters because you can make a new word by taking away a letter from the beginning of a word.
- Say the first word in a pair of words (e.g., *mat* in *mat-at*).
- As you segment the word, put down the corresponding letter for each sound you say. (/m/ /ă/ /t/)
- Blend the sounds (*mat*).
- Say the second word in the pair (*at*).
- Point to the letters as you say the sounds. Remove the letter that represents the deleted sound. (See the illustration below.)
- Tell students the sound you deleted to make the new word. (/m/)
- Add and remove the letter that represents the deleted sound as you say each word (*mat-at*).

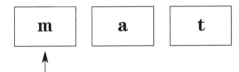

Remove letter to show the sound being deleted.

STUDENT STEPS: Do It

Say the following:
- "Put down one letter for each sound you say in the word _____." (e.g., *mat;* ANSWER: /m/ /ă/ /t/)
- "The new word is _____." (e.g., *at*)
- "Point to the letters as you say the sounds in the word." (/ă/ /t/)
- "Take away the letter that changes _____ to _____." (*mat* to *at;* ANSWER: *m*)

As students become proficient, say the following instead:
- "Use the letter tiles to spell _____." (e.g., *mat*)
- "Change _____ to _____." (*mat* to *at*)

VARIATIONS

- Before putting down a letter for each sound, have students hold a contracted Slinky with one hand on either side. Tell students to pull the ends of the Slinky as they say the sounds in the word and push the ends together as they put the sounds together.

Activity and Word Bank continued on following page

- Before putting down a letter for each sound, ask students to put their hands together in front of them. Tell them to move their hands apart as they break apart the word and clap once as they put the word together.
- Before putting down a letter for each sound, ask students to segment and blend the sounds into a self-phone.
- Before putting down a letter for each sound, ask students to hold one arm out with their palm up. With the opposite hand, have them touch their shoulder as they say the first sound, the middle of their arm as they say the second sound, their wrist as they say the third sound, and their palm if there is a fourth sound. Tell them to slide their hand down their arm as they blend the sounds.
- Instead of using letter tiles, ask students to spell the word on individual white boards.

Word Bank

ad	an	ant	Ed	in	it
bad-ad	ban-an	can't-ant	bed-Ed	bin-in	bit-it
dad-ad	can-an	pant-ant	fed-Ed	fin-in	fit-it
fad-ad	Dan-an	rant-ant	led-Ed	pin-in	hit-it
had-ad	fan-an		Ned-Ed	sin-in	kit-it
lad-ad	man-an	**ask**	red-Ed	tin-in	lit-it
mad-ad	pan-an	mask-ask	Ted-Ed	win-in	pit-it
pad-ad	ran-an	task-ask	wed-Ed		sit-it
sad-ad	tan-an			**ink**	wit-it
		at	**end**	link-ink	
am	**and**	bat-at	bend-end	mink-ink	
ham-am	band-and	cat-at	lend-end	pink-ink	
jam-am	hand-and	fat-at	mend-end	rink-ink	
Pam-am	land-and	hat-at	send-end	sink-ink	
ram-am	sand-and	mat-at	tend-end	wink-ink	
Sam-am		pat-at	vend-end		
		rat-at			
		sat-at			

11 Deleting the First Sound from an Initial Consonant Blend

GOAL

- **Students will spell new words by deleting the first sound from an initial consonant blend.**

MATERIALS

○ Word bank for this activity

○ Letter tiles or letter cards

TEACHER STEPS: Describe It

- Tell students you can do a magic trick with letters because you can make a new word by taking away a letter from the beginning of a word.
- Say the first word in a pair of words (e.g., *trap* in *trap-rap*).
- As you segment the word, put down the corresponding letter for each sound you say (/t/ /r/ /ă/ /p/).
- Blend the sounds (*trap*).
- Say the second word in the pair (*rap*).
- Point to the letters as you say the sounds. Remove the letter that represents the deleted sound. (See the illustration below.)
- Tell students the sound you deleted to make the new word. (/t/)
- Add and remove the letter as you say each word (*trap-rap*).

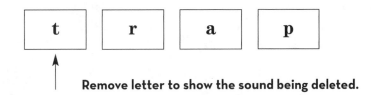

Remove letter to show the sound being deleted.

STUDENT STEPS: Do It

Say the following:
- "Put down one letter for each sound you say in the word _____." (e.g., *trap*; ANSWER: /t/ /r/ /ă/ /p/)
- "The new word is _____." (e.g., *rap*)
- "Point to the letters as you say the sounds in the word." (/r/ /ă/ /p/)
- "Take away the letter that changes _____ to _____." (*trap* to *rap*; ANSWER: *t*)

Say the following:
- "Use the letters to spell _____." (e.g., *trap*)
- "Change _____ to _____." (*trap* to *rap*)

Activity and Word Bank continued on following page

VARIATIONS

- Before putting down a letter for each sound, have students hold a contracted Slinky with one hand on either side. Tell students to pull the ends of the Slinky as they say the sounds in the word and push the ends together as they put the sounds together.
- Before putting down a letter for each sound, ask students to put their hands together in front of them. Tell them to move their hands apart as they break apart the word and clap once as they put the word together.
- Before putting down a letter for each sound, ask students to segment and blend the sounds into a self-phone.
- Before putting down a letter for each sound, ask students to hold one arm out with their palm up. With the opposite hand, have them touch their shoulder as they say the first sound, the middle of their arm as they say the second sound, their wrist as they say the third sound, and their palm if there is a fourth sound. Tell them to slide their hand down their arm as they blend the sounds.
- Instead of using letter tiles, ask students to spell the word on individual white boards.

Word Bank

bl	**cr**	**fl**	**sk**	**sm**	**st**
blend-lend	cram-ram	flap-lap	skid-kid	smug-mug	stop-top
blimp-limp	cramp-ramp	flip-lip	skin-kin		
blink-link	crank-rank		skit-kit	**sn**	**sw**
blot-lot	crib-rib	**gr**		snag-nag	swag-wag
		grant-rant	**sl**	snap-nap	swig-wig
br	**dr**	grip-rip	slap-lap	snip-nip	
brag-rag	draft-raft	grunt-runt	sled-led		**tr**
bran-ran	drank-rank		slid-lid	**sp**	trap-rap
brim-rim	drink-rink	**pl**	slink-link	Spam-Pam	trim-rim
brink-rink	drip-rip	plot-lot	slip-lip	span-pan	trip-rip
	drug-rug	plump-lump	slit-lit	spin-pin	trot-rot
cl	drum-rum		slot-lot	spit-pit	
clamp-lamp			slug-lug	spot-pot	**tw**
clap-lap			slump-lump	spun-pun	twig-wig
clink-link					twin-win
clip-lip					
clot-lot					

12 Deleting the Second Sound from an Initial Consonant Blend

GOAL

- **Students will spell new words by deleting the second sound from an initial consonant blend.**

MATERIALS

○ Word bank for this activity

○ Letter tiles or letter cards

TEACHER STEPS: Describe It

- Tell students you can do a magic trick with letters because you can make a new word by taking away a letter from the beginning of a word.
- Say the first word in a pair of words (e.g., *slip* in *slip-sip*).
- As you segment the word, put down the corresponding letter for each sound you say (/s/ /l/ /ĭ/ /p/).
- Blend the sounds (*slip*).
- Say the second word in the pair (*sip*).
- Point to the letters as you say the sounds. Remove the letter that represents the deleted sound. (See the illustration below.)
- Tell students the sound you deleted to make the new word. (/l/)
- Remove and add the letter that represents the deleted sound as you say each word (*slip-sip*).

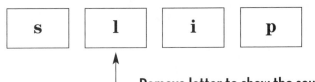

Remove letter to show the sound being deleted.

STUDENT STEPS: Do It

Say the following:
- "Put down one letter for each sound you say in the word _____." (e.g., *slip*; ANSWER: /s/ /l/ /ĭ/ /p/)
- "The new word is _____." (e.g., *sip*)
- "Point to the letters as you say the sounds in the word." (/s/ /ĭ/ /p/)
- "Take away the letter that changes _____ to _____." (*slip* to *sip*; ANSWER: *l*)

As students become proficient, say the following instead:
- "Use the letters to spell _____." (e.g., *slip*)
- "Change _____ to _____." (*slip* to *sip*)

Activity and Word Bank continued on following page

VARIATIONS

- Before putting down a letter for each sound, have students hold a contracted Slinky with one hand on either side. Tell students to pull the ends of the Slinky as they say the sounds in the word and push the ends together as they put the sounds together.
- Before putting down a letter for each sound, ask students to put their hands together in front of them. Tell them to move their hands apart as they break apart the word and clap once as they put the word together.
- Before putting down a letter for each sound, ask students to segment and blend the sounds into a self-phone.
- Before putting down a letter for each sound, ask students to hold one arm out with their palm up. With the opposite hand, have them touch their shoulder as they say the first sound, the middle of their arm as they say the second sound, their wrist as they say the third sound, and their palm if there is a fourth sound. Tell them to slide their hand down their arm as they blend the sounds.
- Instead of using letter tiles, ask students to spell the word on individual white boards.

Word Bank

bl	cr	sk	sn	sw
blend-bend	cramp-camp	skid-Sid	snag-sag	swag-sag
		skin-sin	snap-sap	
br	**dr**	skit-sit	snip-sip	**tr**
brag-bag	draft-daft			trap-tap
	drug-dug	**sl**	**sp**	trim-Tim
		slap-sap	spin-sin	trip-tip
cl	**pl**	slid-Sid	spit-sit	trot-tot
clamp-camp	plant-pant	slink-sink	spun-sun	
clap-cap	plot-pot	slip-sip		**tw**
clot-cot	plump-pump	slit-sit	**st**	twin-tin
			stop-sop	

13 Deleting a Final Consonant Sound

GOAL

- **Students will spell new words by deleting a final consonant sound.**

MATERIALS

○ Word bank for this activity

○ Letter tiles or letter cards

TEACHER STEPS: Describe It

- Tell students you can do a magic trick with letters because you can make a new word by taking away a letter from the end of a word.
- Say the first word in a pair of words (e.g., *and* in *and-an*).
- As you segment the word, put down the corresponding letter for each sound you say (/ă/ /n/ /d/).
- Blend the sounds (*and*).
- Say the second word in the pair (*an*).
- Point to the letters as you say the sounds. Remove the letter that represents the deleted sound. (See the illustration below.)
- Tell students the sound you deleted to make the new word (/d/).
- Add and remove the letter that represents the deleted sound as you say each word (*and-an*).

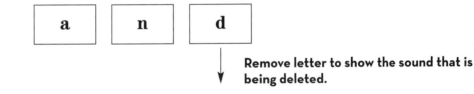

Remove letter to show the sound that is being deleted.

STUDENT STEPS: Do It

Say the following:
- "Put down one letter for each sound you say in the word _____." (e.g., *and*; ANSWER: /ă/ /n/ /d/)
- "The new word is _____." (e.g., *an*)
- "Point to the letters as you say the sounds in the word." (/ă/ /n/)
- "Take away the letter that changes _____ to _____." (*and* to *an*; ANSWER: *d*)

As students become proficient, say the following instead:
- "Use the letters to spell _____." (e.g., *and*)
- "Change _____ to _____." (*and* to *an*)

VARIATIONS

- Before putting down a letter for each sound, have students hold a contracted Slinky with one hand on either side. Tell students to pull the ends of the Slinky as they say the sounds in the word and push the ends together as they put the sounds together.

Activity and Word Bank continued on following page

- Before putting down a letter for each sound, ask students to put their hands together in front of them. Tell them to move their hands apart as they break apart the word and clap once as they put the word together.
- Before putting down a letter for each sound, ask students to segment and blend the sounds into a self-phone.
- Before putting down a letter for each sound, ask students to hold one arm out with their palm up. With the opposite hand, have them touch their shoulder as they say the first sound, the middle of their arm as they say the second sound, their wrist as they say the third sound, and their palm if there is a fourth sound. Tell them to slide their hand down their arm as they blend the sounds.
- Instead of using letter tiles, ask students to spell the word on individual white boards.

Word Bank

and-an	bend-Ben	dent-den	rant-ran	tent-ten
ant-an	bent-Ben	mend-men	stand-Stan	tint-tin
band-ban	bust-bus	pant-pan	tend-ten	

14 Substituting an Initial Consonant Sound

GOAL

- **Students will spell new words by substituting an initial consonant sound.**

MATERIALS

○ Word bank for this activity   ○ Letter tiles or letter cards

TEACHER STEPS: Describe It

- Tell students you can do a magic trick with letters because you can make new words by changing the beginning sound in a word.
- Say a word from the word bank (e.g., *sit*).
- As you segment the word, put down the corresponding letter for each sound you say (/s/ /ĭ/ /t/).
- Blend the sounds (*sit*).
- Say another word (e.g., *hit*).
- Substitute the letter representing the new initial sound (see the illustration below). Point to the letters as you say the sounds.
- Tell students the sound you used to make the new word (/h/).

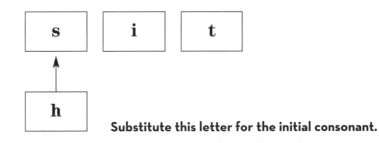

Substitute this letter for the initial consonant.

STUDENT STEPS: Do It

Say the following:
- "Put down one letter for each sound you say in the word _____." (e.g., *sit*; ANSWER: /s/ /ĭ/ /t/)
- "The new word is _____." (e.g., *hit*)
- "Change the letter that will make _____ into _____. (*sit* to *hit*; ANSWER: h)
- "The new word is _____." (e.g., *pit*)
- "Change the letter that will make _____ into _____." (*hit* to *pit*; ANSWER: p)

As students become proficient, say the following instead:
- "Use the letters to spell _____." (e.g., *sit*)
- "Change _____ to _____." (*sit* to *hit*)

Activity and Word Bank continued on following page

CLASSROOM ACTIVITY
ALPHABETIC PRINCIPLE • Substituting Sounds

VARIATIONS

- Before putting down a letter for each sound, have students hold a contracted Slinky with one hand on either side. Tell students to pull the ends of the Slinky as they say the sounds in the word and push the ends together as they put the sounds together.
- Before putting down a letter for each sound, ask students to put their hands together in front of them. Tell them to move their hands apart as they break apart the word and clap once as they put the word together.
- Before putting down a letter for each sound, ask students to segment and blend the sounds into a self-phone.
- Before putting down a letter for each sound, ask students to hold one arm out with their palm up. With the opposite hand, have them touch their shoulder as they say the first sound, the middle of their arm as they say the second sound, their wrist as they say the third sound, and their palm if there is a fourth sound. Tell them to slide their hand down their arm as they blend the sounds.
- Instead of using letter tiles, ask students to spell the word on individual white boards.

Word Bank

ad	an	ask	est	ig	ip	op	um
bad	ban	mask	best	big	dip	hop	bum
dad	can	task	jest	dig	hip	mop	gum
fad	Dan		nest	fig	nip	pop	hum
had	fan	**at**	rest	jig	sip	top	sum
lad	man	bat	test	pig	tip		
mad	pan	cat	vest	rig		**ot**	**un**
pad	ran	fat	west	wig	**it**	cot	bun
sad	tan	hat			bit	dot	fun
		mat	**et**	**im**	fit	got	pun
ag	**and**	pat	bet	dim	hit	hot	run
bag	band	rat	get	him	kit	lot	sun
gag	hand	sat	jet	Tim	lit	not	
lag	land		let		pit	pot	**ut**
nag	sand	**ed**	met	**ink**	sit	rot	cut
rag		bed	net	link	wit		hut
sag	**ank**	fed	pet	mink		**ub**	jut
tag	bank	led	set	pink	**ob**	cub	nut
wag	rank	red	vet	rink	Bob	hub	rut
	sank	wed	wet	sink	cob	rub	
am	tank		yet	wink	job	sub	
ham		**en**			lob	tub	
jam	**ant**	den	**id**	**in**	mob		
Pam	can't	hen	did	bin	rob	**ug**	
ram	pant	men	hid	fin	sob	bug	
Sam	rant	pen	kid	pin		dug	
		ten	lid	sin	**old**	hug	
	ap		rid	tin	bold	jug	
	cap	**end**		win	cold	mug	
	gap	bend			fold	rug	
	lap	lend			gold	tug	
	map	mend			hold		
	nap	send			mold		
	sap	tend			sold		
	tap	vend			told		

15 Substituting a Final Consonant Sound

GOAL

- **Students will spell new words by substituting a final consonant sound.**

MATERIALS

○ Word bank for this activity
○ Letter tiles or letter cards

TEACHER STEPS: Describe It

- Tell students you can do a magic trick with letters because you can make new words by changing the ending sound in a word.
- Say a word from the word bank (e.g., *ran*).
- As you segment the word, put down the corresponding letter for each sound you say (/r/ /ă/ /n/).
- Blend the sounds (*ran*).
- Say another word (e.g., *rag*).
- Point to the letters as you say the sounds. Substitute the letter that represents the new final sound. (See the illustration below.)
- Tell students the sound you used to make the new word. (/g/)

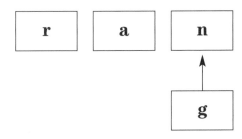

 **Substitute this letter for the final consonant.**

STUDENT STEPS: Do It

Say the following:

- "Put down one letter for each sound you say in the word _____." (e.g., *ran*; ANSWER: /r/ /ă/ /n/)
- "The new word is _____." (e.g., *rag*)
- "Change the letter that will make _____ into _____." (*ran* to *rag*; ANSWER: *g*)
- "The new word is _____." (e.g., *rat*)
- "Change the letter that will make _____ into _____." (*rag* to *rat*; ANSWER: *t*)

As students become proficient, say the following instead:

- "Use the letters to spell _____." (e.g., *ran*)
- "Change _____ to _____." (*ran* to *rag*)

Activity and Word Bank continued on following pages

VARIATIONS

- Before putting down a letter for each sound, have students hold a contracted Slinky with one hand on either side. Tell students to pull the ends of the Slinky as they say the sounds in the word and push the ends together as they put the sounds together.
- Before putting down a letter for each sound, ask students to put their hands together in front of them. Tell them to move their hands apart as they break apart the word and clap once as they put the word together.
- Before putting down a letter for each sound, ask students to segment and blend the sounds into a self-phone.
- Before putting down a letter for each sound, ask students to hold one arm out with their palm up. With the opposite hand, have them touch their shoulder as they say the first sound, the middle of their arm as they say the second sound, their wrist as they say the third sound, and their palm if there is a fourth sound. Tell them to slide their hand down their arm as they blend the sounds.
- Instead of using letter tiles, ask students to spell the word on individual white boards.

Word Bank on following page

Word Bank

ă	ĕ	ĭ	ŏ	ŭ
bad	bed	bib	cob	bud
bag	beg	bid	cod	bug
ban	Ben	big	cog	bum
bat	bet	bin	cop	bun
dad	hem	bit	cot	bus
Dan	hen	did	Dom	but
fad	led	dig	Don	gum
fan	leg	dim	dot	gun
fat	let	din	hop	Gus
had	men	dip	hot	gut
hag	met	fib	job	hub
ham	Ned	fig	jog	hug
has	net	fin	jot	hum
hat	peg	fit	mob	hut
jab	pen	hid	mom	mud
jam	pep	him	mop	mug
Jan	pet	hip	nod	mum
lab	Ted	hit	not	rub
lad	ten	lid	pod	rug
lag	web	lip	pop	run
lap	wed	lit	pot	rut
man	wet	rib	rob	sub
map	yes	rid	Rod	sum
mat	yet	rig	Ron	sun
nab		rim	rot	tub
nag		rip	sob	tug
Nan		Sid	sod	
nap		sin	sop	
pad		sip	Tom	
pal		sit	ton	
Pam		Tim	top	
pan		tin	tot	
pat		tip		
rag		wig		
ram		win		
ran		wit		
rap				
rat				
sad				
sag				
Sam				
sap				
sat				
tab				
tad				
tag				
tan				
tap				

16 Substituting a Medial Vowel Sound

GOAL

- **Students will spell new words by substituting a medial sound.**

MATERIALS

○ Word bank for this activity

○ Letter tiles or letter cards

TEACHER STEPS: Describe It

- Tell students you can do a magic trick with letters because you can make new words by changing the middle sound in a word.
- Say a word from the word bank (e.g., *sat*).
- As you segment the word, put down the corresponding letter for each sound you say (/s/ /ă/ /t/).
- Blend the sounds (*sat*).
- Say another word (e.g., *sit*).
- Point to the letters as you say the sounds. Substitute the letter representing the new medial sound. (See the illustration below.)
- Tell students the sound you used to make the new word (/ĭ/).

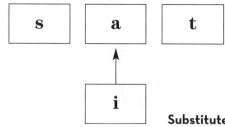

Substitute this letter for the medial vowel.

STUDENT STEPS: Do It

Say the following:
- "Put down one letter for each sound you say in the word _____." (e.g., *sat*; ANSWER: /s/ /ă/ /t/)
- "The new word is _____." (e.g., *sit*)
- "Change the letter that will make _____ into _____." (*sat* to *sit*; ANSWER: *i*)
- "The new word is _____." (e.g., *set*)
- "Change the letter that will make _____ into _____." (*sit* to *set*; ANSWER: e)

As students become proficient, say the following instead:
- "Use the letters to spell _____." (e.g., *sat*)
- Change _____ to _____. (*sat* to *sit*).

Activity and Word Bank continued on following page

VARIATIONS

- Before putting down a letter for each sound, have students hold a contracted Slinky with one hand on either side. Tell students to pull the ends of the Slinky as they say the sounds in the word and push the ends together as they put the sounds together.
- Before putting down a letter for each sound, ask students to put their hands together in front of them. Tell them to move their hands apart as they break apart the word and clap once as they put the word together.
- Before putting down a letter for each sound, ask students to segment and blend the sounds into a self-phone.
- Before putting down a letter for each sound, ask students to hold one arm out with their palm up. With the opposite hand, have them touch their shoulder as they say the first sound, the middle of their arm as they say the second sound, their wrist as they say the third sound, and their palm if there is a fourth sound. Tell them to slide their hand down their arm as they blend the sounds.
- Instead of using letter tiles, ask students to spell the word on individual white boards.

Word Bank

bib	bat	gas	hip	lag	map	pan	red	Sam	tan
Bob	bet	Gus	hop	leg	mop	pen	rid	sum	ten
bit				log		pin	rod		tin
bad	but	get	hat	lug		pun			
bed		got	hit		Ned		rag	sin	tap
bid	dad	gut	hot	lap	nod	pep	rig	sun	tip
bud	did		hut	lip		pop	rug		top
	dud	had		lop	nap	pup		sat	
bag		hid	jam		nip		ran	set	
beg		Jim				pat	Ron	sit	wag
big	Dan			let		pet	run		wig
bog	den	hag		lit	net	pit			
bug	din	hog	jet	lot	not		rap	tab	wet
	Don	hug	jot		nut	pot	rip	tub	wit
			jut			put			
ban		ham		mad					
Ben	fan	hem	lad	mud	Peg	rib	sad		zap
bin	fin	him	led	man	pig	rob	Sid	Tim	zip
bun	fun	hum	lid	men	pug	rub	sod	Tom	

17 Substituting Initial, Medial, and Final Sounds

GOAL

- **Students will spell new words by substituting initial, medial, and final sounds.**

MATERIALS

○ Word bank for this activity

○ Letter tiles or letter cards

TEACHER STEPS: Describe It

- Tell students you can do a magic trick with letters because you can make new words by changing the letters in a word.
- Say a word from the word bank (e.g., *pin*).
- As you segment the word, put down the corresponding letter tile for each sound you say (/p/ /ĭ/ /n/).
- Blend the sounds (*pin*).
- Say another word (e.g., *pit*).
- Point to the letters as you say the sounds. Substitute the letter that represents the new sound (/t/).
- Tell students the sound you used to make the new word (/t/).
- Say another word (e.g., *fit*).
- Point to the letters as you say the sounds. Substitute the letter that represents the new sound (/f/).
- Tell students the sound you used to make a new word (/f/).
- Say another word (e.g., *fat*).
- Point to the letters as you say the sounds. Substitute the letter that represents the new sound (/ă/).
- Tell students the sound you used to make a new word (/ă/).

STUDENT STEPS: Do It

Say the following:
- "Put down one letter for each sound you say in the word _____." (e.g., *pin*; ANSWER: /p/ /ĭ/ /n/)
- "The new word is _____." (e.g., *pit*)
- "Change the letter that will make _____ into _____." (*pin* to *pit*; ANSWER: *t*)
- "The new word is _____." (e.g., *fit*)
- "Change the letter that will make _____ into _____." (*pit* to *fit*; ANSWER: *f*)
- "The new word is _____." (e.g., *fat*)
- Change the letter that will make _____ into _____." (*fit* to *fat*; ANSWER: *a*)

As students become proficient, say the following instead:
- "Use the letters to spell _____." (e.g., *pin*)
- "Change _____ to _____." (*pin* to *pit*)
- "Change _____ to _____." (*pit* to *fit*)
- "Change _____ to _____." (*fit* to *fat*)

Activity and Word Bank continued on following page

VARIATIONS

- Before putting down a letter for each sound, have students hold a contracted Slinky with one hand on either side. Tell students to pull the ends of the Slinky as they say the sounds in the word and push the ends together as they put the sounds together.
- Before putting down a letter for each sound, ask students to put their hands together in front of them. Tell them to move their hands apart as they break apart the word and clap once as they put the word together.
- Before putting down a letter for each sound, ask students to segment and blend the sounds into a self-phone.
- Before putting down a letter for each sound, ask students to hold one arm out with their palm up. With the opposite hand, have them touch their shoulder as they say the first sound, the middle of their arm as they say the second sound, their wrist as they say the third sound, and their palm if there is a fourth sound. Tell them to slide their hand down their arm as they blend the sounds.
- Instead of using letter tiles, ask students to spell the word on individual white boards.

Word Bank

mat	pan	fit	sand	jam	bend	sink	dad
pat	man	wit	send	Jim	band	sank	bad
pet	men	wig	mend	him	sand	sunk	bid
pen	met	big	lend	Tim	send	bunk	bit
ten	let	bag	lent	Tom	sent	bank	pit
tan	set	beg	bent	mom	lent	Hank	pet
tap	sat	leg	bend	mop	tent	rank	get
top	Sam	let	band	top	went	rink	got
tip	sap	lit	land	tip	bent	sink	tot
sip	lap	hit	hand	tin	dent	wink	top
rag	wet	cap	red	hen	best	sent	kid
rat	met	cat	rid	den	pest	send	lid
ran	mat	cot	did	Dan	past	sand	rid
run	bat	cut	dad	dab	last	land	rod
fun	hat	but	mad	cab	cast	lend	rot
fan	hit	bun	mat	cob	fast	mend	dot
fat	hip	run	rat	Bob	fist		got
pat	sip	ran	rut	bib	list	dug	get
pet	sap	ram	but	rib	lint	tug	vet
pen	gap	rim	bit	rub	lent	tub	vat
						rub	
wig	mop	sip	jut	sub	bank	rug	jest
wit	pop	sit	nut	rub	rank	rag	vest
pit	pot	sat	rut	rib	rink	bag	vast
pat	cot	sap	rat	rid	sink	bug	past
fat	cat	nap	ran	lid	sank	big	mast
fan	cab	nip	run	lit	sunk	jig	mask
fun	cub	lip	fun	let	bunk		cask
pun	hub	tip	pun	pet	bank		cast
pen	hut	top	pen	pat			last
pan	hit	tot	pin	pan			list

18 Spelling Words with the Long a Sound

GOAL

- **Students will spell words with the long a sound containing the CVCe, CCVCe, and VCe patterns.**

MATERIALS

○ Word bank for this activity   ○ Letter tiles or letter cards

TEACHER STEPS: Describe It

- Tell students that when there is a silent e at the end of a word, it makes the first vowel say the long sound.
- Say a word from the word bank (e.g., *game*).
- As you spell the word, put down the corresponding letter(s) for each sound you say (/g/ /ā/ /m/). Before putting down the letter e, remind students that adding the silent e makes the a say the long sound.
- Blend the sounds (*game*).
- Follow the same procedure with additional words. When possible, add, delete, or substitute letter(s) to spell new words. (See the illustrations below.)

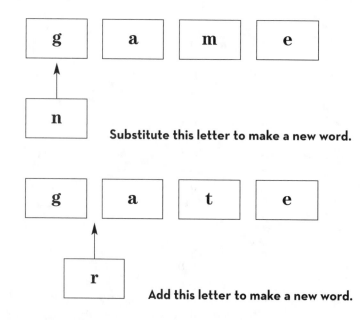

Substitute this letter to make a new word.

Add this letter to make a new word.

STUDENT STEPS: Do It

Say the following:

- "Put down one letter for each sound you say in the word _____." (e.g., *game*; ANSWER: /g/ /ā/ /m/)
- "Which silent letter goes at the end of the word?" (e)
- "What does the silent e do to the first vowel?" (Makes it say the long sound)

Activity and Word Bank continued on following page

Follow the same procedure for additional words. When possible, have students add, delete, or substitute letter(s) to spell new words.

As students become proficient, say a word from the word bank and ask them to spell it with their tiles. When possible, have students add, delete, or substitute letter(s) to spell new words.

VARIATIONS

- Before putting down a letter for each sound, have students hold a contracted Slinky with one hand on either side. Tell students to pull the ends of the Slinky as they say the sounds in the word and push the ends together as they put the sounds together.
- Before putting down a letter for each sound, ask students to put their hands together in front of them. Tell them to move their hands apart as they break apart the word and clap once as they put the word together.
- Before putting down a letter for each sound, ask students to segment and blend the sounds into a self-phone.
- Before putting down a letter for each sound, ask students to hold one arm out with their palm up. With the opposite hand, have them touch their shoulder as they say the first sound, the middle of their arm as they say the second sound, their wrist as they say the third sound, and their palm if there is a fourth sound. Tell them to slide their hand down their arm as they blend the sounds.
- Instead of using letter tiles, ask students to spell the word on individual white boards.

Word Bank

ale	blame	cave	flake	hale	make	plane	shale	snake	tape
ape	brave	dale	gale	hate	male	plate	shame	stale	taste
ate	cake	Dave	game	Jane	name	rake	shave	state	trade
bake	came	fade	gate	Kate	pale	rate	skate	take	waste
bale	cane	fake	gaze	late	pane	safe	slate	tale	wave
blade	cape	fate	grave	made	pave	shake	slave	tame	whale

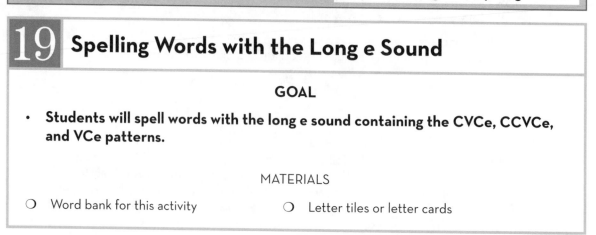

19 Spelling Words with the Long e Sound

GOAL

- **Students will spell words with the long e sound containing the CVCe, CCVCe, and VCe patterns.**

MATERIALS

○ Word bank for this activity   ○ Letter tiles or letter cards

TEACHER STEPS: Describe It

- Tell students that when there is a silent e at the end of a word, it makes the first vowel say the long sound.
- Say a word from the word bank (e.g., *Steve*).
- As you spell the word, put down the corresponding letter(s) for each sound you say (/s/ /t/ /ē/ /v/). Before putting down the second letter e, remind students that adding the silent e makes the first e say the long sound.
- Blend the sounds (*Steve*).
- Follow the same procedure with additional words. When possible, add, delete, or substitute letter(s) to spell new words. (See the illustration below.)

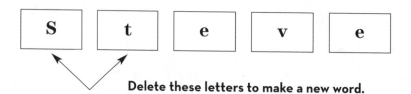

Delete these letters to make a new word.

STUDENT STEPS: Do It

Say the following:
- "Put down one letter for each sound you say in the word _____." (e.g., *Steve*; ANSWER: /s/ /t/ /ē/ /v/)
- "Which silent letter goes at the end of the word?" (e)
- "What does the silent e do to the first vowel?" (Makes it say the long sound)

Follow the same procedure for additional words. When possible, have students add, delete, or substitute letter(s) to spell new words.

As students become proficient, say a word from the word bank and ask them to spell it with their tiles. When possible, have students add, delete, or substitute letter(s) to spell new words.

VARIATIONS

- Before putting down a letter for each sound, have students hold a contracted Slinky with one hand on either side. Tell students to pull the ends of the Slinky as they say the sounds in the word and push the ends together as they put the sounds together.

Activity and Word Bank continued on following page

ALPHABETIC PRINCIPLE · Long Vowel Spelling Patterns   CLASSROOM ACTIVITY

- Before putting down a letter for each sound, ask students to put their hands together in front of them. Tell them to move their hands apart as they break apart the word and clap once as they put the word together.
- Before putting down a letter for each sound, ask students to segment and blend the sounds into a self-phone.
- Before putting down a letter for each sound, ask students to hold one arm out with their palm up. With the opposite hand, have them touch their shoulder as they say the first sound, the middle of their arm as they say the second sound, their wrist as they say the third sound, and their palm if there is a fourth sound. Tell them to slide their hand down their arm as they blend the sounds.
- Instead of using letter tiles, ask students to spell the word on individual white boards.

Word Bank							
cede	Gene	here	mete	plebe	Steve	theme	Zeke
Eve	grebe	mere	Pete	sere	Swede	these	

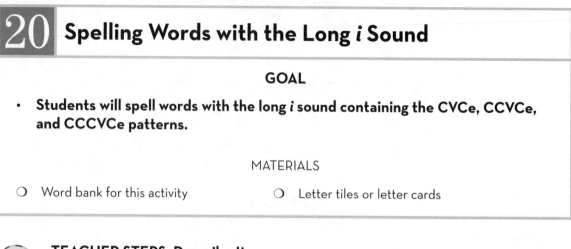

20 Spelling Words with the Long *i* Sound

GOAL

- Students will spell words with the long *i* sound containing the CVCe, CCVCe, and CCCVCe patterns.

MATERIALS

○ Word bank for this activity　　　　○ Letter tiles or letter cards

TEACHER STEPS: Describe It

- Tell students that when there is a silent e at the end of a word, it makes the first vowel say the long sound.
- Say a word from the word bank (e.g., *smile*).
- As you spell the word, put down the corresponding letter(s) for each sound you say (/s/ /m/ /ī/ /l/). Before putting down the letter e, remind students that adding the silent e makes the *i* say the long sound.
- Blend the sounds (*smile*).
- Follow the same procedure with additional words. When possible, add, delete, or substitute letter(s) to spell new words. (See the illustrations below.)

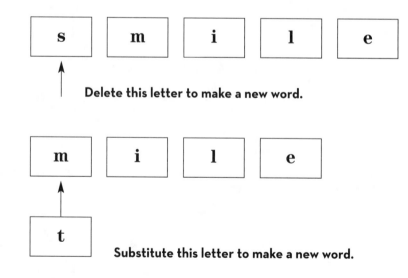

| s | m | i | l | e |

Delete this letter to make a new word.

| m | i | l | e |

| t |

Substitute this letter to make a new word.

STUDENT STEPS: Do It

Say the following:

- "Put down one letter for each sound you say in the word _____." (e.g., *smile*;
  ANSWER: /s/ /m/ /ī/ /l/)
- Which silent letter goes at the end of the word? (e)
- What does the silent e do to the first vowel? (Makes it say the long sound)

Follow the same procedure for additional words. When possible, have students add, delete, or substitute letter(s) to spell new words.

Activity and Word Bank continued on following page

ALPHABETIC PRINCIPLE · Long Vowel Spelling Patterns　　CLASSROOM ACTIVITY

As students become proficient, say a word from the word bank and ask them to spell it with their tiles. When possible, have students add, delete, or substitute letter(s) to spell new words.

VARIATIONS

- Before putting down a letter for each sound, have students hold a contracted Slinky with one hand on either side. Tell students to pull the ends of the Slinky as they say the sounds in the word and push the ends together as they put the sounds together.
- Before putting down a letter for each sound, ask students to put their hands together in front of them. Tell them to move their hands apart as they break apart the word and clap once as they put the word together.
- Before putting down a letter for each sound, ask students to segment and blend the sounds into a self-phone.
- Before putting down a letter for each sound, ask students to hold one arm out with their palm up. With the opposite hand, have them touch their shoulder as they say the first sound, the middle of their arm as they say the second sound, their wrist as they say the third sound, and their palm if there is a fourth sound. Tell them to slide their hand down their arm as they blend the sounds.
- Instead of using letter tiles, ask students to spell the word on individual white boards.

Word Bank

bike	dive	glide	life	mile	prize	size	stride	tire
bite	drive	gripe	like	mine	quite	slide	strike	vine
bride	file	hide	lime	pike	ride	smile	stripe	while
chime	fine	hire	line	pile	ripe	spike	swipe	white
crime	fire	hive	live	pipe	side	spine	tide	wide
dine	five	kite	Mike	pride	sire	spite	tile	wine

21 Spelling Words with the Long o Sound

GOAL

- **Students will spell words with the long o sound containing the CVCe, CCVCe, and CCCVCe patterns.**

MATERIALS

○ Word bank for this activity   ○ Letter tiles or letter cards

TEACHER STEPS: Describe It

- Tell students that when there is a silent e at the end of a word, it makes the first vowel say the long sound.
- Say a word from the word bank (e.g., *spoke*).
- As you spell the word, put down the corresponding letter(s) for each sound you say (/s/ /p/ /ō/ /k/). Before putting down the letter e, remind students that adding the silent e makes the o say the long sound.
- Blend the sounds (*spoke*).
- Follow the same procedure with additional words. When possible, add, delete, or substitute letter(s) to spell new words. (See the illustrations below.)

Delete this letter to make a new word.

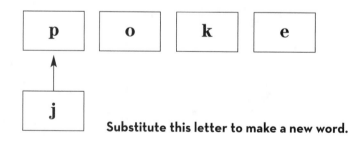

Substitute this letter to make a new word.

STUDENT STEPS: Do It

Say the following:
- "Put down one letter for each sound you say in the word _____." (e.g., *spoke*; ANSWER: /s/ /p/ /ō/ /k/)
- "Which silent letter goes at the end of the word?" (e)
- What does the silent e do to the first vowel? (Makes it say the long sound)

Follow the same procedure for additional words. When possible, have students add, delete, or substitute letter(s) to spell new words.

Activity and Word Bank continued on following page

As students become proficient, say a word from the word bank and ask them to spell it with their tiles. When possible, have students add, delete, or substitute letter(s) to spell new words.

VARIATIONS

- Before putting down a letter for each sound, have students hold a contracted Slinky with one hand on either side. Tell students to pull the ends of the Slinky as they say the sounds in the word and push the ends together as they put the sounds together.
- Before putting down a letter for each sound, ask students to put their hands together in front of them. Tell them to move their hands apart as they break apart the word and clap once as they put the word together.
- Before putting down a letter for each sound, ask students to segment and blend the sounds into a self-phone.
- Before putting down a letter for each sound, ask students to hold one arm out with their palm up. With the opposite hand, have them touch their shoulder as they say the first sound, the middle of their arm as they say the second sound, their wrist as they say the third sound, and their palm if there is a fourth sound. Tell them to slide their hand down their arm as they blend the sounds.
- Instead of using letter tiles, ask students to spell the word on individual white boards.

Word Bank							
bone	cope	froze	joke	poke	score	sore	stove
broke	core	globe	lobe	pole	shore	spoke	throne
choke	dome	grope	mole	robe	slope	stole	tone
chore	dote	grove	mope	rode	smoke	stone	vote
coke	doze	hole	more	rope	snore	store	woke
cone	drove	hope	note	scope	sole		

22 Spelling Words with the Long *u* Sound

GOAL

- **Students will spell words with the long *u* sound containing the CVCe and VCe patterns.**

MATERIALS

○ Word bank for this activity

○ Letter tiles or letter cards

TEACHER STEPS: Describe It

- Tell students that when there is a silent e at the end of a word it makes the first vowel say the long sound.
- Say a word from the word bank (e.g., *cute*).
- As you spell the word, put down the corresponding letter(s) for each sound you say (/k/ /ū/ /t/). Before putting down the letter e, remind students that adding the silent e makes the *u* say the long sound.
- Blend the sounds (*cute*).
  - Follow the same procedure with additional words. When possible, add, delete, or substitute letter(s) to spell new words. (See the illustration below.)

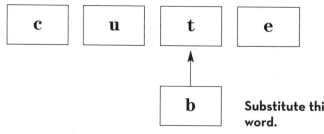

Substitute this letter to make a new word.

STUDENT STEPS: Do It

Say the following:

- "Put down one letter for each sound you say in the word _____." (e.g., *cube*; ANSWER: /k/ /ū/ /b/)
- "Which silent letter goes at the end of the word?" (e)
- "What does the silent e do to the first vowel?" (Makes it say the long sound)

Follow the same procedure for additional words. When possible, have students add, delete, or substitute letter(s) to spell new words.

As students become proficient, say a word from the word bank and ask them to spell it with their tiles. When possible, have students add, delete, or substitute letter(s) to spell new words.

Activity and Word Bank continued on following page

ALPHABETIC PRINCIPLE · Long Vowel Spelling Patterns CLASSROOM ACTIVITY

VARIATIONS

- Before putting down a letter for each sound, have students hold a contracted Slinky with one hand on either side. Tell students to pull the ends of the Slinky as they say the sounds in the word and push the ends together as they put the sounds together.
- Before putting down a letter for each sound, ask students to put their hands together in front of them. Tell them to move their hands apart as they break apart the word and clap once as they put the word together.
- Before putting down a letter for each sound, ask students to segment and blend the sounds into a self-phone.
- Before putting down a letter for each sound, ask students to hold one arm out with their palm up. With the opposite hand, have them touch their shoulder as they say the first sound, the middle of their arm as they say the second sound, their wrist as they say the third sound, and their palm if there is a fourth sound. Tell them to slide their hand down their arm as they blend the sounds.
- Instead of using letter tiles, ask students to spell the word on individual white boards.

Word Bank

cube	cure	fume	huge	muse	pule	use
cuke	cute	fuse	mule	mute	pure	yule

23 Spelling Words with the Long *a, e, i, o, u* Sounds

GOAL

- **Students will spell words with the long *a, e, i, o,* and *u* sounds containing the CVCe, CCVCe, and VCe patterns.**

MATERIALS

- Word bank for this activity
- Letter tiles or letter cards

TEACHER STEPS: Describe It

- Tell students that when there is a silent e in a word, it makes the first vowel say the long sound.
- Say a word from the word bank (e.g., *game*).
- As you spell the word, put down the corresponding letter(s) for each sound you say (/g/ /ā/ /m/). Before putting down the letter e, remind students that adding the silent e makes the first vowel say the long sound.
- Blend the sounds (*game*).
- Follow the same procedure for additional words. When possible, add, delete, or substitute letter(s) to spell new words.

STUDENT STEPS: Do It

Say the following:
- "Put down one letter for each sound you say in the word _____." (e.g., *game*; ANSWER: /g/ /ā/ /m/)
- "Which silent letter goes at the end of the word?" (e)
- "What does the silent e do to the first vowel?" (Makes it say the long sound)

Follow the same procedure for additional words. When possible, have students add, delete, or substitute letter(s) to spell new words.

As students become proficient, say a word from the word bank and ask them to spell it with their tiles. When possible, have students add, delete, or substitute letter(s) to spell new words.

VARIATIONS

- Before putting down a letter for each sound, have students hold a contracted Slinky with one hand on either side. Tell students to pull the ends of the Slinky as they say the sounds in the word and push the ends together as they put the sounds together.
- Before putting down a letter for each sound, ask students to put their hands together in front of them. Tell them to move their hands apart as they break apart the word and clap once as they put the word together.
- Before putting down a letter for each sound, ask students to segment and blend the sounds into a self-phone.

Activity and Word Bank continued on following page

- Before putting down a letter for each sound, ask students to hold one arm out with their palm up. With the opposite hand, have them touch their shoulder as they say the first sound, the middle of their arm as they say the second sound, their wrist as they say the third sound, and their palm if there is a fourth sound. Tell them to slide their hand down their arm as they blend the sounds.
- Instead of using letter tiles, ask students to spell the word on individual white boards.

Word Bank

base	cone	eve	game	make	pile	safe	state	tone
blade	cure	fate	globe	mine	pine	shade	Steve	tube
cane	cute	fine	haze	mope	pole	shave	stone	use
case	date	fire	hive	muse	pride	shine	stove	whale
cave	dime	froze	late	pave	prize	side	swipe	whine
chase	drove	fume	live	Pete	rope	stale	tame	wide

24 Spelling Words with the Long a Sound (More Complex Patterns)

GOAL

- **Students will spell words with the long a sound.**

MATERIALS

○ Word bank for this activity

○ Letter tiles or letter cards

TEACHER STEPS: Describe It

- Tell students that when there are two vowels together in a word, the first vowel usually says the long sound and the second vowel is silent.
- Say a word from the word bank (e.g., *pail*).
- As you spell the word, put down the corresponding letter(s) for each sound you say (/p/ /ā/ /l/). Before putting down the letter *i*, remind students that when *a* and *i* are together, the first vowel says the long sound and the second vowel is silent.
- Blend the sounds (*pail*).
- Follow the same procedure for additional words. When possible, add, delete, or substitute letter(s) to spell new words. (See the illustrations below.)

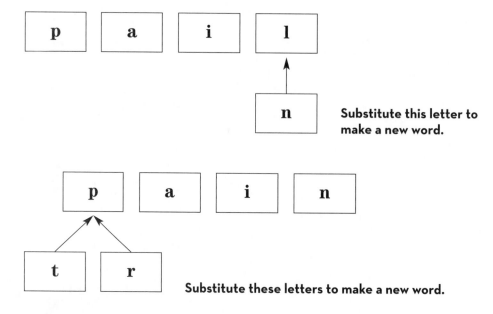

STUDENT STEPS: Do It

Say the following:

- "Put down letters for the first two sounds you say in the word _____." (e.g., *pail*; ANSWER: /p/ /ā/)
- "Which silent letter goes after the *a*?" (*i*)

Activity and Word Bank continued on following page

- "Put down the letter for the last sound." (*l*)
- "What happens when two vowels are together?" (The first one says the long sound.)

Follow the same procedure for additional words. When possible, have students add, delete, or substitute letter(s) to spell new words.

As students become proficient, say a word from the word bank and ask them to spell it with their tiles. When possible, have students add, delete, or substitute letter(s) to spell new words.

VARIATIONS

- Before putting down a letter for each sound, have students hold a contracted Slinky with one hand on either side. Tell students to pull the ends of the Slinky as they say the sounds in the word and push the ends together as they put the sounds together.
- Before putting down a letter for each sound, ask students to put their hands together in front of them. Tell them to move their hands apart as they break apart the word and clap once as they put the word together.
- Before putting down a letter for each sound, ask students to segment and blend the sounds into a self-phone.
- Before putting down a letter for each sound, ask students to hold one arm out with their palm up. With the opposite hand, have them touch their shoulder as they say the first sound, the middle of their arm as they say the second sound, their wrist as they say the third sound, and their palm if there is a fourth sound. Tell them to slide their hand down their arm as they blend the sounds.
- Instead of using letter tiles, ask students to spell the word on individual white boards.

Word Bank

aim	brain	fail	frail	jail	paid	pair	sail	stairs	train
air	chain	faint	gain	maid	pail	plain	saint	strain	vain
bait	chair	fair	grain	mail	pain	quaint	snail	tail	wail
braid	drain	faith	hair	main	paint	rain	stain	trail	

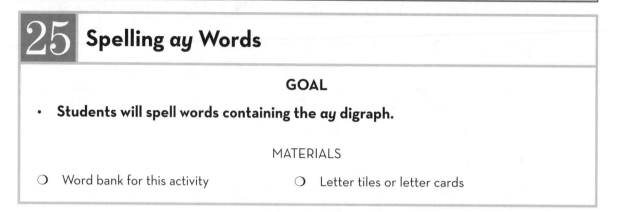

25 Spelling *ay* Words

GOAL

- **Students will spell words containing the *ay* digraph.**

MATERIALS

- Word bank for this activity
- Letter tiles or letter cards

TEACHER STEPS: Describe It

- Tell students that when *a* and *y* are together, they say /ā/ as in *pay*.
- Say a word from the word bank (e.g., *pay*).
- As you spell the word, put down the corresponding letter(s) for each sound you say (/p/ /ā/). Before putting down the letters *a* and *y*, remind students that when these two letters are together, they say /ā/.
- Blend the sounds (*pay*).
- Follow the same procedure for additional words. When possible, add, delete, or substitute letter(s) to spell new words. (See the illustrations below.)

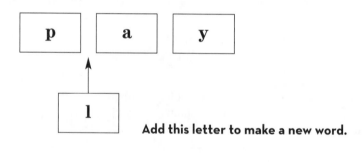

| p | a | y |

↑

| l |

Add this letter to make a new word.

| p | l | a | y |

↑

Delete this letter to make a new word.

STUDENT STEPS: Do It

Say the following:

- "Put down a letter for the first sound you say in the word _____." (e.g., *pay*; ANSWER: /p/)
- "Put down the two letters that say /ā/." (*ay*)

Follow the same procedure for additional words. When possible, have students add, delete, or substitute letter(s) to spell new words.

As students become proficient, say a word from the word bank and ask them to spell it with their tiles. When possible, have students add, delete, or substitute letter(s) to spell new words.

Activity and Word Bank continued on following page

CLASSROOM ACTIVITY

ALPHABETIC PRINCIPLE · Long Vowel Spelling Patterns

VARIATIONS

- Before putting down a letter for each sound, have students hold a contracted Slinky with one hand on either side. Tell students to pull the ends of the Slinky as they say the sounds in the word and push the ends together as they put the sounds together.
- Before putting down a letter for each sound, ask students to put their hands together in front of them. Tell them to move their hands apart as they break apart the word and clap once as they put the word together.
- Before putting down a letter for each sound, ask students to segment and blend the sounds into a self-phone.
- Before putting down a letter for each sound, ask students to hold one arm out with their palm up. With the opposite hand, have them touch their shoulder as they say the first sound, the middle of their arm as they say the second sound, their wrist as they say the third sound, and their palm if there is a fourth sound. Tell them to slide their hand down their arm as they blend the sounds.
- Instead of using letter tiles, ask students to spell the word on individual white boards.

Word Bank

bay	clay	fray	jay	may	play	say	stay	tray
bray	day	gray	Kay	nay	pray	slay	stray	way
cay	Fay	hay	lay	pay	ray	spray	sway	

26 Spelling Words with the Long e Sound (More Complex Patterns)

GOAL

- **Students will spell words with the long e sound.**

MATERIALS

- Word bank for this activity
- Letter tiles or letter cards

TEACHER STEPS: Describe It

- Tell students that when there are two vowels together in a word, the first vowel usually says the long sound and the second vowel is silent.
- Say a word from the word bank (e.g., *beast*).
- As you spell the word, put down the corresponding letter(s) for each sound you say (/b/ /ē/ /s/ /t/). Before putting down the letter *a*, remind students that when *e* and *a* are together, the first vowel says the long sound and the second vowel is silent.
- Blend the sounds (*beast*).
- Follow the same procedure for additional words. When possible, add, delete, or substitute letter(s) to spell new words. (See the illustration below.)

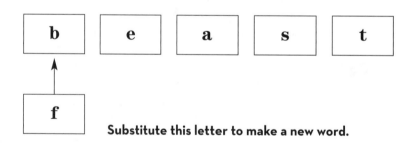

Substitute this letter to make a new word.

STUDENT STEPS: Do It

Say the following:
- "Put down a letter for the first two sounds you say in the word _____." (e.g., *beast*)
- "Which silent letter goes after the e?" (*a*)
- "Put down the letters for the last two sounds." (*st*)
- "What happens when two vowels are together? (The first one has the long sound.)

Follow the same procedure for additional words. When possible, have students add, delete, or substitute letter(s) to spell new words.

As students become proficient, say a word from the word bank and ask them to spell it with their tiles. When possible, have students add, delete, or substitute letter(s) to spell new words.

Activity and Word Bank continued on following page

VARIATIONS

- Before putting down a letter for each sound, have students hold a contracted Slinky with one hand on either side. Tell students to pull the ends of the Slinky as they say the sounds in the word and push the ends together as they put the sounds together.
- Before putting down a letter for each sound, ask students to put their hands together in front of them. Tell them to move their hands apart as they break apart the word and clap once as they put the word together.
- Before putting down a letter for each sound, ask students to segment and blend the sounds into a self-phone.
- Before putting down a letter for each sound, ask students to hold one arm out with their palm up. With the opposite hand, have them touch their shoulder as they say the first sound, the middle of their arm as they say the second sound, their wrist as they say the third sound, and their palm if there is a fourth sound. Tell them to slide their hand down their arm as they blend the sounds.
- Instead of using letter tiles, ask students to spell the word on individual white boards.

Word Bank

beach	beast	deal	heal	leap	peach	scream	steam	treat
bead	cheat	each	Jean	mean	peas	speak	stream	veal
beak	clear	eat	leaf	meat	preach	spear	tea	yeast
beam	cream	gear	lean	near	reap	squeal	teach	zeal

27 Spelling Words with the Long e Sound (More Complex Patterns)

GOAL

- **Students will spell words with the long e sound.**

MATERIALS

- ○ Word bank for this activity
- ○ Letter tiles or letter cards

TEACHER STEPS: Describe It

- Tell students that when there are two vowels together in a word, the first vowel usually says the long sound and the second vowel is silent.
- Say a word from the word bank (e.g., *seed*).
- As you spell the word, put down the corresponding letter(s) for each sound you say (/s/ /ē/ /d/). Before putting down the second e, remind students that when these two vowels are together, the first vowel says the long sound and the second vowel is silent.
- Blend the sounds (*seed*).
- Follow the same procedure for additional words. When possible, add, delete, or substitute letter(s) to spell new words. (See the illustration below.)

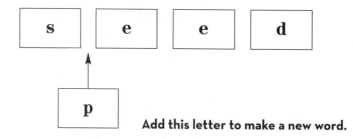

Add this letter to make a new word.

STUDENT STEPS: Do It

Say the following:
- "Put down a letter for the first two sounds you say in the word _____." (e.g., seed)
- "Which silent letter goes after the e?" (e)
- "Put down the letter for the last sound." (d)
- "What happens when two vowels are together?" (The first one says the long sound.)

Follow the same procedure for additional words. When possible, have students add, delete, or substitute letter(s) to spell new words.

As students become proficient, say a word from the word bank and ask them to spell it with their tiles. When possible, have students add, delete, or substitute letter(s) to spell new words.

Activity and Word Bank continued on following page

ALPHABETIC PRINCIPLE • Long Vowel Spelling Patterns

CLASSROOM ACTIVITY

VARIATIONS

- Before putting down a letter for each sound, have students hold a contracted Slinky with one hand on either side. Tell students to pull the ends of the Slinky as they say the sounds in the word and push the ends together as they put the sounds together.
- Before putting down a letter for each sound, ask students to put their hands together in front of them. Tell them to move their hands apart as they break apart the word and clap once as they put the word together.
- Before putting down a letter for each sound, ask students to segment and blend the sounds into a self-phone.
- Before putting down a letter for each sound, ask students to hold one arm out with their palm up. With the opposite hand, have them touch their shoulder as they say the first sound, the middle of their arm as they say the second sound, their wrist as they say the third sound, and their palm if there is a fourth sound. Tell them to slide their hand down their arm as they blend the sounds.
- Instead of using letter tiles, ask students to spell the word on individual white boards.

Word Bank

bee	creep	feet	keep	peep	seed	sheet	sweep	weed
beef	deed	flee	meek	queen	seek	sleep	sweet	week
bees	deep	free	meet	reed	seen	speech	teem	weep
beets	deer	green	need	screen	sheep	steer	three	
cheek	feed	keen	peel	see	sheer	street	tree	

28 Spelling Words with the Long *i* Sound (More Complex Patterns)

GOAL

- **Students will spell words with the long *i* sound.**

MATERIALS

○ Word bank for this activity

○ Letter tiles or letter cards

TEACHER STEPS: Describe It

- Tell students that when there are two vowels together in a word, the first vowel usually says the long sound and the second vowel is silent.
- Say a word from the word bank (e.g., *tie*).
- As you spell the word, put down the corresponding letter(s) for each sound you say (/t/ /ī/). Before putting down the silent e, remind students that when there two vowels together, the first vowel says the long sound.
- As you spell the word, put down the corresponding letter(s) for each sound you say (/t/ /ī/). Before putting down the letter e, remind students that when *i* and *e* are together, the first vowel says the long sound and the second vowel is silent.
- Blend the sounds (*tie*).
- Follow the same procedure for additional words. When possible, add, delete, or substitute letter(s) to spell new words. (See the illustration below.)

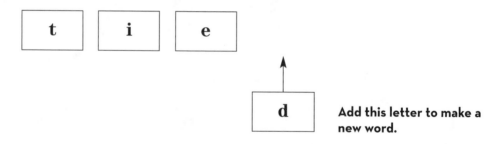

Add this letter to make a new word.

STUDENT STEPS: Do It

Say the following:
- "Put down a letter for the first two sounds you say in the word _____." (e.g., *tied*)
- "Which silent letter goes after the *i*?" (e)
- "Put down the letter for the last sound." (*d*)
- "What happens when two vowels are together?" (The first one says the long sound.)

Follow the same procedure for additional words. When possible, have students add, delete, or substitute letter(s) to spell new words.

As students become proficient, say a word from the word bank and ask them to spell it with their tiles. When possible, have students add, delete, or substitute letter(s) to spell new words.

Activity and Word Bank continued on following page

VARIATIONS

- Before putting down a letter for each sound, have students hold a contracted Slinky with one hand on either side. Tell students to pull the ends of the Slinky as they say the sounds in the word and push the ends together as they put the sounds together.
- Before putting down a letter for each sound, ask students to put their hands together in front of them. Tell them to move their hands apart as they break apart the word and clap once as they put the word together.
- Before putting down a letter for each sound, ask students to segment and blend the sounds into a self-phone.
- Before putting down a letter for each sound, ask students to hold one arm out with their palm up. With the opposite hand, have them touch their shoulder as they say the first sound, the middle of their arm as they say the second sound, their wrist as they say the third sound, and their palm if there is a fourth sound. Tell them to slide their hand down their arm as they blend the sounds.
- Instead of using letter tiles, ask students to spell the word on individual white boards.

Word Bank							
cried	died	dries	fried	lied	spied	tied	vied
cries	dies	fie	fries	lies	spies	ties	vies
die	dried	flies	lie	pie	tie	vie	

29 Spelling Words with the Long o Sound (More Complex Patterns)

GOAL

- **Students will spell words with the long o sound.**

MATERIALS

○ Word bank for this activity

○ Letter tiles or letter cards

TEACHER STEPS: Describe It

- Tell students that when there are two vowels together in a word, the first vowel usually says the long sound and the second vowel is silent.
- Say a word from the word bank (e.g., *road*).
- As you spell the word, put down the corresponding letter(s) for each sound you say (/r/ /ō/ /d/). Before putting down the letter a, remind students that when o and a are together, the first vowel says the long sound and the second vowel is silent.
- Blend the sounds (*road*).
- Follow the same procedure for additional words. When possible, add, delete, or substitute letter(s) to spell new words. (See the illustrations below.)

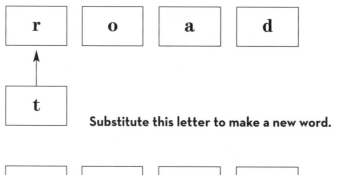

Substitute this letter to make a new word.

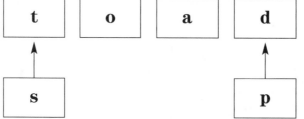

Substitute these letters to make a new word.

STUDENT STEPS: Do It

Say the following:

- "Put down a letter for the first two sounds you say in the word _____." (e.g., *road*)
- "Which silent letter goes after the o?" (*a*)
- "Put down the letter for the last sound." (*d*)
- "What happens when two vowels are together?" (The first one says the long sound.)

Activity and Word Bank continued on following page

Follow the same procedure for additional words. When possible, have students add, delete, or substitute letter(s) to spell new words.

As students become proficient, say a word from the word bank and ask them to spell it with their tiles. When possible, have students add, delete, or substitute letter(s) to spell new words.

VARIATIONS

- Before putting down a letter for each sound, have students hold a contracted Slinky with one hand on either side. Tell students to pull the ends of the Slinky as they say the sounds in the word and push the ends together as they put the sounds together.
- Before putting down a letter for each sound, ask students to put their hands together in front of them. Tell them to move their hands apart as they break apart the word and clap once as they put the word together.
- Before putting down a letter for each sound, ask students to segment and blend the sounds into a self-phone.
- Before putting down a letter for each sound, ask students to hold one arm out with their palm up. With the opposite hand, have them touch their shoulder as they say the first sound, the middle of their arm as they say the second sound, their wrist as they say the third sound, and their palm if there is a fourth sound. Tell them to slide their hand down their arm as they blend the sounds.
- Instead of using letter tiles, ask students to spell the word on individual white boards.

Word Bank						
boast	coat	goal	loaf	oath	roar	soar
boat	croak	goat	loan	oats	roast	throat
coach	float	groan	oak	road	soak	toad
coast	foam	load	oar	roam	soap	toast

30 Spelling Words with the Long o Sound (More Complex Patterns)

GOAL

- **Students will spell words with the long o sound.**

MATERIALS

○ Word bank for this activity　　　　　○ Letter tiles or letter cards

TEACHER STEPS: Describe It

- Tell students that when there are two vowels together in a word, the first vowel usually says the long sound and the second vowel is silent.
- Say a word from the word bank (e.g., *toe*).
- As you spell the word, put down the corresponding letter(s) for each sound you say (/t/ /ō/). Before putting down the letter e, remind students that when o and e are together, the first vowel says the long sound and the second vowel is silent.
- Blend the sounds (*toe*).
- Follow the same procedure for additional words. When possible, add, delete, or substitute letter(s) to spell new words. (See the illustration below.)

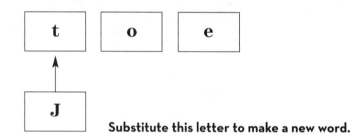

Substitute this letter to make a new word.

STUDENT STEPS: Do It

Say the following:
- "Put down a letter for the first two sounds you say in the word _____." (e.g., *toe*)
- "Which silent letter goes after the *o*?" (e)
- "What happens when two vowels are together?" (The first one says the long sound.)

Follow the same procedure for additional words. When possible, have students add, delete, or substitute letter(s) to spell new words.

As students become proficient, say a word from the word bank and ask them to spell it with their tiles. When possible, have students add, delete, or substitute letter(s) to spell new words.

Activity and Word Bank continued on following page

VARIATIONS

- Before putting down a letter for each sound, have students hold a contracted Slinky with one hand on either side. Tell students to pull the ends of the Slinky as they say the sounds in the word and push the ends together as they put the sounds together.
- Before putting down a letter for each sound, ask students to put their hands together in front of them. Tell them to move their hands apart as they break apart the word and clap once as they put the word together.
- Before putting down a letter for each sound, ask students to segment and blend the sounds into a self-phone.
- Before putting down a letter for each sound, ask students to hold one arm out with their palm up. With the opposite hand, have them touch their shoulder as they say the first sound, the middle of their arm as they say the second sound, their wrist as they say the third sound, and their palm if there is a fourth sound. Tell them to slide their hand down their arm as they blend the sounds.
- Instead of using letter tiles, ask students to spell the word on individual white boards.

Word Bank									
doe	floe	foe	goes	hoe	Joe	roe	toe	toes	woe

31 Spelling ow Words

GOAL

- **Students will spell long o words containing the ow digraph.**

MATERIALS

○ Word bank for this activity

○ Letter tiles or letter cards

TEACHER STEPS: Describe It

- Tell students that when o and w are together, they can say /ō/ as in *mow*.
- Say a word from the word bank (e.g., *mow*).
- As you spell the word, put down the corresponding letter(s) for each sound you say (/m/ /ō/). Before putting down the letters o and w, remind students that when these two letters are together, they can say /ō/.
- Blend the sounds (*mow*).
- Follow the same procedure for additional words. When possible, add, delete, or substitute letter(s) to spell new words. (See the illustration below.)

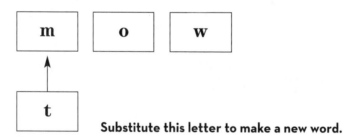

Substitute this letter to make a new word.

STUDENT STEPS: Do It

Say the following:
- "Put down a letter for the first sound you say _____." (e.g., *mow*)
- "Put down the two letters that say /ō/." (ow)

Follow the same procedure for additional words. When possible, have students add, delete, or substitute letter(s) to spell new words.

As students become proficient, say a word from the word bank and ask them to spell it with their tiles. When possible, have students add, delete, or substitute letter(s) to spell new words.

VARIATIONS

Before putting down a letter for each sound, have students hold a contracted Slinky with one hand on either side. Tell students to pull the ends of the Slinky as they say the sounds in the word and push the ends together as they put the sounds together.

Activity and Word Bank continued on following page

- Before putting down a letter for each sound, ask students to put their hands together in front of them. Tell them to move their hands apart as they break apart the word and clap once as they put the word together.
- Before putting down a letter for each sound, ask students to segment and blend the sounds into a self-phone.
- Before putting down a letter for each sound, ask students to hold one arm out with their palm up. With the opposite hand, have them touch their shoulder as they say the first sound, the middle of their arm as they say the second sound, their wrist as they say the third sound, and their palm if there is a fourth sound. Tell them to slide their hand down their arm as they blend the sounds.
- Instead of using letter tiles, ask students to spell the word on individual white boards.

Word Bank

blow	bowl	flow	grow	growth	mow	show	slow	throw
blown	crow	glow	grown	low	row	shown	snow	tow

32 Spelling *ar* Words

GOAL

- **Students will spell words containing the murmur diphthong *ar*.**

MATERIALS

○ Word bank for this activity

○ Letter tiles or letter cards

TEACHER STEPS: Describe It

- Tell students that when *a* and *r* are together, the sound is /ar/ as in *card*.
- Say a word from the word bank (e.g., *card*).
- As you spell the word, put down the corresponding letter(s) for each sound you say (/k/ /ar/ /d/). Before putting down the letters *a* and *r*, remind students that when these two letters are together, they say /ar/.
- Blend the sounds (*card*).
- Follow the same procedure for additional words. When possible, add, delete, or substitute letter(s) to spell new words. (See the illustration below.)

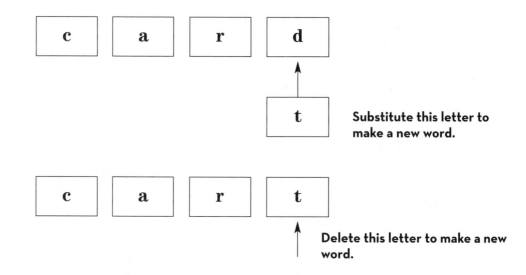

| c | a | r | d |

↑

Substitute this letter to make a new word.

| t |

| c | a | r | t |

↑

Delete this letter to make a new word.

STUDENT STEPS: Do It

Say the following:

- "Put down a letter for the first sound you say in the word _____." (e.g., *card*)
- "Put down the two letters that say /ar/." (*ar*)
- "Put down the letter for the last sound." (*d*)

Follow the same procedure for additional words. When possible, have students add, delete, or substitute letter(s) to spell new words.

Activity and Word Bank continued on following page

ALPHABETIC PRINCIPLE • Variant Vowel Spelling Patterns   CLASSROOM ACTIVITY

As students become proficient, say a word from the word bank and ask them to spell it with their tiles. When possible, have students add, delete, or substitute letter(s) to spell new words.

VARIATIONS

- Before putting down a letter for each sound, have students hold a contracted Slinky with one hand on either side. Tell students to pull the ends of the Slinky as they say the sounds in the word and push the ends together as they put the sounds together.
- Before putting down a letter for each sound, ask students to put their hands together in front of them. Tell them to move their hands apart as they break apart the word and clap once as they put the word together.
- Before putting down a letter for each sound, ask students to segment and blend the sounds into a self-phone.
- Before putting down a letter for each sound, ask students to hold one arm out with their palm up. With the opposite hand, have them touch their shoulder as they say the first sound, the middle of their arm as they say the second sound, their wrist as they say the third sound, and their palm if there is a fourth sound. Tell them to slide their hand down their arm as they blend the sounds.
- Instead of using letter tiles, ask students to spell the word on individual white boards.

Word Bank									
arch	bark	Carl	dark	harm	lark	marsh	shark	spark	start
ark	barn	cart	darn	harp	mar	par	sharp	star	tar
art	car	charm	dart	jar	march	part	smart	starch	yarn
bar	card	chart	hard	lard	mark	scarf			

33 Spelling *or* Words

GOAL

- **Students will spell words containing the murmur diphthong *or*.**

MATERIALS

○ Word bank for this activity

○ Letter tiles or letter cards

TEACHER STEPS: Describe It

- Tell students that when o and *r* are together, the sound is /or/ as in *port*.
- Say a word from the word bank (e.g., *port*).
- As you spell the word, put down the corresponding letter(s) for each sound you say. (/p/ /or/ /t/). Before putting down the letters o and *r*, remind students that when these two letters are together, they say /or/.
- Blend the sounds (*port*).
- Follow the same procedure for additional words. When possible, add, delete, or substitute letter(s) to spell new words. (See the illustrations below.)

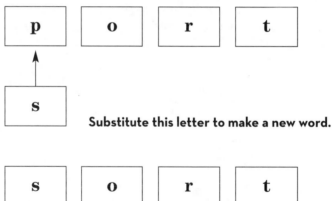

Substitute this letter to make a new word.

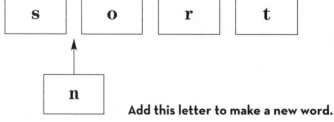

Add this letter to make a new word.

STUDENT STEPS: Do It

Say the following:

- "Put down a letter for the first sound you say in the word _____." (e.g., *port*)
- "Put down the two letters that say /or/." (*or*)
- "Put down the letter for the last sound." (*t*)

Follow the same procedure for additional words. When possible, have students add, delete, or substitute letter(s) to spell new words.

Activity and Word Bank continued on following page

CLASSROOM ACTIVITY

ALPHABETIC PRINCIPLE • Variant Vowel Spelling Patterns

Spelling or Words continued

As students become proficient, say a word from the word bank and ask them to spell it with their tiles. When possible, have students add, delete, or substitute letter(s) to spell new words.

VARIATIONS

- Before putting down a letter for each sound, have students hold a contracted Slinky with one hand on either side. Tell students to pull the ends of the Slinky as they say the sounds in the word and push the ends together as they put the sounds together.
- Before putting down a letter for each sound, ask students to put their hands together in front of them. Tell them to move their hands apart as they break apart the word and clap once as they put the word together.
- Before putting down a letter for each sound, ask students to segment and blend the sounds into a self-phone.
- Before putting down a letter for each sound, ask students to hold one arm out with their palm up. With the opposite hand, have them touch their shoulder as they say the first sound, the middle of their arm as they say the second sound, their wrist as they say the third sound, and their palm if there is a fourth sound. Tell them to slide their hand down their arm as they blend the sounds.
- Instead of using letter tiles, ask students to spell the word on individual white boards.

Word Bank						
born	for	forth	or	scorch	sort	sworn
cord	fork	horn	porch	scorn	sport	thorn
cork	form	lord	pork	short	stork	torch
corn	fort	north	port	snort	storm	worn

34 Spelling *er* Words

GOAL

- **Students will spell words containing the murmur diphthong er.**

MATERIALS

○ Word bank for this activity

○ Letter tiles or letter cards

TEACHER STEPS: Describe It

- Tell students that when *e* and *r* are together, the sound is /er/ as in *herd*.
- Say a word from the word bank (e.g., *herd*).
- As you spell the word, put down the corresponding letter(s) for each sound you say (/h/ /er/ /d/). Before putting down the letters *e* and *r*, remind students that when these two letters are together, they say /er/.
- Blend the sounds (*herd*).

Follow the same procedure for additional words. When possible, add, delete, or substitute letter(s) to spell new words. (See the illustration below.)

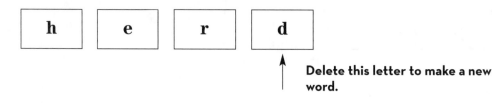

↑ **Delete this letter to make a new word.**

STUDENT STEPS: Do It

Say the following:

- "Put down a letter for the first sound you say in the word _____." (e.g., *herd*)
- "Put down the two letters that say /er/." (*er*)
- "Put down the letter for the last sound." (*d*)

Follow the same procedure for additional words. When possible, have students add, delete, or substitute letter(s) to spell new words.

As students become proficient, say a word from the word bank and ask them to spell it with their tiles. When possible, have students add, delete, or substitute letter(s) to spell new words.

VARIATIONS

- Before putting down a letter for each sound, have students hold a contracted Slinky with one hand on either side. Tell students to pull the ends of the Slinky as they say the sounds in the word and push the ends together as they put the sounds together.
- Before putting down a letter for each sound, ask students to put their hands together in front of them. Tell them to move their hands apart as they break apart the word and clap once as they put the word together.

Activity and Word Bank continued on following page

- Before putting down a letter for each sound, ask students to segment and blend the sounds into a self-phone.
- Before putting down a letter for each sound, ask students to hold one arm out with their palm up. With the opposite hand, have them touch their shoulder as they say the first sound, the middle of their arm as they say the second sound, their wrist as they say the third sound, and their palm if there is a fourth sound. Tell them to slide their hand down their arm as they blend the sounds.
- Instead of using letter tiles, ask students to spell the word on individual white boards.

Word Bank									
clerk	fern	germ	her	herd	jerk	perch	pert	stern	Vern

35 Spelling *ir* Words

GOAL

- **Students will spell words containing the murmur diphthong *ir*.**

MATERIALS

○ Word bank for this activity

○ Letter tiles or letter cards

TEACHER STEPS: Describe It

- Tell students that when *i* and *r* are together, the sound is /ir/ as in *first*.
- Say a word from the word bank (e.g., *first*).
- As you spell the word, put down the corresponding letter(s) for each sound you say (/f/ /ir/ /s/ /t/). Before putting down the letters *i* and *r*, remind students that when these two letters are together, they say /ir/.
- Blend the sounds (*first*).
- Follow the same procedure for additional words. When possible, add, delete, or substitute letter(s) to spell new words. (See the illustration below.)

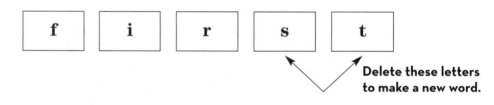

Delete these letters to make a new word.

STUDENT STEPS: Do It

Say the following:
- "Put down a letter for the first sound you say in the word _____." (e.g., *first*)
- "Put down the two letters that say ir." (*ir*)
- "Put down the letters for the remaining sounds." (*st*)

Follow the same procedure for additional words. When possible, have students add, delete, or substitute letter(s) to spell new words.

As students become proficient, say a word from the word bank and ask them to spell it with their tiles. When possible, have students add, delete, or substitute letter(s) to spell new words.

VARIATIONS

- Before putting down a letter for each sound, have students hold a contracted Slinky with one hand on either side. Tell students to pull the ends of the Slinky as they say the sounds in the word and push the ends together as they put the sounds together.
- Before putting down a letter for each sound, ask students to put their hands together in front of them. Tell them to move their hands apart as they break apart the word and clap once as they put the word together.

Activity and Word Bank continued on following page

- Before putting down a letter for each sound, ask students to segment and blend the sounds into a self-phone.
- Before putting down a letter for each sound, ask students to hold one arm out with their palm up. With the opposite hand, have them touch their shoulder as they say the first sound, the middle of their arm as they say the second sound, their wrist as they say the third sound, and their palm if there is a fourth sound. Tell them to slide their hand down their arm as they blend the sounds.
- Instead of using letter tiles, ask students to spell the word on individual white boards.

Word Bank

birch	chirp	firm	girl	shirt	squirm	third	twirl
bird	dirt	first	mirth	sir	squirt	thirst	whirl
birth	fir	flirt	shirk	skirt	stir		

36 Spelling *ur* Words

GOAL

- **Students will spell words containing the murmur diphthong *ur*.**

MATERIALS

○ Word bank for this activity

○ Letter tiles or letter cards

TEACHER STEPS: Describe It

- Tell students that when *u* and *r* are together, the sound is /ur/ as in *turn*.
- Say a word from the word bank (e.g., *turn*).
- As you spell the word, put down the corresponding letter(s) for each sound you say (/t/ /ur/ /n/). Before putting down the letters *u* and *r*, remind students that when these two letters are together, they say /ur/.
- Blend the sounds (*turn*).
- Follow the same procedure for additional words. When possible, add, delete, or substitute letter(s) to spell new words. (See the illustrations below.)

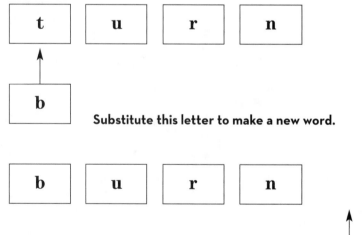

Substitute this letter to make a new word.

Add this letter to make a new word.

STUDENT STEPS: Do It

Say the following:
- "Put down a letter for the first sound you say in the word _____." (e.g., *turn*)
- "Put down the two letters that say /ur/." (*ur*)
- "Put down the letters for the remaining sound." (*n*)

Follow the same procedure for additional words. When possible, have students add, delete, or substitute letter(s) to spell new words.

Activity and Word Bank continued on following page

As students become proficient, say a word from the word bank and ask them to spell it with their tiles. When possible, have students add, delete, or substitute letter(s) to spell new words.

VARIATIONS

- Before putting down a letter for each sound, have students hold a contracted Slinky with one hand on either side. Tell students to pull the ends of the Slinky as they say the sounds in the word and push the ends together as they put the sounds together.
- Before putting down a letter for each sound, ask students to put their hands together in front of them. Tell them to move their hands apart as they break apart the word and clap once as they put the word together.
- Before putting down a letter for each sound, ask students to segment and blend the sounds into a self-phone.
- Before putting down a letter for each sound, ask students to hold one arm out with their palm up. With the opposite hand, have them touch their shoulder as they say the first sound, the middle of their arm as they say the second sound, their wrist as they say the third sound, and their palm if there is a fourth sound. Tell them to slide their hand down their arm as they blend the sounds.
- Instead of using letter tiles, ask students to spell the word on individual white boards.

Word Bank							
burn	burst	churn	curl	furl	hurt	spur	turn
burr	church	curb	fur	hurl	purr	surf	urn

37 Spelling Words with the Short oo Sound

GOAL

- **Students will spell words containing the short oo sound.**

MATERIALS

○ Word bank for this activity

○ Letter tiles or letter cards

TEACHER STEPS: Describe It

- Tell students that when o and o are together, the sound can be /ŏŏ/ as in *book*.
- Say a word from the word bank (e.g., *book*).
- As you segment the word, put down the corresponding letter(s) for each sound you say. (/b/ /ŏŏ/ /k/). Before putting down the letters o and o, remind students that when these two letters are together, they can say /ŏŏ/.
- Blend the sounds (*book*).
- Follow the same procedure for additional words. When possible, add, delete, or substitute letter(s) to spell new words. (See the illustration below.)

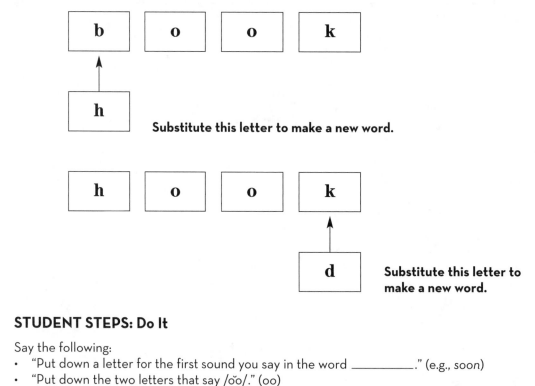

| b | o | o | k |

| h |

Substitute this letter to make a new word.

| h | o | o | k |

| d |

Substitute this letter to make a new word.

STUDENT STEPS: Do It

Say the following:

- "Put down a letter for the first sound you say in the word _____." (e.g., *soon*)
- "Put down the two letters that say /ŏŏ/." (oo)
- "Put down the letter for the last sound." (n)

Activity and Word Bank continued on following page

Follow the same procedure for additional words. When possible, have students add, delete, or substitute letter(s) to spell new words.

As students become proficient, say a word from the word bank and ask them to spell it with their tiles. When possible, have students add, delete, or substitute letter(s) to spell new words.

VARIATIONS

- Before putting down a letter for each sound, have students hold a contracted Slinky with one hand on either side. Tell students to pull the ends of the Slinky as they say the sounds in the word and push the ends together as they put the sounds together.
- Before putting down a letter for each sound, ask students to put their hands together in front of them. Tell them to move their hands apart as they break apart the word and clap once as they put the word together.
- Before putting down a letter for each sound, ask students to segment and blend the sounds into a self-phone.
- Before putting down a letter for each sound, ask students to hold one arm out with their palm up. With the opposite hand, have them touch their shoulder as they say the first sound, the middle of their arm as they say the second sound, their wrist as they say the third sound, and their palm if there is a fourth sound. Tell them to slide their hand down their arm as they blend the sounds.
- Instead of using letter tiles, ask students to spell the word on individual white boards.

Word Bank								
book	cook	foot	hood	hook	nook	soot	took	wool
brook	crook	good	hoof	look	shook	stood	wood	

38 Spelling Words with the Long oo Sound

GOAL

- **Students will spell words containing the long oo sound.**

MATERIALS

○ Word bank for this activity   ○ Letter tiles or letter cards

TEACHER STEPS: Describe It

- Tell students that when o and o are together, the sound can be /o͞o/ as in *soon*.
- Say a word from the word bank (e.g., *soon*).
- As you segment the word, put down the corresponding letter(s) for each sound you say. (/s/ /o͞o/ /n/). Before putting down the letters o and o, remind students that when these two letters are together, they can say /o͞o/.
- Blend the sounds (*soon*).
- Follow the same procedure for additional words. When possible, add, delete, or substitute letter(s) to spell new words. (See the illustration below.)

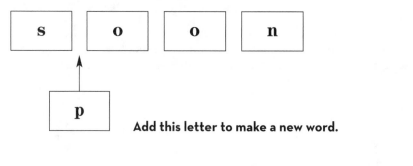

| s | o | o | n |

| p |

Add this letter to make a new word.

| s | p | o | o | n |

| l |

Substitute this letter to make a new word.

STUDENT STEPS: Do It

Say the following:
- "Put down a letter for the first sound you say in the word _____." (e.g., *soon*)
- "Put down the two letters that say /o͞o/." (oo)
- "Put down the letter for the last sound." (*n*)

Follow the same procedure for additional words. When possible, have students add, delete, or substitute letter(s) to spell new words.

Activity and Word Bank continued on following page

As students become proficient, say a word from the word bank and ask them to spell it with their tiles. When possible, have students add, delete, or substitute letter(s) to spell new words.

VARIATIONS

- Before putting down a letter for each sound, have students hold a contracted Slinky with one hand on either side. Tell students to pull the ends of the Slinky as they say the sounds in the word and push the ends together as they put the sounds together.
- Before putting down a letter for each sound, ask students to put their hands together in front of them. Tell them to move their hands apart as they break apart the word and clap once as they put the word together.
- Before putting down a letter for each sound, ask students to segment and blend the sounds into a self-phone.
- Before putting down a letter for each sound, ask students to hold one arm out with their palm up. With the opposite hand, have them touch their shoulder as they say the first sound, the middle of their arm as they say the second sound, their wrist as they say the third sound, and their palm if there is a fourth sound. Tell them to slide their hand down their arm as they blend the sounds.
- Instead of using letter tiles, ask students to spell the word on individual white boards.

Word Bank

boom	broom	droop	moo	poor	shoot	spool	tooth
boost	coo	food	mood	roof	smooth	spoon	troop
boot	cool	fool	moon	room	snoop	too	zoo
booth	coop	hoop	noon	root	soon	tool	
brood	drool	loop	pool	scoop			

39 Spelling Words with the Short and Long oo Sounds

GOAL

- **Students will spell words containing the short and long oo sounds.**

MATERIALS

○ Word bank for this activity   ○ Letter tiles or letter cards

TEACHER STEPS: Describe It

- Tell students that when o and o are together, the sound can be /ŏŏ/ as *book* or /o͞o/ as in *soon*.
- Say a word from the word bank (e.g., *book*).
- As you segment the word, put down the corresponding letter(s) for each sound you say. (/b/ /ŏŏ/ /k/). (See the illustration below.) Before putting down the letters o and o, remind students that when these two letters are together, they can say /ŏŏ/.
- Blend the sounds (*book*).
- Follow the same procedure for additional words. When possible, add, delete, or substitute letter(s) to spell new words.

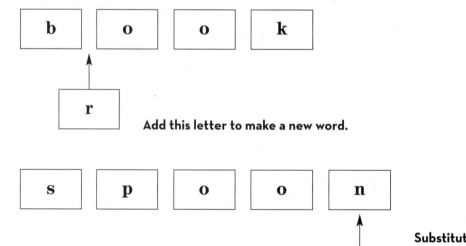

STUDENT STEPS: Do It

Say the following:

- "Put down a letter for the first sound you say in the word _____." (e.g., *book*)
- "Put down the two letters that say /ŏŏ/." (oo)
- "Put down the letter for the last sound." (k)

Follow the same procedure for additional words. When possible, add, delete, or substitute letter(s) to spell new words.

Activity and Word Bank continued on following page

As students become proficient, say a word from the word bank and ask them to spell it with their tiles. When possible, have students add, delete, or substitute letter(s) to spell new words.

VARIATIONS

- Before putting down a letter for each sound, have students hold a contracted Slinky with one hand on either side. Tell students to pull the ends of the Slinky as they say the sounds in the word and push the ends together as they put the sounds together.
- Before putting down a letter for each sound, ask students to put their hands together in front of them. Tell them to move their hands apart as they break apart the word and clap once as they put the word together.
- Before putting down a letter for each sound, ask students to segment and blend the sounds into a self-phone.
- Before putting down a letter for each sound, ask students to hold one arm out with their palm up. With the opposite hand, have them touch their shoulder as they say the first sound, the middle of their arm as they say the second sound, their wrist as they say the third sound, and their palm if there is a fourth sound. Tell them to slide their hand down their arm as they blend the sounds.
- Instead of using letter tiles, ask students to spell the word on individual white boards.

Word Bank

bloom	brook	droop	hood	nook	smooth	stool	tooth
book	broom	food	hoof	pool	spook	stoop	troop
boot	coo	fool	hook	poor	spool	too	wool
booth	coop	foot	hoop	root	spoon	took	zoo
brood	drool	good	loop	scoop	stood	tool	

40 Spelling oy Words

GOAL

- **Students will spell words containing the oy diphthong.**

MATERIALS

○ Word bank for this activity   ○ Letter tiles or letter cards

TEACHER STEPS: Describe It

- Tell students that when o and *y* are together, they say /oy/ as in *toy*.
- Say a word from the word bank (e.g., *toy*).
- As you segment the word, put down the corresponding letter(s) for each sound you say (/b/ /oy/). Before putting down the letters o and *y*, remind students that when these two letters are together, they say /oy/.
- Blend the sounds (*toy*).
- Follow the same procedure for additional words. When possible, add, delete, or substitute letter(s) to spell new words. (See the illustrations below.)

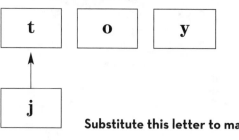

Substitute this letter to make a new word.

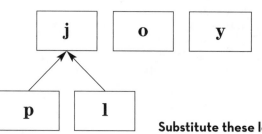

Substitute these letters to make a new word.

STUDENT STEPS: Do It

Say the following:
- "Put down a letter for the first sound you say in the word _____." (e.g., *toy*)
- "Put down the two letters that say /oy/." (oy)

Follow the same procedure for additional words. When possible, have students add, delete, or substitute letter(s) to spell new words.

Activity and Word Bank continued on following page

As students become proficient, say a word from the word bank and ask them to spell it with their tiles. When possible, have students add, delete, or substitute letter(s) to spell new words.

VARIATIONS

- Before putting down a letter for each sound, have students hold a contracted Slinky with one hand on either side. Tell students to pull the ends of the Slinky as they say the sounds in the word and push the ends together as they put the sounds together.
- Before putting down a letter for each sound, ask students to put their hands together in front of them. Tell them to move their hands apart as they break apart the word and clap once as they put the word together.
- Before putting down a letter for each sound, ask students to segment and blend the sounds into a self-phone.
- Before putting down a letter for each sound, ask students to hold one arm out with their palm up. With the opposite hand, have them touch their shoulder as they say the first sound, the middle of their arm as they say the second sound, their wrist as they say the third sound, and their palm if there is a fourth sound. Tell them to slide their hand down their arm as they blend the sounds.
- Instead of using letter tiles, ask students to spell the word on individual white boards.

Word Bank							
boy	cloy	coy	joy	ploy	Roy	soy	toy

41 Spelling *oi* Words

GOAL

- **Students will spell words containing the oi diphthong.**

MATERIALS

○ Word bank for this activity

○ Letter tiles or letter cards

TEACHER STEPS: Describe It

- Tell students that when o and *i* are together, they say /oi/ as in *oil*.
- Say a word from the word bank (e.g., *boil*).
- As you segment the word, put down the corresponding letter(s) for each sound you say. (/b/ /oi/ /l/). Before putting down the letters o and *i*, remind students that when these two letters are together, they say /oi/.
- Blend the sounds (*boil*).
- Follow the same procedure for additional words. When possible, add, delete, or substitute letter(s) to spell new words. (See the illustration below.)

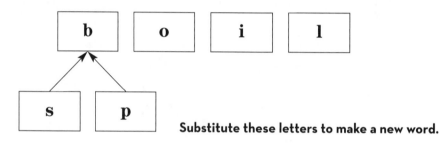

Substitute these letters to make a new word.

STUDENT STEPS: Do It

Say the following:
- "Put down a letter for the first sound you say in the word _____." (e.g., *boil*)
- "Put down the two letters that say /oi/." (*oi*)
- "Put down the letter for the last sound." (*l*)

Follow the same procedure for additional words. When possible, have students add, delete, or substitute letter(s) to spell new words.

As students become proficient, say a word from the word bank and ask them to spell it with their tiles. When possible, have students add, delete, or substitute letter(s) to spell new words.

VARIATIONS

- Before putting down a letter for each sound, have students hold a contracted Slinky with one hand on either side. Tell students to pull the ends of the Slinky as they say the sounds in the word and push the ends together as they put the sounds together.

Activity and Word Bank continued on following page

- Before putting down a letter for each sound, ask students to put their hands together in front of them. Tell them to move their hands apart as they break apart the word and clap once as they put the word together.
- Before putting down a letter for each sound, ask students to segment and blend the sounds into a self-phone.
- Before putting down a letter for each sound, ask students to hold one arm out with their palm up. With the opposite hand, have them touch their shoulder as they say the first sound, the middle of their arm as they say the second sound, their wrist as they say the third sound, and their palm if there is a fourth sound. Tell them to slide their hand down their arm as they blend the sounds.
- Instead of using letter tiles, ask students to spell the word on individual white boards.

Word Bank

boil	coin	foist	join	joist	moist	oink	roil	spoil
broil	foil	hoist	joint	moil	oil	point	soil	toil

42 Spelling *ou* Words

GOAL

- **Students will spell words containing the *ou* diphthong.**

MATERIALS

○ Word bank for this activity   ○ Letter tiles or letter cards

TEACHER STEPS: Describe It

- Tell students that when o and *u* are together, they can say /ou/ as in out.
- Say a word from the word bank (e.g., *out*).
- As you segment the word, put down the corresponding letter(s) for each sound you say. (/ou/ /t/). Before putting down the letters o and *u*, remind students that when these two letters are together, they can say /ou/.
- Blend the sounds (*out*).
- Follow the same procedure for additional words. When possible, add, delete, or substitute letter(s) to spell new words. (See the illustration below.)

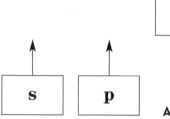

Add these letters to make a new word.

STUDENT STEPS: Do It

Say the following:
- "Put down a letter for the first sound in the word _____." (e.g., *loud*)
- "Put down the two letters that say /ou/." (ou)
- "Put down the letter for the last sound." (*d*)

Follow the same procedure for additional words. When possible, have students add, delete, or substitute letter(s) to spell new words.

As students become proficient, say a word from the word bank and ask them to spell it with their tiles. When possible, have students add, delete, or substitute letter(s) to spell new words.

VARIATIONS

- Before putting down a letter for each sound, have students hold a contracted Slinky with one hand on either side. Tell students to pull the ends of the Slinky as they say the sounds in the word and push the ends together as they put the sounds together.

Activity and Word Bank continued on following page

- Before putting down a letter for each sound, ask students to put their hands together in front of them. Tell them to move their hands apart as they break apart the word and clap once as they put the word together.
- Before putting down a letter for each sound, ask students to segment and blend the sounds into a self-phone.
- Before putting down a letter for each sound, ask students to hold one arm out with their palm up. With the opposite hand, have them touch their shoulder as they say the first sound, the middle of their arm as they say the second sound, their wrist as they say the third sound, and their palm if there is a fourth sound. Tell them to slide their hand down their arm as they blend the sounds.
- Instead of using letter tiles, ask students to spell the word on individual white boards.

Word Bank

bound	flour	loud	pound	shout	spout
cloud	foul	mouth	pout	snout	sprout
couch	grouch	ouch	proud	sound	stout
count	ground	out	round	sour	trout
crouch	hound	pouch	scout	south	

43 Spelling ow Words

GOAL

- **Students will spell words containing the ow diphthong.**

MATERIALS

○ Word bank for this activity

○ Letter tiles or letter cards

TEACHER STEPS: Describe It

- Tell students that when o and *w* are together, they can say /ou/ as in *clown*.
- Say a word from the word bank (e.g., *clown*).
- As you segment the word, put down the corresponding letter(s) for each sound you say. (/k/ /l/ /ou/ /n/). Before putting down the letters o and *w*, remind students that when these two letters are together, they can say /ou/.
- Blend the sounds (*clown*).
- Follow the same procedure for additional words. When possible, add, delete, or substitute letter(s) to spell new words. (See the illustration below.)

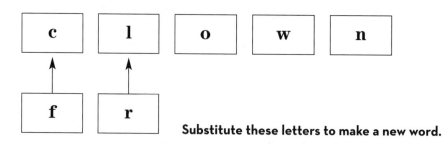

Substitute these letters to make a new word.

STUDENT STEPS: Do It

Say the following:
- "Put down the two letters that say the first two sounds in the word _____." (e.g., *clown*)
- "Put down the two letters that make the next sound." (ow)
- "Put down the letter for the last sound." (n)

Follow the same procedure for additional words. When possible, have students add, delete, or substitute letter(s) to spell new words.

As students become proficient, say a word from the word bank and ask them to spell it with their tiles. When possible, have students add, delete, or substitute letter(s) to spell new words.

VARIATIONS

- Before putting down a letter for each sound, have students hold a contracted Slinky with one hand on either side. Tell students to pull the ends of the Slinky as they say the sounds in the word and push the ends together as they put the sounds together.

Activity and Word Bank continued on following page

- Before putting down a letter for each sound, ask students to put their hands together in front of them. Tell them to move their hands apart as they break apart the word and clap once as they put the word together.
- Before putting down a letter for each sound, ask students to segment and blend the sounds into a self-phone.
- Before putting down a letter for each sound, ask students to hold one arm out with their palm up. With the opposite hand, have them touch their shoulder as they say the first sound, the middle of their arm as they say the second sound, their wrist as they say the third sound, and their palm if there is a fourth sound. Tell them to slide their hand down their arm as they blend the sounds.
- Instead of using letter tiles, ask students to spell the word on individual white boards.

Word Bank								
brow	clown	cowl	down	fowl	gown	how	now	town
brown	cow	crown	drown	frown	growl	howl	owl	

44 Spelling ew Words

GOAL

- **Students will spell words containing the ew digraph.**

MATERIALS

○ Word bank for this activity   ○ Letter tiles or letter cards

TEACHER STEPS: Describe It

- Tell students that when e and w are together, they can say /ew/ as in *new*.
- Say a word from the word bank (e.g., *new*).
- As you spell the word, put down the corresponding letter(s) for each sound you say (/n/ /ew/). Before putting down the letters e and w, remind students that when these two letters are together, they can say /ew/.
- Blend the sounds (*new*).
- Follow the same procedure for additional words. When possible, add, delete, or substitute letter(s) to spell new words. (See the illustration below.)

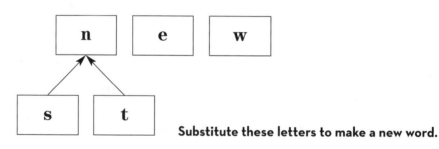

Substitute these letters to make a new word.

STUDENT STEPS: Do It

Say the following:
- "Put down a letter for the first sound you say in the word _____." (e.g., *new*)
- "Put down the two letters that say /ew/." (ew)

Follow the same procedure for additional words. When possible, have students add, delete, or substitute letter(s) to spell new words.

As students become proficient, say a word from the word bank and ask them to spell it with their tiles. When possible, have students add, delete, or substitute letter(s) to spell new words.

VARIATIONS

- Before putting down a letter for each sound, have students hold a contracted Slinky with one hand on either side. Tell students to pull the ends of the Slinky as they say the sounds in the word and push the ends together as they put the sounds together.

Activity and Word Bank continued on following page

- Before putting down a letter for each sound, ask students to put their hands together in front of them. Tell them to move their hands apart as they break apart the word and clap once as they put the word together.
- Before putting down a letter for each sound, ask students to segment and blend the sounds into a self-phone.
- Before putting down a letter for each sound, ask students to hold one arm out with their palm up. With the opposite hand, have them touch their shoulder as they say the first sound, the middle of their arm as they say the second sound, their wrist as they say the third sound, and their palm if there is a fourth sound. Tell them to slide their hand down their arm as they blend the sounds.
- Instead of using letter tiles, ask students to spell the word on individual white boards.

Word Bank

blew	chew	dew	new	screw	strewn
brew	crew	drew	news	stew	threw

45 Spelling *au* Words

GOAL

- **Students will spell words containing the *au* digraph.**

MATERIALS

○ Word bank for this activity

○ Letter tiles or letter cards

TEACHER STEPS: Describe It

- Tell students that when *a* and *u* are together, they say /au/ as in *Paul*.
- Say a word from the word bank (e.g., *Paul*).
- As you spell the word, put down the corresponding letter(s) for each sound you say. Before putting down the letters *a* and *u*, remind students that when these two letters are together, they say /au/.
- Blend the sounds (*Paul*).
- Follow the same procedure for additional words. When possible, add, delete, or substitute letter(s) to spell new words. (See the illustration below.)

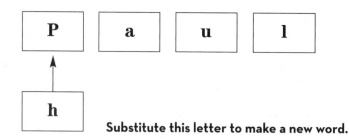

Substitute this letter to make a new word.

STUDENT STEPS: Do It

Say the following:
- "Put down a letter for the first sound you say in the word _____." (e.g., *Paul*)
- "Put down the two letters that say /au/." (*au*)
- "Put down the letter for the last sound." (*l*)

Follow the same procedure for additional words. When possible, have students add, delete, or substitute letter(s) to spell new words.

As students become proficient, say a word from the word bank and ask them to spell it with their tiles. When possible, have students add, delete, or substitute letter(s) to spell new words.

VARIATIONS

- Before putting down a letter for each sound, have students hold a contracted Slinky with one hand on either side. Tell students to pull the ends of the Slinky as they say the sounds in the word and push the ends together as they put the sounds together.

Activity and Word Bank continued on following page

ALPHABETIC PRINCIPLE · Variant Vowel Spelling Patterns

CLASSROOM ACTIVITY

- Before putting down a letter for each sound, ask students to put their hands together in front of them. Tell them to move their hands apart as they break apart the word and clap once as they put the word together.
- Before putting down a letter for each sound, ask students to segment and blend the sounds into a self-phone.
- Before putting down a letter for each sound, ask students to hold one arm out with their palm up. With the opposite hand, have them touch their shoulder as they say the first sound, the middle of their arm as they say the second sound, their wrist as they say the third sound, and their palm if there is a fourth sound. Tell them to slide their hand down their arm as they blend the sounds.
- Instead of using letter tiles, ask students to spell the word on individual white boards.

Word Bank									
auk	fault	flaunt	Gaul	haunt	laud	Maud	Paul	squall	taut
daub	faun	fraud	haul	jaunt	launch	maul	Saul	taunt	vault

Fluency Development

INTRODUCTION

Fluency development begins at the word level with high-frequency words and continues with connected text. A high-frequency word is one recognized immediately as a whole and without detailed analysis. High-frequency words are recognized at sight or with automaticity. The more high-frequency words a reader knows, the fewer times he or she will stop reading to figure out the unknown words, thus increasing reading fluency. This ultimately helps to achieve our overall reading goal of good reading comprehension.

High-frequency words are often confused with one another, such as *them* for *then*, *was* for *saw*, and *their* for *there*. These examples illustrate why it is so important to explicitly teach high-frequency words through direct instruction: They can be visually similar. High-frequency words are best learned through a lot of contextual reading because students will encounter these high-frequency words often. Teachers can reinforce these words by developing a high-frequency word wall. Five to seven words can be added to the word wall weekly and practiced during free moments during the school day. One way to practice the new high-frequency words is when preparing to leave the classroom for recess or lunch. Have students read the new list of high-frequency words from the wall as a group. The new high-frequency words that have been added that week can be posted both inside and outside of the door. In order to leave or enter the room, students must read the list of new high-frequency words posted for that week. At the end of the week, this new list of words can be added to the classroom word wall.

As mentioned in Chapter 4, in preparation for the Home–School Connection fluency activities, two fluency kits can be assembled for each student so that the students can use one kit in the classroom and one kit at home. Chapter 4 describes the preparation and organization of the fluency kit materials in detail. The appendix contains photocopiable templates for some of the kit materials, such as a high-frequency word bank and high-frequency word cards. Alternatively, you can use a high-frequency word bank from your core reading program. Additional lists of high-frequency words can be constructed using the words that appear on the high-frequency word cards.

Fluency is the ability to read with "speed, accuracy, and appropriate expression" that aids in comprehension of text (NICHD, 2000, p. 3-1). When teachers think about fluency, oral reading is often emphasized, but fluency also pertains to silent reading. In early reading instruction, oral reading is emphasized (Johns & Berglund, 2002), which is the focus of this chapter of interventions.

Speed is the rate of reading, usually expressed in words correct per minute (WCPM). Directions for calculating speed are included in the second intervention, One Minute, Please!

Accuracy is explained when a student recognizes most words in a text with automaticity or little effort or decoding. The formula for calculating reading accuracy can be found on page 222. When students are at a primary reading level, you can expect that they will make some reading errors or miscues, by inserting words, repeating words, mispronouncing, and/or omitting words. A general rule of thumb is that if a student misses more than 10% of the words in a given passage, the text is probably too difficult to use for instructional purposes (Dowhower, 1994).

Appropriate expression means that a student reads with prosody or correct intonation, phrasing, and pitch so that their oral reading sounds conversational (Dowhower, 1994).

Comprehension is understanding what one reads. Without comprehension, reading is just an exercise in decoding or word calling. Comprehension can be measured through story retelling, oral discussions, answering questions, or drawing pictures or any combination of the aforementioned activities.

According to LaBerge and Samuels (1974), fluency is essential to achieving good comprehension because it frees the reader to focus on the text meaning and not on word reading. Therefore exercises in the mastery of high-frequency words and reading and rereading passages to achieve fluency are not wasted exercises but have a payoff later in good comprehension.

The next few pages of this chapter contain tools to assist you in setting up a fluency program in your classroom. Calculating reading fluency and accuracy will help you get baseline data on students' reading fluency levels. On the basis of the results from the assessment, you will be able to place students in the appropriate text level. In addition, the procedures for pairing students will assist when you conduct reading fluency interventions during the school day. These partners can also be used for other reading activities. The proper pairing of students ensures that every student can benefit from partner reading at some level of challenge.

How to Calculate Reading Fluency and Accuracy

How to determine fluency:

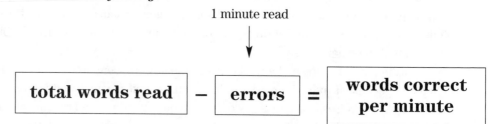

Example: 62 words read − 7 errors = 55 words correct per minute (WCPM)

How to determine reading accuracy and the appropriate level of text for a student:

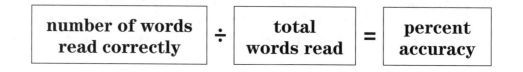

Example: 145 words correct ÷ 156 total words read = 92.9% (93%) accuracy

Choosing the Level of Text Challenge

Independent	**Instructional**	**Frustration**
97%–100% accuracy	94%–96% accuracy	93% accuracy and below
(excellent/good	(good/satisfactory	(satisfactory/fair/poor
comprehension)	comprehension)	comprehension)

Procedure for Pairing Students for Fluency Interventions

1. Rank order students according to reading fluency.

2. Split the class list in half.

3. Pair the top-ranked student in top half (TH) with the top-ranked student in the bottom half (BH). Follow the same procedure for the two students who are second from the top in each half; continue this process until all students have partners.

Top half	**Bottom half**	**Pairs**
Top-ranked student in TH	Top-ranked student in BH	Pair A
Second-ranked student in TH	Second-ranked student in BH	Pair B
Third-ranked student in TH	Third-ranked student in BH	Pair C

Oral Reading Fluency Benchmarks, Grades 1–8

In order to help students with reading fluency, you must first know students' oral reading accuracy and rate. State standards include current benchmarks to assess student reading progress. Ongoing progress monitoring will assist you in accurately determining whether the interventions are helping students to meet benchmark standards.

Assessment of oral reading fluency is scored as words correct per minute (WCPM), but if a teacher wants to get a more detailed score of a student's reading, reading accuracy also needs to be calculated. We recommend using three passages to avoid having the content of any one passage affecting the student's fluency score. Have the student read each passage for 1 minute, and record all three scores. The median or middle score is the student's fluency score for that testing period. For example, if the student scores 38, 47, and 53, her fluency score is 47. Use different sets of three passages for testing in the fall, winter, and spring.

		Oral reading fluency norms, grades 1–8		
Grade	Percentile	Fall WCPM	Winter WCPM	Spring WCPM
1	90		81	111
	75		47	82
	50		23	53
	25		12	28
	10		6	15
	SD		32	39
	Count		16,950	19,434
2	90	106	125	142
	75	79	100	117
	50	51	72	89
	25	25	42	61
	10	11	18	31
	SD	37	41	42
	Count	15,896	18,229	20,128
3	90	128	146	162
	75	99	120	137
	50	71	92	107
	25	44	62	78
	10	21	36	48
	SD	40	43	44
	Count	16,988	17,383	18,372
4	90	145	166	180
	75	119	139	152
	50	94	112	123
	25	68	87	98
	10	45	61	72
	SD	40	41	43
	Count	16,523	14,572	16,269
5	90	166	182	194
	75	139	156	168
	50	110	127	139
	25	85	99	109
	10	61	74	83
	SD	45	44	45
	Count	16,212	13,331	15,292
6	90	177	195	204
	75	153	167	177
	50	127	140	150
	25	98	111	122
	10	68	82	93
	SD	42	45	44
	Count	10,520	9,218	11,290
7	90	180	192	202
	75	156	165	177
	50	128	136	150
	25	102	109	123
	10	79	88	98
	SD	40	43	41
	Count	6,482	4,058	5,998
8	90	185	199	199
	75	161	173	177
	50	133	146	151
	25	106	115	124
	10	77	84	97
	SD	43	45	41
	Count	5,546	3,496	5,335

Table from Hasbrouck, J., & Tindal, G.A. (2006). Oral reading fluency norms: A valuable assessment tool for reading teachers. *The Reading Teacher, 59,* 639–644. Reprinted with permission of the International Reading Association.

Classroom Management Tool: Fluency Kits

GOAL

- **Implement a management system to aid in the increase of students' reading fluency and accuracy.**

MATERIALS

- ○ Gallon-size zip-top bags (one per student)
- ○ Reading passage with word count at the end of each row
- ○ High-frequency word bank (a template appears in the appendix)
- ○ Leveled readers at students' instructional and independent levels
- ○ Fluency graph (a template appears in the appendix)
- ○ Decodable passage or book
- ○ Timer

TEACHER STEPS: Describe It

- Constructs fluency kits so that material placed in the kit is based on students' reading fluency and accuracy levels. (See Chapter 4 for a detailed description of preparing fluency kits and other intervention materials.)
- Teach students how to use their fluency kit during independent work time or during a workshop.
- Fluency kits are a way to organize these materials and make it easy for students to carry the kits from an independent center to a teacher workstation.
- Pair students using the pairing procedure described previously in this chapter, or group students by ability for intervention work.
- Students can practice the fluency interventions using the materials that are in their fluency kit.

STUDENT STEPS: Do It

- Distribute a fluency kit to each student.
- Say the following:
    - "Partner up, and you'll play One Minute, Please!, reading from the passage in your fluency kit." (Each week, give a new passage to each student at his or her instructional level.)
    - "When I say go, Partner One will read for 1 minute."
    - "Ready, go!" (Begin timing for 1 minute.)
    - "Now it's time for Partner Two to read; ready, go." (Begin timing for 1 minute.)
    - "Count the number of words read correctly in 1 minute for your partners, then record the number on your fluency graphs."

VARIATIONS

- Subject matter reading passages can be added to the fluency kit (e.g., science, social studies, literature stories).
- Vocabulary cards or lists for science, social studies, or other subjects can be included in the fluency kit.

Classroom Management Tool: Eight Pennies

GOAL

- **Implement activities to ensure that enough fluency practice takes place during the school day.**

MATERIALS

- High-frequency word bank (a template appears in the appendix)
- Paragraphs at students' instructional level
- Reading passages at students' independent level
- High-frequency word wall
- Favorite book passages
- Fluency kits

TEACHER STEPS: Describe It

- Place eight pennies in one pocket at the beginning of each school day.
- Each penny represents one fluency intervention activity.
- Reach for a penny from your pocket when it is time for a fluency activity.
- Begin the morning by taking out the first penny and announcing the first Eight Penny intervention activity.
- Students perform the intervention and then move on to whatever is planned for the students at that time.
- After waiting about one half-hour, reach for another penny, and introduce another intervention activity.
- Continue this during the school day until you have transferred all eight pennies from one pocket to another.

STUDENT STEPS: Do It

- Say the following:
  - "First penny!"
  - "Let's play High-Speed Words."
- Students take out a word bank from their fluency kits. "When I say begin, start reading your word bank as quickly as you can. At the end of 1 minute, we'll count the number of words read correctly. Ready? Begin."
- Set the timer for 1 minute. When the timer sounds, say "Stop!"
- Students count the number of words read at the end of that minute and record it on their fluency graph.

VARIATIONS

- As an alternative, you can place eight plastic bangle bracelets on your arm at the beginning of the school day and transfer them to the other arm as you conduct intervention activities.
- Other activities can include choral reading, reading from patterned or predictable books, and using audiobooks as a method of helping students practice fluent reading skills.

AUDIOBOOK RESOURCES

Agency for Instructional Technology
Post Office Box 1397
1800 North Stonelake Drive
Bloomington, IN 47404
800-457-4509
www.ait.net

Audio Bookshelf
174 Prescott Hill Road
Northport, ME 4849
800-234-1713

BDD Audio
1540 Broadway
New York, NY 10063
800-223-6834

Blackboard Entertainment
2647 International Boulevard
Suite 853
Oakland, CA 94601
800-968-2261
www.blackboardkids.com

Books on Tape
Post Office Box 7900
Newport Beach, CA 92658
800-223-6834

DK Multimedia
95 Madison Avenue
New York, NY 10016
800-356-6575
www.dk.com

The Learning Company
6493 Kaiser Drive
Fremont, CA 94555
510-792-2101
www.learningco.com

Listening Library
One Park Avenue
Old Greenwich, CT 06870
800-243-4504

READ 180 Audiobooks
Scholastic
557 Broadway
New York, NY 10012
800-724-6527
www.scholastic.com

Weston Woods
12 Oakwood Avenue
Norwalk, CT 06850
800-243-5020
http://teacher.scholastic.com/products/westonwoods/
    index.htm

BIG IDEA: Fluency with Connected Text

1 What's in the Box?

GOAL

- **Students will write, read, and recognize high-frequency words with mastery and fluency.**

MATERIALS

○ What's in the Box? worksheet (one for each student and one for the teacher; a template appears in the appendix)*

○ High-frequency word bank (a template appears in the appendix) or high-frequency word wall

○ Letter tiles or paper letter tiles

*If you will be asking students and parents to work on the corresponding home activity, be sure to provide a copy of the worksheet for the child to take home with the What's in the Box? Home–School Connection activity page.

TEACHER STEPS: Describe It

- Tell the students that they are going to read high-frequency words aloud in a fun and different way.
- Place the What's in the Box? worksheet in front of you. Put down a tile for the letter that is missing in a high-frequency word on the worksheet (e.g., possibilities for the ☐ are the**m**, the**n**, the**y**, the**e**).
- Say the word(s) aloud.

STUDENT STEPS: Do It

Say the following:
- "Put down the letter that is missing in the high-frequency word." (e.g., possibilities for the ☐ are the**m**, the**n**, the**y**, the**e**).
- "Say the word aloud."
- "Sometimes there is more than one right answer. Find as many answers for one word as you can" (e.g., possibilities for a ☐ are *am*, *an*, *at*, *as*)
- "Continue this procedure until all of the words have been completed on the What's in the Box? worksheet."

ANSWER KEY FOR THE WHAT'S IN THE BOX? WORKSHEET

Possible answers (reading across rows): *an*, *them*, *then*, *with*, *when*, *before*, *are*, *from*, *like*, *give*, *does*, *gave*, *said*, *into*, *look*, *little*, *out* (or *our*), *where*, *which*, *your*, *she*, *they*, *what*, *you'd*

VARIATION

- Take the words completed from the worksheet and have students use the newly formed words to fill in sentences. Students can consult the high-frequency word bank or high-frequency word wall while filling in the sentences.

2 Partner Up: Paired Repeated Readings

GOAL

- **Students will increase reading fluency and accuracy.**

MATERIALS

○ Reading passage at the students' instructional and independent levels

TEACHER STEPS: Describe It

- Students take out reading passages from their fluency kits.
- Students have an instructional and independent passage in their fluency kits so that you can decide which level of reading to focus on during the activity.
- Pair students (refer to the pairing procedure described early in this chapter).
- Partners number off (e.g., 1 and 2) to determine which partners will read first and second.
- Partner One reads a passage three times aloud to his or her partner, and then the partners change roles and Partner Two does the same.
- The partners may give feedback to each other and assist one another during the reading of the passage.

STUDENT STEPS: Do It

Say the following:
- "Take out your fluency kits and remove an instructional passage to prepare for Partner Up."
- "Partner One reads the instructional passage for 1 minute."
- "Partner Two can give feedback to Partner One in the form of positive reinforcement or suggestions for the second reading, like "Great reading!" or "Slow down a little so that you can read the harder words.")
- "Partner One reads the same instructional passage for 1 minute while Partner Two listens and reads along silently."
- "Partner Two can give feedback to Partner One in the form of positive reinforcement or suggestions for the third reading."
- "Partner One reads the same passage for a third time, while Partner Two listens and reads along silently."

This procedure is repeated with Partner Two as the reader.

VARIATIONS

- Partner Up can be integrated into the intervention program with students using an audiotaped story instead of another student as the reading partner.
- The student reads along with the tape and can rewind and play the tape two or three times to build fluency.

BIG IDEA: Fluency with Connected Text

3 High-Speed Words

GOAL

- **Students will read high-frequency words accurately and fluently.**

MATERIALS

- High-frequency word cards (templates appear in the appendix)
- High-frequency word bank (a template appears in the appendix)
- High-frequency word wall
- Timer (optional)

TEACHER STEPS: Describe It

- Pair able students with students who need practice reading high-frequency words.
- Have the pairs take turns reading the high-frequency word cards. Students set the timer and ask their partners to read as many words as they can in 1 minute.
- Students can track their progress by keeping a log with the date and the number of words read per minute or by graphing the number of words read per minute.
- Students begin this activity with high-frequency word cards.
- Students can repeat this activity using a high-frequency word bank at their desk or while standing in front of the high-frequency word wall.

STUDENT STEPS: Do It

Say the following:
- "Partner up to play High Speed Words. When I say begin, Partner One will read as many high frequency words as possible in 1 minute.
- "Place words read correctly in one pile, and words read incorrectly in another. Begin."
- "Now switch and Partner 2 will read the word cards." (Repeat until everyone has had a chance to read for 1 minute.)
- "Take out your fluency graphs and record the number of words you read correctly at the end of the minute."

4 Up Against the Wall

GOAL

- **Students will read and recognize high-frequency words with mastery and fluency.**

MATERIALS

- High-frequency word wall
- Post-it notes with students' names written on them
- Timer

TEACHER STEPS: Describe It

- Tell a student that he or she is going to read high-frequency words from the word wall for 20 seconds. At the end of 20 seconds, the student places his or her Post-it note next to the last word read.
- The student will have 20 seconds to read the words a second time to try to surpass where he or she left off at the end of the first timed period.
- Students are paired and time each other daily until they master all high-frequency words on the word wall.

STUDENT STEPS: Do It

Say the following:

- "I need a volunteer to play Up Against the Wall."
- "When I say begin, start reading the words on the word wall." (The student reads words for 20 seconds.)
- "Place your name on the Post-it note next to the last word you read."
- "I'll set the timer for 20 more seconds, and I want you to try and read more words than you read the first time. Ready, go!" (Repeat this sequence to see if the student can surpass where he or she left off at the end of the first timed period.)

Students partner up and continue this activity throughout the day/week.

BIG IDEA: Fluency with Connected Text

5 Shout It Out

GOAL

- **Students will read and recognize high-frequency words with mastery and fluency.**

MATERIALS

○ High-frequency word bank (a template appears in the appendix) or a high-frequency word bank from your core reading program

○ Index cards
○ Rings or yarn
○ Hole puncher

TEACHER STEPS: Describe It

- Prepare index cards with a hole punched in the upper left hand corner.
- Have students write 10 high-frequency words on index cards. (More advanced students can prepare 15 cards, and students in need of more intensive help can prepare just 5 cards.)
- Fasten all cards together with a ring or yarn.
- Using a matching set of cards, hold up one card at a time. If students recognize the word, they shout it out.
- Students are then divided into pairs for this activity.
- Partner One holds up high-frequency words, one card at a time.
- Partner Two shouts it out if he or she recognizes the word. Partners switch at the end of 1 minute.
- You can conduct this as a whole-class activity using a timer to control the time for each partner to read, with all pairs doing the activity at the same time. Or, students can work in partners during independent work time; when students recognize a word, instead of shouting it out, they whisper.

STUDENT STEPS: Do It

Say the following:

- "We're going to play Shout It Out, so everyone take out your high-frequency word cards from your fluency kits."
- "You will play this game with your partner. Partner One will read first while Partner Two flashes the high-frequency word cards for 1 minute. At the end of one minute you'll switch and Partner Two will read."
- "Begin!"

At the end of 1 minute, remind the students to record their score on the fluency graph.

VARIATION

- This activity is ideal for periods when students need to focus as a whole group. You can flash the high-frequency word cards for a period of 1 minute, and when students recognize a word, they can shout it out.

6 Knock, Knock, Who's There?

GOAL

- **Students will read and recognize high-frequency words with mastery and fluency.**

MATERIALS

○ Two high-frequency word banks with 5–10 words each

○ Chart paper

TEACHER STEPS: Describe It

- List 5–10 high-frequency words on a small piece of chart paper. Create an identical list on another piece of chart paper. (Each week, a different list can be used. Examples of three lists appear below.)
- Tape one high-frequency word chart on the door inside the classroom.
- Tape the second high-frequency word chart on the outside of the classroom door.
- Selected students read the words each time they enter and leave the classroom.
- Repeat this procedure when lining up to leave the classroom.

STUDENT STEPS: Do It

Say the following:
- "The only way to exit and enter the classroom is to read the words on the door."
- "I'll read the words first, then you repeat them after me."
- "Who would like to volunteer to read the words on the door?"

This continues until either all of the children read the words individually, if time permits, or groups of children read the words together (e.g., boys; girls; students wearing red, green, or blue).

Week 1	Week 2	Week 3
a	another	been
about	any	before
across	are	began
after	around	best
again	as	better
all	ask	big
always	at	black
am	away	blue

VARIATION

- For students identified as needing additional help, time the students while reading the high-frequency word bank. The object is for each of these students to improve his or her time with each subsequent reading of the lists, not to compete with the other students.

BIG IDEA: Fluency with Connected Text

7 Concentration

GOAL

- **Students will read and recognize high-frequency words with mastery and fluency.**

MATERIALS

○ Two sets of high-frequency word cards (templates appear in the appendix). Each set contains the same words. The sets can be color coded to distinguish one set from another (e.g., one white set and one yellow set).

TEACHER STEPS: Describe It

- Tell the students you are going to play a matching game with high-frequency word cards.
- Each set of cards is placed face down in rows (e.g., a row of white cards and a row of yellow cards).
- One card is turned over from the first colored set and held up for all students to see (e.g., *was*).
- "Raise your hand if you can read the high-frequency word."
- Call on someone whose hand is raised.
- "What is the word?" (*was*)
- If the word is read correctly, the student who responded gets a turn to choose another high-frequency word card from the second set of cards. If the student chooses a card that matches the first card, he or she chooses the next student.
- If the cards do not match, the cards are returned to their original location, and the next student begins his or her turn.
- Continue this procedure until there are no cards left on the table.

STUDENT STEPS: Do It

Say the following:
- "We're going to play Concentration, a matching game."
- "Partner Up, and take your high-frequency word cards out of your fluency kits." (Be sure to specify which words to use since the partners' cards must match.)
- "Turn your cards face down on your table, and Partner Two will go first."
- "Turn over one card from your own pile and one from your partner's. You want to find the matches. Read each word aloud as you turn it over. If the words match, you keep the match. If they don't match, turn them back over in their place, and it's your partner's turn to play."
- "The game is over when all of the cards are matched. The winner is the one who has the most matches at the end of play."

8 You're It!

GOAL

- **Students will read and recognize high-frequency words with mastery and fluency.**

MATERIALS

❍ High-frequency word cards (templates appear in the appendix)

❍ Box

❍ "You're it!" cards (a template appears in the appendix)*

*A set of "You're it!" cards should be included in the materials provided to students and parents, for use in the matching Home–School Connection activity.

TEACHER STEPS: Describe It

- Tell students that you are going to choose words from the box and read them aloud.
- When you choose a card that says, "You're it!" read all of the high-frequency word cards you have chosen thus far as fast as you can.
- Then return all of the cards to the box to continue the game.
- Pull high-frequency words out of the box one at a time, showing each word to the class.
- Students say each word aloud.
- When a card saying, "You're it!" is pulled from the box, the class reads each of the words that are outside of the box as you hold them up.
- All cards are returned to the box after each round of You're It!
- After the class has done a round of You're It! reading words as a group, have the class play the game with only one student at a time reading words (see Student Steps: Do It).

STUDENT STEPS: Do It

- Say the following:
  - "We're going to play You're It!"
- Call on someone to pull high-frequency words out of the box.
  - "Show each card to the class and we'll read each word aloud."
  - "If you pull out the card that says 'You're it!' you must read all of the high-frequency words pulled out of the box so far."
- After the student takes a turn, choose another student, and play continues.

VARIATIONS

- Students can work in partners.
- The entire class can play while sitting in a circle on the floor. The box is passed around the circle. Each student chooses words from the box and places them on the floor in front of him or her. Limit each student to five cards to ensure that all students have a turn. If a student does not choose a "You're it!" card, he or she keeps the cards out of the box and passes the box to the next person. The game ends after all students have had a turn or when there are no cards left.

9 All Aboard the High-Frequency Word Train

GOAL

- **Students will read and recognize high-frequency words with mastery and fluency.**

MATERIALS

○ High-frequency word cards (templates appear in the appendix)

○ Matching list of high-frequency words from the cards, posted in a visible location in the classroom.

TEACHER STEPS: Describe It

- Invite one student to read the first high-frequency word.
- That student stands up as the first car on the High-Frequency Word Train and reads the first word. If the student reads the word incorrectly, read the word and the student repeats the word after you.
- After the student has read the first word correctly or has repeated the word, the student chooses the next student to read another high-frequency word.
- Continue with each successive student holding up a word card and inviting another student to read it and get aboard the High-Frequency Word Train. Students grab the waist of the student in front of them when they join the train.
- When all students are part of the High-Frequency Word Train, the train travels around the room celebrating the high-frequency words learned during this activity. Using the list of words posted in the classroom, point to each word learned during the activity. The students say each word four times. For example, "Could could could could, he he he he, an an an an, done done done done . . . "

STUDENT STEPS: Do It

- Say the following:
  - "Raise your hand if you can read the high-frequency word."
- Call on someone whose hand is raised.
  - "What is the word?" (*the*)
- Invite the student to come to the front of the class and get aboard the High-Frequency Word Train.
- The student shows another high-frequency word card.
- The student calls on someone whose hand is raised to read the next word (e.g., *with*).
- Invite this student to come to the front of the class and get aboard the High-Frequency Word Train.
- Continue this sequence until all students are aboard the High-Frequency Word Train.
- When all students have been chosen to read a high-frequency word, the first person who began the activity can say, "All aboard the high-frequency word train." Then the class can choo-choo around the classroom to celebrate the new high-frequency words learned.

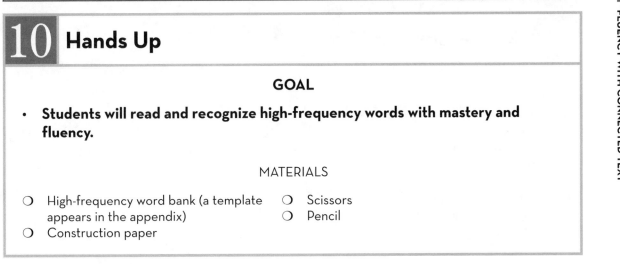

10 Hands Up

GOAL

- **Students will read and recognize high-frequency words with mastery and fluency.**

MATERIALS

- ○ High-frequency word bank (a template appears in the appendix)
- ○ Construction paper
- ○ Scissors
- ○ Pencil

TEACHER STEPS: Describe It

- Students are going to learn 10 high-frequency words in a fun and different way.
- Give students a precut template of a pair of hands.
- Students write their name on the palms of the hands.
- Students write one of the high-frequency word on each finger.
- Students read each high-frequency word aloud.

STUDENT STEPS: Do It

- Say the following:
  - "Write your name in the palm of each hand."
  - "Write this word on the thumb." (e.g., *the*)
  - "Continue with words until all 10 fingers have a word."
  - "Let's read each word together."
- Hands can be placed up on a bulletin board when the activity is over.

VARIATIONS

- Students can read the words on the hands as a fluency activity.
- Students can make their Hands Up high-frequency words using a precut template during independent work time and then practice them for fluency.

BIG IDEA: Fluency with Connected Text

11 Shake, Spill, and Say

GOAL

- **Students will read and recognize high-frequency words with mastery and fluency.**

MATERIALS

○ High-frequency word cards (templates appear in the appendix)   ○ Container with a lid

TEACHER STEPS: Describe It

- Tell the students that they are going to read high-frequency words aloud in a fun and different way.
- Place the high-frequency word cards in a container with a lid.
- Shake the container.
- Spill all of the cards on the table, reading only the cards that are face up.
- This activity is best played with groups of two to four students.

STUDENT STEPS: Do It

- Say to students, "I need two volunteers to play Shake, Spill, and Say."
- Say to the first student, "Shake up the words and spill them on the table or floor."
- Say to the second student, "Read only the words that landed face up, and place them in a pile after you read them."
- "Partner up." Have two sets of partners (four students) play together after students are familiar with the activity.
- This activity works best with groups of two to four students so that no player has to wait too long to take another turn.
- Continue this procedure until all students have a turn to play Shake, Spill, and Say.

VARIATION

- Write high-frequency words on blank dice and play Shake, Spill, and Say.

12 The Magic Hat

GOAL

- **Students will read and recognize high-frequency words with mastery and fluency.**

MATERIALS

- ○ High-frequency word cards (templates appear in the appendix)
- ○ Magic hat
- ○ Magic wand

TEACHER STEPS: Describe It

- Make a magic hat by cutting a black tag board brim to fit around the top of an oatmeal box that has been painted black.
- Make a magic wand by cutting out a star and decorating it with glitter, gluing it to a ruler, and then tying curly ribbon to it.
- Place the high-frequency word cards in the magic hat.
- Tell the students that they are going to read high-frequency words aloud in a fun and different way.
- Wave the wand over the hat and say "Alacazam, alacazee, which high-frequency word can I read with great speed?"
- Pick one high-frequency word card out of the magic hat (e.g., *with*).
- Read the card quickly.
- Pass the magic hat and the magic wand to the next student.

STUDENT STEPS: Do It

- Say the following:
    - "Today we're going to read high frequency words aloud in a fun and different way."
    - "Who would like to be the first magician today?" (Choose one student to demonstrate.)
- Call on someone to say the chant and choose the first high-frequency word from the hat: "Alacazam, alacazee, which high-frequency word can I read with great speed?"
- Pass the magic hat and wand to the next student.
- Continue this procedure until all students have had a chance to pull a word from the magic hat.
- This activity works best with groups of two to four students so that no player has to wait too long to take another turn.

BIG IDEA: Fluency with Connected Text

13 One Minute, Please!

GOAL

- **Students will increase reading fluency and accuracy.**

MATERIALS

- ❍ Reading material at the students' independent and instructional level
- ❍ Timer

- ❍ Fluency graph (a template appears in the appendix)

TEACHER STEPS: Describe It

- This activity can be conducted in pairs or classwide.
- Tell the students they are going to read for speed and accuracy in a fun and different way.
- Students are given a passage at their instructional level first and partnered so that one student is the reader and one is the listener.
- The timer is set for 1 minute, and Partner One begins to read first.
- After 1 minute, the number of words read correctly is recorded on the student's fluency graph.
- Set the timer for 1 minute. Partner Two begins to read.
- Number of words read correctly is recorded on the student's fluency graph.

STUDENT STEPS: Do It

- Say the following:
  - "Partner up because we're going to read for 1 minute."
- Give students an instructional passage with a word count at the end of each line.
- Students are paired in advance (refer to the pairing procedure described early in this chapter).
  - "Partner One starts reading when I give the signal to begin by saying, 'One minute, please.'"
  - "At the end of 1 minute, Partner Two counts and records the number of words read correctly on Partner One's fluency graph."
  - "Then we'll switch roles and Partner Two will read, and Partner One will count and record the number of words read correctly on Partner Two's fluency graph."

VARIATIONS

- This activity can be used with reading passages from a variety of subjects across the curriculum to include passages in social studies, science, language arts, and so forth.
- One Minute, Please! can also be used with the high-frequency word bank or with a high-frequency nouns word wall. (See the appendix for a photocopiable list of high-frequency nouns.)

14 Echo Reading

GOAL

- **Students will increase reading fluency and accuracy.**

MATERIALS

- ○ Paragraph at the students' instructional level

TEACHER STEPS: Describe It

- You or a student reads the first phrase or sentence from the paragraph. The other student reads the same material.
- Continue this procedure to the end of the paragraph. Then, switch roles.
- The other student reads and you or another student rereads until the end of the paragraph.
- Students place these stories in their fluency kits.

STUDENT STEPS: Do It

Classwide

- Tell all students, "Remove the paragraph from your fluency kits for Echo Reading."
- Say, "I will read the first phrase or sentence, and you repeat it after me." Students reread the same material.
- This procedure continues until you reach the end of the paragraph.

In Pairs

- Partner One reads the first phrase or sentence.
- Partner Two reads the same material.
- Continue this procedure until the paragraph is read.
- Students switch roles.

15 Hello/Goodbye

GOAL

- **Students will increase reading fluency and accuracy.**

MATERIALS

○ Copies of a paragraph at the students' independent level, taped to the inside and outside of the classroom door

TEACHER STEPS: Describe It

- Each week a paragraph will be taped inside and outside of the classroom door.
- Students must read the paragraph before they go to an intervention group or before they enter or leave the classroom.
- Ask specific students to read each time until everyone gets a turn, or the entire class can read together in a choral reading activity.
- Students are lined up at the door for this activity.
- Students say "hello" or "goodbye" to you after reading the paragraph.
- Hello/Goodbye can be practiced each time students are lined up to enter or leave the classroom (e.g., leaving/returning for recess/lunch).

STUDENT STEPS: Do It

- Say the following:
    - "Line up at the door, and I will choose one student to read the paragraph on the door."
- Select one student to read the paragraph aloud.
    - "Now let's read the paragraph together as a class."
- If time permits, select another student to read the paragraph.
- After students read the paragraph, they may say "hello" or "goodbye" to you depending on whether the students are entering or leaving the room.

VARIATION

- Paragraphs can be placed in strategic places in the school for further practice (e.g., lunch line, restroom door, library door, office door).

16 Choral Reading

GOAL

- **Students will increase reading fluency and accuracy.**

MATERIALS

- ○ Paragraph/text at the students' instructional level (poetry or a book with predictable story patterns, repeated phrases, or refrains work very well)
- ○ Transparencies or chart paper

TEACHER STEPS: Describe It

- Select a text for use in the Choral Reading intervention.
- Provide copies of the text for everyone in the class.
- Make a transparency of the text and show it on the overhead projector or write the text on chart paper so that all of the students can view it.
- Read the text aloud to the students, emphasizing expression and pauses and intonation changes indicated by punctuation.
- After modeling, ask the students to read aloud with you. Practice reading together chorally several times.
- Students place these stories in their fluency kits for future practice.

STUDENT STEPS: Do It

Classwide

Say the following:
- "Take out your choral reading passage from your fluency kit."
- "I will read the text one time to you while you follow along silently."
- "Now it's your turn to read aloud chorally with me."

When done, students place these stories in their fluency kits for future practice.

BIG IDEA: Fluency with Connected Text

17 Repeated Readings

GOAL

- **Students will increase reading fluency and accuracy.**

MATERIALS

- ○ Paragraph/text at the students' instructional level (poetry or a book with predictable story patterns, repeated phrases, or refrains work very well)
- ○ Timer

TEACHER STEPS: Describe It

- Select a text for use in the Repeated Readings intervention. This can be from the core reading program or any preselected passage.
- Provide copies of the text for a student. (This activity is typically conducted one-to-one with a student rather than with multiple students.)
- Time the student reading for 1 minute. Mark the stopping point on your copy of the text.
- Tell the student how many words he or she read correctly in 1 minute, and correct any errors in reading specific words.
- Record the number of words read correctly on the student's fluency graph.
- Have the student practice reading the text again, and repeat the process of correcting errors and recording the number of words correct per minute on the fluency graph.
- The student repeats this until he or she reads the text without errors.
- The student places this text in his or her fluency kit for future practice.

STUDENT STEPS: Do It

Say the following:
- "The goal is to read a passage many times until you can read it with fluency."
- Ask the student to remove the text from his or her fluency kit for Repeated Readings.
  - "I'm going to set the timer for 1 minute, and we'll count the number of words you read correctly at the end of that minute."
- Set the timer for 1 minute.
- The student reads the text aloud for 1 minute.
- Correct errors and record the number of words read correctly in 1 minute on the student's fluency graph.
- The procedure is repeated until the student can read the text without errors.
- The student places these stories in his or her fluency kit for future practice.

18 Reader's Theater

GOAL

- **Students will increase reading fluency and accuracy.**

MATERIALS

○ A passage chosen by students from their favorite play, poem, or story

TEACHER STEPS: Describe It

- Students choose a passage from a favorite play, poem, or story they have been reading.
- Students practice reading the passage aloud until they are confident they can read it in front of the class or intervention group.
- Students then volunteer to read to the class or the intervention group.
- Give the class time to practice during intervention or workshop time, or assign this practice as homework.

STUDENT STEPS: Do It

- Ask students to take out their favorite passage that they have prepared to read to the class.
- Ask for a student volunteer to read his or her passage aloud.
- Introduce the student by saying, "Ladies and gentlemen, presenting _____ [student's name] who will be reading _____ [title of selection]."
- The student stands in front of the class or in front of the class or intervention group and reads the passage.
- Students applaud when the student is finished, and another student is chosen to read.

VARIATION

- Reader's Theater can also be done in partners. This can be particularly useful when students' favorite passages come from plays.

THEATER WEB SITE RESOURCES

http://bms.westport.k12.ct.us/mccormick/rt/whatrt.htm
http://loiswalker.com/catalog/teach.html
http://www.aaronshep.com/rt/
http://www.aaronshep.com/rt/RTE.html
http://www.fictionteachers.com/classroomtheater/whatis.html
http://www.lisablau.com/scriptomonth.html
http://www.proteacher.com/070173.shtml
http://www.readingonline.org/electronic/elec_index.asp?HREF=carrick/index.html
http://www.stemnet.nf.ca/CITE/langrt.htm
http://www.teachingheart.net/readerstheater.htm

19 Poetry Theater

GOAL

- **Students will increase reading fluency and accuracy.**

MATERIALS

○ A favorite poem chosen by students

TEACHER STEPS: Describe It

- Students choose a favorite poem.
- Students practice reading the poem aloud until they are confident they can read it in front of the class or intervention group.
- Students then volunteer to read to the class or the intervention group.
- Give the class time to practice during intervention, workshop time, or for homework.

STUDENT STEPS: Do It

- Ask students to take out their favorite poem that they have prepared to read to the class.
- Ask for a student volunteer to read his or her poem aloud.
- Introduce the student by saying, "Ladies and gentlemen, presenting _____ [student's name] who will be reading _____ [title of selection]."
- The student stands in front of the class or in front of the class or intervention group and reads the poem.
- Students applaud when the student is finished, and another student is chosen to read.

VARIATION

- Poetry Theater can also be done in partners. Partners can read to each other, or partners can support one another and read chorally in front of the class.

Integrating Vocabulary Development and Comprehension Instruction into Intervention

The five Big Ideas of reading—phonological awareness, alphabetic principle, fluency with connected text, vocabulary development, and comprehension—are essential ingredients of a beginning reading program. For intervention, teachers need to focus on the critical skills that individual students need to be successful in the general reading curriculum. In this book, we provide a set of intervention activities to boost students' skills in specific aspects of phonemic awareness, decoding (alphabetic principle), and oral reading fluency. Vocabulary development and comprehension, the remaining two Big Ideas of reading (National Institute of Child Health and Human Development, 2000; Simmons & Kame'enui, 1998), are different from the other Big Ideas. Like the other Big Ideas, they provide a foundation for later literacy learning, but unlike the other areas, they continue to develop throughout the school years and become the main focus of reading instruction by the intermediate grades.

Because vocabulary development and comprehension are not easily broken into component subskills as are the other areas of reading, they are typically taught throughout the reading curriculum and even across the curriculum in other subject areas. Teachers continually highlight and reinforce students' understanding of vocabulary words, passage comprehension, and strategies for independent reading. Rather than design intervention activities that focus solely on vocabulary development or comprehension, in this chapter we demonstrate how to integrate vocabulary development and comprehension activities into intervention lessons. Each section begins with a description of a lesson design that you can use to plan your vocabulary development and comprehension instruction. The lesson design is followed by a discussion of several research-based strategies.

English language learners often experience significant challenges in learning English vocabulary while learning to read in English. These students will benefit from extensive vocabulary and comprehension support during reading instruction. Teachers often integrate the teaching of English vocabulary and language structure into their reading lessons. For struggling readers who are also ELLs, intervention time is a good time to reinforce their vocabulary and comprehension development. Chapter 2 explains the STAR strategy, a simple approach to systematic vocabulary and English language support for English language learners.

VOCABULARY DEVELOPMENT

The vocabulary development strategies described in this chapter can be integrated into your phonemic awareness, alphabetic principle, and fluency intervention instruction. It is important to teach and reinforce vocabulary before, during, and after instruction. In this portion of the chapter you will learn how to design effective vocabulary lessons and implement engaging instructional activities.

Designing Effective Vocabulary Development Instruction

The following lesson design is based on current research in vocabulary instruction. Each of the seven steps is described first to orient you to the process. An example of how to apply this design to teach the word *favorite* follows the description of the seven steps.

1. Develop Student-Friendly Definitions

Effective vocabulary instruction must begin with a student-friendly definition that conveys the connotation of the target word (how it is typically used) in easy-to-understand, everyday language (Beck et al., 2002).

2. Provide Examples

In this step, students are given examples of the target word. It is critical that the students understand and are able to relate to the examples.

3. Provide Non-examples

Non-examples, or contrasting examples, pinpoint the definition by providing instances in which the definition does not apply. Use non-examples to help clarify any misunderstandings regarding the connotation of the target word.

4. Discuss the Word with Students

Incorporate students' background knowledge by asking them to discuss what they know about the target word. Students benefit from the contributions of their classmates. Students who have no knowledge of the word's meaning learn a great deal from their peers during these discussions.

5. Check for Understanding

As you proceed through the vocabulary lesson and at the end of the lesson, be sure to periodically review the target word's meanings.

6. Provide Multiple Exposures to the Word

Students must have meaningful multiple exposures for a word to become part of their listening, speaking, reading, and writing vocabularies. Several vocabulary strategies are described later in this chapter that will help you accomplish this goal.

7. Discuss the Word in Context

For words that students read in context, be sure to discuss each word as students encounter the word in the selection. Relate the word to the student-friendly definition and examples you used to teach the word.

Example: Teaching the Word *Favorite*

1. Develop Student-Friendly Definitions

"Your favorite is something or someone you like the *most*."

2. Provide Examples

"For example, reading was my favorite subject in school. It is the subject that I liked the *most*. When you read, you can learn so many new and interesting things."

"I have other favorite things. The ice cream flavor I like the *most* is rocky road. It's my favorite because it is chocolate ice cream, the flavor I like the most, with marshmallows and nuts mixed in."

"My favorite place to go on the weekends is the beach. I like it the *most* because of the sound of the waves, the fresh air, and the feel of the sand on my bare feet."

3. Provide Non-examples

"The opposite of your favorite thing is something you don't like or dislike the *most*. For example, the vegetable I dislike the *most* is Brussels sprouts because they taste bitter to me."

"One thing I have to do everyday that I don't like or dislike the *most* is driving on the freeway. I dislike it the most because there is always so much traffic. It takes me a long time to get where I am going, and it is boring sitting in the car."

4. Discuss the Word with Students

"Tell me about a person, place, or thing that is your favorite."

5. Check for Understanding

"Before we go on to the next word, let's review the meanings of the word you just learned."

6. Provide Multiple Exposures to the Word

"I am going to say the names of things people like to do. First, listen to all of them. Then, I will say them again. The second time I say them I want you to raise your hand when you hear the name of your *favorite* thing to do. Be ready to tell me why it is your *favorite*."
Ride a bicycle
Play games
Watch television
Read a book
Listen to CDs

7. Discuss the Word in Context

"In our story, Jake said that the giraffe was his favorite animal at the zoo. If the giraffe is his favorite animal, it means he likes it the most of all the animals he saw at the zoo that day."

Vocabulary Strategies

Many strategies will help you provide the practice and multiple exposures students need to learn a word well. A few of these strategies are explained next.

Semantic Feature Analysis

Semantic feature analysis (SFA) is a strategy that addresses associations among semantically related words. An SFA chart consists of semantically related words and semantic features. These features are words or phrases that describe characteristics shared by some of the words. Semantic features also distinguish a word from other meanings.

To construct an SFA chart, do the following:

1. Write the semantically related words along the left-hand side.

2. Write the semantic features along the top.

3. At point where the word and feature intersect, help students determine the extent of the relationship using the following scale:
    +   The feature applies to the word.
    −   There is no relationship between the feature and the word.
    ?   No decision can be made without more information.
    0   The feature applies sometimes.

	wheels	wings	land	water	air
bicycle	+	–	+	–	–
car	+	–	+	–	–
bus	+	–	+	–	–
train	+	–	+	–	–
truck	+	–	+	–	–
boat	0	–	–	+	–
helicopter	–	–	–	0	+
airplane	+	+	0	0	+
space shuttle	–	–	–	–	+

Figure 9. Semantic feature analysis.

In the SFA chart shown in Figure 9, students determine the relationship of modes of transportation to five semantic features.

Semantic Mapping

Semantic maps provide a visual depiction of the relationships between words (see Figure 10 for an example). To develop a semantic map, the major concept or key word is placed in the center. Related terms are placed in squares, rectangles, and/or circles and connected with lines to illustrate the relationships to the major concept. Additional information such as characteristics and examples can also be added.

Word Map

Word maps (Schwartz & Raphael, 1985) help illustrate the connotation or function of the word (see Figure 11 for an example). Generally, word maps include a simple definition, attributes or characteristics, examples, and non-examples for the target word.

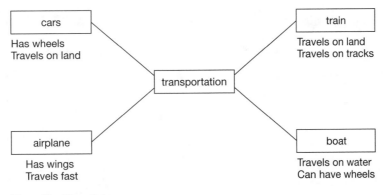

Figure 10. Semantic map.

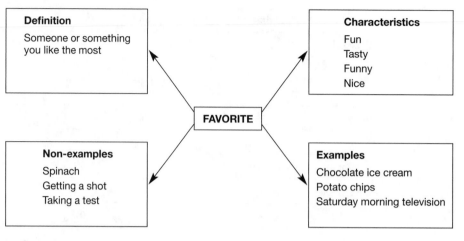

Definition	Characteristics
Someone or something you like the most	Fun Tasty Funny Nice

FAVORITE

Non-examples	Examples
Spinach Getting a shot Taking a test	Chocolate ice cream Potato chips Saturday morning television

Figure 11. Word map.

Frayer Model

The Frayer model (Buehl, 1995) is a variation on the word map that uses a slightly different visual organization (see Figure 12 for an example of the Frayer model).

Venn Diagram

A Venn diagram is used to compare and contrast two concepts or key ideas (see Figure 13 for an example). To construct a Venn diagram, draw two interconnecting circles. Above each circle, write the terms that are being compared and contrasted. The unique characteristics of each concept are written in the large portion of the circle. Characteristics that are common to both concepts are listed where the circles intersect.

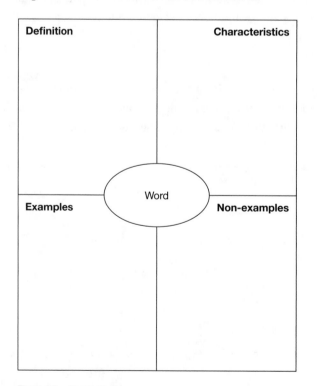

Figure 12. Frayer model.

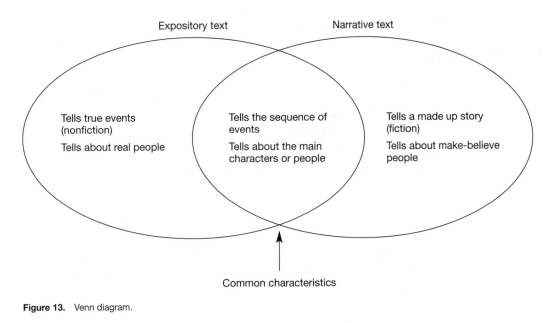

Figure 13. Venn diagram.

Learning Vocabulary from Context: Fix-Up Strategies

Extensive reading is an effective way to increase vocabulary knowledge. For this method to be effective, students must be taught how to derive meaning from words in the text. Klingner, Vaughn, and Schumm (1998) identified four fix-up strategies that can help students with this task:

1. Reread the sentence with the word and look for key ideas to help you figure it out. Think about what makes sense.

2. Reread the sentences before and after the word looking for clues.

3. Look for a prefix or suffix in the word that might help.

4. Break apart the word and look for smaller words you know.

When students encounter a word they do not know, they start with the first fix-up strategy and work their way through until they find the one that helps them determine the word's meaning. The first two strategies are based on context clues, whereas the third and fourth strategies are based on structural analysis. The fix-up strategies cannot be used when the context in which the word appears or the structure of the word does not lend itself to determining its meaning. Those words, if conceptually central to understanding the selection, must be explicitly taught.

Generative-Level Strategies

Generative activities are higher-order thinking activities requiring students to apply the information about a word's meaning in unique ways resulting in responses that demonstrate their understanding of the word. Beck and her colleagues (2002) have developed several engaging generative-level activities. Four are explained next.

Questions, Reasons, and Examples

This activity requires children to answer a question about the target word and give reasons for their responses.

"I'm going to ask you some questions about your *favorite* things. Be ready to tell me why they are your favorite."

"What is your favorite book? Why?"

"What is your favorite TV show? Why?"

"What is your favorite thing to do when you are not in school? Why?"

Word Associations

After teaching three or four words, students are to link a new word by answering questions. The following is an example of a word association activity after teaching the words *favorite, rapidly, cheerful,* and *frequently*.

"Which word goes with *airplane?* Why?"

"Which word goes with *chocolate ice cream?* Why?"

"Which word goes with *smiling?* Why?"

Idea Completion

Idea completion requires students to integrate student-friendly definitions into context. Below is an example of idea completion using the target words *favorite, rapidly, cheerful,* and *frequently*.

"Gil's mother made him a chocolate cake for his birthday because . . . "

"Everyone liked Mrs. Taylor because . . . "

"The principal knew Tyler very well because . . . "

"Celeste won the race because . . . "

Making Choices

In this activity, children are asked to make choices and justify or explain why they made those choices. In the following example, students identify their favorite activity at school and explain why the activity is their favorite.

"I am going to say the names of some things you do at school. First, listen to all of the names. Then, I will say them again. The second time I say them I want you to raise your hand when you hear your favorite. Be ready to tell me why it is your *favorite*."

Reading

Arithmetic

P.E.

Taking a test

Science

COMPREHENSION

This section describes a lesson design that will help you teach comprehension strategies explicitly and describes research-based comprehension strategies. The strategies can be implemented in a large-group setting or in small groups with students who need reading comprehension intervention.

Designing Effective Explicit Reading Comprehension Instruction

Comprehension is defined as students' ability to construct meaning from text. Students comprehend a text when they set a purpose for reading, integrate background knowledge with new information, monitor their comprehension, use comprehension strategies, and tap their knowledge of vocabulary and the structure of language.

Reading comprehension strategy instruction must be explicit. To accomplish this goal, teachers must incorporate metacognitive knowledge into their instruction by telling students what the strategy is and when, why, and how it is used. Metacognitive knowledge is taught by using the three phases of scaffolded instruction: modeling using think-alouds, teacher-assisted or guided practice, and independent practice.

Metacognitive Knowledge

Simply stated, metacognition is thinking about one's thinking. Metacognitive knowledge refers to a reader's ability to know and use strategies he or she needs to successfully understand the text. There are three categories of metacognitive knowledge: declarative, procedural, and conditional knowledge.

Declarative knowledge consists of facts, rules, concepts, and strategies that are stored in the reader's long-term memory. Examples of declarative knowledge include students' knowledge and understanding of reading comprehension strategies, the steps of the writing process, or the rules of grammar.

Procedural knowledge pertains to how declarative knowledge is implemented. For example, students who can state the steps of the strategy for writing a summary have shown declarative knowledge, whereas students who use the steps to compose an appropriate summary have demonstrated procedural knowledge.

Conditional knowledge involves knowing when or under what conditions a strategy should be used. For example, after reading a portion of a selection, skilled readers know they should summarize what they have read or generate questions to monitor their comprehension.

Phases of Scaffolded Instruction

Effective explicit reading comprehension strategy lessons are designed using the three phases of scaffolded instruction.

1. *Modeling phase:* The teacher makes the thinking process public by modeling each step of the strategy while thinking aloud.

2. *Teacher-assisted or guided practice phase:* The teacher facilitates students' learning by guiding them through the strategy.

3. *Independent practice phase:* The students complete the strategy on their own.

Reading Comprehension Strategies

The comprehension strategies in this chapter are categorized within the three phases of reading instruction: before reading, during reading, and after reading. Most of the strategies can be used in more than one phase. For example, background knowledge statements and predictions students make before reading can be reviewed and, if necessary, revised as the selection is being read and/or after the entire selection is read. Similarly, graphic organizers or story maps can be completed during and/or after reading the text.

Strategies to Implement Before Reading

Strategies implemented before reading help students set the purpose for reading by accessing their background knowledge and allowing them to make predictions about what they might learn and what they want to learn from the selection.

K-W-L: What I Know, What I Want to Know, What I Learned

Several strategies can be used both to access students' background knowledge and pique their interested in reading the selection by asking them what they want to learn. The most well-known and widely used is Ogle's (1986) K-W-L strategy (What I Know, What I Want to Know, What I Learned). You can use the K-W-L strategy by following these steps in conjunction with a K-W-L chart (see Figure 14):

1. In the *K* column, record what students think they know about the selection.

2. In the *W* column, record what students want to learn.

What I Know K	What I Want to Know W	What I Learned L
You can call 911 to get help when there is a fire. Fires can kill people. Firefighters work in the fire station. Fire trucks have loud sirens.	What kinds of equipment do they need to put out a fire? What are their clothes made of so that they won't catch on fire? How do they get someone out of a house that is on fire?	Firefighters have to go to school to learn how to do their jobs. Firefighters work as a team to save people. Their clothes are heavy and are made of material that won't catch on fire.

Figure 14. K-W-L chart.

3. After students have read the entire selection or a portion of it, return to the KWL chart to confirm or amend the information in the *K* column (What I Know).

4. Complete the *L* column (What I Learned) by writing the students' answers to the questions in the *W* column (What I Want to Know) and entering other pertinent information students have learned from the selection.

Preview Strategy

The preview strategy, developed by Klingner and colleagues (1998), is a variation on the theme of accessing background knowledge and determining what students want to learn. The preview strategy consists of two parts: brainstorm (think about what you already know about the topic) and predict (think about what you might learn).

Implement the preview strategy by following these steps:

1. Have students preview what they are going to read by looking at the title, subheadings, illustrations, graphs, and skimming the text for key words.

2. Ask students to brainstorm by thinking about what they have already learned about the topic.

3. Record students' responses on the board or on chart paper.

4. Ask students to predict what they think they might learn.

5. Record students' responses on the board or on chart paper.

6. Review the brainstorm and predictions after students have read a portion or all of the selection. Revise any statements that were not accurate.

Strategies to Implement During and After Reading

The strategies described in this section can be implemented during and/or after reading. You may stop at any point in a reading selection and ask students to generate a main idea, answer questions, summarize what they have read, or add information to a story map or a graphic organizer.

Main Idea Strategy

Generating main idea statements is a strategy that promotes "deep processing" (Armbruster & Wilkinson, 1991) of text, which helps students understand and remember what they have read. Deep processing involves selecting, organizing, and integrating information. *Selecting* refers to a reader's ability to focus on important information. *Organizing* involves arranging the information into a meaningful structure. The process of linking the information to one's background knowledge is referred to as *integrating*.

The main idea strategy is based on the work of Klingner and colleagues (1998), who labeled it "get the gist," and Fuchs, Fuchs, Mathes, and Simmons (1997), who coined the term "paragraph shrinking." When students generate main idea statements, they read, identify the most important information in the paragraph and state that idea in a concise sentence containing 10 or fewer words.

The strategy consists of three steps:

1. Name who or what the paragraph is mostly about.

2. Tell the most important information about the who or what.

3. State or write the main idea in 10 words or fewer.

Retelling

Fuchs and colleagues (1997) developed a strategy to help students retell the sequence of events in a story or information they learned from expository text. In this simple strategy, the teacher asks two questions: "What did you learn first? What did you learn next?" The teacher continues asking the second question until the students have completed retelling the events.

Summarizing

The critical attribute that differentiates retelling from summarizing is conciseness. Typically, when retelling, students recount everything they can remember from the passage. A summary, by contrast, is a condensed version of the main ideas in the passage. An effective way to teach summarization is to combine it with the main idea strategy, whereby the main ideas from the text can be crafted into a concise summary (see Figure 15 for an example).

Asking Questions

Teacher- and student-generated questions help students think about and monitor their comprehension of the important ideas, concepts, and facts in a passage. Asking questions also helps students prepare for tests and class discussions.

For students to be successful in this comprehension-monitoring activity, they need to learn how to generate and answer literal, inferential, and evaluative questions. That is, some questions should address information that is stated explicitly in the text, whereas other questions require students to integrate what they have read with their background knowledge. Students must also be prepared to respond to questions whose answers depend solely on the students' background knowledge.

Main ideas
1. Mammals have fur. 2. Mammals have babies and take care of them. 3. Mammals have to keep warm in cold weather. 4. Mammals are all different sizes.
Summary
Mammals are different-sized furry animals that have to protect their babies and stay warm in winter.

Figure 15. Main ideas and summary.

Raphael (1986) developed a strategy called Question–Answer Relationships (QAR), which is based on a taxonomy of questions developed by Pearson and Johnson (1978). The taxonomy classifies questions according to their relationship to two sources of information that will help the reader answer the questions. These sources are the text and the reader's background knowledge. Raphael translated the theory behind these classifications and developed four question types: Right There, Think and Search, Author and You, and On My Own.

1. *Right There:* The answer is easy to find in the reading. The words used to make up the question and the words used to answer the question are *right there* in the same sentence.

   Example: *What color was the car?*

2. *Think and Search:* The answer to the question is in the reading. The answer is made up of information that comes from more than one sentence or paragraph. You have to put together information from different parts of the reading to find the answer.

   Example: *Where were the three places Jake looked to try to find his wallet?*

3. *Author and You:* The answer to the question is not in the reading. Think about what the author tells you and what you already know.

   Example: *How did Pam feel about being alone in the house?*

4. *On My Own:* The answer to the question is not in the reading. You can answer the question by thinking about what you already know.

   Example: *What favorite things would you take if you were going on a long trip?*

Think-Pair-Share

Think–Pair–Share (McTighe & Lyman, 1988) is designed to increase the likelihood that students will participate in class discussions by providing them with time to discuss the material with a partner first. This strategy is particularly helpful for English language learners who may need time to rehearse their responses with a partner before stating them orally to the entire class. The Think–Pair–Share strategy can be used to discuss comprehension questions during and after reading.

Think: Students individually think about the answer to the question.

Pair: Students talk about their thoughts with a partner. Both students must be prepared to share their thoughts with the class.

Share: Students share their responses during the class discussion.

Graphic Organizers

Over the years, a variety of names have been given to graphic representations of text: graphic organizer, semantic map, information organizer, tree diagram, branching diagram, and so forth. Although the names are different, the purpose is essentially the same: to improve stu-

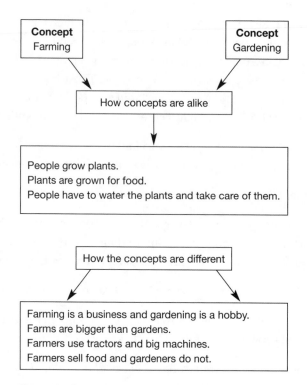

Figure 16. Compare/contrast graphic organizer.

dents' comprehension by illustrating relationships between and among critical concepts. Two types of graphic organizers are discussed next.

- *Compare/contrast:* In the compare/contrast graphic organizer, the two concepts being compared are written at the top of the organizer (see Figure 16). Through discussion, students determine how these concepts are alike and different. This organizer is flexible in that it can be used for both narrative (fiction) and expository (informational) text. For example, students can compare and contrast two stories, two characters, or two social studies or science concepts.

- *Story map:* Story maps are used for narrative text. Story mapping is based on research conducted by cognitive psychologists and anthropologists who developed a set of rules (story grammar) by analyzing folktales. Simply put, the main character has a problem, goal, or conflict. After making attempts to resolve the problem or conflict or to reach the goal, the protagonist either succeeds or fails to do so. Story mapping can be used for conducting character analysis, analyzing characters' reactions, and determining themes.

  Although there are many variations of story maps, they are usually divided into sections, each containing one story grammar element. An example is provided in Figure 17. Teachers may ask students to complete a story map during or after a selection is read. Students can complete maps as a class, in pairs, in small groups, or independently.

Main character(s)
Setting
Problem/goal/conflict
Plot
Attempts at resolution 1. 2. 3. 4. 5.
Resolution/conclusion Resolution: The problem/conflict is solved or the goal is achieved. Conclusion: The problem/conflict is not solved or the goal is not achieved.
Theme

Figure 17. Story map.

Comprehending Narrative Text: Story Grammar Questions

The questions below address story grammar elements. They can be asked during and/or after reading narrative text. They are designed to check comprehension, stimulate class discussion, and help your students complete a story map.

Main Character

Who is the main character?

Who is telling the story?

Who is the character you know most about?

Who is the most important character in this story?

Around whom does the problem/conflict revolve?

Who is trying to achieve a goal?

Setting

When does the story take place?

Where does the story take place?

Problem/Goal/Conflict

What problem did the main character face?

What is the main character's goal?

What was the main character trying to accomplish?

What does the main character want to do?

What type of conflict is the main character facing?

What is the main character's conflict?

Attempts

How does the main character try to solve the problem?

How does the main character try to achieve his goal?

How does the main character try to resolve the conflict?

Resolution

How does the main character solve the problem?

How is the problem solved?

How does the main character achieve the goal?

How does the main character resolve the conflict?

Conclusions

What happened at the end of the story?

How did the story end?

Theme

What is the author trying to tell us?

What is the author trying to say?

Why do you think the author wrote this story?

What did the main character learn at the end of the story?

Retelling the Story

Students can use the information from a story map to retell a story (see Figure 18). Charting the story's beginning, middle, and end helps students organize their thoughts by breaking down the retell into three main parts, each addressing at least one story grammar element.

Comprehending Expository Text

Following is an example of how comprehension strategies can be integrated into instruction when using expository or informational text.

Before Reading

Look at the title and pictures.

What do you already know about the topic?

What have you read, heard, or seen about this topic?

What do you want to learn about the topic?

During and After Reading

The following strategies can be used while reading portions of the text and after reading the entire selection:

Summarization
Tell what you have learned.

Generating Questions
Think of a question you would like one of your classmates to answer. Be ready to say whether the answer is correct.

Beginning	Middle	End
Who is the main character?	How did the main character try to solve the problem, achieve the goal or resolve the conflict?	How was the problem/conflict solved or the goal achieved?
Where did the story take place?		What happened at the end of the story?
What is the problem/goal/conflict?		

Figure 18. Story map for retelling a story.

Think of a question and its answer. Be ready to share the question and answer with the class.

What questions do you want to ask to help you understand the topic?

Main Idea

What is the main who or what of the paragraph we just read?

What is the most important information?

Say the main idea in 10 words or fewer.

Comprehension Questions

(Ask students questions that address the four question types: Right There, Think and Search, Author And You, and On My Own.)

Background Knowledge/Predictions

Review information students knew about the topic.

Confirm or revise the statements based on the information read.

Discuss information students wanted to learn about the topic.

Graphic Organizer

Add information to the graphic organizer.

SUMMARY

This chapter has presented a variety of vocabulary and reading comprehension strategies that will help your students understand narrative and expository text. It is important to teach the strategies explicitly, one at a time. Once students are able to complete a strategy with little prompting from you, teach them a new one. Teaching students a few new strategies simultaneously is confusing and increases the amount of time it will take for them to use the strategies independently. Remember, less is more!

Home-School
Connection Activities

The Home-School Connection activity numbers correspond with the classroom activity numbers in Chapters 5–7. The numbering of the home activities is not consecutive because some classroom activities do not have a matching home activity.

PHONOLOGICAL AWARENESS

FOCUS ON: Rhyming

FOCUS ON: Onset-Rime and Phonemic Awareness

FOCUS ON: Segmenting and Blending

ALPHABETIC PRINCIPLE

FOCUS ON: Letter-Sound Correspondence

FOCUS ON: Adding Sounds

FOCUS ON: Deleting Sounds

FOCUS ON: Substituting Sounds

FOCUS ON: Long Vowel Spelling Patterns

FOCUS ON: Variant Vowel Spelling Patterns

FLUENCY

② Rhyming Word Families

GOAL

- The student will develop an understanding of the concepts of rhyme and rhyming and how rhyme is typically used.

MATERIALS

○ Word bank for this activity

MODEL

Say the following:
- "I'm going to say a word and rhyme it with as many words as I can, using the alphabet as my guide: *bowl/coal, hole/mole, pole/poll, role/roll, sole/soul.*"

NOW IT'S YOUR TURN

Say the following:
- "I'm going to say a word, and you rhyme it with as many words as you can, using the alphabet as your guide." (Say a word from the word bank.)
- "What's the word?"

EXTRA SUPPORT

- If the child has difficulty rhyming, model the correct response and ask the child to repeat it after you.

Word Bank: Words with Possible Rhyming Answers

1. bowl (coal, hole, mole, pole/poll, role/roll, sole/soul)
2. cat (at, bat, fat, hat, mat, pat, rat, sat, vat)
3. spoon (baboon, cartoon, dune, goon, June, moon, noon, raccoon)
4. flour (cower, glower, hour, our, power, scour, sour, tower)
5. egg (beg, leg, peg)
6. milk (bilk, ilk, silk; not many others)
7. butter (apple butter, bread and butter, cutter, clutter, flutter, gutter, mutter, peanut butter, shutter)
8. pan (an, Ann, bran, can, Dan, fan, flan, Japan, man, pecan, pelican, plan, ran, tan, van)
9. spatula (Ashtabula, Dracula, hula)
10. stove (cove, dove, drove, grove, wove)
11. syrup (cheer up, I give up)
12. batter (chatter, clatter, fatter, matter, patter)
13. flipper (clipper, dipper, hipper, kipper, nipper, ripper, slipper, zipper)

Interventions for Reading Success by Diane Haager, Joseph A. Dimino, and Michelle Pearlman Windmueller

Rhyming Match

GOAL

- **The student will practice recognizing rhyming word pairs.**

MATERIALS

❍ Word bank for this activity

❍ 20 index cards, with hand-drawn or clip art pictures of words in word bank attached to the cards

MODEL

- Show each picture card to the child, and have him or her name each picture.
- Demonstrate how each picture rhymes with one other picture.
- Explain that you are going to play a matching game with the picture cards.
- Mix up the cards. Place them face down on the table in neat rows.
- Play the game like Concentration, turning over two cards in each turn. If the cards rhyme, they are a match and the student may keep the pair.

NOW IT'S YOUR TURN

- Say the following:
  - "Today we are going to play a matching game. Each person is going to have a turn. When it is your turn, you will turn over two cards. If the pictures on the cards rhyme, you have made a match and you can keep the cards. If the pictures do not rhyme, you must turn them back over in exactly the same place. The person with the most rhyming pairs is the winner. Watch me take a turn."
- Turn over two cards and say the words. Show how to compare the words to see if they rhyme. Replace the cards, and remix them if necessary.

VARIATION

You can add more picture cards to make the game harder or to accommodate a larger group.

Word Bank: Words with Possible Rhyming Answers			
bed	head	dog	log
bell	well	dot	pot
bone	phone	man	can
car	jar	pin	fin
cat	bat	ten	pen

Rhyme Around the Room

GOAL

- **The student will make rhymes using objects around the room.**

MATERIALS

○ Timer

MODEL

- Tell the child you are going to play a game using objects around the room.
- Tell the child that when you set the timer and say, "Go," he or she will have 3 minutes to get objects in the room.
- Explain that there are three important rules for playing the game. First, the child can only bring an object to you if he or she can think of a *real* word that rhymes with it. When the child returns, he or she will have to say the name of the object and its rhyming word. Second, the child must move carefully around the room so as not to break anything or hurt him or herself. Third, the child must return the objects to their proper place when the game is finished.
- Be sure to tell the child that he or she can just point to an object if it cannot be moved. For example, the light on the ceiling might rhyme with *kite*.

NOW IT'S YOUR TURN

- Demonstrate by quietly getting an object such as a pen and giving a rhyming word such as hen.
- To demonstrate the rule that the child must think of a rhyming word, give him or her an untimed opportunity to practice by finding one object and saying its rhyme. Give feedback as necessary. Practice until the child understands the concept.
- Set the timer, and say, "Go."

VARIATION

Have the child find pairs of objects that rhyme. The child may only bring back objects if he or she can find another object in the room that rhymes with it (e.g., *fan/can*).

Segmenting and Blending Words with Onsets and Rimes

GOAL

- **The student will segment and blend onsets and rimes.**

MATERIALS

- ○ Word bank for this activity
- ○ Blank colored tiles, small blocks, or paper squares

MODEL

- Say the following:
- "I'm going to break apart the word *fox*: /f/ /ŏx/."
- "Listen and watch while I move one square down for each part I say: /f/ /ŏx/."

 **/f/ /ŏx/**

- "The word is *fox*."
- Say the word while pushing the squares together.

NOW IT'S YOUR TURN

Say the following:
- "Use your squares to show the sounds in _____." (Choose a word from Column 1. See the answer in Column 2.)
- "Push the squares together and blend the sounds."
- "What's the word?"

EXTRA SUPPORT

- If your child has trouble breaking apart and/or blending the parts of the word, model the correct response and ask the child to repeat it after you.

Word Bank on following page

Interventions for Reading Success by Diane Haager, Joseph A. Dimino, and Michelle Pearlman Windmueller

Word Bank

1. Word	2. Sounds	1. Word	2. Sounds
base	/b/ /ās/	lamb	/l/ /ăm/
bone	/b/ /ōn/	lie	/l/ /ī/
can	/k/ /ăn/	mat	/m/ /ăt/
cone	/k/ /ōn/	meat	/m/ /ēt/
dear	/d/ /ēr/	pat	/p/ /ăt/
doe	/d/ /ō/	pin	/p/ /ĭn/
fan	/f/ /ăn/	rice	/r/ /īs/
fill	/f/ /ĭl/	row	/r/ /ō/
game	/g/ /ām/	sand	/s/ /ănd/
gill	/g/ /ĭl/	soap	/s/ /ōp/
hat	/h/ /ăt/	toe	/t/ /ō/
jam	/j/ /ăm/	wake	/w/ /āk/
kit	/k/ /ĭt/	year	/y/ /ēr/

(10) Adding an Initial Consonant Sound

GOAL

- **The student will identify the initial sound that has been added to a word to make a new word.**

MATERIALS

- Word bank for this activity
- Blank colored tiles, small blocks, or paper squares

MODEL

- Say the following:
  - "old-mold"
  - "Listen and watch while I move one square down for each part I say: /m/ /ōld/."
- As you break apart the second word, put down one square for each part you say. Use a square of a different color to represent the first sound.
- Say "old-mold." Remove the first square as you say the first word. Add it back as you say the second word.

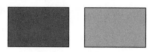 **/m/ /ōld/**

- Say, "When I add the sound /m/ to *old*, the word is *mold*."

NOW IT'S YOUR TURN

Say the following:
- "The words are _____." (Choose a word pair from Column 1.)
- "Put down one square for each part in the word." (Say the second word in the pair.)
- "Break apart the word." (See the answer in Column 2.)
- "What sound did you add to change _____ to _____?" (See the answer in Column 3.)

EXTRA SUPPORT

- If your child has trouble breaking apart the word and/or determining the added sound, model the correct response and ask the child to repeat it after you.

Word Bank on following page

Word Bank

1. Word pairs	2. Sounds	3. Added sound
at-bat	/b/ /ăt/	/b/
eat-beat	/b/ /ēt/	/b/
ice-dice	/d/ /īs/	/d/
oil-foil	/f/ /oil/	/f/
am-ham	/h/ /ăm/	/h/
old-hold	/h/ /ōld/	/h/
ash-cash	/k/ /ăsh/	/k/
oil-coil	/k/ /oil/	/k/
it-kit	/k/ /ĭt/	/k/
and-land	/l/ /ănd/	/l/
owe-low	/l/ /ow/	/l/
ate-mate	/m/ /āt/	/m/
old-mold	/m/ /ōld/	/m/
aim-name	/n/ /ām/	/n/
odd-nod	/n/ /ŏd/	/n/
ace-pace	/p/ /ās/	/p/
am-ram	/r/ /ăm/	/r/
ink-rink	/r/ /ĭnk/	/r/
am-Sam	/s/ /ăm/	/s/
ink-sink	/s/ /ĭnk/	/s/
old-told	/t/ /ōld/	/t/
ink-wink	/w/ /ĭnk/	/w/

Adding a Final Consonant Sound

GOAL

- **The student will identify the final sound that has been added to a word to make a new word.**

MATERIALS

○ Word bank for this activity

○ Blank colored tiles, small blocks, or paper squares

MODEL

- Say a pair of words in which the second word is identical to the first word except that a final consonant sound has been added. Accentuate the final sound as you say the second word: "*bell-bel**t**.*"
- Listen and watch while I move one square down for each part I say: /bĕl/ /t/."
- As you break apart the second word, put down one square for each part you say. Use a square of a different color to represent the second sound.

 **/bĕl/ /t/**

- Say "*bell-belt.*" (Remove the second square when you say the first word, and add it back as you say the second word.)
- "When I add the sound /t/ to *bell,* the word is *belt.*"

NOW IT'S YOUR TURN

Say the following:
- "The words are _____." (Choose a word pair from Column 1.)
- "Put down one square for each part in the word." (Say the second word in the pair.)
- "Break apart the word." (See the answer in Column 2.)
- "What sound did you add to change _____ to _____?" (See the answer in Column 3.)

EXTRA SUPPORT

- If your child has trouble breaking apart the word and/or determining the added sound, model the correct response and ask the child to repeat it after you.

Word Bank on following page

Word Bank

1. Word pairs	2. Sounds	3. Added sound
an-and	/ăn/ /d/	/d/
bee-beef	/bē/ /f/	/f/
for-fork	/for/ /k/	/k/
see-seal	/sē/ /l/	/l/
she-sheet	/shē/ /p/	/p/
say-save	/sā/ /v/	/v/
how-house	/hou/ /s/	/s/
tie-time	/tī/ /m/	/m/
say-save	/sā/ /v/	/v/
my-mine	/mī/ /n/	/n/
free-freeze	/frē/ /z/	/z/
car-card	/kar/ /d/	/d/
say-safe	/sā/ /f/	/f/
bee-beak	/bē/ /k/	/k/
may-mail	/mā/ /l/	/l/
lamb-lamp	/lăm/ /p/	/p/
teach-teacher	/tēch/ /r/	/r/
high-hive	/hī/ /v/	/v/
no-note	/nō/ /t/	/t/
me-mean	/mē/ /n/	/n/

(12) Deleting an Initial Consonant Sound

GOAL

- **The student will identify the initial sound that has been deleted from a word to make a new word.**

MATERIALS

○ Word bank for this activity

○ Blank colored tiles, small blocks, or paper squares

MODEL

- Say "*sit-it.*"
- "Listen and watch while I move one square down for each part I say: /s/ /ĭt/."
- As you break apart the first word, put down one square for each part you say. Use a square of a different color to represent the first sound.

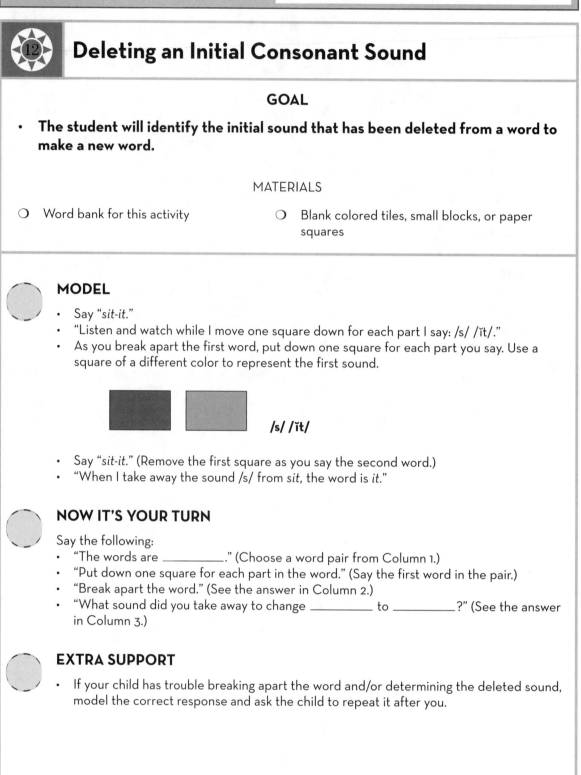

/s/ /ĭt/

- Say "*sit-it.*" (Remove the first square as you say the second word.)
- "When I take away the sound /s/ from *sit*, the word is *it*."

NOW IT'S YOUR TURN

Say the following:
- "The words are _____." (Choose a word pair from Column 1.)
- "Put down one square for each part in the word." (Say the first word in the pair.)
- "Break apart the word." (See the answer in Column 2.)
- "What sound did you take away to change _____ to _____?" (See the answer in Column 3.)

EXTRA SUPPORT

- If your child has trouble breaking apart the word and/or determining the deleted sound, model the correct response and ask the child to repeat it after you.

Word Bank on following page

Word Bank

1. Word pairs	2. Sounds	3. Deleted sound
bat-at	/b/ /ăt/	/b/
beat-eat	/b/ /ēt/	/b/
dice-ice	/d/ /īs/	/d/
foil-oil	/f/ /oil/	/f/
ham-am	/h/ /ăm/	/h/
hold-old	/h/ /ōld/	/h/
cash-ash	/k/ /ăsh/	/k/
coil-oil	/k/ /oil/	/k/
kit-it	/k/ /ĭt/	/k/
land-and	/l/ /ănd/	/l/
low-owe	/l/ /ō/	/l/
mat-at	/m/ /ăt/	/m/
mold-old	/m/ /ōld/	/m/
name-aim	/n/ /ām/	/n/
nod-odd	/n/ /ŏd/	/n/
pace-ace	/p/ /ās/	/p/
ram-am	/r/ /ăm/	/r/
rink-ink	/r/ /ĭnk/	/r/
Sam-am	/S/ /ăm/	/s/
sink-ink	/s/ /ĭnk/	/s/
told-old	/t/ /ōld/	/t/
wink-ink	/w/ /ĭnk/	/w/

13 Deleting a Final Consonant Sound

GOAL

- **The student will identify the final sound that has been deleted from a word to make a new word.**

MATERIALS

❍ Word bank for this activity

❍ Blank colored tiles, small blocks, or paper squares

MODEL

- Say the following:
  - "beet-bee"
  - "Listen and watch while I move one square down for each part I say: /bē/ /t/."
- As you break apart the first word, put down one square for each part you say. Use a square of a different color to represent the first sound.

 **/bē/ /t/**

  - "*beet-bee*" (Remove the second square as you say the second word.)
  - "When I take away the sound /t/ from *beet*, the word is *bee*."

NOW IT'S YOUR TURN

Say the following:
- "The words are _____-_____." (Choose a word pair from Column 1.)
- "Put down one square for each part in the word _____." (Say the first word in the pair.)
- "Break apart the word." (See the answer in Column 2.)
- "What sound did you take away to change _____ to _____?" (See the answer in Column 3.)

EXTRA SUPPORT

- If your child has trouble breaking apart the word and/or determining the deleted sound, model the correct response and ask the child to repeat it after you.

Word Bank on following page

Word Bank

1. Word pairs	2. Sounds	3. Deleted sound
band-ban	/băn/ /d/	/d/
card-car	/kar/ /d/	/d/
self-sell	/sĕl/ /f/	/f/
bake-bay	/bā/ /k/	/k/
bark-bar	/bar/ /k/	/k/
fork-for	/for/ /k/	/k/
hail-hay	/hā/ /l/	/l/
heal-he	/hē/ /l/	/l/
form-for	/for/ /m/	/m/
dime-die	/dī/ /m/	/m/
farm-far	/far/ /m/	/m/
barn-bar	/bar/ /n/	/n/
bean-bee	/bē/ /n/	/n/
grape-gray	/grā/ /p/	/p/
hope-hoe	/hō/ /p/	/p/
tire-tie	/tī/ /r/	/r/
wire-why	/wī/ /r/	/r/
goose-goo	/gōo/ /s/	/s/
house-how	/hou/ /s/	/s/
meet-me	/mē/ /t/	/t/
beet-bee	/bē/ /t/	/t/
belt-bell	/bĕl/ /t/	/t/
dive-die	/dī/ /v/	/v/
hive-high	/hī/ /v/	/v/
freeze-free	/frē/ /z/	/z/
prize-pry	/prī/ /z/	/z/

16 Segmenting and Blending Two-Sound Words

GOAL

- **The student will segment and blend words with two sounds.**

MATERIALS

○ Word bank for this activity   ○ Blank tiles, small blocks, or paper squares

MODEL

Say the following:
- "I'm going to break apart the word see."
- "Listen and watch while I put down one square for each sound I say: /s/ /ē/."
- "The word is see." (Say the word while pushing the squares together.)

NOW IT'S YOUR TURN

- Say the following:
  - "Put down one square for each sound in the word _____." (Say a word from Column 1. See the answer in Column 2.)
- Say the word and push the squares together.

EXTRA SUPPORT

- If the child has difficulty moving one square for each sound, model the correct response and ask the child to repeat after you.

Word Bank			
1. Word	**2. Sounds**	**1. Word**	**2. Sounds**
bee	/b/ /ē/	low	/l/ /ō/
boo	/b/ /o͞o/	may	/m/ /ā/
day	/d/ /ā/	me	/m/ /ē/
die	/d/ /ī/	moo	/m/ /o͞o/
do	/d/ /o͞o/	my	/m/ /ī/
fee	/f/ /ē/	no	/n/ /ō/
go	/g/ /ō/	pay	/p/ /ā/
guy	/g/ /ī/	pie	/p/ /ī/
hay	/h/ /ā/	ray	/r/ /ā/
he	/h/ /ē/	say	/s/ /ā/
hi	/h/ /ī/	see	/s/ /ē/
hoe	/h/ /ō/	show	/sh/ /ō/
lie	/l/ /ī/	toe	/t/ /ō/

(18) Segmenting and Blending Three-Sound Words

GOAL

- **The student will segment and blend words with three sounds.**

MATERIALS

○ Word bank for this activity   ○ Blank tiles, small blocks, or paper squares

MODEL

Say the following:
- "I'm going to break apart the word *sat*."
- "Listen and watch while I put down one square for each sound I say: /s /ă/ /t/."
- "The word is *sat*." (Say the word while pushing the squares together.)

NOW IT'S YOUR TURN

- Say the following:
  - "Put down one square for each sound in the word _____." (Say a word from Column 1. See the answer in Column 2.)
- Say the word and push the squares together.

EXTRA SUPPORT

- If the child has difficulty moving one square for each sound, model the correct response and ask the child to repeat after you.

HOME-SCHOOL CONNECTION ACTIVITY
PHONOLOGICAL AWARENESS · Segmenting and Blending

Word Bank			
1. Word	**2. Sounds**	**1. Word**	**2. Sounds**
bait	/b/ /ā/ /t/	ham	/h/ /ă/ /m/
ban	/b/ /ă/ /n/	heat	/h/ /ē/ /t/
bill	/b/ /ĭ/ /l/	jam	/j/ /ă/ /m/
bit	/b/ /ĭ/ /t/	lad	/l/ /ă/ /d/
bone	/b/ /ō/ /n/	late	/l/ /ā/ /t/
chin	/ch/ /ĭ/ /n/	mad	/m/ /ă/ /d/
cup	/c/ /ŭ/ /p/	man	/m/ /ă/ /n/
Dan	/d/ /ă/ /n/	meat	/m/ /ē/ /t/
dash	/d/ /ă/ /sh/	mice	/m/ /ī/ /s/
deal	/d/ /ē/ /l/	nice	/n/ /ī/ /s/
fan	/f/ /ă/ /n/	pup	/p/ /ŭ/ /p/
feel	/f/ /ē/ /l/	rice	/r/ /ī/ /s/
fill	/f/ /ĭ/ /l/	rich	/r/ /ĭ/ /ch/
gate	/g/ /ā/ /t/	win	/w/ /ĭ/ /n/

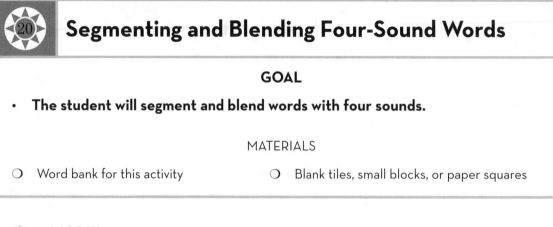

20   Segmenting and Blending Four-Sound Words

GOAL

- **The student will segment and blend words with four sounds.**

MATERIALS

○ Word bank for this activity   ○ Blank tiles, small blocks, or paper squares

MODEL

Say the following:
- "I am going to break apart the word *fast*."
- "Listen and watch while I put down one square for each sound I say: /f/ /ă/ /s/ /t/."
- "The word is *fast*." (Say the word while pushing the squares together.)

NOW IT'S YOUR TURN

- Say the following:
  - "Put down one square for each sound in the word _____." (Say a word from Column 1. See the answer in Column 2.)
- Push the squares together and blend the sounds.

EXTRA SUPPORT

- If the child has difficulty moving one square for each sound, model the correct response and ask the child to repeat after you.

Word Bank

1. Word	2. Sounds	1. Word	2. Sounds
brag	/b/ /r/ /ă/ /g/	sand	/s/ /ă/ /n/ /d/
crash	/c/ /r/ /ă/ /sh/	slime	/s/ /l/ /ī/ /m/
drum	/d/ /r/ /ŭ/ /m/	smile	/s/ /m/ /ī/ /l/
flake	/f/ /l/ /ā/ /k/	snail	/s/ /n/ /ā/ /l/
flame	/f/ /l/ /ā/ /m/	speak	/s/ /p/ /ē/ /k/
flat	/f/ /l/ /ă/ /t/	spill	/s/ /p/ /ĭ/ /l/
great	/g/ /r/ /ā/ /t/	steak	/s/ /t/ /ā/ /k/
groan	/g/ /r/ /ō/ /n/	steal	/s/ /t/ /ē/ /l/
pinch	/p/ /ĭ/ /n/ /ch/	steer	/s/ /t/ /ē/ /r/
place	/p/ /l/ /ā/ /s/	stone	/s/ /t/ /ō/ /n/
plane	/p/ /l/ /ā/ /n/	stool	/s/ /t/ /o͞o/ /l/
plate	/p/ /l/ /ā/ /t/	trace	/t/ /r/ /ā/ /s/
price	/p/ /r/ /ī/ /s/	train	/t/ /r/ /ā/ /n/

Interventions for Reading Success by Diane Haager, Joseph A. Dimino, and Michelle Pearlman Windmueller

29. Adding an Initial Consonant Sound

GOALS

- **The student will segment and blend words with two, three, and four sounds.**
- **The student will identify the initial sound that has been added to a word to make a new word.**

MATERIALS

○ Word bank for this activity

○ Blank colored tiles, small blocks, or paper squares

MODEL

Say the following:
- "I am going to break apart the word *at*."
- "Listen and watch while I put down one square for each sound I say: /ă/ /t/."
- "The new word is *sat*."
- "Listen and watch." Put down one square for every sound you say (/s/ /ă/ /t/). Use a square of a different color to represent the first sound. Place these squares under the first set of squares. (See the illustration below.)
- "I added the sound /s/ to change *at* to *sat*."

/ă/ /t/   **Use tiles of the same color to segment the first word.**

/m/ /ă/ /t/   **Use a tile of a different color to indicate the added sound.**

NOW IT'S YOUR TURN

Say the following:
- "Put down one square for each sound in the word _____." (Say the first word from a pair in Column 1. See the answer in Column 2.)
- "The new word is _____." (Say the second word in the pair.)
- "Put down one square for each sound in the word. Use a square of a different color to show the first sound. Put the squares under the first set of squares." (See the answer in Column 3.)
- "What sound did you add to change _____ to _____?" (See the answer in Column 4.)

EXTRA SUPPORT

- If the child has trouble breaking apart the word and/or determining the added sound, model the correct response and ask the child to repeat after you.

Word Bank on following page

HOME-SCHOOL CONNECTION ACTIVITY
PHONOLOGICAL AWARENESS · Segmenting and Blending

Word Bank

1. Word pairs	2. Sounds	3. Sounds	4. Added sound
ad-bad	/ă/ /d/	/b/ /ă/ /d/	/b/
end-bend	/ĕ/ /n/ /d/	/b/ /ĕ/ /n/ /d/	/b/
it-fit	/ĭ/ /t/	/f/ /ĭ/ /t/	/f/
and-hand	/ă/ /n/ /d/	/h/ /ă/ /n/ /d/	/h/
am-jam	/ă/ /m/	/j/ /ă/ /m/	/j/
at-mat	/ă/ /t/	/m/ /ă/ /t/	/m/
ask-mask	/ă/ /s/ /k/	/m/ /ă/ /s/ /k/	/m/
an-pan	/ă/ /n/	/p/ /ă/ /n/	/p/
ant-pant	/ă/ /n/ /t/	/p/ /ă/ /n/ /t/	/p/
ink-pink	/ĭ/ /n/ /k/	/p/ /ĭ/ /n/ /k/	/p/
and-sand	/ă/ /n/ /d/	/s/ /ă/ /n/ /d/	/s/
am-Sam	/ă/ /m/	/S/ /ă/ /m/	/s/
ink-sink	/ĭ/ /n/ /k/	/s/ /ĭ/ /n/ /k/	/s/
end-send	/ĕ/ /n/ /d/	/s/ /ĕ/ /n/ /d/	/s/
in-win	/ĭ/ /n/	/w/ /ĭ/ /n/	/w/

Adding a Sound to Form an Initial Consonant Blend

GOALS

- **The student will segment and blend words with two, three, and four sounds.**
- **The student will identify the initial sound that has been added to a word to make a new word.**

MATERIALS

○ Word bank for this activity

○ Blank colored tiles, small blocks, or paper squares

MODEL

Say the following:

- "I am going to break apart the word *low*."
- "Listen and watch while I put one square down for each sound I say: /l/ /ō/."
- "The new word is *glow*."
- "Listen and watch." Put down one square for every sound you say, /g/ /l/ /ō/. Use a square of a different color to represent the first sound. Place these squares under the first set of squares. (See the illustration below.)
- "I added the sound /g/ to change *low* to *glow*."

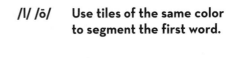

/l/ /ō/   **Use tiles of the same color to segment the first word.**

/g/ /l/ /ō/   **Use a tile of a different color to indicate the added sound.**

NOW IT'S YOUR TURN

Say the following:

- "Put down one square for each sound in the word _____." (Say the first word from a pair in Column 1. See the answer in Column 2.)
- "The new word is _____." (Say the second word in the pair.)
- "Put down one square for each sound. Use a square of a different color to show the first sound. Put the squares under the first set of squares." (See the answer in Column 3.)
- "What sound did you add to change _____ to _____?" (See the answer in Column 4.)

Activity and Word Bank continued on following page

Interventions for Reading Success by Diane Haager, Joseph A. Dimino, and Michelle Pearlman Windmueller

287

EXTRA SUPPORT

- If the child has trouble breaking apart the word and/or determining the added sound, model the correct response and ask the child to repeat after you.

Word Bank

1. Word pairs	2. Sounds	3. Sounds	4. Added sound
lack-black	/l/ /ă/ /k/	/b/ /l/ /ă/ /k/	/b/
rag-brag	/r/ /ă/ /g/	/b/ /r/ /ă/ /g/	/b/
lap-clap	/l/ /ă/ /p/	/k/ /l/ /ă/ /p/	/k/
lame-flame	/l/ /ā/ /m/	/f/ /l/ /ā/ /m/	/f/
lass-glass	/l/ /ă/ /s/	/g/ /l/ /ă/ /s/	/g/
row-grow	/r/ /ō/	/g/ /r/ /ō/	/g/
lane-plane	/l/ /ā/ /n/	/p/ /l/ /ā/ /n/	/p/
low-slow	/l/ /ō/	/s/ /l/ /ō/	/s/
tick-stick	/t/ /ĭ/ /k/	/s/ /t/ /ĭ/ /k/	/s/
weep-sweep	/w/ /ē/ /p/	/s/ /w/ /ē/ /p/	/s/
nail-snail	/n/ /ā/ /l/	/s/ /n/ /ā/ /l/	/s/
key-ski	/k/ /ē/	/s/ /k/ /ē/	/s/
rip-trip	/r/ /ĭ/ /p/	/t/ /r/ /ĭ/ /p/	/t/
win-twin	/w/ /ĭ/ /n/	/t/ /w/ /ĭ/ /n/	/t/

31 Adding a Second Sound to Form an Initial Consonant Blend

GOALS

- **The student will segment and blend words with two, three, and four sounds.**
- **The student will identify the sound that has been added to a word to make a new word.**

MATERIALS

○ Word bank for this activity

○ Blank colored tiles, small blocks, or paper squares

MODEL

Say the following:
- "I am going to break apart the word *cap*."
- "Listen and watch while I put down one square for each sound I say: /c/ /ă/ /p/."
- "The new word is *clap*."
- "Listen and watch." Point to the squares as you say the sounds (/c/ /l/ /ă/ /p/). Insert a square of a different color to represent the added sound. (See the illustration below.)
- "I added the sound /l/ to change *cap* to *clap*."

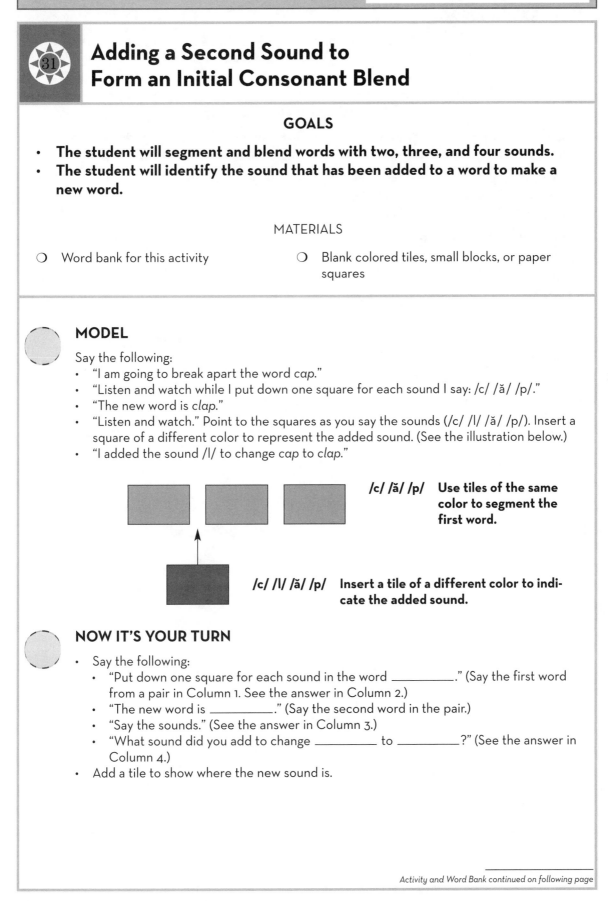

/c/ /ă/ /p/   **Use tiles of the same color to segment the first word.**

/c/ /l/ /ă/ /p/   **Insert a tile of a different color to indicate the added sound.**

NOW IT'S YOUR TURN

- Say the following:
  - "Put down one square for each sound in the word _____." (Say the first word from a pair in Column 1. See the answer in Column 2.)
  - "The new word is _____." (Say the second word in the pair.)
  - "Say the sounds." (See the answer in Column 3.)
  - "What sound did you add to change _____ to _____?" (See the answer in Column 4.)
- Add a tile to show where the new sound is.

Activity and Word Bank continued on following page

EXTRA SUPPORT

· If the child has trouble breaking apart the word and/or determining the added sound, model the correct response and ask the child to repeat after you.

Word Bank

1. Word pairs	2. Sounds	3. Sounds	4. Added sound
back-black	/b/ /ă/ /k/	/b/ /l/ /ă/ /k/	/l/
bag-brag	/b/ /ă/ /g/	/b/ /r/ /ă/ /g/	/r/
cap-clap	/k/ /ă/ /p/	/k/ /l/ /ă/ /p/	/l/
fame-flame	/f/ /ā/ /m/	/f/ /l/ /ā/ /m/	/l/
gas-glass	/g/ /ă/ /s/	/g/ /l/ /ă/ /s/	/l/
go-grow	/g/ /ō/	/g/ /r/ /ō/	/r/
pane-plane	/p/ /ā/ /n/	/p/ /l/ /ā/ /n/	/l/
see-ski	/s/ /ē/	/s/ /k/ /ē/	/k/
sew-slow	/s/ /ō/	/s/ /l/ /ō/	/l/
sail-snail	/s/ /ā/ /l/	/s/ /n/ /ā/ /l/	/n/
sick-stick	/s/ /ĭ/ /k/	/s/ /t/ /ĭ/ /k/	/t/
seep-sweep	/s/ /ē/ /p/	/s/ /w/ /ē/ /p/	/w/
tip-trip	/t/ /ĭ/ /p/	/t/ /r/ /ĭ/ /p/	/r/
tin-twin	/t/ /ĭ/ /n/	/t/ /w/ /ĭ/ /n/	/w/

33 Deleting an Initial Consonant Sound

GOALS

- **The student will segment and blend words with two, three, and four sounds.**
- **The student will identify the initial sound that has been deleted from a word to make a new word.**

MATERIALS

○ Word bank for this activity   ○ Blank colored tiles, small blocks, or paper squares

MODEL

Say the following:
- "I am going to break apart the word *sat.*"
- "Listen and watch while I put down one square for each sound I say: /s/ /ă/ /t/." Use a square of a different color to represent the first sound. (See the illustration below.)
- "The new word is *at.*"
- "Listen and watch." Put down one square for every sound you say: /ă/ /t/. Place these squares under the first set of squares. (See the illustration below.)
- "I took away the sound /s/ to change *sat* to *at.*"

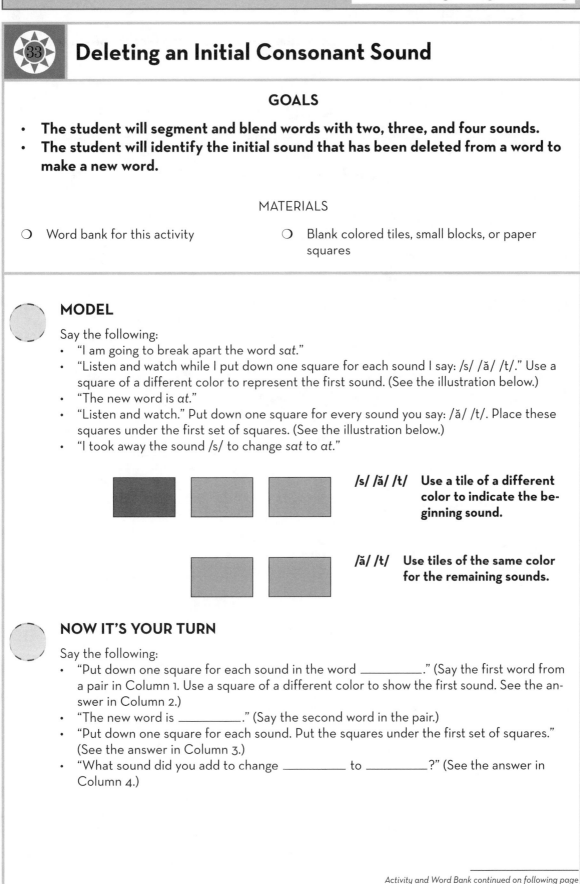

/s/ /ă/ /t/   **Use a tile of a different color to indicate the beginning sound.**

/ă/ /t/   **Use tiles of the same color for the remaining sounds.**

NOW IT'S YOUR TURN

Say the following:
- "Put down one square for each sound in the word _____." (Say the first word from a pair in Column 1. Use a square of a different color to show the first sound. See the answer in Column 2.)
- "The new word is _____." (Say the second word in the pair.)
- "Put down one square for each sound. Put the squares under the first set of squares." (See the answer in Column 3.)
- "What sound did you add to change _____ to _____?" (See the answer in Column 4.)

Activity and Word Bank continued on following page

EXTRA SUPPORT

- If the child has trouble breaking apart the word and/or determining the deleted sound, model the correct sound and ask the child to repeat after you.

Word Bank

1. Word pairs	2. Sounds	3. Sounds	4. Deleted sound
bad-ad	/b/ /ă/ /d/	/ă/ /d/	/b/
bend-end	/b/ /ĕ/ /n/ /d/	/ĕ/ /n/ /d/	/b/
fit-it	/f/ /ĭ/ /t/	/ĭ/ /t/	/f/
hand-and	/h/ /ă/ /n/ /d/	/ă/ /n/ /d/	/h/
jam-am	/j/ /ă/ /m/	/ă/ /m/	/j/
mat-at	/m/ /ă/ /t/	/ă/ /t/	/m/
mask-ask	/m/ /ă/ /s/ /k/	/ă/ /s/ /k/	/m/
pan-an	/p/ /ă/ /n/	/ă/ /n/	/p/
pant-ant	/p/ /ă/ /n/ /t/	/ă/ /n/ /t/	/p/
pink-ink	/p/ /ĭ/ /n/ /k/	/ĭ/ /n/ /k/	/p/
sand-and	/s/ /ă/ /n/ /d/	/ă/ /n/ /d/	/s/
Sam-am	/S/ /ă/ /m/	/ă/ /m/	/s/
sink-ink	/s/ /ĭ/ /n/ /k/	/ĭ/ /n/ /k/	/s/
send-end	/s/ /ĕ/ /n/ /d/	/ĕ/ /n/ /d/	/s/
win-in	/w/ /ĭ/ /n/	/ĭ/ /n/	/w/

34 Deleting the First Sound from an Initial Consonant Blend

GOALS

- **The student will segment and blend words with two, three, and four sounds.**
- **The student will identify the initial sound that has been deleted from a word to make a new word.**

MATERIALS

○ Word bank for this activity

○ Blank colored tiles, small blocks, or paper squares

MODEL

Say the following:
- "I am going to break apart the word *snow*."
- "Listen and watch while I put down one square for each sound I say: /s/ /n/ /ō/."
- "The new word is *no*."
- "Listen and watch." Put down one square for every sound you say: /n/ /ō/. Place these squares under the first set of squares. (See the illustration below.)
- "I took away the sound /s/ to change *snow* to *no*."

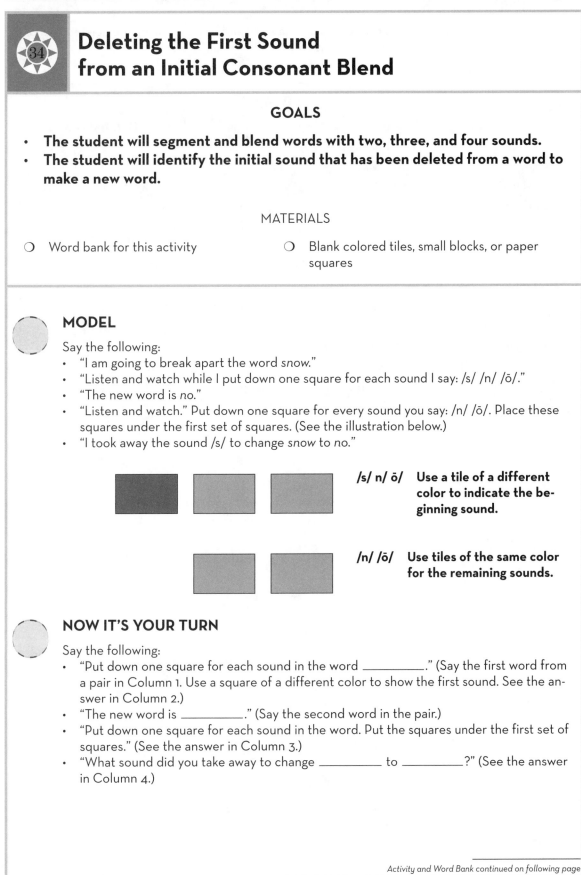

/s/ n/ ō/ Use a tile of a different color to indicate the beginning sound.

/n/ /ō/ Use tiles of the same color for the remaining sounds.

NOW IT'S YOUR TURN

Say the following:
- "Put down one square for each sound in the word _____." (Say the first word from a pair in Column 1. Use a square of a different color to show the first sound. See the answer in Column 2.)
- "The new word is _____." (Say the second word in the pair.)
- "Put down one square for each sound in the word. Put the squares under the first set of squares." (See the answer in Column 3.)
- "What sound did you take away to change _____ to _____?" (See the answer in Column 4.)

Activity and Word Bank continued on following page

EXTRA SUPPORT

- If the child has trouble breaking apart the word and/or determining the deleted sound, model the correct response and ask the child to repeat after you.

Word Bank

1. Word pairs	2. Sounds	3. Sounds	4. Deleted sound
black-lack	/b / /l/ /ă/ /k/	/l/ /ă/ /k/	/b/
brag-rag	/b/ /r/ /ă/ /g/	/r /ă/ /g/	/b/
clap-lap	/k/ /l/ /ă/ /p/	/l/ /ă/ /p/	/k/
flame-lame	/f/ /l/ /ā/ /m/	/l/ /ā/ /m/	/f/
glass-lass	/g/ /l/ /ă/ /s/	/l/ /ă/ /s/	/g/
grow-row	/g/ /r/ /ō/	/r/ /ō/	/g/
plane-lane	/p/ /l/ /ā/ /n/	/l/ /ā/ /n/	/p/
slow-low	/s/ /l/ /ō/	/l/ /ō/	/s/
stick-tick	/s/ /t/ /ĭ/ /k/	/t/ /ĭ/ /k/	/s/
sweep-weep	/s/ /w/ /ē/ /p/	/w/ /ē/ /p/	/s/
snail-nail	/s/ /n/ /ā/ /l/	/n/ /ā/ /l/	/s/
ski-key	/s/ /k/ /ē/	/k/ /ē/	/s/
trip-rip	/t/ /r/ /ĭ/ /p/	/r/ /ĭ/ /p/	/t/
twin-win	/t/ /w/ /ĭ/ /n/	/w/ /ĭ/ /n/	/t/

Interventions for Reading Success by Diane Haager, Joseph A. Dimino, and Michelle Pearlman Windmueller

Deleting the Second Sound from an Initial Consonant Blend

GOALS

- **The student will segment and blend words with two, three, and four sounds.**
- **The student will identify the sound that has been deleted from a word to make a new word.**

MATERIALS

- ❍ Word bank for this activity
- ❍ Blank tiles, small blocks, or paper squares

MODEL

Say the following:
- "I am going to break apart the word *slide.*"
- "Listen and watch while I move down one square for each sound I say: /s/ /l/ /ī/ /d/."
- "The new word is *side.*"
- "Listen and watch." Point to the squares as you say the sounds: /s/ /ī/ /d/. Remove the square representing the deleted sound. (See the illustration below.)
- "I took away the sound /l/ to change *slide* to *side.*"

NOW IT'S YOUR TURN

Say the following:
- "Put down one square for each sound in the word _____." (Say the first word from a pair in Column 1. See the answer in Column 2.)
- "The new word is _____." (Say the second word in the pair.)
- "Say the sounds _____." (See the answer in Column 3.)
- "What sound did you take away to change _____ to _____?" (See the answer in Column 4.)
- "Take away the tile."

Arrangement of tiles for segmenting the sounds in *slide:*

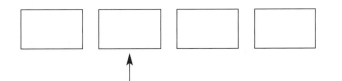

Remove the second tile when segmenting the second word in the pair.

EXTRA SUPPORT

- If the child has trouble breaking apart the word and/or determining the deleted sound, model the correct response and ask the child to repeat after you.

Word Bank on following page

Interventions for Reading Success by Diane Haager, Joseph A. Dimino, and Michelle Pearlman Windmueller

295

Word Bank

1. Word pairs	2. Sounds	3. Sounds	4. Deleted sound
black-back	/b/ /l/ /ă/ /k/	/b/ /ă/ /k/	/l/
brag-bag	/b/ /r/ /ă/ /g/	/b/ /ă/ /g/	/r/
clap-cap	/k/ /l/ /ă/ /p/	/k/ /ă/ /p/	/l/
flame-fame	/f/ /l/ /ā/ /m/	/f/ / /ā/ /m/	/l/
glass-gas	/g/ /l/ /ă/ /s/	/g/ /ă/ /s/	/l/
grow-go	/g/ /r/ /ō/	/g/ /ō/	/r/
plane-pane	/p/ /l/ /ā/ /n/	/p/ /ā/ /n/	/l/
snail-sail	/s/ /n/ /ā/ /l/	/s/ /ā/ /l/	/n/
ski-see	/s/ /k/ /ē/	/s/ /ē/	/k/
sweep-seep	/s/ /w/ /ē/ /p/	/s/ /ē/ /p/	/w/
stick-sick	/s/ /t/ /ĭ/ /k/	/s/ /ĭ/ /k/	/t/
slow-sow	/s/ /l/ /ō/	/s/ /ō/	/l/
twin-tin	/t/ /w/ /ĭ/ /n/	/t/ /ĭ/ /n/	/w/
trip-tip	/t/ /r/ /ĭ/ /p/	/t/ /ĭ/ /p/	/r/

36   Substituting an Initial Consonant Sound

GOALS

- **The student will identify the initial consonant sound that has been substituted to make a new word.**

MATERIALS

○ Word bank for this activity

○ Blank colored tiles, small blocks, or paper squares

MODEL

Say the following:

- "I am going to break apart the word *sit*."
- "Listen and watch while I move down one square for each sound I say: /s/ /ĭ/ /t/."
- "The new word is *pit*."
- "Listen and watch." Point to the squares as you say the sounds: /p/ /ĭ/ /t/. Substitute a square of a different color to represent the new sound. (See the illustration below.)
- "*sit-pit* . . . I changed the sound /s/ to /p/."

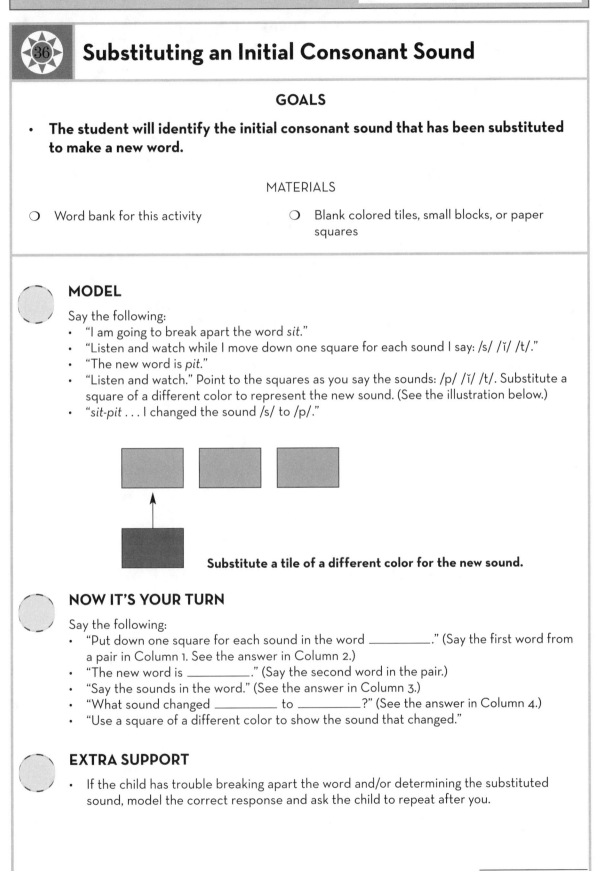

Substitute a tile of a different color for the new sound.

NOW IT'S YOUR TURN

Say the following:

- "Put down one square for each sound in the word _____." (Say the first word from a pair in Column 1. See the answer in Column 2.)
- "The new word is _____." (Say the second word in the pair.)
- "Say the sounds in the word." (See the answer in Column 3.)
- "What sound changed _____ to _____?" (See the answer in Column 4.)
- "Use a square of a different color to show the sound that changed."

EXTRA SUPPORT

- If the child has trouble breaking apart the word and/or determining the substituted sound, model the correct response and ask the child to repeat after you.

Word Bank on following page

Interventions for Reading Success by Diane Haager, Joseph A. Dimino, and Michelle Pearlman Windmueller

Word Bank

1. Word pairs	2. Sounds	3. Sounds	4. Substituted sound
bit-fit	/b/ /ĭ/ /t/	/f/ /ĭ/ /t/	/f/
had-bad	/h/ /ă/ /d/	/b/ /ă/ /d/	/b/
jam-Sam	/j/ /ă/ /m/	/S/ /ă/ /m/	/s/
land-sand	/l/ /ă/ /n/ /d/	/s/ /ă/ /n/ /d/	/s/
lend-send	/l/ /ĕ/ /n/ /d/	/s/ /ĕ/ /n/ /d/	/s/
man-pan	/m/ /ă/ /n/	/p/ /ă/ /n/	/p/
mend-bend	/m/ /ĕ/ /n/ /d/	/b/ /ĕ/ /n/ /d/	/b/
mink-pink	/m/ /ĭ/ /n/ /k/	/p/ /ĭ/ /n/ /k/	/p/
Pam-jam	/P/ /ă/ /m/	/j/ /ă/ /m/	/j/
rant-pant	/r/ /ă/ /n/ /t/	/p/ /ă/ /n/ /t/	/p/
sand-hand	/s/ /ă/ /n/ /d/	/h/ /ă/ /n/ /d/	/h/
sat-mat	/s/ /ă/ /t/	/m/ /ă/ /t/	/m/
task-mask	/t/ /ă/ /s/ /k/	/m/ /ă/ /s/ /k/	/m/
tin-win	/t/ /ĭ/ /n/	/w/ /ĭ/ /n/	/w/
wink-sink	/w/ /ĭ/ /n/ /k/	/s/ /ĭ/ /n/ /k/	/s/

37 Substituting a Final Consonant Sound

GOAL

- **The student will identify the final consonant sound that has been substituted to make a new word.**

MATERIALS

○ Word bank for this activity

○ Blank colored tiles, small blocks, or paper squares

MODEL

Say the following:

- "I am going to break apart the word *sit*."
- "Listen and watch while I put down one square for each sound I say: /s/ /ĭ/ /t/."
- "The new word is *sip*."
- "Listen and watch." Point to the squares as you say the sounds: /s/ /ĭ/ /p/. Substitute a square of a different color to represent the new sound. (See the illustration below.)
- "*sit–sip* . . . I changed the sound /t/ to /p/."

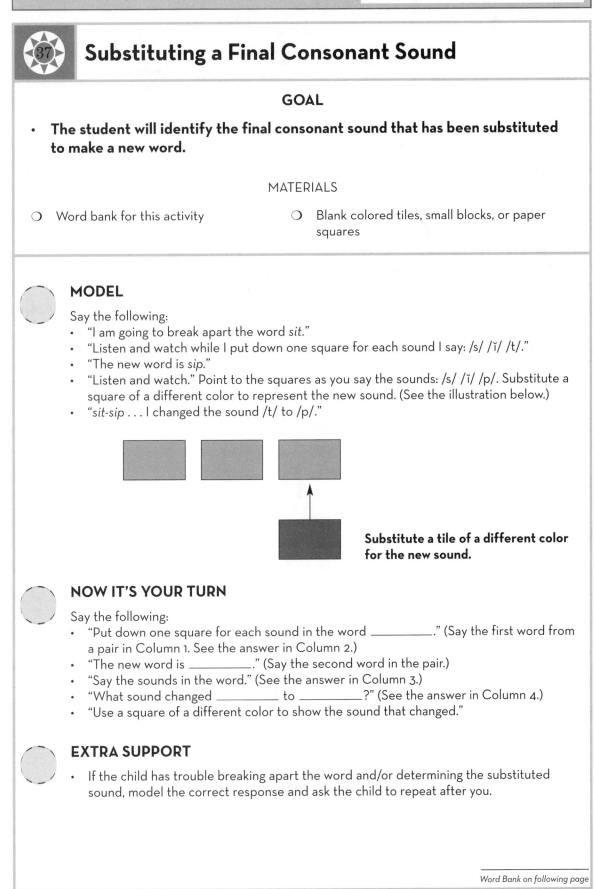

Substitute a tile of a different color for the new sound.

NOW IT'S YOUR TURN

Say the following:

- "Put down one square for each sound in the word _____." (Say the first word from a pair in Column 1. See the answer in Column 2.)
- "The new word is _____." (Say the second word in the pair.)
- "Say the sounds in the word." (See the answer in Column 3.)
- "What sound changed _____ to _____?" (See the answer in Column 4.)
- "Use a square of a different color to show the sound that changed."

EXTRA SUPPORT

- If the child has trouble breaking apart the word and/or determining the substituted sound, model the correct response and ask the child to repeat after you.

Word Bank on following page

Word Bank

1. Word pairs	2. Sounds	3. Sounds	4. Substituted sound
Ben-bed	/b/ /ĕ/ /n/	/b/ /ĕ/ /d/	/d/
bus-bug	/b/ /ŭ/ /s/	/b/ /ŭ/ /g/	/g/
fan-fat	/f/ /ă/ /n/	/f/ /ă/ /t/	/t/
hit-him	/h/ /ĭ/ /t/	/h/ /ĭ/ /m	/m/
hot-hop	/h/ /ŏ/ /t/	/h/ /ŏ/ /p/	/p/
hug-hum	/h/ /ŭ/ /g/	/h/ /ŭ/ /m/	/m/
Jan-jam	/j/ /ă/ /n/	/j/ /ă/ /m/	/m/
mat-man	/m/ /ă/ /t/	/m/ /ă/ /n/	/n/
mop-mom	/m/ /ŏ/ /p/	/m/ /ŏ/ /m/	/m/
pet-pen	/p/ /ĕ/ /t/	/p/ /ĕ/ /n/	/n/
rug-run	/r/ /ŭ/ /g/	/r/ /ŭ/ /n/	/n/
sad-sat	/s/ /ă/ /d/	/s/ /ă/ /t/	/t/
sip-sit	/s/ /ĭ/ /p/	/s/ /ĭ/ /t/	/t/
win-wig	/w/ /ĭ/ /n/	/w/ /ĭ/ /g/	/g/
yes-yet	/y/ /ĕ/ /s/	/y/ /ĕ/ /t/	/t/

38 Substituting a Medial Vowel Sound

GOAL

- **The student will identify the medial sound that has been substituted to make a new word.**

MATERIALS

○ Word bank for this activity

○ Blank colored tiles, small blocks, or paper squares

MODEL

Say the following:
- "I am going to break apart the word *sit.*"
- "Listen and watch while I put down one square for each sound I say: /s/ /ĭ/ /t/."
- "The new word is *sat.*"
- "Listen and watch." Point to the squares as you say the sounds: /s/ /ă/ /t/. Substitute a square of a different color to represent the new sound. (See the illustration below.)
- "*sit-sat . . .* I changed the sound /ĭ/ to /ă/."

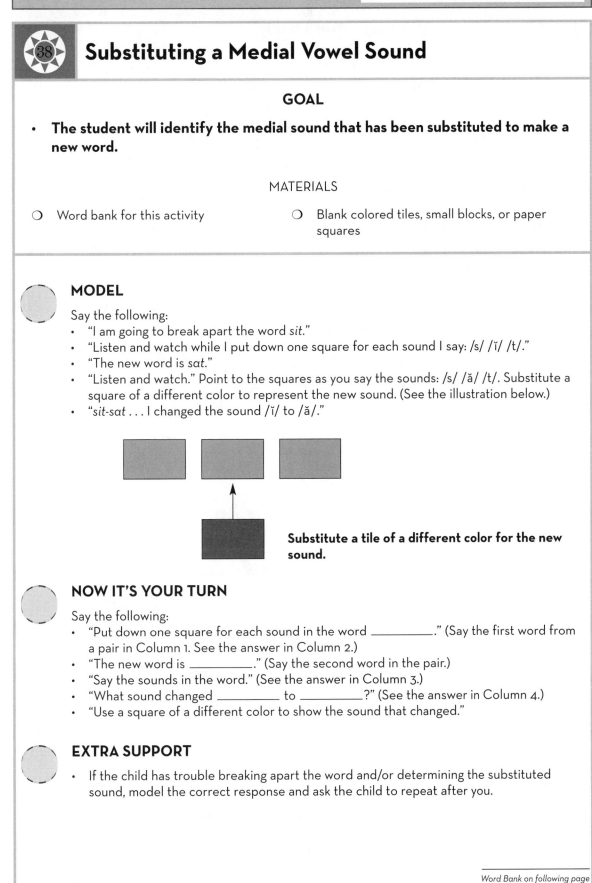

Substitute a tile of a different color for the new sound.

NOW IT'S YOUR TURN

Say the following:
- "Put down one square for each sound in the word _____." (Say the first word from a pair in Column 1. See the answer in Column 2.)
- "The new word is _____." (Say the second word in the pair.)
- "Say the sounds in the word." (See the answer in Column 3.)
- "What sound changed _____ to _____?" (See the answer in Column 4.)
- "Use a square of a different color to show the sound that changed."

EXTRA SUPPORT

- If the child has trouble breaking apart the word and/or determining the substituted sound, model the correct response and ask the child to repeat after you.

Word Bank on following page

Word Bank

1. Word pairs	2. Sounds	3. Sounds	4. Substituted sound
beg-big	/b/ /ĕ/ /g/	/b/ /ĭ/ /g/	/ĭ/
Bob-bib	/b/ /ŏ/ /b/	/b/ /ĭ/ /b/	/ĭ/
fan-fin	/f/ /ă/ /n/	/f/ /ĭ/ /n/	/ĭ/
fan-fun	/f/ /ă/ /n/	/f/ /ŭ/ /n/	/ŭ/
ham-him	/h/ /ă/ /m/	/h/ /ĭ/ /m/	/ĭ/
hip-hop	/h/ /ĭ/ /p/	/h/ /ŏ/ /p/	/ŏ/
Jim-jam	/j/ /ĭ/ /m/	/j/ /ă/ /m/	/ă/
lad-lid	/l/ /ă/ /d/	/l/ /ĭ/ /d/	/ĭ/
lap-lip	/l/ /ă/ /p/	/l/ /ĭ/ /p/	/ĭ/
man-men	/m/ /ă/ /n/	/m/ /ĕ/ /n/	/ĕ/
map-mop	/m/ /ă/ /p/	/m/ /ŏ/ /p/	/ŏ/
rub-rib	/r/ /ŭ/ /b/	/r/ /ĭ/ /b/	/ĭ/
run-ran	/r/ /ŭ/ /n/	/r/ /ă/ /n/	/ă/
tin-ten	/t/ /ĭ/ /n/	/t/ /ĕ/ /n/	/ĕ/
wig-wag	/w/ /ĭ/ /g/	/w/ /ă/ /g/	/ă/

① Spelling Two-Sound Words

GOAL

- **The student will spell two-sound words in which each sound is represented by one letter.**

MATERIALS

○ Word bank for this activity

○ Magnetic letters, paper letters, or letter tiles

MODEL

Say the following:
- "I'm going to spell the word *up*."
- "Listen and watch while I put down one letter for each sound I say: /ŭ/ /p/." (Put down the corresponding letter for each sound you say.)

u	p

- Blend the sounds (*up*).

NOW IT'S YOUR TURN

Say the following:
- "Put down the letter for each sound in the word _____." (Say a word from the word bank.)
- "What's the word?"

EXTRA SUPPORT

- If your child has difficulty putting down the correct letter for a sound, model the correct response and ask the child to repeat after you.

Word Bank				
Short *a*	**Short *e***	**Short *i***	**Short *o***	**Short *u***
ad	Ed	if	on	up
am		in		us
an		it		
at				

② Spelling Three-Sound Words

GOAL

- **The student will spell three-sound words in which each sound is represented by one letter.**

MATERIALS

○ Word bank for this activity

○ Magnetic letters, paper letters, or letter tiles

MODEL

Say the following:
- "I'm going to spell the word *bug*."
- "Listen and watch while I put down one letter for each sound I say: /b/ /ŭ/ /g/." (Put down the corresponding letter for each sound you say.)

- Blend the sounds. (*bug*)

NOW IT'S YOUR TURN

Say the following:
- "Put down the letter for each sound in the word _____." (Say a word from the word bank.)
- "What's the word?"

EXTRA SUPPORT

- If your child has difficulty putting down the correct letter for a sound, model the correct response and ask the child to repeat after you.

Word Bank on following page

Word Bank

Short *a*	Short *e*	Short *i*	Short *o*	Short *u*
bag	beg	bib	Bob	bud
bat	Ben	big	cod	bug
Dan	bet	bin	Don	bun
fan	den	bit	dot	bus
had	get	did	got	but
ham	hen	dip	hop	fun
jam	jet	fib	hot	gum
lap	leg	fig	job	gun
mad	let	hit	lot	Gus
map	men	lid	mop	hug
mat	net	lip	nod	hum
nap	peg	lit	not	hut
pan	pen	nip	pop	mud
pat	pet	rib	pot	nut
rag	red	rip	rob	rub
ran	set	sin	sob	rug
rap	Ted	sit	Tom	run
sad	ten	Tim	top	sum
tag	web	tip		sun
tan	wet	wig		tub
tap	yes	win		
wag	yet	zip		

3 Spelling Four-Sound Words

GOAL

- **The student will spell four-sound words in which each sound is represented by one letter.**

MATERIALS

○ Word bank for this activity

○ Magnetic letters, paper letters, or letter tiles

MODEL

Say the following:
- "I'm going to spell the word *list*."
- "Listen and watch while I put down one letter for each sound I say: /l/ /ĭ/ /s/ /t/." (Put down the corresponding letter for each sound you say.)

| l | i | s | t |

- Blend the sounds. (*list*)

NOW IT'S YOUR TURN

Say the following:
- "Put down the letter for each sound in the word _____." (Say a word from the word bank.)
- What's the word?

EXTRA SUPPORT

- If your child has difficulty putting down the correct letter for a sound, model the correct response and ask the child to repeat after you.

Word Bank on following page

Word Bank

Short *a*	Short *e*	Short *i*	Short *o*	Short *u*
bank	beds	drip	drop	bump
brag	best	flip	mops	club
camp	fled	grin	plot	cups
cats	fret	grip	snob	drug
clap	hens	limp	spot	drum
crab	jest	link	stop	grub
cram	lend	list	tops	hump
damp	nest	mink	trot	lump
drag	rest	pigs		plug
fans	sled	pink		plum
flab	vest	rink		pump
flag	webs	sink		rugs
flap		skid		slug
flat		skin		snug
glad		skip		spun
hand		skit		stub
hats		slid		
lamp		slip		
land		slit		
last		spin		
maps		spit		
pans		trim		
plan		trip		
raft		twig		
ramp		twin		
rank		wigs		
sand		wink		
sank				
scab				
scan				
slab				
slam				
slap				
snag				
snap				
swag				
tank				
trap				

(5) Adding an Initial Consonant Sound

GOAL

- **The student will spell new words by adding an initial consonant sound.**

MATERIALS

○ Word bank for this activity

○ Magnetic letters, paper letters, or letter tiles

MODEL

Say the following:
- "I'm going to spell the word *it*."
- "Listen and watch while I put down one letter for each sound I say: /ĭ/ /t/." (Put down the corresponding letter for each sound you say.)
- "The new word is *sit*."
- "Listen and watch." (Add the letter representing the first sound. Point to the remaining letters as you say the sounds, /s/ /ĭ/ /t/. See the illustration below.)
- "When I add the sound /s/ to *it*, the word is *sit*."

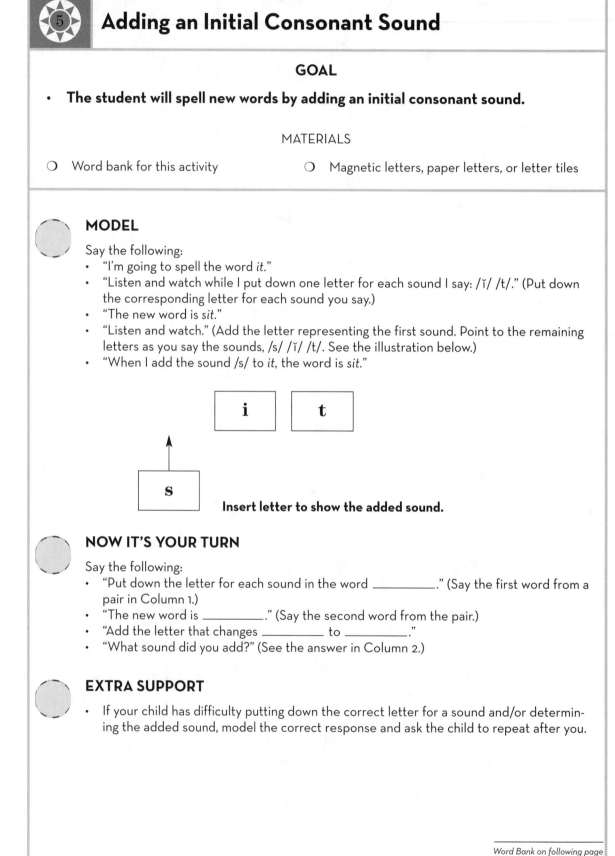

Insert letter to show the added sound.

NOW IT'S YOUR TURN

Say the following:
- "Put down the letter for each sound in the word _____." (Say the first word from a pair in Column 1.)
- "The new word is _____." (Say the second word from the pair.)
- "Add the letter that changes _____ to _____."
- "What sound did you add?" (See the answer in Column 2.)

EXTRA SUPPORT

- If your child has difficulty putting down the correct letter for a sound and/or determining the added sound, model the correct response and ask the child to repeat after you.

Word Bank on following page

Word Bank

1. Word pairs	2. Added sound	1. Word pairs	2. Added sound
ad-bad	/b/	ask-mask	/m/
ad-dad	/d/	ask-task	/t/
ad-fad	/f/	at-bat	/b/
ad-had	/h/	at-cat	/k/
ad-lad	/l/	at-fat	/f/
ad-mad	/m/	at-hat	/h/
ad-pad	/p/	at-mat	/m/
am-ham	/h/	at-pat	/p/
am-jam	/j/	at-rat	/r/
am-Pam	/p/	at-sat	/s/
am-ram	/r/	end-bend	/b/
am-Sam	/s/	end-lend	/l/
an-ban	/b/	end-mend	/m/
an-can	/k/	end-send	/s/
an-Dan	/d/	end-tend	/t/
and-band	/b/	end-vend	/v/
and-hand	/h/	ink-link	/l/
and-land	/l/	ink-mink	/m/
and-sand	/s/	ink-pink	/p/
an-fan	/f/	ink-rink	/r/
an-man	/m/	ink-sink	/s/
an-pan	/p/	ink-wink	/w/
an-ran	/r/	it-bit	/b/
an-tan	/t/	it-fit	/f/
ant-can't	/k/	it-lit	/l/
ant-pant	/p/	it-pit	/p/
ant-rant	/r/	it-sit	/s/

6 Adding a Final Consonant Sound

GOAL

- **The student will spell new words by adding a final consonant sound.**

MATERIALS

○ Word bank for this activity

○ Magnetic letters, paper letters, or letter tiles

MODEL

Say the following:
- "I'm going to spell the word *an*."
- "Listen and watch while I put down one letter for each sound I say: /ă/ /n/." (Put down the corresponding letter for each sound you say.)
- "The new word is *and*."
- "Listen and watch." (Point to the letters as you say the sounds, /ă/ /n/ /d/. Insert the letter that represents the added sound. See the illustration below.)
- "When I add the sound /d/ to *an*, the word is *and*."

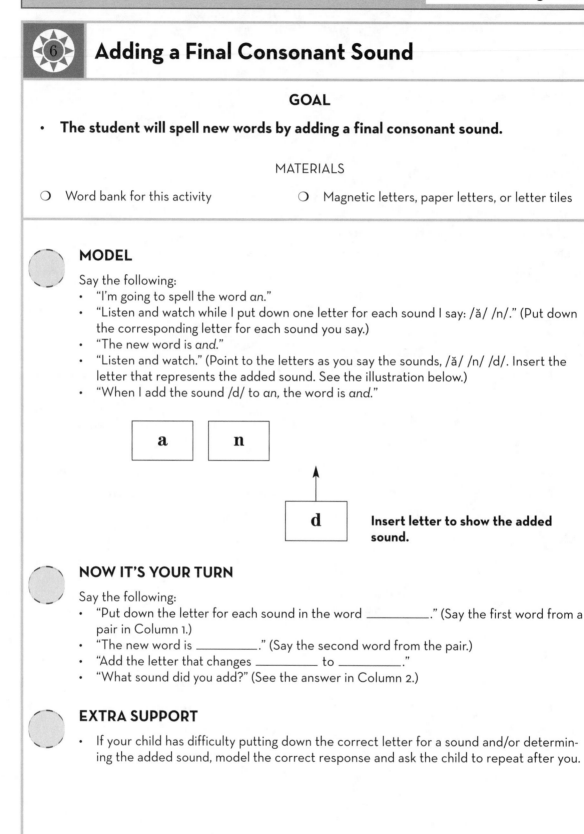

Insert letter to show the added sound.

NOW IT'S YOUR TURN

Say the following:
- "Put down the letter for each sound in the word _____." (Say the first word from a pair in Column 1.)
- "The new word is _____." (Say the second word from the pair.)
- "Add the letter that changes _____ to _____."
- "What sound did you add?" (See the answer in Column 2.)

EXTRA SUPPORT

- If your child has difficulty putting down the correct letter for a sound and/or determining the added sound, model the correct response and ask the child to repeat after you.

Word Bank on following page

Word Bank

1. Word pairs	2. Added sound	1. Word pairs	2. Added sound
an-and	/d/	men-mend	/d/
an-ant	/t/	pan-pant	/t/
ban-band	/d/	ran-rant	/t/
Ben-bent	/t/	Stan-stand	/d/
Ben-bend	/d/	ten-tent	/t/
bus-bust	/t/	ten-tend	/d/
den-dent	/t/	tin-tint	/t/

Adding a Sound to Form an Initial Consonant Blend

(7)

GOAL

- The student will spell new words by adding a sound to form an initial consonant blend.

MATERIALS

○ Word bank for this activity

○ Magnetic letters, paper letters, or letter tiles

MODEL

Say the following:

- "I'm going to spell the word *lap*."
- "Listen and watch while I put down one letter for each sound I say: /l/ /ă/ /p/." (Put down the corresponding letter for each sound you say.)
- "The new word is *clap*."
- "Listen and watch." (Point to the letters as you say the sounds, (/k/ /l/ /ă/ /p/). Insert the letter that represents the added sound. See the illustration below.)
- "Listen and watch." (Add the letter representing the first sound. Point to the remaining letters as you say the sounds, /k/ /l/ /ă/ /p/. See the illustration below.)
- "When I add the sound /k/ to *lap*, the word is *clap*."

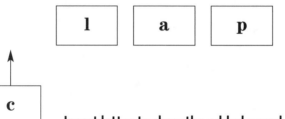

Insert letter to show the added sound.

NOW IT'S YOUR TURN

Say the following:

- "Put down the letter for each sound in the word _____." (Say the first word from a pair in Column 1.)
- "The new word is _____." (Say the second word from the pair.)
- "Add the letter that changes _____ to _____."
- "What sound did you add?" (See the answer in Column 2.)

EXTRA SUPPORT

- If your child has difficulty putting down the correct letter for a sound and/or determining the added sound, model the correct response and ask the child to repeat after you.

Word Bank on following page

Word Bank

1. Word pairs	2. Added sound	1. Word pairs	2. Added sound
can-scan	/s/	Pam-spam	/s/
kid-skid	/s/	pan-span	/s/
kin-skin	/s/	pin-spin	/s/
kit-skit	/s/	pit-spit	/s/
lamp-clamp	/k/	pot-spot	/s/
lap-clap	/k/	pun-spun	/s/
lap-flap	/f/	rag-brag	/b/
lap-slap	/s/	ram-cram	/k/
lend-blend	/b/	ran-bran	/b/
lid-slid	/s/	rank-prank	/p/
limp-blimp	/b/	rant-grant	/g/
link-blink	/b/	rap-trap	/t/
link-clink	/k/	rib-crib	/k/
link-slink	/s/	rim-brim	/b/
lip-flip	/f/	rim-trim	/t/
lip-slip	/s/	rip-drip	/d/
lit-slit	/s/	rip-grip	/g/
lot-blot	/b/	rip-trip	/t/
lot-clot	/k/	rot-trot	/t/
lot-plot	/p/	rug-drug	/d/
lump-plump	/p/	runt-grunt	/g/
lump-slump	/s/	top-stop	/s/
mug-smug	/s/	wag-swag	/s/
nag-snag	/s/	wig-swig	/s/
nap-snap	/s/	wig-twig	/t/
nip-snip	/s/	win-twin	/t/

⑧ Adding an Initial Consonant Blend

GOAL

- **The student will spell new words by adding an initial consonant blend.**

MATERIALS

○ Word bank for this activity

○ Magnetic letters, paper letters, or letter tiles

MODEL

Say the following:
- "I'm going to spell the word *in*."
- "Listen and watch while I put down one letter for each sound I say: /ĭ/ /n/." (Say the word sound by sound. Put down the corresponding letter for each sound you say.)
- "The new word is *spin*."
- "Listen and watch." (Add the letters representing the first two sounds. Point to the remaining letters as you say the sounds, /s/ /p/ /ĭ/ /n/. See the illustration below.)
- "When I add the sounds /s/ /p/ to *in*, the word is *spin*."

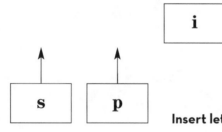

Insert letters to show the added sounds.

NOW IT'S YOUR TURN

Say the following:
- "Put down the letter for each sound in the word _____." (Say the first word from a pair in column 1.)
- "The new word is _____." (Say the second word from the pair.)
- "Add the letters that change _____ to _____."
- "What sound did you add?" (See the answer in Column 2.)

EXTRA SUPPORT

- If your child has difficulty putting down the correct letter for a sound and/or determining the added sounds, model the correct response and ask the child to repeat after you.

Word Bank on following page

Word Bank

1. Word Pairs	2. Added sounds	1. Word Pairs	2. Added sounds
am-clam	/k/ /l/	Ed-fled	/f/ /l/
am-cram	/k/ /r/	Ed-sled	/s/ /l/
am-slam	/s/ /l/	end-blend	/b/ /l/
am-spam	/s/ /p/	end-trend	/t/ /r/
am-swam	/s/ /w/	in-grin	/g/ /r/
am-tram	/t/ /r/	ink-blink	/b/ /l/
an-bran	/b/ /r/	ink-clink	/k/ /l/
an-clan	/k/ /l/	ink-drink	/d/ /r/
an-plan	/p/ /l/	ink-slink	/s/ /l/
an-Stan	/s/ /t/	ink-stink	/s/ /t/
ant-grant	/g/ /r/	in-skin	/s/ /k/
ant-plant	/p/ /l/	in-spin	/s/ /p/
ant-slant	/s/ /l/	in-twin	/t/ /w/
at-brat	/b/ /r/	it-skit	/s/ /k/
at-flat	/f/ /l/	it-slit	/s/ /l/
at-slat	/s/ /l/	it-spit	/s/ /p/
at-spat	/s/ /p/	us-plus	/p/ /l/
Ed-bled	/b/ /l/		

9

Adding a Second Sound to Form an Initial Consonant Blend

GOAL

- **The student will spell new words by adding a sound to form an initial consonant blend.**

MATERIALS

○ Word bank for this activity

○ Magnetic letters, paper letters, or letter tiles

MODEL

Say the following:
- "I'm going to spell the word *tin*."
- "Listen and watch while I put down one letter for each sound I say: /t/ /ĭ/ /n/." (Put down the corresponding letter for each sound you say.)
- "The new word is *twin*."
- "Listen and watch." (Point to the letters as you say the sounds, /t/ /w/ /ĭ/ /n/. Insert the letter that represents the added sound. See the illustration below.)
- "When I add the sound /w/ to *tin*, the word is *twin*."

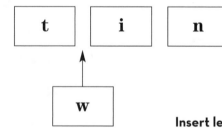

| t | i | n |

| w |

Insert letter to show the added sound.

NOW IT'S YOUR TURN

Say the following:
- "Put down the letter for each sound in the word _____." (Say the first word from a pair in Column 1.)
- "The new word is _____." (Say the second word from the pair.)
- "Add the letter that changes _____ to _____."
- "What sound did you add?" (See the answer in Column 2.)

EXTRA SUPPORT

- If your child has difficulty putting down the correct letter for a sound and/or determining the added sound, model the correct response and ask the child to repeat after you.

Word Bank on following page

Word Bank

1. Word pairs	2. Added sounds	1. Word pairs	2. Added sounds
bag-brag	/r/	Sid-slid	/l/
bend-blend	/l/	sink-slink	/l/
camp-clamp	/l/	sin-skin	/k/
camp-cramp	/r/	sin-spin	/p/
cap-clap	/l/	sip-slip	/l/
cot-clot	/l/	sit-skit	/k/
daft-draft	/r/	sit-slit	/l/
dug-drug	/r/	sit-spit	/p/
pant-plant	/l/	sop-stop	/t/
pot-plot	/l/	sun-spun	/p/
pump-plump	/l/	tap-trap	/r/
sag-snag	/n/	Tim-trim	/r/
sag-swag	/w/	tin-twin	/w/
sap-slap	/l/	tip-trip	/r/
Sid-skid	/k/	tot-trot	/r/

(10) Deleting an Initial Consonant Sound

GOAL

• **The student will spell new words by deleting an initial consonant sound.**

MATERIALS

○ Word bank for this activity

○ Magnetic letters, paper letters, or letter tiles

MODEL

Say the following:

• "I'm going to spell the word *mat*."
• "Listen and watch while I put down one letter for each sound I say: /m/ /ă/ /t/." (Put down the corresponding letter for each sound you say.)
• "The new word is *at*."
• "Listen and watch." (Point to the letters as you say the sounds, /ă/ /t/. Remove the letter that represents the deleted sound. See the illustration below.)
• "I took away the sound /m/ to change *mat* to *at*."

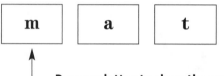

| m | a | t |

Remove letter to show the sound being deleted.

NOW IT'S YOUR TURN

Say the following:

• "Put down the letter for each sound in the word _____." (Say the first word from a pair in Column 1.)
• "The new word is _____." (Say the second word from the pair.)
• "Take away the letter that changes _____ to _____."
• "What sound did you take away?" (See the answer in Column 2.)

EXTRA SUPPORT

• If your child has difficulty putting down the correct letter for a sound and/or determining the deleted sound, model the correct response and ask the child to repeat after you.

Word Bank on following page

Word Bank

1. Word pairs	2. Deleted sound	1. Word pairs	2. Deleted sound
bad-ad	/b/	mat-at	/m/
ban-an	/b/	mend-end	/m/
band-and	/b/	mink-ink	/m/
bat-at	/b/	Ned-Ed	/n/
bed-Ed	/b/	pad-ad	/p/
bend-end	/b/	Pam-am	/p/
bin-in	/b/	pan-an	/p/
bit-it	/b/	pant-ant	/p/
can-an	/k/	pat-at	/p/
can't-ant	/k/	pin-in	/p/
cat-at	/k/	pink-ink	/p/
dad-ad	/d/	pit-it	/p/
Dan-an	/d/	ram-am	/r/
fad-ad	/f/	ran-an	/r/
fan-an	/f/	rant-ant	/r/
fat-at	/f/	rat-at	/r/
fed-Ed	/f/	red-Ed	/r/
fin-in	/f/	rink-ink	/r/
fit-it	/f/	sad-ad	/s/
had-ad	/h/	Sam-am	/s/
ham-am	/h/	sand-and	/s/
hand-and	/h/	sat-at	/s/
hat-at	/h/	send-end	/s/
hit-it	/h/	sink-ink	/s/
jam-am	/j/	sit-it	/s/
kit-it	/k/	tan-an	/t/
lad-ad	/l/	task-ask	/t/
land-and	/l/	Ted-Ed	/t/
led-Ed	/l/	tend-end	/t/
lend-end	/l/	tin-in	/t/
link-ink	/l/	vend-end	/v/
lit-it	/l/	wed-Ed	/w/
mad-ad	/m/	win-in	/w/
man-an	/m/	wink-ink	/w/
mask-ask	/m/	wit-it	/w/

11 Deleting the First Sound from an Initial Consonant Blend

GOAL

- The student will spell new words by deleting the first sound from an initial consonant blend.

MATERIALS

○ Word bank for this activity

○ Magnetic letters, paper letters, or letter tiles

MODEL

Say the following:
- "I'm going to spell the word *trap*."
- "Listen and watch while I put down one letter for each sound I say: /t/ /r/ /ă/ /p/." (Put down the corresponding letter for each sound you say.)
- "The new word is *rap*."
- "Listen and watch." (Point to the letters as you say the sounds, /r/ /ă/ /p/. Remove the letter that represents the deleted sound. See the illustration below.)
- "I took away the sound /t/ to change *trap* to *rap*."

Remove letter to show the sound being deleted.

NOW IT'S YOUR TURN

Say the following:
- "Put down the letter for each sound in the word _____." (Say the first word from a pair in column 1.)
- "The new word is _____." (Say the second word from the pair.)
- "Take away the letter that changes _____ to _____."
- "What sound did you take away?" (See the answer in Column 2.)

EXTRA SUPPORT

- If your child has difficulty putting down the correct letter for a sound and/or determining the deleted sound, model the correct response and ask the child to repeat after you.

Word Bank on following page

Word Bank

1. Word pairs	2. Deleted sound	1. Word pairs	2. Deleted sound
blend-lend	/b/	skin-kin	/s/
blimp-limp	/b/	skit-kit	/s/
blink-link	/b/	slap-lap	/s/
blot-lot	/b/	sled-led	/s/
brag-rag	/b/	slid-lid	/s/
bran-ran	/b/	slink-link	/s/
brim-rim	/b/	slip-lip	/s/
brink-rink	/b/	slit-lit	/s/
clap-lap	/k/	slot-lot	/s/
clink-link	/k/	slug-lug	/s/
clip-lip	/k/	slump-lump	/s/
clot-lot	/k/	snag-nag	/s/
cram-ram	/k/	snap-nap	/s/
cramp-ramp	/k/	snip-nip	/s/
crank-rank	/k/	span-pan	/s/
crib-rib	/k/	spin-pin	/s/
draft-raft	/d/	spit-pit	/s/
drink-rink	/d/	spot-pot	/s/
drip-rip	/d/	spun-pun	/s/
drug-rug	/d/	stop-top	/s/
drum-rum	/d/	swig-wig	/s/
flap-lap	/f/	trap-rap	/t/
flip-lip	/f/	trim-rim	/t/
grip-rip	/g/	trip-rip	/t/
grunt-runt	/g/	trot-rot	/t/
plot-lot	/p/	twig-wig	/t/
plump-lump	/p/	twin-win	/t/
skid-kid	/s/		

Deleting the Second Sound from an Initial Consonant Blend

GOAL

- The student will spell new words by deleting the second sound from an initial consonant blend.

MATERIALS

○ Word bank for this activity

○ Magnetic letters, paper letters, or letter tiles

MODEL

Say the following:
- "I'm going to spell the word *slip*."
- "Listen and watch while I put down one letter for each sound I say: /s/ /l/ /ĭ/ /p/." (Put down the corresponding letter for each sound you say.)
- "The new word is *sip*."
- "Listen and watch." (Point to the letters as you say the sounds, /s/ /ĭ/ /p/. Remove the letter that represents the deleted sound. See the illustration below.)
- "I took away the sound /l/ to change *slip* to *sip*."

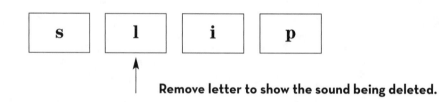

Remove letter to show the sound being deleted.

NOW IT'S YOUR TURN

Say the following:
- "Put down the letter for each sound in the word _____." (Say the first word from a pair in Column 1.)
- "The new word is _____." (Say the second word from the pair.)
- "Take away the letter that changes _____ to _____."
- "What sound did you take away?" (See the answer in Column 2.)

EXTRA SUPPORT

- If your child has difficulty putting down the correct letter for a sound and/or determining the deleted sound, model the correct response and ask the child to repeat after you.

Word Bank on following page

Word Bank

1. Word pairs	2. Deleted sound	1. Word pairs	2. Deleted sound
blend-bend	/l/	snag-sag	/n/
brag-bag	/r/	snap-sap	/n/
clamp-camp	/l/	snip-sip	/n/
clap-cap	/l/	spin-sin	/p/
cramp-camp	/r/	spit-sit	/p/
plant-pant	/l/	spun-sun	/p/
plot-pot	/l/	trap-tap	/r/
plump-pump	/l/	trim-Tim	/r/
skid-Sid	/k/	trip-tip	/r/
skin-sin	/k/	trot-tot	/r/
skit-sit	/k/	twin-tin	/w/
slap-sap	/l/		

⑬ Deleting a Final Consonant Sound

GOAL

- **The student will spell new words by deleting a final consonant sound.**

MATERIALS

○ Word bank for this activity   ○ Magnetic letters, paper letters, or letter tiles

MODEL

Say the following:
- "I'm going to spell the word *and.*"
- "Listen and watch while I put down one letter for each sound I say: /ă/ /n/ /d/." (Put down the corresponding letter for each sound you say.)
- "The new word is *an.*"
- "Listen and watch." (Point to the letters as you say the sounds, /ă/ /n/. Remove the letter that represents the deleted sound. See the illustration below.)
- "I took away the sound /d/ to change *and* to *an.*"

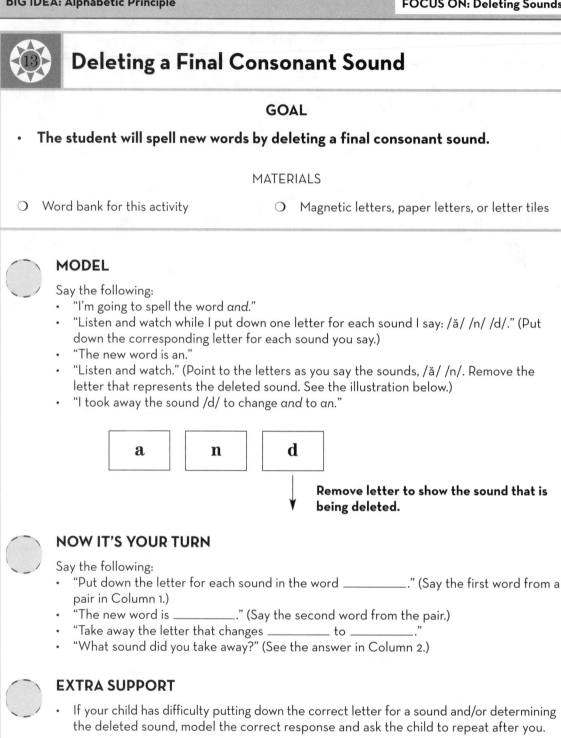

| a | n | d |

↓ **Remove letter to show the sound that is being deleted.**

NOW IT'S YOUR TURN

Say the following:
- "Put down the letter for each sound in the word _____." (Say the first word from a pair in Column 1.)
- "The new word is _____." (Say the second word from the pair.)
- "Take away the letter that changes _____ to _____."
- "What sound did you take away?" (See the answer in Column 2.)

EXTRA SUPPORT

- If your child has difficulty putting down the correct letter for a sound and/or determining the deleted sound, model the correct response and ask the child to repeat after you.

Word Bank on following page

Word Bank

1. Word pairs	2. Deleted sound	1. Word pairs	2. Deleted sound
and-an	/d/	rant-ran	/t/
ant-an	/t/	stand-Stan	/d/
bend-Ben	/d/	tend-ten	/d/
bust-bus	/t/	tent-ten	/t/
dent-den	/t/	tint-tin	/t/
mend-men	/d/		

(14) Substituting an Initial Consonant Sound

GOAL

- **The student will spell new words by substituting an initial consonant sound.**

MATERIALS

○ Word bank for this activity

○ Magnetic letters, paper letters, or letter tiles

MODEL

Say the following:
- "I'm going to spell the word *sit*."
- "Listen and watch while I put down one letter for each sound I say: /s/ /ĭ/ /t/." (Put down the corresponding letter for each sound you say.)
- "The new word is *hit*."
- "Listen and watch." (Substitute the letter that represents the new sound. Point to the letters as you say the sounds, /h/ /ĭ/ /t/. See the illustration below.)
- "I changed the sound /s/ to /h/ to make *sit* into *hit*."

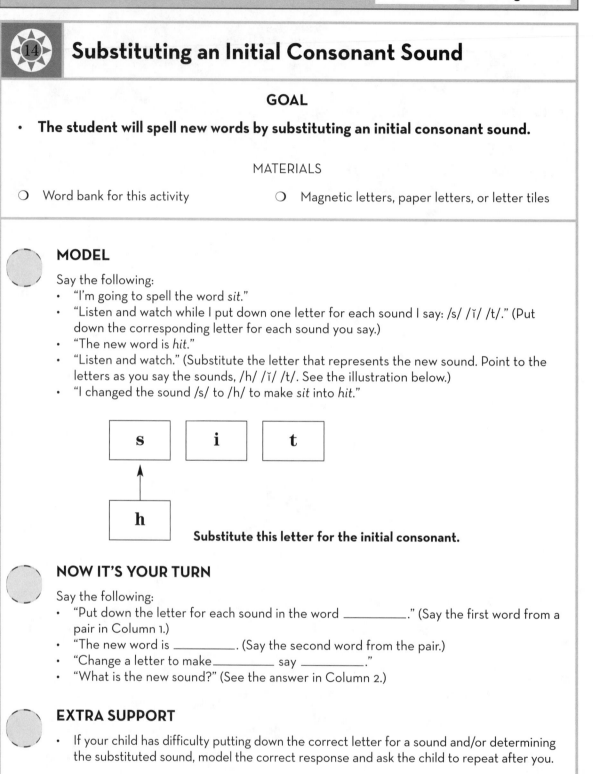

Substitute this letter for the initial consonant.

NOW IT'S YOUR TURN

Say the following:
- "Put down the letter for each sound in the word _____." (Say the first word from a pair in Column 1.)
- "The new word is _____. (Say the second word from the pair.)
- "Change a letter to make _____ say _____."
- "What is the new sound?" (See the answer in Column 2.)

EXTRA SUPPORT

- If your child has difficulty putting down the correct letter for a sound and/or determining the substituted sound, model the correct response and ask the child to repeat after you.

Word Bank on following page

Word Bank

1. Word pairs	2. Substituted sound	1. Word pairs	2. Substituted sound
bag-tag	/t/	men-ten	/t/
bed-red	/r/	nut-cut	/k/
best-nest	/n/	pan-man	/m/
bet-set	/s/	pant-rant	/r/
big-fig	/f/	pig-jig	/j/
bit-kit	/k/	pit-fit	/f/
can-ran	/r/	rub-sub	/s/
cap-map	/m/	rut-hut	/h/
cat-rat	/r/	sad-mad	/m/
cot-hot	/h/	Sam-Pam	/p/
dad-pad	/p/	sand-hand	/h/
dig-wig	/w/	sap-tap	/t/
dip-sip	/s/	sat-hat	/h/
dot-pot	/p/	sink-pink	/p/
ham-jam	/j/	sit-hit	/h/
hen-pen	/p/	tan-fan	/f/
hip-lip	/l/	Tim-him	/h/
hop-mop	/m/	tub-cub	/k/
jet-pet	/p/	wag-rag	/r/
lad-had	/h/	west-test	/t/
land-band	/b/	wet-vet	/v/
mask-task	/t/	wink-mink	/m/
mat-fat	/f/		

Interventions for Reading Success by Diane Haager, Joseph A. Dimino, and Michelle Pearlman Windmueller

HOME-SCHOOL CONNECTION ACTIVITY
ALPHABETIC PRINCIPLE • Substituting Sounds

(15) Substituting a Final Consonant Sound

GOAL

- **The student will spell new words by substituting a final consonant sound.**

MATERIALS

○ Word bank for this activity ○ Magnetic letters, paper letters, or letter tiles

MODEL

Say the following:
- "I'm going to spell the word *ran*."
- "Listen and watch while I put down one letter for each sound I say: /r/ /ă/ /n/." (Put down the corresponding letter for each sound you say.)
- "The new word is *rag*."
- "Listen and watch." (Substitute the letter that represents the new sound. Point to the letters as you say the sounds, /r/ /ă/ /g/. See the illustration below.)
- "I changed the sound /n/ to /g/ to change *ran* to *rag*."

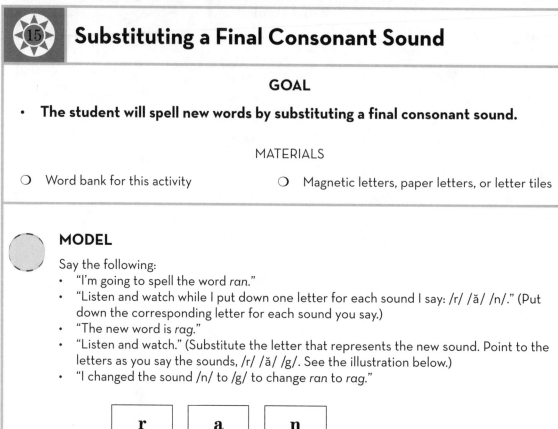

Substitute this letter for the final consonant.

NOW IT'S YOUR TURN

Say the following:
- "Put down the letter for each sound in the word _____." (Say the first word from a pair in Column 1.)
- "The new word is _____." (Say the second word from the pair.)
- "Change a letter to make_____ say _____."
- "What is the new sound?" (See the answer in Column 2.)

EXTRA SUPPORT

- If your child has difficulty putting down the correct letter for a sound and/or determining the substituted sound, model the correct response and ask the child to repeat after you.

Word Bank on following page

Interventions for Reading Success by Diane Haager, Joseph A. Dimino, and Michelle Pearlman Windmueller
Copyright © 2007 by Paul H. Brookes Publishing Co., Inc. All rights reserved.

Word Bank

1. Word pairs	2. Substituted sound	1. Word pairs	2. Substituted sound
bat-bag	/g/	net-Ned	/d/
Ben-beg	/g/	not-nod	/d/
bit-big	/g/	Pam-Pat	/t/
bug-bus	/s/	pen-pet	/t/
cot-cob	/b/	rat-ran	/n/
dot-Don	/n/	rib-rip	/p/
fan-fat	/t/	Sam-sap	/p/
fit-fig	/g/	sat-sad	/d/
gum-gun	/n/	sit-Sid	/d/
hat-ham	/m/	sun-sum	/m/
hug-hum	/m/	tap-tag	/g/
jog-jot	/t/	tip-Tim	/m/
lip-lid	/d/	Tom-top	/p/
mat-man	/n/	wet-web	/b/
mug-mud	/d/	yet-yes	/s/

Interventions for Reading Success by Diane Haager, Joseph A. Dimino, and Michelle Pearlman Windmueller

16 Substituting a Medial Vowel Sound

GOAL

- **The student will spell new words by substituting a medial sound.**

MATERIALS

- ○ Word bank for this activity
- ○ Magnetic letters, paper letters, or letter tiles

MODEL

Say the following:
- "I'm going to spell the word *sat*."
- "Listen and watch while I put down one letter for each sound I say: /s/ /ă/ /t/." (Put down the corresponding letter for each sound you say.)
- "The new word is *sit*."
- "Listen and watch." (Point to the letters as you say the sounds, /s/ /ĭ/ /t/. Substitute the letter that represents the new medial sound. See the illustration below.)
- "Listen and watch." (Substitute the letter that represents the new sound. Point to the letters as you say the sounds, /s/ /ĭ/ /t/. See the illustration below.)
- "I changed the sound /ă/ to /ĭ/ to change *sat* to *sit*."

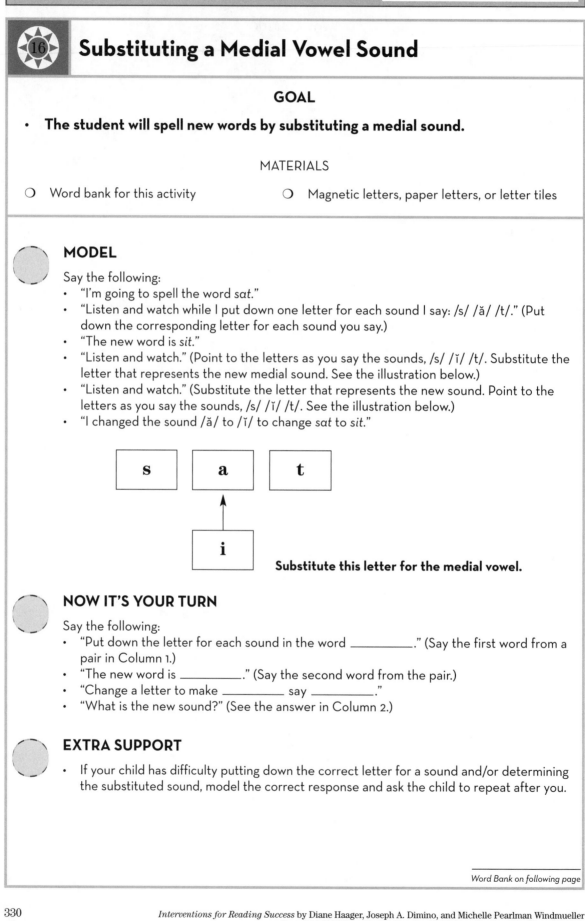

Substitute this letter for the medial vowel.

NOW IT'S YOUR TURN

Say the following:
- "Put down the letter for each sound in the word _____." (Say the first word from a pair in Column 1.)
- "The new word is _____." (Say the second word from the pair.)
- "Change a letter to make _____ say _____."
- "What is the new sound?" (See the answer in Column 2.)

EXTRA SUPPORT

- If your child has difficulty putting down the correct letter for a sound and/or determining the substituted sound, model the correct response and ask the child to repeat after you.

Word Bank on following page

Word Bank

1. Word pairs	2. Substituted sound	1. Word pairs	2. Substituted sound
big-beg	/ĕ/	map-mop	/ŏ/
bun-Ben	/ĕ/	mud-mad	/ă/
den-Dan	/ă/	pin-pen	/ĕ/
did-dad	/ă/	pop-pup	/ŭ/
fan-fin	/ĭ/	rib-rob	/ŏ/
Gus-gas	/ă/	rod-red	/ĕ/
ham-him	/ĭ/	Ron-run	/ŭ/
hit-hot	/ŏ/	rug-rag	/ă/
hog-hug	/ŭ/	Sam-sum	/ŭ/
hop-hip	/ĭ/	set-sit	/ĭ/
hug-hog	/ŏ/	tab-tub	/ŭ/
lip-lap	/ă/	tan-ten	/ĕ/

Reading and Spelling Words with the Long a Sound

Your child has learned to read and spell words in which a silent e makes the first vowel say the long sound as in the word *name*.

GOAL

- **The student will read and spell words with the long a sound containing the CVCe, CCVCe, and VCe patterns.**

MATERIALS

- Word bank for this activity
- Magnetic letters, paper letters, or letter tiles
- Timer

READ

MODEL

- Read the word bank for this activity with your child in two different ways. First read across rows, then read down each column.

NOW IT'S YOUR TURN

- Ask your child to read the words across and down.
- Time your child for 1 minute as your child reads the words across the rows. Count the number of words read. The purpose of this exercise is to see how many words your child can read correctly in 1 minute. After your child reads the words across the rows, count the words. Write the number on a sheet of paper.
- Time your child for 1 minute as your child reads the words down the columns. Count the number of words read. The goal is for your child to read more words the second time.

EXTRA SUPPORT

- If your child has difficulty reading a word, say the word and ask the child to repeat it.

SPELL

MODEL

- Say a word from the word bank.
- Spell the word with the letter tiles.

NOW IT'S YOUR TURN

- Say a word from the word bank.
- Ask your child to spell the word with the letter tiles.

Activity and Word Bank continued on following page

Interventions for Reading Success by Diane Haager, Joseph A. Dimino, and Michelle Pearlman Windmueller

EXTRA SUPPORT

- If your child has difficulty spelling a word, model the correct response and ask the child to repeat after you.

Word Bank

fake	shame	safe	skate	name
waste	pane	bake	slave	shave
male	grave	gate	cape	slate
trade	late	hate	came	stale
plane	pave	tame	fade	brave
tape	make	snake	taste	pale
fate	wave	take	made	cane
blade	blame	ate	flake	Dave
Jane	game	ape	rate	cave
plate	gaze	shake	Kate	rake
cake	state	gale	dale	shale
ale	bale	tale	whale	hale

Interventions for Reading Success by Diane Haager, Joseph A. Dimino, and Michelle Pearlman Windmueller
Copyright © 2007 by Paul H. Brookes Publishing Co., Inc. All rights reserved.

HOME-SCHOOL CONNECTION ACTIVITY
ALPHABETIC PRINCIPLE · Long Vowel Spelling Patterns

Reading and Spelling Words with the Long e Sound

Your child has learned to read and spell words in which a silent e makes the first vowel say the long sound as in the word *Steve*.

GOAL

- **The student will read and spell words with the long e sound containing the CVCe and CCVe patterns.**

MATERIALS

- ○ Word bank for this activity
- ○ Magnetic letters, paper letters, or letter tiles

- ○ Timer

READ

MODEL

- Read the word bank for this activity with your child in two different ways. First read across rows, then read down each column.

NOW IT'S YOUR TURN

- Ask your child to read the words across and down.
- Time your child for 1 minute as your child reads the words across the rows. Count the number of words read. The purpose of this exercise is to see how many words your child can read correctly in 1 minute. After your child reads the words across the rows, count the words. Write the number on a sheet of paper.
- Time your child for 1 minute as your child reads the words down the columns. Count the number of words read. The goal is for your child to read more words the second time.

EXTRA SUPPORT

- If your child has difficulty reading a word, say the word and ask the child to repeat it.

SPELL

MODEL

- Say a word from the word bank.
- Spell the word with the letter tiles.

NOW IT'S YOUR TURN

- Say a word from the word bank.
- Ask your child to spell the word with the letter tiles.

Activity and Word Bank continued on following page

Interventions for Reading Success by Diane Haager, Joseph A. Dimino, and Michelle Pearlman Windmueller

EXTRA SUPPORT

- If your child has difficulty spelling a word, model the correct response and ask the child to repeat after you.

Word Bank				
Pete	Eve	Steve	here	grebe
plebe	cede	Swede	Mede	Zeke
theme	Gene	mere	sere	these
mete	Pete	Eve	Steve	here
grebe	plebe	cede	Swede	these
Zeke	theme	Gene	mere	sere
these	mete	Pete	Eve	Steve
here	grebe	plebe	cede	Swede
mere	Zeke	theme	Gene	mere
sere	mere	mete	Pete	Eve
Steve	here	grebe	plebe	cede

Reading and Spelling Words with the Long *i* Sound

Your child has learned to read and spell words in which a silent e makes the first vowel say the long sound as in the word *smile*.

GOAL

- **The student will read and spell words with the long *i* sound containing the CCCVCe, CVCe, and CCVe patterns.**

MATERIALS

- Word bank for this activity
- Magnetic letters, paper letters, or letter tiles

- Timer

READ

MODEL

- Read the word bank for this activity with your child in two different ways. First read across rows, then read down each column.

NOW IT'S YOUR TURN

- Ask your child to read the words across and down.
- Time your child for 1 minute as your child reads the words across the rows. Count the number of words read. The purpose of this exercise is to see how many words your child can read correctly in 1 minute. After your child reads the words across the rows, count the words. Write the number on a sheet of paper.
- Time your child for 1 minute as your child reads the words down the columns. Count the number of words read. The goal is for your child to read more words the second time.

EXTRA SUPPORT

- If your child has difficulty reading a word, say the word and ask the child to repeat it.

SPELL

MODEL

- Say a word from the word bank.
- Spell the word with the letter tiles.

NOW IT'S YOUR TURN

- Say a word from the word bank.
- Ask your child to spell the word with the letter tiles.

Activity and Word Bank continued on following page

Interventions for Reading Success by Diane Haager, Joseph A. Dimino, and Michelle Pearlman Windmueller

EXTRA SUPPORT

- If your child has difficulty spelling a word, model the correct response and ask the child to repeat after you.

Word Bank

bite	live	ripe	tide	while
dine	prize	hive	fine	white
sire	spite	smile	swipe	bike
like	glide	Mike	drive	side
life	pike	spine	crime	stride
quite	tile	kite	spike	mine
pipe	five	mile	wine	pile
file	slide	line	strike	ride
fire	hire	dive	vine	gripe
hide	bride	lime	stripe	chime
tire	pride	vile	wide	size

HOME-SCHOOL CONNECTION ACTIVITY
ALPHABETIC PRINCIPLE • Long Vowel Spelling Patterns

Reading and Spelling Words with the Long o Sound

Your child has learned to read and spell words in which a silent e makes the first vowel say the long sound as in the word *joke*.

GOAL

- **The student will read and spell words with the long o sound containing the CVCe, CCVe, and VCe patterns.**

MATERIALS

○ Word bank for this activity
○ Magnetic letters, paper letters, or letter tiles

○ Timer

READ

MODEL

- Read the word bank for this activity with your child in two different ways. First read across rows, then read down each column.

NOW IT'S YOUR TURN

- Ask your child to read the words across and down.
- Time your child for 1 minute as your child reads the words across the rows. Count the number of words read. The purpose of this exercise is to see how many words your child can read correctly in 1 minute. After your child reads the words across the rows, count the words. Write the number on a sheet of paper.
- Time your child for 1 minute as your child reads the words down the columns. Count the number of words read. The goal is for your child to read more words the second time.

EXTRA SUPPORT

- If your child has difficulty reading a word, say the word and ask the child to repeat it.

SPELL

MODEL

- Say a word from the word bank.
- Spell the word with the letter tiles.

NOW IT'S YOUR TURN

- Say a word from the word bank.
- Ask your child to spell the word with the letter tiles.

Activity and Word Bank continued on following page

Interventions for Reading Success by Diane Haager, Joseph A. Dimino, and Michelle Pearlman Windmueller

EXTRA SUPPORT

- If your child has difficulty spelling a word, model the correct response and ask the child to repeat after you.

		Word Bank		
note	mope	vote	robe	stole
tone	lobe	hole	globe	shore
poke	sole	rope	more	snore
slope	drove	chore	stove	throne
smoke	grope	snore	bone	cone
woke	store	mope	cope	tone
froze	choke	sore	slope	score
cope	joke	store	stole	rode
stone	woke	score	core	scope
broke	grove	hope	sole	dome
vote	coke	doze	pole	grope
mole	dote	spoke	spoke	smoke

Interventions for Reading Success by Diane Haager, Joseph A. Dimino, and Michelle Pearlman Windmueller

HOME-SCHOOL CONNECTION ACTIVITY
ALPHABETIC PRINCIPLE • Long Vowel Spelling Patterns

Reading and Spelling Words with the Long *u* Sound

Your child has learned to read and spell words in which a silent e makes the first vowel say the long sound as in the word *cute*.

GOAL

- **The student will read and spell words with the long *u* sound containing the CVCe, CCVe, and VCe patterns.**

MATERIALS

- ○ Word bank for this activity
- ○ Magnetic letters, paper letters, or letter tiles
- ○ Timer

READ

MODEL

- Read the word bank for this activity with your child in two different ways. First read across rows, then read down each column.

NOW IT'S YOUR TURN

- Ask your child to read the words across and down.
- Time your child for 1 minute as your child reads the words across the rows. Count the number of words read. The purpose of this exercise is to see how many words your child can read correctly in 1 minute. After your child reads the words across the rows, count the words. Write the number on a sheet of paper.
- Time your child for 1 minute as your child reads the words down the columns. Count the number of words read. The goal is for your child to read more words the second time.

EXTRA SUPPORT

- If your child has difficulty reading a word, say the word and ask the child to repeat it.

SPELL

MODEL

- Say a word from the word bank.
- Spell the word with the letter tiles.

NOW IT'S YOUR TURN

- Say a word from the word bank.
- Ask your child to spell the word with the letter tiles.

Activity and Word Bank continued on following page

EXTRA SUPPORT

- If your child has difficulty spelling a word, model the correct response and ask the child to repeat after you.

Word Bank

cute	cure	mule	use	pure
fume	cube	cures	mules	fumes
cubes	muse	huge	cuke	pule
cukes	yule	mute	fuse	cute
fuses	cure	mule	use	pure
cute	fume	cube	cures	mules
fumes	cubes	muse	huge	cuke
pule	cukes	yule	mute	fuse
cute	fuses	cure	mule	use
pure	cute	fume	cube	cures
mules	fumes	cubes	muse	huge

Reading and Spelling Words with the Long *a, e, i, o, u* Sounds

Your child has learned to read and spell words in which a silent e makes the first vowel say the long sound as in the words *name, Steve, smile, joke,* and *cute.*

GOAL

- **The student will read and spell words with the long *a, e, i, o,* and *u* sounds containing the CVCe, CCVe, and VCe patterns.**

MATERIALS

○ Word bank for this activity
○ Magnetic letters, paper letters, or letter tiles

○ Timer

READ

MODEL

- Read the word bank for this activity with your child in two different ways. First read across rows, then read down each column.

NOW IT'S YOUR TURN

- Ask your child to read the words across and down.
- Time your child for 1 minute as your child reads the words across the rows. Count the number of words read. The purpose of this exercise is to see how many words your child can read correctly in 1 minute. After your child reads the words across the rows, count the words. Write the number on a sheet of paper.
- Time your child for 1 minute as your child reads the words down the columns. Count the number of words read. The goal is for your child to read more words the second time.

EXTRA SUPPORT

- If your child has difficulty reading a word, say the word and ask the child to repeat it.

SPELL

MODEL

- Say a word from the word bank.
- Spell the word with the letter tiles.

NOW IT'S YOUR TURN

- Say a word from the word bank.
- Ask your child to spell the word with the letter tiles.

Activity and Word Bank continued on following page

Interventions for Reading Success by Diane Haager, Joseph A. Dimino, and Michelle Pearlman Windmueller
Copyright © 2007 by Paul H. Brookes Publishing Co., Inc. All rights reserved.

EXTRA SUPPORT

- If your child has difficulty spelling a word, model the correct response and ask the child to repeat after you.

Word Bank

rope	whale	live	stale	pine
cave	fume	wide	stove	mine
state	cone	blade	drove	base
muse	name	whine	fate	use
froze	swipe	late	shine	pave
haze	mope	cane	globe	side
tone	tube	dime	cute	chase
fine	case	fire	pole	make
cure	shave	prize	pile	date
Steve	hive	safe	eve	stone
pride	glare	shade	Pete	tame

Reading and Spelling Words with the Long a Sound (More Complex Patterns)

Your child has learned to read and spell words containing two vowels in which the first vowel says the long sound and the second vowel is silent as in the word *pail*.

GOAL

- **The student will read and spell words with the long a sound containing the *ai* digraph.**

MATERIALS

○ Word bank for this activity   ○ Timer
○ Magnetic letters, paper letters, or
   letter tiles

READ

MODEL

- Read the word bank for this activity with your child in two different ways. First read across rows, then read down each column.

NOW IT'S YOUR TURN

- Ask your child to read the words across and down.
- Time your child for 1 minute as your child reads the words across the rows. Count the number of words read. The purpose of this exercise is to see how many words your child can read correctly in 1 minute. After your child reads the words across the rows, count the words. Write the number on a sheet of paper.
- Time your child for 1 minute as your child reads the words down the columns. Count the number of words read. The goal is for your child to read more words the second time.

EXTRA SUPPORT

- If your child has difficulty reading a word, say the word and ask the child to repeat it.

SPELL

MODEL

- Say a word from the word bank.
- Spell the word with the letter tiles.

NOW IT'S YOUR TURN

- Say a word from the word bank.
- Ask your child to spell the word with the letter tiles.

Activity and Word Bank continued on following page

Interventions for Reading Success by Diane Haager, Joseph A. Dimino, and Michelle Pearlman Windmueller

EXTRA SUPPORT

- If your child has difficulty spelling a word, model the correct response and ask the child to repeat after you.

Word Bank				
train	braid	mail	stain	main
pair	stairs	faint	sail	fail
plain	tail	saint	quaint	bait
grain	pail	brain	frail	faith
chair	wail	maid	pain	fair
gain	jail	strain	paid	trail
braid	drain	maid	paint	fail
faith	maid	tail	aim	snail
chain	rain	air	hair	vain
aim	grain	plain	faint	pail

HOME-SCHOOL CONNECTION ACTIVITY
ALPHABETIC PRINCIPLE • Long Vowel Spelling Patterns

25 Reading and Spelling *ay* Words

Your child has learned to read and spell words in which *ay* makes the sound /ā/ as in *pay*.

GOAL

- **The student will read and spell words containing the *ay* digraph.**

MATERIALS

- ○ Word bank for this activity
- ○ Magnetic letters, paper letters, or letter tiles
- ○ Timer

READ

MODEL

- Read the word bank for this activity with your child in two different ways. First read across rows, then read down each column.

NOW IT'S YOUR TURN

- Ask your child to read the words across and down.
- Time your child for 1 minute. Count the number of words read. The purpose of this exercise is to see how many words your child can read correctly in 1 minute. After your child reads the words across the rows, count the words. Write the number on a sheet of paper.
- Time your child for 1 minute as your child reads the words down the columns. Count the number of words read. The goal is for your child to read more words the second time.

EXTRA SUPPORT

- If your child has difficulty reading a word, say the word and ask the child to repeat it.

SPELL

MODEL

- Say a word from the word bank.
- Spell the word with the letter tiles.

NOW IT'S YOUR TURN

- Say a word from the word bank.
- Ask your child to spell the word with the letter tiles.

Activity and Word Bank continued on following page

Interventions for Reading Success by Diane Haager, Joseph A. Dimino, and Michelle Pearlman Windmueller

EXTRA SUPPORT

- If your child has difficulty spelling a word, model the correct response and ask the child to repeat after you.

Word Bank

may	lay	day	spray	say
pay	bay	way	stray	jay
bray	hay	sway	pray	may
clay	slay	ray	bay	gray
play	pray	say	clay	spray
tray	stay	fray	cay	Fay
Kay	nay	may	lay	day
spray	say	pay	bay	way
stray	jay	bray	hay	sway
pray	may	clay	slay	ray

Reading and Spelling Words with the Long e Sound (More Complex Patterns)

Your child has learned to read and spell words containing two vowels in which the first vowel says the long sound and the second vowel is silent as in the word *beast*.

GOAL

- **The student will use vowel digraphs to read and spell words with the long e sound containing the ea digraph.**

MATERIALS

- ○ Word bank for this activity
- ○ Magnetic letters, paper letters, or letter tiles

- ○ Timer

READ

MODEL

- Read the word bank for this activity with your child in two different ways. First read across rows, then read down each column.

NOW IT'S YOUR TURN

- Ask your child to read the words across and down.
- Time your child for 1 minute as your child reads the words across the rows. Count the number of words read. The purpose of this exercise is to see how many words your child can read correctly in 1 minute. After your child reads the words across the rows, count the words. Write the number on a sheet of paper.
- Time your child for 1 minute as your child reads the words down the columns. Count the number of words read. The goal is for your child to read more words the second time.

EXTRA SUPPORT

- If your child has difficulty reading a word, say the word and ask the child to repeat it.

SPELL

MODEL

- Say a word from the word bank.
- Spell the word with the letter tiles.

NOW IT'S YOUR TURN

- Say a word from the word bank.
- Ask your child to spell the word with the letter tiles.

Activity and Word Bank continued on following page

EXTRA SUPPORT

- If your child has difficulty spelling a word, model the correct response and ask the child to repeat after you.

Word Bank

each	peas	heal	reap	speak
veal	squeal	mean	Jean	leap
leaf	beach	teach	stream	deal
bead	preach	tea	meat	cheat
cream	spear	steam	treat	zeal
lean	gear	peach	cream	eat
beak	clear	beam	near	yeast
scream	peas	heal	reap	speak
leap	jean	mean	squeal	veal
cheat	meat	tea	preach	bead

HOME-SCHOOL CONNECTION ACTIVITY
ALPHABETIC PRINCIPLE • Long Vowel Spelling Patterns

Reading and Spelling Words with the Long e Sound (More Complex Patterns)

Your child has learned to read and spell words containing two vowels in which the first vowel says the long sound and the second vowel is silent as in the word *seed*.

GOAL

- **The student will use vowel digraphs to read and spell words with the long e sound containing the ee digraph.**

MATERIALS

- ○ Word bank for this activity
- ○ Magnetic letters, paper letters, or letter tiles

- ○ Timer

READ

MODEL

- Read the word bank for this activity with your child in two different ways. First read across rows, then read down each column.

NOW IT'S YOUR TURN

- Ask your child to read the words across and down.
- Time your child for 1 minute as your child reads the words across the rows. Count the number of words read. The purpose of this exercise is to see how many words your child can read correctly in 1 minute. After your child reads the words across the rows, count the words. Write the number on a sheet of paper.
- Time your child for 1 minute as your child reads the words down the columns. Count the number of words read. The goal is for your child to read more words the second time.

EXTRA SUPPORT

- If your child has difficulty reading a word, say the word and ask the child to repeat it.

SPELL

MODEL

- Say a word from the word bank.
- Spell the word with the letter tiles.

NOW IT'S YOUR TURN

- Say a word from the word bank.
- Ask your child to spell the word with the letter tiles.

Activity and Word Bank continued on following page

EXTRA SUPPORT

- If your child has difficulty spelling a word, model the correct response and ask the child to repeat after you.

		Word Bank		
keep	need	weed	seen	sheer
steer	peep	sheet	sweep	sweet
free	three	sheep	feet	weep
seed	tree	bees	cheek	green
deep	creep	feed	screen	deer
peel	flee	meet	week	eel
feed	screen	speech	queen	street
seek	bee	deed	deed	need
keen	beef	reed	creep	feet
beets	sleep	meek	weeds	see

Interventions for Reading Success by Diane Haager, Joseph A. Dimino, and Michelle Pearlman Windmueller
Copyright © 2007 by Paul H. Brookes Publishing Co., Inc. All rights reserved.

Reading and Spelling Words with the Long *i* Sound (More Complex Patterns)

Your child has learned to read and spell words containing two vowels in which the first vowel says the long sound and the second vowel is silent as in the word *tie*.

GOAL

- **The student will use vowel digraphs to read and spell words with the long *i* sound containing the *ie* digraph.**

MATERIALS

○ Word bank for this activity
○ Magnetic letters, paper letters, or letter tiles

○ Timer

READ

MODEL

- Read the word bank for this activity with your child in two different ways. First read across rows, then read down each column.

NOW IT'S YOUR TURN

- Ask your child to read the words across and down.
- Time your child for 1 minute as your child reads the words across the rows. Count the number of words read. The purpose of this exercise is to see how many words your child can read correctly in 1 minute. After your child reads the words across the rows, count the words. Write the number on a sheet of paper.
- Time your child for 1 minute as your child reads the words down the columns. Count the number of words read. The goal is for your child to read more words the second time.

EXTRA SUPPORT

- If your child has difficulty reading a word, say the word and ask the child to repeat it.

SPELL

MODEL

- Say a word from the word bank.
- Spell the word with the letter tiles.

NOW IT'S YOUR TURN

- Say a word from the word bank.
- Ask your child to spell the word with the letter tiles.

Activity and Word Bank continued on following page

Interventions for Reading Success by Diane Haager, Joseph A. Dimino, and Michelle Pearlman Windmueller

EXTRA SUPPORT

- If your child has difficulty spelling a word, model the correct response and ask the child to repeat after you.

Word Bank

pie	die	flies	died	lie
dried	lies	cries	spies	fried
fie	vie	dies	lied	spied
die	flies	died	lie	pie
tie	cried	spies	fried	dried
vie	ties	lied	spied	fie
flies	died	dies	pie	die
cries	spies	fries	dries	lies
dies	tied	spied	fie	vied
ties	lie	pie	die	flies

Reading and Spelling Words with the Long o Sound (More Complex Patterns)

Your child has learned to read and spell words containing two vowels in which the first vowel says the long sound and the second vowel is silent as in the word *road*.

GOAL

- **The student will use vowel digraphs to read and spell words with the long o sound containing the oa digraph.**

MATERIALS

- ❍ Word bank for this activity
- ❍ Magnetic letters, paper letters, or letter tiles
- ❍ Timer

READ

MODEL

- Read the word bank for this activity with your child in two different ways. First read across rows, then read down each column.

NOW IT'S YOUR TURN

- Ask your child to read the words across and down.
- Time your child for 1 minute as your child reads the words across the rows. Count the number of words read. The purpose of this exercise is to see how many words your child can read correctly in 1 minute. After your child reads the words across the rows, count the words. Write the number on a sheet of paper.
- Time your child for 1 minute as your child reads the words down the columns. Count the number of words read. The goal is for your child to read more words the second time.

EXTRA SUPPORT

- If your child has difficulty reading a word, say the word and ask the child to repeat it.

SPELL

MODEL

- Say a word from the word bank.
- Spell the word with the letter tiles.

NOW IT'S YOUR TURN

- Say a word from the word bank.
- Ask your child to spell the word with the letter tiles.

Activity and Word Bank continued on following page

EXTRA SUPPORT

- If your child has difficulty spelling a word, model the correct response and ask the child to repeat after you.

Word Bank				
loan	goal	roast	loaf	throat
boat	oak	foam	coast	oats
roam	roar	coach	toad	boat
goat	soar	oath	road	float
load	croak	groan	boast	soak
soap	coat	oar	toast	loan
goal	roast	loaf	throat	oak
foam	coast	oats	roam	roar
soar	oath	road	float	load
coat	oar	toast	loan	foam

Reading and Spelling Words with the Long o Sound (More Complex Patterns)

Your child has learned to read and spell words containing two vowels in which the first vowel says the long sound and the second vowel is silent as in the word *toe*.

GOAL

- **The student will use vowel digraphs to read and spell words with the long o sound containing the oe digraph.**

MATERIALS

- ◯ Word bank for this activity
- ◯ Magnetic letters, paper letters, or letter tiles

- ◯ Timer

READ

MODEL

- Read the word bank for this activity with your child in two different ways. First read across rows, then read down each column.

NOW IT'S YOUR TURN

- Ask your child to read the words across and down.
- Time your child for 1 minute as your child reads the words across the rows. Count the number of words read. The purpose of this exercise is to see how many words your child can read correctly in 1 minute. After your child reads the words across the rows, count the words. Write the number on a sheet of paper.
- Time your child for 1 minute as your child reads the words down the columns. Count the number of words read. The goal is for your child to read more words the second time.

EXTRA SUPPORT

- If your child has difficulty reading a word, say the word and ask the child to repeat it.

SPELL

MODEL

- Say a word from the word bank.
- Spell the word with the letter tiles.

NOW IT'S YOUR TURN

- Say a word from the word bank.
- Ask your child to spell the word with the letter tiles.

Activity and Word Bank continued on following page

HOME-SCHOOL CONNECTION ACTIVITY

ALPHABETIC PRINCIPLE · Long Vowel Spelling Patterns

EXTRA SUPPORT

- If your child has difficulty spelling a word, model the correct response and ask the child to repeat after you.

Word Bank				
toe	doe	foe	goes	roe
woe	hoe	roe	floe	toe
doe	foe	goes	doe	woe
hoe	roe	floe	toe	hoe
roe	floe	toe	doe	foe

(31) Reading and Spelling ow Words

Your child has learned to read and spell words in which ow makes the sound /ō/ as in *mow*.

GOAL

- **The student will read and spell words with the long o sound containing the ow digraph.**

MATERIALS

- Word bank for this activity
- Magnetic letters, paper letters, or letter tiles
- Timer

READ

MODEL

- Read the word bank for this activity with your child in two different ways. First read across rows, then read down each column.

NOW IT'S YOUR TURN

- Ask your child to read the words across and down.
- Time your child for 1 minute as your child reads the words across the rows. Count the number of words read. The purpose of this exercise is to see how many words your child can read correctly in 1 minute. After your child reads the words across the rows, count the words. Write the number on a sheet of paper.
- Time your child for 1 minute as your child reads the words down the columns. Count the number of words read. The goal is for your child to read more words the second time.

EXTRA SUPPORT

- If your child has difficulty reading a word, say the word and ask the child to repeat it.

SPELL

MODEL

- Say a word from the word bank.
- Spell the word with the letter tiles.

NOW IT'S YOUR TURN

- Say a word from the word bank.
- Ask your child to spell the word with the letter tiles.

Activity and Word Bank continued on following page

EXTRA SUPPORT

- If your child has difficulty spelling a word, model the correct response and ask the child to repeat after you.

Word Bank

mow	blown	shown	blow	slow
glow	low	grow	row	grown
throw	crow	show	growth	snow
flow	bowl	tow	mow	blown
shown	blow	slow	glow	low
grow	row	grown	flow	bowl
tow	mow	blown	shown	blow
slow	glow	low	grow	row
grown	flow	bowl	tow	mow
blown	shown	blow	slow	glow

HOME-SCHOOL CONNECTION ACTIVITY
ALPHABETIC PRINCIPLE • Variant Vowel Spelling Patterns

Reading and Spelling *ar* Words

Your child has learned to read and spell words in which *ar* makes the sound /ar/ as in card.

GOAL

• **The student will read and spell words containing the /ar/ sound.**

MATERIALS

○ Word bank for this activity
○ Magnetic letters, paper letters, or letter tiles

○ Timer

READ

MODEL

• Read the word bank for this activity with your child in two different ways. First read across rows, then read down each column.

NOW IT'S YOUR TURN

• Ask your child to read the words across and down.
• Time your child for 1 minute as your child reads the words across the rows. Count the number of words read. The purpose of this exercise is to see how many words your child can read correctly in 1 minute. After your child reads the words across the rows, count the words. Write the number on a sheet of paper.
• Time your child for 1 minute as your child reads the words down the columns. Count the number of words read. The goal is for your child to read more words the second time.

EXTRA SUPPORT

• If your child has difficulty reading a word, say the word and ask the child to repeat it.

SPELL

MODEL

• Say a word from the word bank.
• Spell the word with the letter tiles.

NOW IT'S YOUR TURN

• Say a word from the word bank.
• Ask your child to spell the word with the letter tiles.

Activity and Word Bank continued on following page

EXTRA SUPPORT

· If your child has difficulty spelling a word, model the correct response and ask the child to repeat after you.

Word Bank

car	bark	dark	barn	charm
dart	Carl	bar	chart	cart
part	lark	spark	lard	starch
harm	ark	yarn	tar	par
art	harm	scarf	smart	scarf
sharp	march	harp	jar	mark
hard	darn	star	shark	dart
arch	marsh	start	mar	yarn
car	bark	dark	barn	charm
dart	Carl	bar	chart	cart

33 Reading and Spelling *or* Words

Your child has learned to read and spell words in which *or* makes the sound /or/ as in *port*.

GOAL

- **The student will read and spell words containing the /or/ sound.**

MATERIALS

- ❍ Word bank for this activity
- ❍ Magnetic letters, paper letters, or letter tiles
- ❍ Timer

READ

MODEL

- Read the word bank for this activity with your child in two different ways. First read across rows, then read down each column.

NOW IT'S YOUR TURN

- Ask your child to read the words across and down.
- Time your child for 1 minute as your child reads the words across the rows. Count the number of words read. The purpose of this exercise is to see how many words your child can read correctly in 1 minute. After your child reads the words across the rows, count the words. Write the number on a sheet of paper.
- Time your child for 1 minute as your child reads the words down the columns. Count the number of words read. The goal is for your child to read more words the second time.

EXTRA SUPPORT

- If your child has difficulty reading a word, say the word and ask the child to repeat it.

SPELL

MODEL

- Say a word from the word bank.
- Spell the word with the letter tiles.

NOW IT'S YOUR TURN

- Say a word from the word bank.
- Ask your child to spell the word with the letter tiles.

Activity and Word Bank continued on following page

 Interventions for Reading Success by Diane Haager, Joseph A. Dimino, and Michelle Pearlman Windmueller

EXTRA SUPPORT

- If your child has difficulty spelling a word, model the correct response and ask the child to repeat after you.

Word Bank

or	horn	torch	port	sort
sworn	worn	snort	stork	thorn
short	porch	cord	form	fork
born	lord	corn	for	north
sport	storm	scorch	cork	fort
cork	scorn	pork	forth	short
or	horn	torch	port	sort
sworn	short	born	horn	porch
lord	snort	cord	corn	stork
form	for	thorn	fork	north

34 Reading and Spelling *er* Words

Your child has learned to read and spell words in which er makes the sound /er/ as in *herd*.

GOAL

- **The student will read and spell words containing the /er/ sound.**

MATERIALS

- ❍ Word bank for this activity
- ❍ Magnetic letters, paper letters, or letter tiles
- ❍ Timer

READ

MODEL

- Read the word bank for this activity with your child in two different ways. First read across rows, then read down each column.

NOW IT'S YOUR TURN

- Ask your child to read the words across and down.
- Time your child for 1 minute as your child reads the words across the rows. Count the number of words read. The purpose of this exercise is to see how many words your child can read correctly in 1 minute. After your child reads the words across the rows, count the words. Write the number on a sheet of paper.
- Time your child for 1 minute as your child reads the words down the columns. Count the number of words read. The goal is for your child to read more words the second time.

EXTRA SUPPORT

- If your child has difficulty reading a word, say the word and ask the child to repeat it.

SPELL

MODEL

- Say a word from the word bank.
- Spell the word with the letter tiles.

NOW IT'S YOUR TURN

- Say a word from the word bank.
- Ask your child to spell the word with the letter tiles.

Activity and Word Bank continued on following page

Interventions for Reading Success by Diane Haager, Joseph A. Dimino, and Michelle Pearlman Windmueller

HOME-SCHOOL CONNECTION ACTIVITY
ALPHABETIC PRINCIPLE • Variant Vowel Spelling Patterns

EXTRA SUPPORT

- If your child has difficulty spelling a word, model the correct response and ask the child to repeat after you.

Word Bank

fern	herd	her	perch	stern
her	clerk	jerk	fern	germ
pert	Vern	fern	herd	her
stern	fern	herd	her	perch
clerk	jerk	fern	germ	her
Vern	fern	herd	her	pert
herd	her	perch	stern	jerk
clerk	jerk	fern	germ	her
Vern	fern	herd	her	pert
fern	herd	her	perch	stern

35 Reading and Spelling *ir* Words

Your child has learned to read and spell words in which *ir* makes the sound /ir/ as in *first*.

GOAL

- **The student will read and spell words containing the /ir/ sound.**

MATERIALS

- ❍ Word bank for this activity
- ❍ Magnetic letters, paper letters, or letter tiles
- ❍ Timer

READ

MODEL

- Read the word bank for this activity with your child in two different ways. First read across rows, then read down each column.

NOW IT'S YOUR TURN

- Ask your child to read the words across and down.
- Time your child for 1 minute as your child reads the words across the rows. Count the number of words read. The purpose of this exercise is to see how many words your child can read correctly in 1 minute. After your child reads the words across the rows, count the words. Write the number on a sheet of paper.
- Time your child for 1 minute as your child reads the words down the columns. Count the number of words read. The goal is for your child to read more words the second time.

EXTRA SUPPORT

- If your child has difficulty reading a word, say the word and ask the child to repeat it.

SPELL

MODEL

- Say a word from the word bank.
- Spell the word with the letter tiles.

NOW IT'S YOUR TURN

- Say a word from the word bank.
- Ask your child to spell the word with the letter tiles.

Activity and Word Bank continued on following page

EXTRA SUPPORT

- If your child has difficulty spelling a word, model the correct response and ask the child to repeat after you.

Word Bank

girl	birch	girl	firm	stir
squirt	shirk	third	sir	skirt
birth	bird	first	whirl	fir
squirm	chirp	twirl	thirst	dirt
shirt	flirt	first	whirl	fir
girl	birch	girl	firm	stir
squirt	shirk	third	sir	skirt
birth	bird	first	whirl	fir
squirm	chirp	twirl	thirst	dirt
shirt	flirt	girl	birch	firm

HOME-SCHOOL CONNECTION ACTIVITY
ALPHABETIC PRINCIPLE • Variant Vowel Spelling Patterns

36 Reading and Spelling *ur* Words

Your child has learned to read and spell words in which *ur* makes the sound /ur/ as in *turn*.

GOAL

- **The student will read and spell words containing the /ur/ sound.**

MATERIALS

- ❍ Word bank for this activity
- ❍ Magnetic letters, paper letters, or letter tiles
- ❍ Timer

READ

MODEL

- Read the word bank for this activity with your child in two different ways. First read across rows, then read down each column.

NOW IT'S YOUR TURN

- Ask your child to read the words across and down.
- Time your child for 1 minute as your child reads the words across the rows. Count the number of words read. The purpose of this exercise is to see how many words your child can read correctly in 1 minute. After your child reads the words across the rows, count the words. Write the number on a sheet of paper.
- Time your child for 1 minute as your child reads the words down the columns. Count the number of words read. The goal is for your child to read more words the second time.

EXTRA SUPPORT

- If your child has difficulty reading a word, say the word and ask the child to repeat it.

SPELL

MODEL

- Say a word from the word bank.
- Spell the word with the letter tiles.

NOW IT'S YOUR TURN

- Say a word from the word bank.
- Ask your child to spell the word with the letter tiles.

Activity and Word Bank continued on following page

EXTRA SUPPORT

- If your child has difficulty spelling a word, model the correct response and ask the child to repeat after you.

Word Bank

hurt	furl	turn	spur	curb
hurl	curl	burn	burr	burst
surf	churn	fur	church	purr
furl	fur	hurt	furl	turn
furl	turn	spur	curb	hurt
burn	burr	burst	curl	hurl
church	purr	surf	churn	fur
spur	curb	hurt	furl	turn
burr	burst	hurl	curl	burn
purr	surf	churn	fur	church

Reading and Spelling
Words with the Short oo Sound

Your child has learned to read and spell words in which oo makes the sound /ŏŏ/ as in *book*.

GOAL

- **The student will read and spell words containing the short oo sound.**

MATERIALS

○ Word bank for this activity
○ Magnetic letters, paper letters, or letter tiles

○ Timer

READ

MODEL

- Read the word bank for this activity with your child in two different ways. First read across rows, then read down each column.

NOW IT'S YOUR TURN

- Ask your child to read the words across and down.
- Time your child for 1 minute as your child reads the words across the rows. Count the number of words read. The purpose of this exercise is to see how many words your child can read correctly in 1 minute. After your child reads the words across the rows, count the words. Write the number on a sheet of paper.
- Time your child for 1 minute as your child reads the words down the columns. Count the number of words read. The goal is for your child to read more words the second time.

EXTRA SUPPORT

- If your child has difficulty reading a word, say the word and ask the child to repeat it.

SPELL

MODEL

- Say a word from the word bank.
- Spell the word with the letter tiles.

NOW IT'S YOUR TURN

- Say a word from the word bank.
- Ask your child to spell the word with the letter tiles.

Activity and Word Bank continued on following page

Interventions for Reading Success by Diane Haager, Joseph A. Dimino, and Michelle Pearlman Windmueller

EXTRA SUPPORT

- If your child has difficulty spelling a word, model the correct response and ask the child to repeat after you.

		Word Bank		
wood	good	hoof	stood	hook
wool	cook	good	wood	soot
crook	shook	nook	book	hood
foot	book	nook	took	look
hood	stood	foot	hoof	wool
good	hoof	stood	hook	wood
cook	good	wood	soot	crook
brook	nook	took	look	stood
foot	shook	nook	book	hood
hood	stood	foot	hoof	wool

Reading and Spelling Words with the Long oo Sound

Your child has learned to read and spell words in which oo makes the long /o͞o/ as in soon.

GOAL

- **The student will read and spell words containing the long oo sound.**

MATERIALS

- ❍ Word bank for this activity
- ❍ Magnetic letters, paper letters, or letter tiles
- ❍ Timer

READ

MODEL

- Read the word bank for this activity with your child in two different ways. First read across rows, then read down each column.

NOW IT'S YOUR TURN

- Ask your child to read the words across and down.
- Time your child for 1 minute as your child reads the words across the rows. Count the number of words read. The purpose of this exercise is to see how many words your child can read correctly in 1 minute. After your child reads the words across the rows, count the words. Write the number on a sheet of paper.
- Time your child for 1 minute as your child reads the words down the columns. Count the number of words read. The goal is for your child to read more words the second time.

EXTRA SUPPORT

- If your child has difficulty reading a word, say the word and ask the child to repeat it.

SPELL

MODEL

- Say a word from the word bank.
- Spell the word with the letter tiles.

NOW IT'S YOUR TURN

- Say a word from the word bank.
- Ask your child to spell the word with the letter tiles.

Activity and Word Bank continued on following page

Interventions for Reading Success by Diane Haager, Joseph A. Dimino, and Michelle Pearlman Windmueller

EXTRA SUPPORT

- If your child has difficulty spelling a word, model the correct response and ask the child to repeat after you.

Word Bank

root	tooth	pool	smooth	broom
scoop	shoot	snoop	room	booth
coop	spoon	cool	boost	noon
boom	zoo	food	drool	spool
too	poor	fool	moon	tool
loop	troop	brood	droop	boot
moo	roof	mood	soon	hoop
coo	fool	booth	coop	spoon
shoot	snoop	root	tooth	pool
smooth	broom	scoop	booth	room

Reading and Spelling Words with the Short and Long oo Sounds

Your child has learned to read and spell words in which oo makes the sound /ŏŏ/ as in *book* and the sound /ōō/ as in *soon*.

GOAL

- **The student will read and spell words containing the short and long sound of oo.**

MATERIALS

- ○ Word bank for this activity
- ○ Magnetic letters, paper letters, or letter tiles
- ○ Timer

READ

MODEL

- Read the word bank for this activity with your child in two different ways. First read across rows, then read down each column.

NOW IT'S YOUR TURN

- Ask your child to read the words across and down.
- Time your child for 1 minute as your child reads the words across the rows. Count the number of words read. The purpose of this exercise is to see how many words your child can read correctly in 1 minute. After your child reads the words across the rows, count the words. Write the number on a sheet of paper.
- Time your child for 1 minute as your child reads the words down the columns. Count the number of words read. The goal is for your child to read more words the second time.

EXTRA SUPPORT

- If your child has difficulty reading a word, say the word and ask the child to repeat it.

SPELL

MODEL

- Say a word from the word bank.
- Spell the word with the letter tiles.

NOW IT'S YOUR TURN

- Say a word from the word bank.
- Ask your child to spell the word with the letter tiles.

Activity and Word Bank continued on following page

Interventions for Reading Success by Diane Haager, Joseph A. Dimino, and Michelle Pearlman Windmueller

EXTRA SUPPORT

- If your child has difficulty spelling a word, model the correct response and ask the child to repeat after you.

Word Bank

troop	brood	nook	tool	hoof
root	scoop	book	wood	droop
tooth	too	spoon	boot	booth
fool	stool	stoop	spool	pool
smooth	drool	hoop	hook	coo
stood	loop	foot	food	took
broom	coop	hood	good	boot
pool	zoo	poor	root	hoof
foot	bloom	book	smooth	good
hoop	droop	nook	spook	wool

40 Reading and Spelling *oy* Words

Your child has learned to read and spell words in which *oy* makes the sound /oy/ as in *toy*.

GOAL

- **The student will read and spell words containing the oy diphthong.**

MATERIALS

- ○ Word bank for this activity
- ○ Magnetic letters, paper letters, or letter tiles
- ○ Timer

READ

MODEL

- Read the word bank for this activity with your child in two different ways. First read across rows, then read down each column.

NOW IT'S YOUR TURN

- Ask your child to read the words across and down.
- Time your child for 1 minute as your child reads the words across the rows. Count the number of words read. The purpose of this exercise is to see how many words your child can read correctly in 1 minute. After your child reads the words across the rows, count the words. Write the number on a sheet of paper.
- Time your child for 1 minute as your child reads the words down the columns. Count the number of words read. The goal is for your child to read more words the second time.

EXTRA SUPPORT

- If your child has difficulty reading a word, say the word and ask the child to repeat it.

SPELL

MODEL

- Say a word from the word bank.
- Spell the word with the letter tiles.

NOW IT'S YOUR TURN

- Say a word from the word bank.
- Ask your child to spell the word with the letter tiles.

Activity and Word Bank continued on following page

 Interventions for Reading Success by Diane Haager, Joseph A. Dimino, and Michelle Pearlman Windmueller

EXTRA SUPPORT

- If your child has difficulty spelling a word, model the correct response and ask the child to repeat after you.

		Word Bank		
toy	coy	joy	boy	boys
ploy	Roy	ploy	toys	toy
soy	joy	boy	cloy	ploy
Roy	ploy	toys	toy	soy
joy	boy	cloy	ploy	joy
boy	cloy	ploy	joy	toy
coy	joy	boy	cloy	ploy
Roy	ploy	toys	toy	soy
joy	boy	cloy	ploy	joy
boy	cloy	toy	toys	soy

(41) Reading and Spelling *oi* Words

Your child has learned to read and spell words in which *oy* makes the sound /oi/ as in *boil*.

GOAL

- **The student will read and spell words containing the *oi* diphthong.**

MATERIALS

○ Word bank for this activity   ○ Timer
○ Magnetic letters, paper letters, or
  letter tiles

READ

MODEL

- Read the word bank for this activity with your child in two different ways. First read across rows, then read down each column.

NOW IT'S YOUR TURN

- Ask your child to read the words across and down.
- Time your child for 1 minute as your child reads the words across the rows. Count the number of words read. The purpose of this exercise is to see how many words your child can read correctly in 1 minute. After your child reads the words across the rows, count the words. Write the number on a sheet of paper.
- Time your child for 1 minute as your child reads the words down the columns. Count the number of words read. The goal is for your child to read more words the second time.

EXTRA SUPPORT

- If your child has difficulty reading a word, say the word and ask the child to repeat it.

SPELL

MODEL

- Say a word from the word bank.
- Spell the word with the letter tiles.

NOW IT'S YOUR TURN

- Say a word from the word bank.
- Ask your child to spell the word with the letter tiles.

Activity and Word Bank continued on following page

Interventions for Reading Success by Diane Haager, Joseph A. Dimino, and Michelle Pearlman Windmueller

EXTRA SUPPORT

- If your child has difficulty spelling a word, model the correct response and ask the child to repeat after you.

Word Bank

coin	point	hoist	toil	join
moist	foist	boil	soil	joint
foil	roil	oil	spoil	broil
moil	hoist	oink	joist	coin
foist	boil	soil	joint	moist
coin	oil	spoil	broil	foil
hoist	toil	join	coin	point
boil	soil	joint	moist	foist
oil	spoil	broil	foil	coin
toil	join	coin	point	hoist

Reading and Spelling *ou* Words

Your child has learned to read and spell words in which *ou* makes the sound /ou/ as in *out*.

GOAL

- **The student will read and spell words containing the *ou* diphthong.**

MATERIALS

○ Word bank for this activity
○ Magnetic letters, paper letters, or letter tiles

○ Timer

READ

MODEL

- Read the word bank for this activity with your child in two different ways. First read across rows, then read down each column.

NOW IT'S YOUR TURN

- Ask your child to read the words across and down.
- Time your child for 1 minute as your child reads the words across the rows. Count the number of words read. The purpose of this exercise is to see how many words your child can read correctly in 1 minute. After your child reads the words across the rows, count the words. Write the number on a sheet of paper.
- Time your child for 1 minute as your child reads the words down the columns. Count the number of words read. The goal is for your child to read more words the second time.

EXTRA SUPPORT

- If your child has difficulty reading a word, say the word and ask the child to repeat it.

SPELL

MODEL

- Say a word from the word bank.
- Spell the word with the letter tiles.

NOW IT'S YOUR TURN

- Say a word from the word bank.
- Ask your child to spell the word with the letter tiles.

Activity and Word Bank continued on following page

EXTRA SUPPORT

- If your child has difficulty spelling a word, model the correct response and ask the child to repeat after you.

Word Bank

sound	foul	ground	flour	proud
spout	couch	sour	snout	bound
round	grouch	pound	crouch	loud
out	scout	south	pout	ouch
cloud	trout	stout	sprout	sour
hound	shout	mouth	pouch	count
sound	spout	round	out	foul
couch	grouch	scout	ground	sour
pound	south	flour	snout	crouch
pout	proud	bound	ouch	foul

Reading and Spelling ow Words

Your child has learned to read and spell words in which *ow* makes the sound /ow/ as in *clown*.

GOAL

- **The student will read and spell words containing the ow diphthong.**

MATERIALS

- ○ Word bank for this activity
- ○ Magnetic letters, paper letters, or letter tiles

READ

MODEL

- Read the word bank for this activity with your child in two different ways. First read across rows, then read down each column.

NOW IT'S YOUR TURN

- Ask your child to read the words across and down.
- Time your child for 1 minute as your child reads the words across the rows. Count the number of words read. The purpose of this exercise is to see how many words your child can read correctly in 1 minute. After your child reads the words across the rows, count the words. Write the number on a sheet of paper.
- Time your child for 1 minute as your child reads the words down the columns. Count the number of words read. The goal is for your child to read more words the second time.

EXTRA SUPPORT

- If your child has difficulty reading a word, say the word and ask the child to repeat it.

SPELL

MODEL

- Say a word from the word bank.
- Spell the word with the letter tiles.

NOW IT'S YOUR TURN

- Say a word from the word bank.
- Ask your child to spell the word with the letter tiles.

EXTRA SUPPORT

- If your child has difficulty spelling a word, model the correct response and ask the child to repeat after you.

Word Bank on following page

Word Bank

now	drown	clown	owl	town
crown	howl	frown	how	fowl
brown	cow	growl	gown	down
drown	clown	owl	town	now
howl	frown	how	fowl	crown
cow	growl	gown	down	brown
frown	how	fowl	crown	how
now	crown	brown	drown	howl
cow	clown	frown	growl	owl
how	gown	town	fowl	down

HOME-SCHOOL CONNECTION ACTIVITY
ALPHABETIC PRINCIPLE • Variant Vowel Spelling Patterns

44 Reading and Spelling ew Words

Your child has learned to read and spell words in which *ew* makes the sound /ew/ as in *new*.

GOAL

- **The student will read and spell words containing the ew digraph.**

MATERIALS

- Word bank for this activity
- Magnetic letters, paper letters, or letter tiles

- Timer

READ

MODEL

- Read the word bank for this activity with your child in two different ways. First read across rows, then read down each column.

NOW IT'S YOUR TURN

- Ask your child to read the words across and down.
- Time your child for 1 minute as your child reads the words across the rows. Count the number of words read. The purpose of this exercise is to see how many words your child can read correctly in 1 minute. After your child reads the words across the rows, count the words. Write the number on a sheet of paper.
- Time your child for 1 minute as your child reads the words down the columns. Count the number of words read. The goal is for your child to read more words the second time.

EXTRA SUPPORT

- If your child has difficulty reading a word, say the word and ask the child to repeat it.

SPELL

MODEL

- Say a word from the word bank.
- Spell the word with the letter tiles.

NOW IT'S YOUR TURN

- Say a word from the word bank.
- Ask your child to spell the word with the letter tiles.

Activity and Word Bank continued on following page

EXTRA SUPPORT

- If your child has difficulty spelling a word, model the correct response and ask the child to repeat after you.

Word Bank

new	stew	blew	crew	strewn
chew	news	screw	strew	dew
drew	strewn	threw	new	stew
blew	crew	strewn	chew	news
screw	brew	dew	brew	dew
pew	threw	new	stew	drew
new	stew	blew	crew	strewn
news	screw	brew	dew	drew
blew	crew	strewn	chew	news
threw	new	stew	stew	chew

HOME-SCHOOL CONNECTION ACTIVITY
ALPHABETIC PRINCIPLE • Variant Vowel Spelling Patterns

㊟ Reading and Spelling *au* Words

Your child has learned to read and spell words in which *au* makes the sound /au/ as in *Paul.*

GOAL

- **The student will read and spell words containing the *au* digraph.**

MATERIALS

- Word bank for this activity
- Magnetic letters, paper letters, or letter tiles
- Timer

READ

MODEL
- Read the word bank for this activity with your child in two different ways. First read across rows, then read down each column.

NOW IT'S YOUR TURN
- Ask your child to read the words across and down.
- Time your child for 1 minute as your child reads the words across the rows. Count the number of words read. The purpose of this exercise is to see how many words your child can read correctly in 1 minute. After your child reads the words across the rows, count the words. Write the number on a sheet of paper.
- Time your child for 1 minute as your child reads the words down the columns. Count the number of words read. The goal is for your child to read more words the second time.

EXTRA SUPPORT
- If your child has difficulty reading a word, say the word and ask the child to repeat it.

SPELL

MODEL
- Say a word from the word bank.
- Spell the word with the letter tiles.

NOW IT'S YOUR TURN
- Say a word from the word bank.
- Ask your child to spell the word with the letter tiles.

Activity and Word Bank continued on following page

EXTRA SUPPORT

- If your child has difficulty spelling a word, model the correct response and ask the child to repeat after you.

Word Bank

haul	Paul	fraud	squall	Saul
taunt	fault	launch	auk	maul
daub	faun	Gaul	laud	flaunt
taut	vaunt	flaunt	haul	Paul
fraud	squall	Saul	taunt	fault
launch	auk	maul	daub	faun
Gaul	laud	flaunt	taut	vaunt
flaunt	haul	Paul	fraud	squall
Saul	taunt	fault	launch	auk
maul	daub	faun	Gaul	laud

HOME-SCHOOL CONNECTION ACTIVITY
ALPHABETIC PRINCIPLE · Variant Vowel Spelling Patterns

1 What's in the Box?

GOAL

- **The student will write, read, and recognize high-frequency words with mastery and fluency.**

MATERIALS

- What's in the Box worksheet
- High-frequency word bank
- Letter tiles or paper letters
- Timer

MODEL

Say the following:
- "We're going to work together on the high-frequency word worksheet titled What's in the Box?"
- "I'm going to set the timer and complete the worksheet with as many words as possible."
- "I am going to use the high-frequency word bank and the letter tiles to fill in the blank letter that is missing from the first word." (a☐)
- "There may be more than one answer for this word, so let's think of as many answers as we can." (Possibilities for a☐ are *am, an, as, at.*)

NOW IT'S YOUR TURN

Say the following:
- "What's in the box for the second word?" (Possibilities for *the*☐ are *them, then, they, thee.*)
- "Be sure to use the word bank to help you figure out the new words."
- "What's the word?"

EXTRA SUPPORT

- If the child has difficulty putting down the correct letter to complete the word, model the correct response and ask the child to repeat after you.

ANSWER KEY FOR THE WHAT'S IN THE BOX? WORKSHEET

Possible answers (reading across rows): *an, them, then, with, when, before, are, from, like, give, does, gave, said, into, look, little, out* (or *our*), *where, which, your, she, they, what, you'd*

Interventions for Reading Success by Diane Haager, Joseph A. Dimino, and Michelle Pearlman Windmueller

② Partner Up: Paired Repeated Readings

GOAL

- **The student will increase reading fluency and accuracy.**

MATERIALS

○ Reading passage at the child's instructional level

MODEL

Say the following:
- "I am Partner One and you are Partner Two."
- "I am going to read this passage once aloud while you listen."
- "Afterward, you'll read the passage aloud three times while I listen."

NOW IT'S YOUR TURN

- Read the passage one time aloud.
- Say the following:
  - "Now it's your turn to read."
  - "Read this passage three times."

EXTRA SUPPORT

- If the child has difficulty reading the passage, you read it again and then have your child read the passage three times for repeated practice.

③ High-Speed Words

GOAL

- **The student will read high-frequency words accurately and fluently.**

MATERIALS

- High-frequency word cards
- High-frequency word lists (containing 10 words per list)
- High-frequency word wall
- Timer (optional)

MODEL

Say the following:
- "I'm going to be your partner."
- "Listen and watch, while I put down one word card at a time and read it aloud." (Put down one card and read it out loud.)
- "Now I'm going to put down more words just a little faster." (Put down additional cards, reading the words aloud faster.)

NOW IT'S YOUR TURN

- Say the following:
  - "Listen and watch, while I put down one word card."
  - "What's the word?"
  - "Keep going while I flash the word cards for you."
- Do the same thing with the high-frequency word bank. Set the timer for 1 minute.
- Have your child read as many words as he or she can in 1 minute, moving down the list. (For variety, have your child move across the list.)

EXTRA SUPPORT

- If the child has difficulty reading the word cards, model the correct response and ask the child to repeat after you.

④ Up Against the Wall

GOAL

- **The student will read and recognize high-frequency words with mastery and fluency.**

MATERIALS

- ○ High-frequency words posted on the wall or the refrigerator
- ○ Post-it notes with the child's name on it
- ○ Timer

MODEL

Say the following:
- "I'm going to set the timer for 1 minute."
- "When I say 'Begin' I will start reading the list of words as carefully and quickly as I can."
- "After 1 minute, I will place a Post-it note next to the last word I read."

NOW IT'S YOUR TURN

Say the following:
- "When I say 'Begin' you will start reading the list of words as carefully and quickly as you can."
- "After one minute, you can place a Post-it note next to the last word you read."

EXTRA SUPPORT

- If the child has difficulty reading the words, read the list together, and then ask the child to read the list alone.

⑤ Shout It Out

GOAL

- **The student will read and recognize high-frequency words with mastery and fluency.**

MATERIALS

- ○ List of 10 high-frequency words, high-frequency word bank, and/or high-frequency noun list*
- ○ Index cards
- ○ Rings or yarn
- ○ Hole puncher

*If the child is a kindergarten or first-grade student, use a high-frequency list of 10 words and choose 5–10 of those words to work on. For first graders, add words as the child is more able to read these words. If your child is in second grade or higher, use words from the high-frequency word bank and the high-frequency noun list.

MODEL

Say the following:
- "I'm going to flash some high-frequency words."
- "Watch while I read each word and shout it out."

NOW IT'S YOUR TURN

Say the following:
- "I'm going to flash some high-frequency words for you to read."
- "Watch for the word and shout it out."

EXTRA SUPPORT

- If the child has difficulty reading the word correctly, model the correct response and ask the child to repeat after you.

⑥ Knock, Knock, Who's There?

GOAL

- **The student will read and recognize high-frequency words with mastery and fluency.**

MATERIALS

○ Two copies of a high-frequency word list with 5–10 words each. If doing this activity during different weeks, switch lists from week to week so that the child works on mastering different words. (Examples of three lists appear below.)

MODEL

- Read aloud the list of high-frequency words posted on the refrigerator.

NOW IT'S YOUR TURN

Say the following:
- "While I'm making dinner, read the words that are posted on the refrigerator."

EXTRA SUPPORT

- If the child has difficulty reading the words independently, model the correct response and ask the child to repeat after you.

Week 1	Week 2	Week 3
a	another	been
about	any	before
across	are	began
after	around	best
again	as	better
all	ask	big
always	at	black
am	away	blue

⑦ Concentration

GOAL

- **The student will read and recognize high-frequency words with mastery and fluency.**

MATERIALS

○ Two sets of high-frequency word cards. Each set contains the same words. The sets can be color coded to distinguish one set from another (one white set and one yellow set).

MODEL

- Say the following:
  - "I'm going to place some word cards face down."
  - "I'm going to choose one card from each color and see if they match."
- Read the words aloud.
- If they match, keep the cards in your pile and choose two more cards.
- If they do not match, return the cards to their original location, and let the child take a turn.

NOW IT'S YOUR TURN

Say the following:
- "Choose two word cards, one from each color."
- "What are the words?"
- "Do they match?"
- "If so, read the words out loud, keep the match, and take another turn."

EXTRA SUPPORT

- If the child has difficulty reading the words out loud correctly, model the correct response and ask the child to repeat after you.

8 You're It!

GOAL

- **The student will read and recognize high-frequency words with mastery and fluency.**

MATERIALS

- High-frequency word cards
- Box
- "You're it!" cards

MODEL

- Say the following:
  - "I'm going to take words out of this box."
  - "Each time I'm going to read the word out loud."
  - "If I take a card that says "You're it!" then I'll read all of the words I have taken out of the box as quickly as I can."
  - "Listen and watch."
- Put down the word cards one at a time and read them aloud. When you take a "You're it!" card, read all of the cards you have taken out of the box as quickly as you can. When you are done reading the cards you have taken out of the box, leave them out of the box.

NOW IT'S YOUR TURN

- Say the following:
  - "Take word cards out of the box one at a time and read each one out loud."
- Have the child continue to do this until he or she takes out a "You're it!" card.
- Say the following:
  - "Read all of the words that you took out of the box, as quickly as you can."
- When the child has finished reading all of the cards he or she has taken out of the box, the cards are left out of the box.
- The child continues this activity until all of the cards have been taken out of the box.

EXTRA SUPPORT

- If the child has difficulty reading the word cards, model the correct response and ask the child to repeat after you.

⑪ Shake, Spill, and Say

GOAL

- **The student will read and recognize high-frequency words with mastery and fluency.**

MATERIALS

○ High-frequency word cards ○ Container with a lid

MODEL

Say the following:
- "I'm going to shake these words up and spill them out on the table."
- "Listen and watch, while I read only the words that land face up on the table."

NOW IT'S YOUR TURN

Say the following:
- "Shake the container and spill out all of the words."
- "Read only the words that land face up on the table."

EXTRA SUPPORT

- If the child has difficulty reading the words, model the correct response and ask the child to repeat after you.

13 One Minute, Please!

GOAL

- **The student will increase reading fluency and accuracy.**

MATERIALS

- ○ Reading material at the child's independent and instructional level
- ○ Timer
- ○ Fluency graph

MODEL

Say the following:
- "I'm going to set the timer for 1 minute."
- "Start reading when I say, 'Begin.'"
- "Read carefully and quickly until I say, 'Stop.'"
- "At the end of 1 minute we'll count the number of words you read and write it down on your fluency graph."

NOW IT'S YOUR TURN

- Say the following:
  - "The timer is set for 1 minute."
  - "Ready to read? Begin."
- Tell the child how many words he or she read in 1 minute, and correct any errors in reading specific words. Ask the child to record the number of words read correctly on his or her fluency graph.

EXTRA SUPPORT

- If your child is having difficulty getting started, read along with him or her for 1 minute. Then have your child read alone.

14 Echo Reading

GOAL

- **The student will increase reading fluency and accuracy.**

MATERIALS

○ Paragraph at the child's instructional level

MODEL

- Say the following:
  - "I'm going to read a sentence. Then, I want you to read the same sentence."
  - "We're going to read this entire paragraph in this way."
- Once you have modeled this activity for the child, the child reads a sentence first and you echo what the child has read (see below in Now It's Your Turn).

NOW IT'S YOUR TURN

Say the following:
- "Read the first sentence of your paragraph and I'll read after you."
- "Read this way until you reach the end of the passage."

EXTRA SUPPORT

- If the child has difficulty reading the sentences, model the activity again for the child and ask the child to repeat after you.

Interventions for Reading Success by Diane Haager, Joseph A. Dimino, and Michelle Pearlman Windmueller

16 Choral Reading

GOAL

- **The student will increase reading fluency and accuracy.**

MATERIALS

- ○ Text at the child's instructional level (poetry or a book with predictable story patterns, repeated phrases, or refrains works very well)

MODEL

Say the following:
- "I'm going to read from a text."
- "Then, I want you to read the same text together with me aloud."
- "After that, we're going to read this same text two more times together aloud."

NOW IT'S YOUR TURN

Say the following:
- "Read the text with me aloud."
- "Now, let's read this same text two more times together aloud."

EXTRA SUPPORT

- If the child has difficulty reading, you may tape record the passage being read aloud and the child can read along with the tape.

17 Repeated Readings

GOAL

- **The student will increase reading fluency and accuracy.**

MATERIALS

○ Text at the child's instructional level (poetry or a book with predictable story patterns, repeated phrases, or refrains works very well)

MODEL

- Say the following:
  - "I'm going to set the timer for 1 minute."
  - "You read the text for 1 minute, and I'll mark the stopping point on my copy of the text at the end of the minute."
  - "I will record the number of words read correctly on your fluency graph."
  - "I want you to read the text repeatedly until you can read it without errors."
- The child repeats this until the text is read without errors.
- The child places this text in his or her fluency kit for future practice.

NOW IT'S YOUR TURN

- Say the following:
  - "Read the text aloud for 1 minute."
- Tell the child how many words he or she read in 1 minute, and correct any errors in reading specific words.
- Record the number of words read correctly per minute on the child's fluency graph.
  - "The goal is to read this story without any mistakes. Let's keep going until you can do this!"

EXTRA SUPPORT

- If the child has difficulty reading the text, model the activity for the child again and ask the child to repeat after you.

Interventions for Reading Success by Diane Haager, Joseph A. Dimino, and Michelle Pearlman Windmueller

References

Armbruster, B.B., & Wilkinson, I.A.G. (1991). Silent reading, oral reading, and learning from text. *The Reading Teacher, 45,* 154–155.

Beck, I.L., McKeown, M.G., & Kucan, L. (2002). *Bring words to life: Robust vocabulary instruction.* New York: The Guilford Press.

Buehl, D., (1995). *Classroom strategies for interactive learning.* West Allis: Wisconsin State Reading Association.

Chard, D.J., & Dickson, S.V. (1999). *Phonological awareness: Instructional and assessment guidelines.* Retrieved August 3, 2006, from http://www.ldonline.org/article/6254

Dimino, J. (2004, April). *The click of reading comprehension: Collaborative Strategic Reading.* The Council for Exceptional Children annual conference, New Orleans.

Dowhower, S.L. (1994). Repeated reading revisited: Research into practice. *Reading and Writing Quarterly, 10,* 343–358.

Foorman, B.R., Francis, D.J., Fletcher, J.M., Schatschneider, C., & Mehta, P. (1998). The role of instruction in learning to read: Preventing reading failure in at-risk children. *Journal of Educational Psychology, 90,* 37–55.

Francis, D.J., Shaywitz, S.E., Stuebing, K.K., Shaywitz, B.A., & Fletcher, J.M. (1996). Developmental lag versus deficit models of reading disability: A longitudinal, individual growth curves analysis. *Journal of Educational Psychology, 88,* 3–17.

Fuchs, D., Fuchs, L. S., Mathes, P. H., & Simmons, D.C. (1997). Peer-assisted strategies: Making classrooms more responsive to diversity. *American Educational Research Journal, 34*(1), 174–206.

Good, R.H., & Kaminski, R.A. (Eds.). (2002). *Dynamic Indicators of Basic Early Literacy Skills* (6th ed.). Eugene, OR: Institute for Development of Educational Achievement.

Good, R.H., III, Simmons, D., & Kame'enui, E.J. (2001). The importance and decision-making utility of a continuum of fluency-based indicators of foundational reading skills for third-grade high-stakes reading outcomes. *Scientific Studies of Reading, 5*(3), 257–288.

Haager, D. (2006). *Early reading intervention in urban schools: General education teachers as interventionists.* Paper presented at the 2006 OSEP Project Directors' Conference, Washington, DC.

Haager, D., Klingner, J., & Vaughn, S. (Eds.). (2007). *Evidence-based reading practices for response to intervention.* Baltimore: Paul H. Brookes Publishing Co.

Haager, D., & Windmueller, M. (2001). Early literacy intervention for English language learners at-risk for learning disabilities: Student and teacher outcomes in an urban school. *Learning Disabilities Quarterly, 24,* 235–250.

Hasbrouck, J., & Tindal, G. A. (2006). Oral reading fluency norms: A valuable assessment tool for reading teachers. *The Reading Teacher, 59,* 636–644.

Hunt, N., & Marshall, K. (2006). *Exceptional children and youth* (4th ed.). Boston: Houghton Mifflin.

Johns, J.L., & Berglund, R.L. (2002). *Fluency: Answers, questions, evidence-based strategies.* Dubuque, IA: Kendall/Hunt.

Juel, C. (1988). Learning to read and write: A longitudinal study of 54 children from first through fourth grades. *Journal of Educational Psychology, 80,* 437–447.

Kaminski, R.A., & Good, R.H., III. (1996). Toward a technology for assessing basic early literacy skills. *School Psychology Review, 25,* 215–227.

Klingner, J.K., Vaughn, S., & Schumm, J.S. (1998). Collaborative strategic reading during social studies in heterogeneous fourth-grade classrooms. *Elementary School Journal, 99*(1), 3–22.

LaBerge, D., & Samuels, S.J. (1974). Toward a theory of automatic information processing in reading. *Cognitive Psychology, 6,* 293–323.

McTighe, J., & Lyman, F.T., Jr. (1988). Cueing thinking in the classroom: The promise of theory-based tools. *Educational Leadership, 45*(7), 18–24.

National Assessment of Educational Progress. (2005). *The nation's report card: Reading 2005.* Washington, DC: National Center for Educational Statistics.

National Institute of Child Health and Human Development. (2000). *Report of the National Reading Panel. Teaching children to read: An evidence-based assessment of the scientific research literature on reading and its implications for reading instruction: Reports of the subgroups* (NIH Publication No. 00-4754). Washington, DC: U.S. Government Printing Office. Also available on-line: http://www.nichd.nih.gov/publications/nrp/report.htm

National Research Council, Division of Behavioral and Social Sciences and Education, Committee on Minority Representation in Special Education. (2002). *Minority students in special and gifted education.* Washington, DC: National Academies Press.

No Child Left Behind Act of 2001, PL 107-110, 115 Stat. 1425, 20 U.S.C. §§ 6301 *et seq.*

O'Connor, R.E. (2000). Increasing the intensity of intervention in kindergarten and first grade. *Learning Disabilities Research and Practice, 15,* 43–54.

O'Connor, R.E., & Jenkins, J.R. (2002). Early identification and intervention for young children with reading/learning disabilities. In R. Bradley, L. Danielson, & D.P. Hallahan (Eds.), *Identification of learning disabilities: Research to practice* (pp. 99–149). Mahwah, NJ: Lawrence Erlbaum Associates.

Ogle, D.M. (1986). K-W-L: A teaching model that develops active reading of expository text. *The Reading Teacher, 39,* 564–570.

Oh, D.M., Haager, D., & Windmueller, M.P. (April, 2006). *A longitudinal study predicting reading success for English learners from kindergarten to first grade.* Paper presented at the annual meeting of the American Educational Research Association, San Francisco.

Pearson, P.D., & Johnson, D.W. (1978). *Teaching reading comprehension.* New York: Holt, Rinehart & Winston.

Pinnell, G.S., Lyons, C.A., DeFord, D.E., Bryk, A.S., & Seltzer, M. (1994). Comparing instructional models for the literacy education of high-risk first graders. *Reading Research Quarterly, 29*(1), 9–40.

Raphael, T.E. (1986). Teaching question-answer relationships revisited. *The Reading Teacher, 39,* 516–522.

Schwartz, R.M., & Raphael, T.E. (1985). Concept of definition: A key to improving students' vocabulary. *The Reading Teacher, 39,* 198–205.

Simmons, D.C., & Kame'enui, E.J. (1998). Introduction. In D.C. Simmons & E.J. Kame'enui (Eds.), *What reading research tells us about children with diverse learning needs: Bases and basics.* Mahwah, NJ: Lawrence Erlbaum Associates.

Snow, C.E., Burns, M.S., & Griffin, P. (Eds.). (1998). *Preventing reading difficulties in young children.* Washington, DC: National Academies Press.

Stanovich, K.E. (1986). Matthew effects in reading: Some consequences of individual differences in the acquisition of literacy. *Reading Research Quarterly, 21,* 360–406.

Stanovich, P.J., & Stanovich, K.E. (2003, May). *Using research and reason in education: How teachers can use scientifically based research to make curricular and instructional decisions.* Retrieved August 5, 2003, from http://www.nifl.gov/partnershipforreading/publications/k-3.html

Texas Education Agency. (2003). *3-tier reading model: A prevention model for reducing reading difficulties in kindergarten through third grade students.* Retrieved July 6, 2005, from http://www.tea.state.tx.us/reading/readingfirst/3tiemodreainsint.pdf

Torgesen, J.K. (1998, Spring–Summer). Catch them before they fall: Identification and assessment to prevent reading failure in children [Electronic version]. *American Educator.*

Torgesen, J.K., & Burgess, S.R. (1998). Consistency of reading-related phonological processes throughout early childhood: Evidence from longitudinal-correlational and instructional studies. In J. Metsala & L. Ehri (Eds.), *Word recognition in beginning reading.* Mahwah, NJ: Lawrence Erlbaum Associates.

University of Oregon Center on Teaching and Learning. (n.d.). *DIBELS benchmark goals and indicators of risk: Three assessment periods per year.* Retrieved August 24, 2006, from http://dibels.uoregon .edu/benchmarkgoals.pdf

U.S. Department of Education. (2002). *Helping your children with homework.* Washington, DC: Author.

Vaughn, S., Linan-Thompson, S., & Hickman, P. (2003). Response to instruction as a means of identifying students with reading/learning disabilities. *Learning Disabilities Research and Practice, 69,* 391–409.

Photocopiable Templates

INTRODUCTION

This appendix contains photocopiable templates that you can use to make many of the materials and worksheets that you will need for the interventions in this book. Chapter 4 describes preparing and organizing the materials in detail, including how to assemble kits for students to take home with them so that they have all the items needed for the Home-School Connection activities that they will be doing with their parents.

This appendix also contains a letter to parents that you can photocopy and give to parents who attend an orientation session to explain the intervention activities as well as to parents who are unable to attend the orientation session. The letter explains the purpose of the activities and gives parents hints on how to do the activities with their child.

Bingo Board

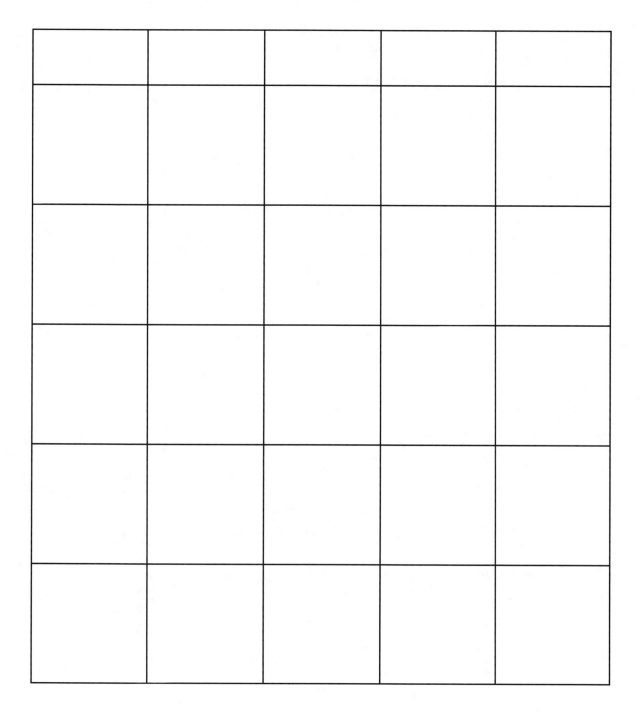

Color Tile Template

a	b	c	d	e
f	g	h	i	j
k	l	m	n	o
p	q	r	s	t
u	v	w	x	y
z	a	a	a	a

Lowercase Letter Tiles

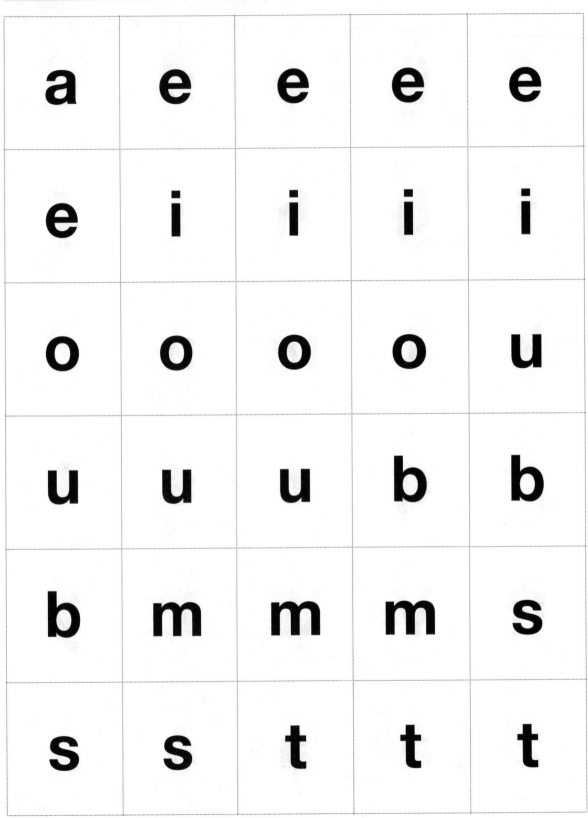

a	e	e	e	e
e	i	i	i	i
o	o	o	o	u
u	u	u	b	b
b	m	m	m	s
s	s	t	t	t

A	B	C	D	E
F	G	H	I	J
K	L	M	N	O
P	Q	R	S	T
U	V	W	X	Y
Z	A	A	A	A

Interventions for Reading Success by Diane Haager, Joseph A. Dimino, and Michelle Pearlman Windmueller

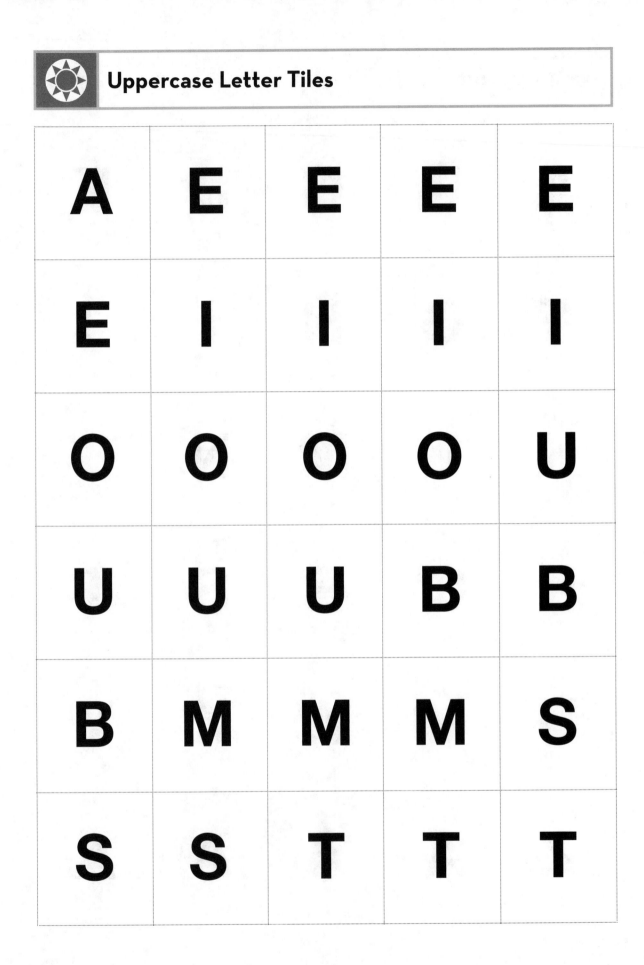

A	E	E	E	E
E	I	I	I	I
O	O	O	O	U
U	U	U	B	B
B	M	M	M	S
S	S	T	T	T

Two-Sound Template

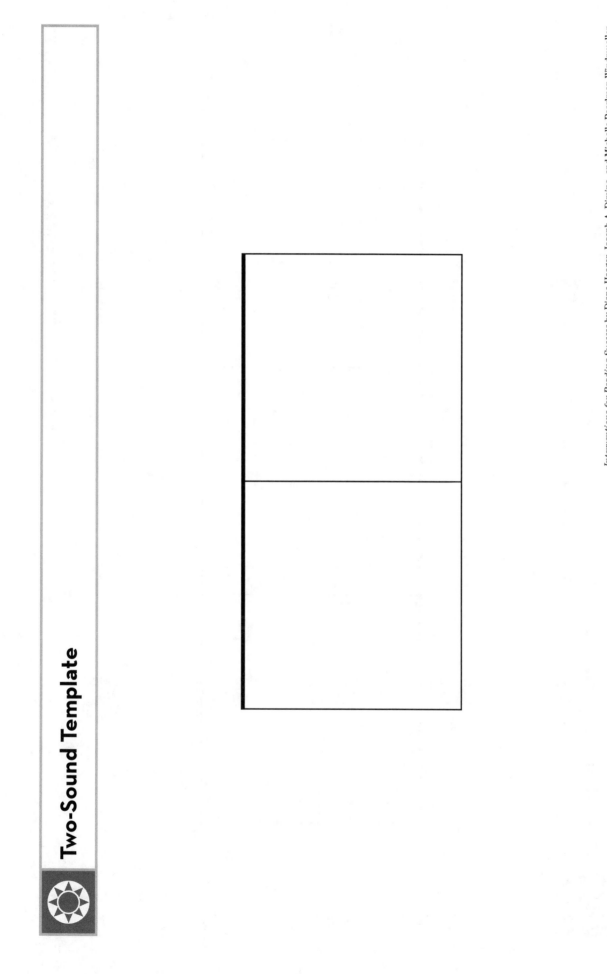

Three-Sound Template

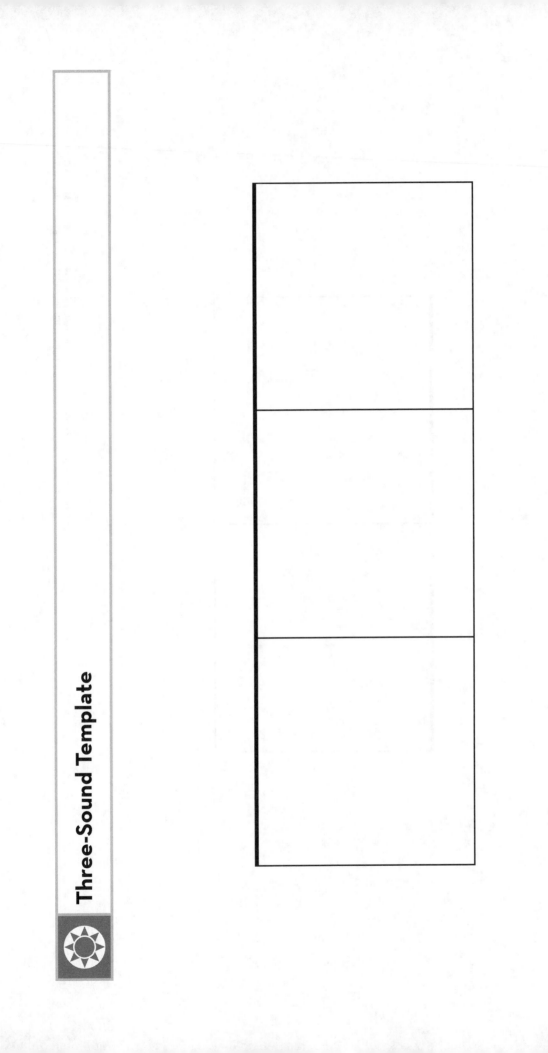

Four-Sound Template

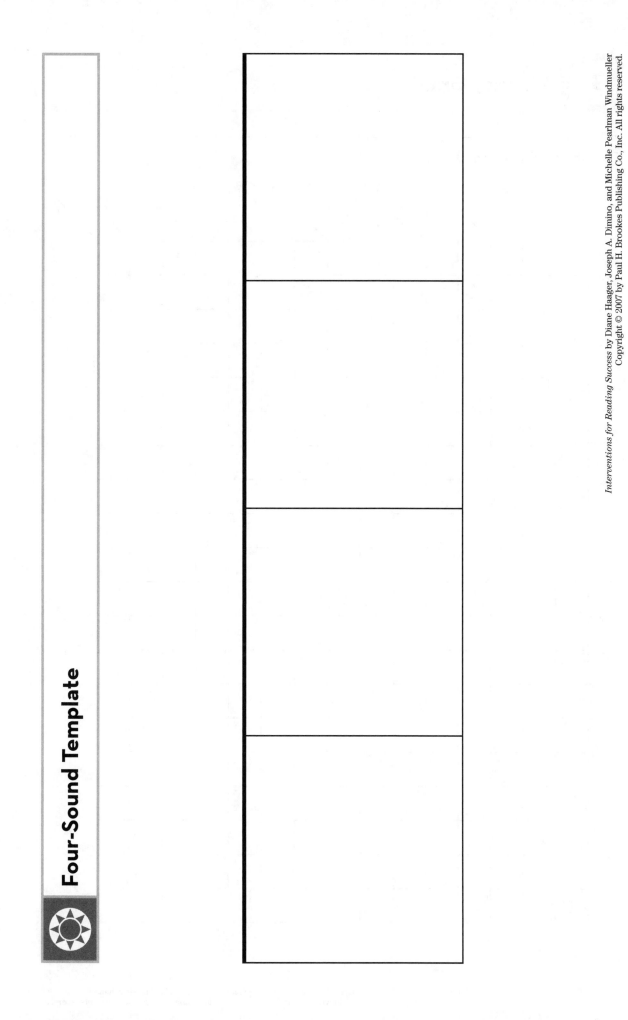

Fluency Graph

Name: _____

(Place dates in diagonal slots.)

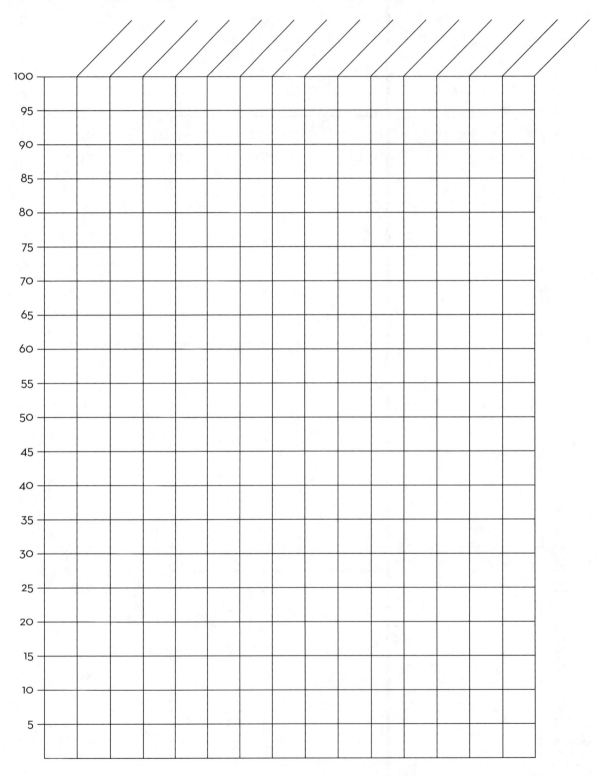

Interventions for Reading Success by Diane Haager, Joseph A. Dimino, and Michelle Pearlman Windmueller

High-Frequency Word Bank

a	could	he	might	same	too
about	cut	heard	more	saw	took
across	did	help	most	say	toward
after	didn't	her	much	see	try
again	do	here	must	she	turn
all	does	high	my	short	two
always	done	him	near	should	under
am	don't	his	need	show	up
an	down	hold	never	six	upon
and	draw	hot	new	small	us
another	eat	how	next	so	use
any	enough	I	no	some	very
are	even	if	not	soon	walk
around	every	I'm	now	start	want
as	far	in	of	still	warm
ask	fast	into	off	stop	was
at	find	is	oh	take	we
away	first	it	old	tell	well
be	five	its	on	ten	went
because	for	just	once	than	were
been	found	keep	one	that	what
before	four	kind	only	the	when
began	from	know	open	their	where
best	full	last	or	them	which
better	gave	leave	other	then	while
big	get	left	our	there	white
black	give	let	out	these	who
blue	go	light	over	they	why
both	going	like	own	think	will
bring	gone	little	play	this	with
but	good	long	put	those	work
by	got	look	ran	thought	would
call	green	made	read	three	yes
came	grow	make	red	through	yet
can	had	many	right	to	you
close	hard	may	round	today	your
cold	has	me	run	together	
come	have	mean	said	told	

Interventions for Reading Success by Diane Haager, Joseph A. Dimino, and Michelle Pearlman Windmueller
Copyright © 2007 by Paul H. Brookes Publishing Co., Inc. All rights reserved.

a	always	are
about	am	around
across	an	as
after	and	ask
again	another	at
all	any	away

be	better	but
because	big	by
been	black	call
before	blue	came
began	both	can
best	bring	close

cold	do	eat
come	does	enough
could	don't	even
cut	done	every
did	down	far
didn't	draw	fast

find	from	going
first	full	gone
five	gave	good
for	get	got
found	give	green
four	go	grow

had	help	hold
hard	her	hot
has	here	how
have	high	I
he	him	I'm
heard	his	if

in	keep	let
into	kind	light
is	know	like
it	last	little
its	leave	long
just	left	look

made	might	near
make	more	need
many	most	never
may	much	new
me	must	next
mean	my	no

not	on	other
now	once	our
of	one	out
off	only	over
oh	open	own
old	or	play

425

put	run	she
ran	said	short
read	same	should
red	saw	show
right	say	six
round	see	small

so	take	their
some	tell	them
soon	ten	then
start	than	there
still	that	these
stop	the	they

think	to	toward
this	today	try
those	together	turn
thought	told	two
three	too	under
through	took	up

upon	warm	what
us	was	when
use	we	where
very	well	which
walk	went	while
want	were	white

who	yes	
why	yet	
will	you	
with	your	
work		
would		

High-Frequency Nouns

air	girl	nothing
back	group	people
book	hand	place
boy	head	road
car	home	room
children	house	school
city	man	side

What's in the Box?

a ☐   the ☐   the ☐

wit ☐   whe ☐   befor ☐

ar ☐   fro ☐   lik ☐

giv ☐   doe ☐   gav ☐

sai ☐   int ☐   loo ☐

littl ☐   ou ☐   wher ☐

whic ☐   you ☐   sh ☐

the ☐   wha ☐   you ☐

You're it!	You're it!	You're it!
You're it!	You're it!	You're it!
You're it!	You're it!	You're it!
You're it!	You're it!	You're it!
You're it!	You're it!	You're it!
You're it!	You're it!	You're it!

Dear Parent or Guardian,

I would like to tell you about the Home-School Connection activities your child will be bringing home this year. These are activities for parents and children to do together to practice important reading skills learned at school. After I teach the skill at school, I will send home a Home-School Connection activity page that has simple instructions on how to do the activity.

These activities are simple games that reinforce basic skills with letters, sounds, and words. I encourage you to make this a fun parent–child time. However, don't be fooled by the game style of the activities—they really are teaching important skills. It will be helpful to find a time and place where you will not be interrupted by the television, the radio, or other children. Also, be sure to do the activities when you and your child aren't too tired. It will be best to do the activities at a table where you can spread out the materials. Some activities involve the use of letter tiles. I will send tiles home for you to use. Please do not use letters from word games you might have at home because these games usually include only capital letters.

Each activity follows the same format. Here is a description of what you will find on each Home–School Connection activity page:

Goal:	This describes the skill to be learned in this activity.
Materials:	This will tell you what you need, either materials that I send home or objects you are likely to have already.
Model:	This section tells you exactly how to demonstrate the skill. It is important for you to show your child what to do rather than just tell her or him. Model the skill two or three times.
Now It's Your Turn:	This section explains how the student will do what you have modeled in the previous step.
Extra Support:	If your child has difficulty with the task, this section gives some ideas for breaking it down into simpler steps.
Word Bank:	Most of the activities use words or the sounds in words. The word bank gives you a list of words that have the right sounds or letters for the activity so that you won't have to think of them yourself.

On the Home-School Connection activity pages that you will receive, some words are written with slash marks, such as /k/ /ă/ /n/ for the word can. Whenever you see the slash marks, you should say the *sounds* of the letters, not the letter names. Some of these activities are word games that involve breaking words down into their individual sounds, like saying /k/ /ă/ /n/ for the word *can*. Other activities involve the opposite skills—blending individual sounds into whole words. Short vowel sounds are marked with the ˘ symbol, such as /ĕ/ for the vowel sound in the word *bet*, and long vowel sounds are marked with the ¯ symbol, such as /ō/ for the vowel sound in the word *snow*. The vowel sound in certain unstressed syllables, such as the last sound in the word *umbrella*, is indicated with this symbol ə.

Learning to read is the single most important skill your child will learn in elementary school. Children are more successful when they have an opportunity to practice their new skills. I appreciate your support as we work together to help your child become a successful reader.

Sincerely,

Your Child's Teacher

Index

Page references followed by *f* and *t* indicate figures and tables, respectively.